ALSO BY SHERRY TURKLE
PSYCHOANALYTIC POLITICS: Freud's French Revolution

THE SECOND SELF

COMPUTERS
AND THE
HUMAN SPIRIT

by Sherry Turkle

A TOUCHSTONE BOOK
Published by
SIMON & SCHUSTER, INC.
NEW YORK

First Touchstone Edition, 1985

Published by Simon & Schuster, Inc.
Simon & Schuster Building
Rockefeller Center
1230 Avenue of the Americas
New York, New York 10020

TOUCHSTONE and colophon are registered trademarks of
Simon & Schuster, Inc.

Manufactured in the United States of America

10 9 8 7 6 5 4 3 2 1
10 9 8 7 6 5 4 3 2   Pbk.

Library of Congress Cataloging in Publication Data
Turkle, Sherry.
   The second self.
   Includes bibliographical references and index.
   1. Computers. 2. Electronic data processing—
Psychological aspects.   I. Title
QA76.T85   1984   001.64   83-27102
ISBN 0-671-46848-0
ISBN 0-671-60602-6 Pbk.

To Robert Bonowitz
and
Mildred Bonowitz

ACKNOWLEDGMENTS

I have worked on this book for six years and I have accumulated many debts. My first, of course, is to my informants who generously allowed me to share in their lives. My second debt is not to individuals but to an institution. This is the Massachusetts Institute of Technology.

It was at MIT that I first met up with the computer culture and it was at MIT that I found help and support to pursue my understanding of it.

Two people gave me early encouragement that helped to get my project underway: Harold J. Hanham, the Dean of the School of Humanities and Social Sciences, and Michael Dertouzos, Director of the Laboratory for Computer Science. In the Laboratory for Computer Science, J. C. R. Licklieder, Robert Fano, and Joseph Weizenbaum were early guides to important issues, as were Patrick Winston, Marvin Minsky, Seymour Papert, and Gerald Sussman in the Artificial Intelligence Laboratory, and Benson Snyder in the Division for Study and Research in Education. I owe a special debt to Professors Abelson, Fano, Seering, and Sussman of MIT as well as to Professor William H. Bossert of Harvard for making it possible for me to study the progress of students in their introductory programming courses. At MIT my academic home is in the Program for Science, Technology, and Society. My colleagues there read the earliest drafts of research proposals and reports that grew into this book; they helped me formulate my ideas. I thank all of them, with particular thanks to Carl Kaysen, Kenneth Keniston, Leo Marx, and Michael Piore. I have a special debt to Professor Keniston. For several years he and I have taught the course "Technology and the Individual." Some of the material in this book was presented there and gained enormously from his reflections, as it did from the reactions of our students.

My students have played a very special role in this project, particularly the students who have taken my "Computers and People" seminar through the years. My work required me to learn many things about electronics, computers, and programming languages, all of which were new to me. In my students I found tireless teachers. Beyond helping me to learn what I needed to know technically, they helped me to see the depth of feeling and involvement that people develop when they interact with technical objects: bicycles, radios, and model trains as well as computers. Without this understanding I would not have been able to write this book.

My intellectual debts extend beyond MIT. This book is an outgrowth of a previous project—a sociological study of psychoanalysis. What seemed like a shift of interest to many of my friends and colleagues felt to me like the pursuit of the same goal: to understand how ideas move out from a sophisticated technical world into the culture as a whole and, once there, how they shape the way people think about themselves. And so I owe a debt to several sociologists who had a formative influence on my earlier work— Daniel Bell, George Homans, and David Riesman, all of whom encouraged me in this new project and supported my sense of its intellectual continuity with what I had done before.

Listening was at the heart of this research, and I must thank my colleagues in the Mental Health Service of the Harvard University Health Service who helped me to become a better clinician, that is to say a better listener.

Several readers of my manuscript made important contributions. At a crucial point in the process of rewriting, Janet Sand encouraged me to go beyond what I then thought were my best efforts. Cynthia Merman offered that mix of moral support and practical suggestion that marks a fine editor. Jaffray Cuyler, Craig Decker, Elaine Douglass, Erwin Glikes, Ann Godoff, Sani Kirmani, Rob Kling, Martin Krieger, Pearl Levy, Justin Marble, Artemis Papert, Christopher Stacy, Lloyd Tennenbaum, and Deborah Wilkes all made suggestions that found their way into the finished product.

This work is a field study based on many thousands of hours of interviews and observations all over the United States. The freedom to work, to travel, to transcribe, to write and rewrite is costly. I was in a position to pursue this research because of the material support of three organizations: the National Science Foundation, which funded the first three years of my fieldwork, and the Guggenheim and Rockefeller Foundations, which provided me with fellowship support in later phases of research and writing.

I have three final debts to acknowledge—to Nancy Rosenblum, whose commitment to me and to this project has filled me with wonder and gratitude, to John Berlow, a co-investigator in the Austen School study of children and computers, and to Seymour Papert, who first encouraged me to consider the proposition that when computers become expressive instruments in the hands of children the machines enter into the process of growing up. More than anyone else, he impressed me with the idea—an idea that informs every page of this book—of how arbitrary are the lines that we use to divide thought and feeling. These three worked with me, with patience and tolerance, during long hours of brainstorming, writing, and editing. Their contributions did more than increase the scope and clarity of this book. Their presence decreased the loneliness and the doubts that went along with writing it. I thank them from the bottom of my heart.

SHERRY TURKLE

Boston, Massachusetts
December 1983

CONTENTS

PART III
INTO A NEW AGE

NOTES

The Evocative Object

On a cold January dawn in 1800, a boy of about thirteen came out of the woods near the village of Saint-Sernin in the Aveyron region of southern France. No one knew where he had come from. To all appearances he had survived alone, finding food and shelter in an inhospitable mountain climate since early childhood. He could not speak, and he made only weird meaningless cries.

The Wild Child was human, yet he had lived apart from culture and language. He walked out of the woods to enter history and, what is perhaps more to the point, to enter modern mythology as someone with a secret to tell. As a human being who had lapsed back to the animal condition, he was thought to embody the "natural." His way of thinking, if he could be taught to communicate, would testify to the condition of "man in nature." The life of the Wild Child became the occasion for what has been called "the forbidden experiment," the experiment that would reveal what human beings really are beneath the overlay of society and culture.[1] Are people "blank slates," malleable, infinitely perfectible, or is there a human nature that constrains human possibility? And if there is a human nature, what is it? Are we gentle creatures ill-equipped for the strains of life in society? Or are we brutish and aggressive animals barely tamed by the demands of social life?

A young French doctor, Jean-Marc-Gaspard Itard, tried to teach the Wild Child, rechristened as Victor. He undertook the forbidden experiment. But even after seven years of the most painstaking, systematic, and often inspired pedagogy, the boy never learned to speak, to read, or to write. He never told what he knew. He never told if he knew.

Although the experiment resolved nothing, the story of the Wild Child did not lose its power. The forbidden experiment did not settle opposing views about nature and nurture, about the innate and the social, but it provided a concrete image with which to think about them. People could imagine themselves in the story, they could say, "I am Itard. I have the job of teaching the Wild Child. What am I going to try? What do I think will happen? And why?" And when they went through the thought experiment, their ideas about what people are and how they develop came to the surface.

The Wild Child appeared soon after the French Revolution. It was a time when theories about human nature seemed up for grabs. It mattered desperately whether our nature was forever fixed or could be reformed. Fascination with the forbidden experiment and fascination with playing through its possibilities in one's mind were fed by widespread uncertainties. Now, as during that time, we are plagued with questions about who we are. Now, as then, we are drawn to whatever permits us, or forces us, to think the problem through. Not surprisingly, we have of late "rediscovered" Victor's story. There has been a flood of new studies of the Wild Child: historical, literary, psychological. The story is still evocative, "good to think with." But there is something new. There is a new focus for a forbidden experiment. A new mind that is not yet a mind. A new object, betwixt and between, equally shrouded in superstition as well as science. This is the computer.

We asked of the Wild Child to speak to us about our relationship to nature. But of the computer we ask more. We ask not just about where we stand in nature, but about where we stand in the world of artifact. We search for a link between who we are and what we have made, between who we are and what we might create, between who we are and what, through our intimacy with our own creations, we might become.

The schoolbook history of new technologies concentrates on the practical. In these accounts, the telescope led to the discovery of new stars, the railroad to the opening of new territories. But there is another history whose consequences are deep and far-reaching. A new sense of the earth's place in the solar system made it necessary to rethink our relation to God; the ability to cross a continent within days meant a new notion of distance and communication. Clocks brought more than the ability to measure time precisely; they made time into something "divisible" and abstract.[2] Time was no longer what it took to get a job done. Time was no longer tied to the movement of the sun or the moon or to the changing of a season. Time was what it took for hands to move on a mechanism. With digital timekeeping devices, our notion of time is once more being touched by technical changes. Time is made more abstract still. Time is no longer a process; time is information.

Technology catalyzes changes not only in what we do but in how we think. It changes people's awareness of themselves, of one another, of their relationship with the world. The new machine that stands behind the flashing digital signal, unlike the clock, the telescope, or the train, is a machine that "thinks." It challenges our notions not only of time and distance, but of mind.

Most considerations of the computer concentrate on the "instrumental computer," on what work the computer will do. But my focus here is on something different, on the "subjective computer." This is the machine as it enters into social life and psychological development, the computer as it affects the way that we think, especially the way we think about ourselves. I believe that what fascinates me is the unstated question that lies behind much of our preoccupation with the computer's capabilities. That question is not what will the computer be like in the future, but instead, what will *we* be like? What kind of people are we becoming?

Most considerations of the computer describe it as rational, uniform, constrained by logic. I look at the computer in a different light, not in terms of its nature as an "analytical engine," but in terms of its "second nature" as an evocative object, an object that fascinates, disturbs equanimity, and precipitates thought.

Computers call up strong feelings, even for those who are not in direct contact with them. People sense the presence of something new and exciting. But they fear the machine as powerful and threatening. They read newspapers that speak of "computer widows" and warn of "computer addiction." Parents are torn about their children's involvement not only with computers but with the machines' little brothers and sisters, the new generation of electronic toys. The toys hold the attention of children who never before sat quietly, even in front of a television screen. Parents see how the toys may be educational, but fear the quality of children's engagement with them. "It's eerie when their playmates are machines." "I wish my son wouldn't take his 'Little Professor' to bed. I don't mind a book, would welcome a stuffed animal—but taking the machine to bed gives me a funny feeling." I sit on a park bench with the mother of a six-year-old girl who is playing a question-and-answer game with a computer-controlled robot. The child talks back to the machine when it chides her for a wrong answer or congratulates her for a right one. "My God," says the mother, "she treats that thing like a person. Do you suppose she thinks that people are machines?"

This mother shows us the shock of a first encounter. But the computer is evocative in an even more profound way for those who know it well, who interact with it directly, who are in a position to experience its second nature.

From them, there is testimony about the computer's "holding power." They say the machine is fascinating. They say it is hard to put away. For some, the "hold" is a source of puzzled amusement: a lawyer whose Wall Street firm has installed a computer system in the office and who finds himself "making work" to use it comments, "It's a cross between the Sunday *Times* crossword and Rubik's Cube." For others, the feelings are more intense, even threatening. They speak of being grabbed in a more compelling, even more intimate way than by almost anything else they have ever known. A variety of people, ranging from virtuoso programmers to those whose contact with computers goes no further than playing video games, compare their experiences with computers to sex, to drugs, or to transcendental meditation. The computer's reactivity and complexity stimulate a certain extravagance of description. "When I play pinball," says a thirty-five-year-old account executive who plays several hours of video games a day, "I am playing with a material. When I play Asteroids, it's like playing with a mind."

The computer is evocative not only because of its holding power, but because holding power creates the condition for other things to happen. An analogy captures the first of these: the computer, like a Rorschach inkblot test, is a powerful projective medium. Unlike stereotypes of a machine with which there is only one way of relating—stereotypes built from images of workers following the rhythm of a computer-controlled machine tool or children sitting at computers that administer math problems for drill—we shall see the computer as partner in a great diversity of relationships.

In this book, the diversity is dramatic because I choose to look at settings where the computer can be taken up as an expressive medium. Not all encounters between people and computers are as open. But as computers become commonplace objects in daily life —in leisure and learning as well as in work—everyone will have the opportunity to interact with them in ways where the machine can act as a projection of part of the self, a mirror of the mind.

The Rorschach provides ambiguous images onto which different forms can be projected. The computer too takes on many shapes and meanings. In what follows, we shall see that, as with the Rorschach, what people make of the computer speaks of their larger concerns, speaks of who they are as individual personalities.

When different people sit down at computers, even when they sit down at the same computer to do the "same" job, their styles of interacting with the machine are very different. Nowhere is this more true than when they program. For many, computer programming is experienced as creating a world apart. Some create worlds that are highly predictable and use their experiences in them to develop a sense of themselves as capable of exerting firm control. Others have different needs, different desires, and create worlds whose complexity is always on the verge of getting out of hand, worlds where they can feel themselves to be wizards of brinkmanship.

But of course there is a difference between the computer and the Rorschach. The blots stay on the page. The computer becomes part of everyday life. It is a constructive as well as a projective medium. When you create a programmed world, you work in it, you experiment in it, you live in it. The computer's chameleonlike quality, the fact that when you program it, it becomes your creature, makes it an ideal medium for the construction of a wide variety of private worlds and, through them, for self-exploration.[3] Computers are more than screens onto which personality is projected. They have already become a part of how a new generation is growing up. For adults and for children who play computer games, who use the computer for manipulating words, information, visual images, and especially for those who learn to program, computers enter into the development of personality, of identity, and even of sexuality.

As this happens, experiences with computers become reference points for thinking and talking about other things. Computers provoke debate about education, society, politics, and, most central to the theme of this book, about human nature. In this, the computer is a "metaphysical machine." Children too are provoked. The computer creates new occasions for thinking through the fundamental questions to which childhood must give a response, among them the question "What is life?"[4]

In the adult world, experts argue about whether or not computers will ever become true "artificial intelligences," themselves capable of autonomous, humanlike thought. But irrespective of the future of machine intelligence, computers are affecting how today's children think, influencing how they construct such concepts as animate and inanimate, conscious and not conscious.

Some objects, and in our time the computer is preeminent among them, provoke reflection on fundamentals. Children playing with toys that they imagine to be alive and adults playing with the idea of mind as program are both drawn by the computer's ability to provoke and to color self-reflection. The computer is a "metaphysical machine," a "psychological machine," not just because it might be said to have a psychology, but because it influences how we think about our own.

I came to this study of computers and people six years ago after joining the faculty at MIT. I was struck by the psychological discourse that surrounded computers, and by the extent to which it was used by my students and my faculty colleagues to describe the machine's processes. A chess program wasn't working. Its programmers spoke of its problems as follows: "When it feels threatened, under attack, it wants to advance its king. It confuses value and power, and this leads to self-destructive behavior." Even the most technical discussions about computers use terms borrowed from human mental functioning. In the language of their creators, programs have intentions, try their best, are more or less intelligent or stupid, communicate with one another, and become confused. This psychological vocabulary should not be surprising. Many people think of computers as mathematical objects, but when you get closer to them you realize that they are information objects, manipulators of symbols, of language. You inevitably find yourself interacting with a computer as you would with a mind, even if a limited one. This is why the language that grows up around computers has a special flavor. Computer jargon is specifically "mind jargon."

And not only is the computer thought of in human mental terms. There is movement in the other direction as well. People are thinking of themselves in computational terms. A computer scientist says, "my next lecture is hardwired," meaning that he can deliver it without thinking, and he refuses to be interrupted during an excited dinner conversation, insisting that he needs "to clear his buffer." Another refers to psychotherapy as "debugging," the technique used to clean out the final errors from almost-working programs and to her "default solutions" for dealing with men.

These people are not just using computer jargon as a manner of speaking. Their language carries an implicit psychology that equates the processes that take place in people to those that take place in machines. It suggests that we are information systems whose thought is carried in "hardware," that we have a buffer, a mental terrain that must be cleared and crossed before we can interact with other people, that for every problem there is a pre-programmed solution on which we can fall back "by default," and that emotional problems are errors that we can extirpate.

"Hardwired," "buffer," "default," "debug"—these were among the computer metaphors I met within the MIT computer culture. Others, that came before them, have already moved out into the common language, for example the very notion of programming. When I was in the earliest stages of writing this book I had lunch with a friend to whom I tried to explain this process of computational ideas moving out. My problem was solved when two young women sat down at the table next to us. "The hard part," said one to the other, "is reprogramming yourself to live alone." The language of computers has moved out so effectively that we forget its origins. But although we may forget, we do not so easily escape the new assumptions that our language carries about what we are and how we can change.

Amid this discussion of minds as machines and of machines having minds I felt some of the dislocation and change of perspective that can make being a stranger in a foreign place both difficult and exciting. For the anthropologist this experience brings more than the shock of the new. There is a privilege and a responsibility to see the new world through a prism not available to its members, and (and this is the part that is often the most difficult) to use the new lenses to see one's own world differently as well. In this book

I try to meet both of these responsibilities. And in the end, the second became even more central to my concerns than the first. Because as I worked, it became clear that what I was studying was not confined to computer experts and computer professionals. The computer was moving out into the culture as a whole.

When I began my work, studying the computer culture meant working with easily identifiable groups of people, among these virtuoso programmers known as "hackers," members of the artificial intelligence community, and the first generation of people who owned home computers. But my subject had a special quality. Unlike most ethnographies, which explore a well-defined and delimited community, whether it be a primitive society or a rural commune, I was studying a moving target. When I began my work, personal computers had just come on the market. The first computer toys and games had not yet appeared. Most people had never heard the phrase "artificial intelligence." As this book goes to press, computer toys are commonplace in toddler playrooms, college freshmen arrive on campus with computers rather than electric typewriters, and the importance of a "fifth-generation" supercomputer has become a theme of public debate.

Thus, this book became a study of a culture in the making. A computer culture that in one way or another touches us all. And because it affects our lives in so many ways, this book takes its questions about this nascent culture from many perspectives.

From the perspective of psychological development I ask how computers enter into the process of growing up. Computers affect children very differently at different ages.

I found three stages in children's relationships with computers. First there is a "metaphysical" stage: when very young children meet computers they are concerned with whether the machines think, feel, are alive. Older children, from age seven or eight on, are less concerned with speculating about the nature of the world than with mastering it. For many of them, the first time they stand in front of a computer they can master is when they play their first video game. I discuss games—the computational medium that first made it into the general culture—and then I follow elementary-school-age children out of the games arcade and into the classroom, where they are learning to master computers by programming them. These children are all involved with the question of their own competence and effectiveness. When they work with computers they don't want to philosophize, they want to win. The second stage is one of mastery.[5]

In adolescence, experience is polarized around the question of identity, and the child's relation to the computer takes on a third character.[6] Some adolescents adopt the computer as their major activity, throwing themselves into programming the way others devote themselves to fixing cars. But there is a more subtle and widespread way that computers enter the adolescent's world of self-definition and self-creation. A computer program is a reflection of its programmer's mind. If you are the one who wrote it, then working with it can mean getting to know yourself differently. We shall see that in adolescence computers become part of a return to reflection, this time not about the machine but about oneself.

A psychological perspective also led me to study what computers come to mean for different kinds of people. I look at differences of gender, of personality, and I look most carefully at what seems to place some people "at risk." In particular, there is the risk of forming a relationship with the computer that will close rather than open opportunities for personal development. While for some children the computer enhances personal growth, for others it becomes a place to "get stuck." For adults as well as children, computers, reactive and interactive, offer companionship without the mutuality and complexity of a human relationship. They seduce because they provide a chance to be in complete control, but they can trap people into an infatuation with control, with building one's own private world.

I describe metaphysics, mastery, and identity as organizing issues for children as they grow up. I return to them from another perspective, an anthropological one, when I write about cultures within the computer world where one or another of these issues emerges as a central theme. I look at the culture of artificial intelligence, the culture of virtuoso programmers, and the culture of personal computer owners.

The connection between artificial intelligence and the "metaphysical computer" is apparent. As soon as you take seriously the idea of creating an artificial intelligence, you face questions such as whether we have any more than sentimental reasons to believe that there is something about people that makes it impossible to capture our intelligence in machines. Can an intelligence without a living body, without sexuality, ever really understand human beings? Artificial intelligence researchers study minds in order to build programs, and they use programs to think about mind. In the course of exercising their profession, they have made questions about human intelligence and human essence their stock in trade. For the "hacker," the virtuoso programmer, what is most important about the computer is what you can make it do. Hackers use their mastery over the machine to build a culture of prowess that defines itself in terms of winning over ever more complex systems. And in talking to personal computer owners I heard echoes of the search for identity. I found that for them the computer is important not just for what it does but for how it makes you feel. It is described as a machine that lets you see yourself differently, as in control, as "smart enough to do science," as more fully participant in the future.

My style of inquiry here is ethnographic. My goal: to study computer cultures by living within them, participating when possible in their lives and rituals, and by interviewing people who could help me understand things from the inside.

The people I describe in the chapters on computer cultures are not "average" computer users. Computers are a larger part of their lives than for most people. I write about them in order to present portraits of what can happen when people enter very close relationships with this machine. My method shares the advantage of using "ideal types"—examples that present reality in a form larger than life.[7] Ideal types are usually constructed fictions. My examples are real. Yet they isolate and highlight particular aspects of the computer's influence because I have chosen to write about people in computer cultures that amplify different aspects of the machine's personality. Studying people within these cultures allows us to look at the issues of metaphysics, mastery, and identity in adults' relationships with computers in a sharp, clear way. But what we see today "larger than life" within computer cultures will not remain within their confines. As the computer presence becomes more widespread, relationships between people and computers that now take place within them prefigure changes for our culture as a whole—new forms of intimacy with machines, and a new model of mind as machine.

Because the computer is no longer confined to expert subcultures, this book addresses yet another kind of question: How do ideas born within the technical communities around computation find their way out to the culture beyond? This is the province of the sociology of knowledge. Ideas that begin their life in the world of science can move out; they are popularized and simplified, often only half understood, but they can have a profound effect on how people think. This diffusion has special importance in the case of the computer. The computer is a "thinking" machine. Ideas about computation come to influence our ideas about mind. So, above all, what "moves out" is the notion of mind as program, carried beyond the academy not only by the spoken and written word, but because it is embedded in an actual physical object: the computer.

My approach to theories about mind as program is not that of a philosopher. My concern is not with the truth of such theories, but with the way in which they capture the popular imagination. What happens when people consider the computer as a model of human mind? What happens when people begin to think that they are machines? I report what people think, what they say, how they struggle to find new resolutions. When I look at computational ideas as they move out, I explore a "sociology of superficial knowledge": the study of how such knowledge plays a role in the lives of individuals and cultures that is not at all superficial.

These efforts to capture the impact of the computer on people involve me in a long-standing debate about the relationship between technology and culture. At one pole there is "technological determinism," the assertion that technology itself has a determinative impact, that understanding a technology allows us to predict its effects. "What does television do to children?" The question assumes that television, independent of its content or its social context, has an effect, for example that it creates a passive viewer, or that it breaks down the linear way of thinking produced by the printed word. At the opposite pole is the idea that the influence of a technology can be understood only in terms of the meanings people give it. What does it come to represent? How is it woven into a web of other representations, other symbols?[8]

My method, attentive to the detail of specific relationships with computers as they take place within cultures, provides a kind of evidence that undermines both extreme positions. Technological determinism is certainly wrong: there can be no simple answer to the question "What is the effect of the computer on how people think?" As we shall see, computers evoke rather than determine thinking. The consequences of interaction with them are dramatically different for different people. But the idea that what is changing is "all in the mind" does not hold up, either. The impact of the computer is constrained by its physical realities. One such reality is the machine's physical opacity. If you open a computer or a computer toy, you see no gears that turn, no levers that move, no tubes that glow. Most often, you see some wires and one black chip. Children faced with wires and a chip, and driven by their need to ask how things work, can find no simple physical explanation. Even with considerable sophistication, the workings of the computer present no easy analogies with objects or processes that came before, except for analogies with people and their mental processes. In the world of children and adults, the physical opacity of this machine encourages it to be talked about and thought about in psychological terms.

In my interviews I heard discourse about computers being used to think about free will and determinism, about consciousness and intelligence. We shall see that this is not surprising from a philosophical point of view. But I was not talking to philosophers. I was talking to sophomores in high-school computer clubs, five-year-olds playing with computer games and toys, college freshmen taking their first programming course, engineers in industrial settings, and electronics hobbyists who had recently switched from building model trains to building computers from kits. In this book I report on interviews with over four hundred people, about half of them children and half of them adults. The computer brought many of them to talk about things they might otherwise not have discussed. It provided a descriptive language that gave them the means to do so. The computer has become an "object-to-think-with."[9] It brings philosophy into everyday life.

For children a computer toy that steadily wins at tic-tac-toe can spark questions about consciousness and intention. For adults such primitive machines do not have this power. Since almost everyone knows a mechanical strategy for playing tic-tac-toe, the game can easily be brought under the reassuring dictum that "machines do only what they are programmed to do." Tic-tac-toe computers are not metaphysically "evocative objects" for adults. But other computers are. Conversations about computers that play chess, about robotics, about computers that might display judgment, creativity, or wit lead to heated discussions of the limits of machines and the uniqueness of the human mind. In the past, this debate has been carried on in academic circles, among philosophers, cognitive psychologists, and researchers working on the development of intelligent machines. The growing computer presence has significantly widened the circle of debate. It is coming to include us all.

Steve is a college sophomore, an engineering student who had never thought much about psychology. In the first month of an introductory computer-science course he saw how seemingly intelligent and autonomous systems could be programmed.* This led him to the idea that there might be something illusory in his own subjective sense of autonomy and self-determination.

Steve's classmate Paul had a very different reaction. He too came to ask whether free will was illusory. The programming course was his first brush with an idea that many other people encounter through philosophy, theology, or psychoanalysis: the idea that the conscious ego might not be a free agent. Having seen this possibility, he rejected it, with arguments about free will and the irreducibility of people's conscious sense of themselves. In his reaction to the computer, Paul made explicit a commitment to a concept of his own nature to which he had never before felt the need to pay any deliberate attention. For Paul, the programmed computer became the very antithesis of what it is to be human. The programmed computer became part of Paul's identity as not-computer.

Paul and Steve disagree. But their disagreement is really not about computers. It is about determinism and free will. At different points in history this same debate has played on different stages. Traditionally a theological issue, in the first quarter of this century it was played out in debate about psychoanalysis. In the last quarter of this century it looks as though it is going to be played out in debate about machines.

The analogy with psychoanalysis goes further. For several generations, popular language has been rich in terms borrowed from psychoanalysis, terms like "repression," "the unconscious," "the Oedipus complex" and, of course, "the Freudian slip." These ideas make a difference in how people think about their pasts, their

---

* Steve is a made-up name. My policy in this book has been to provide pseudonyms for my informants and, where necessary, change the details of descriptive materials that would identify them. I use real names when I cite published material and when I cite extracts from interviews with members of the scientific community.

presents, and their possibilities for change. They influence people who have never seen a psychoanalyst, who scarcely understand Freudian theory, and who are thoroughly skeptical about its "truth." So, when we reflect on the social impact of psychoanalysis, it makes more sense to speak of the development of a psychoanalytic culture than to talk about the truth of particular psychoanalytic ideas.[10] What fueled the development of a psychoanalytic culture is not the validity of psychoanalysis as a science, but the power of its psychology of everyday life. Freud's theory of dreams, jokes, puns, and slips allows people to take it up as a fascinating plaything. The theory is evocative. It gives people new ways to think about themselves. Interpreting dreams and slips allows us all to have contact with taboo preoccupations, with our sexuality, our aggression, our unconscious wishes.

My interpretation of the computer's cultural impact rests on its ability to do something of the same sort. For me, one of the most important cultural effects of the computer presence is that the machines are entering into our thinking about ourselves. If behind popular fascination with Freudian theory there was a nervous, often guilty preoccupation with the self as sexual, behind increasing interest in computational interpretations of mind is an equally nervous preoccupation with the idea of self as machine.

The debate about artificial intelligence has centered on the question "Will machines think like people?" For our nascent computer culture another question is more relevant: not whether machines will ever think like people, but whether people have always thought like machines. And if the latter is true, is this the most important thing about us? Is this what is most essential about being human?

The computer stands betwixt and between.[11] In some ways on the edge of mind, it raises questions about mind itself. Other marginal objects carry their own questions: the figure of the clown and the madman, both within and outside the normal social order, the myths of Dracula and Frankenstein, both within and outside our normal categories of what is alive. And then, on the border between nature and culture, there is the image of the Wild Child of Aveyron, the child who grew up in nature, never, it was believed, having had the influence of society, language, and civilization.

The Wild Child of Aveyron was an evocative object, inciting self-reflection, not because of anything that he did, but because of who he was, because of his position on the border between nature and culture. The computer too stands on a border. Its evocative nature does not depend on assumptions about the eventual success of artificial intelligence researchers in actually making machines that duplicate people. It depends on the fact that people tend to perceive a "machine that thinks" as a "machine who thinks." They begin to consider the workings of that machine in psychological terms. Why this happens, how this happens, and what it means for all of us is the subject of this book.

PART I

GROWING UP WITH COMPUTERS: THE ANIMATION OF THE MACHINE

CHAPTER 1

Child Philosophers:
Are Smart Machines Alive?

It is summer. Robert, seven, is part of a play group at the beach. I have been visiting the group every day. I bring a carton filled with small computer toys and games and a tape recorder to capture the children's reactions as they meet these toys. Robert is playing with Merlin, a computer toy that plays tic-tac-toe. Robert's friend Craig has shown him how to "beat" Merlin. There is a trick: Merlin follows an optimal strategy most of the time, and if neither player makes a bad move every game will end in a draw. But Merlin is programmed to make a slip every once in a while. Children discover a strategy that will sometimes allow them to win, but then when they try it a second time it usually doesn't work. The machine gives the impression of not being "dumb enough" to let down its defenses twice. Robert has watched Craig perform the "winning trick" and now he wants to try it himself. He plays his part perfectly, but on this round Merlin too plays a perfect game, which leads to a draw. Robert accuses it of being a "cheating machine." "And if you cheat you're alive." Children are used to machines being predictable. The surprising is associated with the world of the living. But this is a machine that surprises.

Robert throws Merlin into the sand in anger and frustration. "Cheater. I hope your brains break." He is overheard by Craig and Greg, aged six and eight, who sense that this may be a good moment to reclaim Merlin for themselves. They salvage the by now very sandy toy and take it upon themselves to set Robert straight.

Craig: "Merlin doesn't know if it cheats. It won't know if it breaks. It doesn't know if you break it, Robert. It's not alive."

Greg: "Someone taught Merlin to play. But he doesn't know if he wins or loses."

Robert: "Yes, he does know if he loses. He makes different noises."

Greg: "No, stupid. It's smart. It's smart enough to make the right kinds of noises. But it doesn't really know if it loses. That's how you can cheat it. It doesn't know you are cheating. And when it cheats it doesn't even know it's cheating."

Jenny, six, interrupts with disdain. "Greg, to cheat you have to know you are cheating. Knowing is part of cheating."

The conversation is over. I found it a striking scene. Four young children stand in the surf amid their shoreline sand castles and argue the moral and metaphysical status of a machine on the basis of its psychology: does the machine know what it is doing? does it have intentions, consciousness, feelings?

What is important here is not the yes or no of whether children think computers cheat or even whether computers are alive. What is important is the quality of the conversation, both psychological and philosophical, that the objects evoke.

Millions of parents have bought computer toys hoping they will encourage their children to practice spelling, arithmetic, and hand—eye coordination. But in the hands of the child they do something else as well: they become the occasion for theorizing, for fantasizing, for thinking through metaphysically charged questions to which childhood searches for a response.

It was Jean Piaget who discovered the child as metaphysician. Beginning in the 1920s, Piaget studied children's emerging way of understanding such aspects of the world as causality, life, and consciousness.[1] Children begin by understanding the world in terms of what they know best: themselves. Why does the stone roll down the slope? "To get to the bottom," says the young child, as though the ball had its own desires. Childhood animism, this attribution of the properties of life to inanimate objects, is only gradually displaced by new ways of understanding the physical world in terms of physical processes. In time the child learns that the stone falls because of gravity; intentions have nothing to do with it. And so a dichotomy is constructed: physical and psychological properties stand opposed to one another in two great systems. The physical is used to understand things, the psychological to understand people and animals. But the computer is a new kind of object—psychological, yet a thing.

Marginal objects, objects with no clear place, play important roles. On the lines between categories, they draw attention to how we have drawn the lines. Sometimes in doing so they incite us to reaffirm the lines, sometimes to call them into question, stimulating different distinctions. They are the growing point for new learning, new theory building. Computers, as marginal objects on the boundary between the physical and the psychological, force thinking about matter, life, and mind. Children use them to build theories about the animate and the inanimate and to develop their ideas about thought itself.

Marginal objects are not neutral presences. They upset us because they have no home and because they often touch on highly charged issues of transition. Sit silently and watch children pulling the wings off butterflies, staring at the creatures with awesome concentration. When they do this, children are not simply being thoughtless or cruel. They are not playing with butterflies as much as with their own evolving ideas, fears, and fantasies about life and death, about what is allowed and what is not allowed, about what can be controlled and what is beyond control.

Piaget discovered the child as metaphysician and set a style for investigating children's thinking. He tried to understand children's theories in intellectual terms.[2] Piaget interviewed children, asking them, for example, whether clouds, dogs, rocks, and many other familiar objects were alive. Or he gave them problems and examined their solutions. His style of inquiry tries to probe what children think. I follow his example, but I also have another concern. Beyond what children think, I am interested in what they feel, and how what they feel enters into the development of their thought. The development of logic is pushed forward by children's emotional as well as intellectual needs. There is passion behind theory construction.

In my research on how computers enter children's thinking, my method is like Piaget's in that I asked children direct questions, but I did something else as well. I observed what children did with computers and computer toys in natural settings where computers provoked excitement, conversation, and disagreement. Sometimes children who would say computers were "not alive" betrayed more complex feelings by treating them as though they were.

The butterfly can play its role as an evocative object because it is on a threshold, alive enough to fly, yet seemingly far enough from being alive in the way that a person is alive to make its mutilation and killing almost acceptable. And when the butterfly's wings have been torn from it, it is placed in another situation betwixt and between. When does it stop being a butterfly? At what point is it dead? The computer too evokes feelings and thoughts related to life, death, and the limits of permissibility and control. It too is seen as marginal, in some ways alive and in many not. Thus it is like bugs and butterflies. But it introduces something very new.

The world of bugs and butterflies is like the world of Humpty-Dumpty: "All the King's horses and all the King's men couldn't put Humpty together again." Computers belong to a different world. They offer an experience of restoring "life" as well as ending it. The computer's interactivity and complexity—the fact that it is "smart" and "talks back"—make some children see it as one of those things on the margin of being alive. It is also possible to play with the idea of "killing" the computer. Certain inputs will "crash" it: the program, unable to cope, is thrown into a nonfunctioning state. The crash, an event often accompanied by a violent burst of gibberish on the screen, can carry a high emotional charge. Watching children go through cycles of crashing and reviving, of "killing" and "resuscitating" their machines, suggests that they are using them to work through feelings about endings and beginnings, about life and death.

In this chapter I first look at a number of such situations where the computer, marginal and evocative, provokes strong emotions, even fear. Later I shall talk about how children develop theories that among other purposes may serve to banish their fears. Through the construction of concepts the child tries to put order where there was disorder. The computer, standing between the physical and the psychological, between the animate and the inanimate, creates a new disorder and provokes the child to new conceptualizations.

Why the Computer Disturbs

Matthew, a good-natured and precocious child of five, was eagerly learning to write computer programs to make graphic designs on the screen. His mood changed abruptly and he left the computer in tears when he understood how to make a recursive program: a program whose action includes setting in motion an exactly similar program whose action includes setting in motion an exactly similar program, and so on. Once started, the program will (if it has no "stop rule") go on "forever," limited only by the hardware, the amount of "memory" of the machine.

It is not enough to say that Matthew was afraid. His experience was complex and confusing, one that many people have shared. When I was a little girl I had a book on the cover of which was a picture of a little girl looking at the cover of the same book, on which, ever so small, one could still discern a picture of a girl looking at the cover, and so on. I found the cover compelling, yet somehow it frightened me. Where did the little girls end? How small could they get? When my mother took me to a photographer for a portrait, I made him take a picture of me reading the book. That made matters even worse. Whenever I looked at the photograph or the book I couldn't stop thinking about them, yet could find no way to capture for myself or for anyone else exactly what it was that was so upsetting and so gripping for me.

Other children meet this experience in the form of questions about where the stars end or whether there is ever a final image when mirrors reflect mirrors. In all of these cases, what disturbs is closely tied to what fascinates and what fascinates is deeply rooted in what disturbs.

When I was in trouble with self-referential pictures I could get no help. The adults around me were no better able to handle the infinite series of ever smaller little girls than I was, except to assert their authority by telling me not to think about such things. Children's encounters with ideas like self-reference, infinity, and paradox are disturbing and exciting and are made all the more mysterious by the fact that appeals to parents about them are likely to provoke frustrating admonitions not to think about such slippery questions.[3] Yet such questions become storm centers in the mind.

The computer touches on several of these slippery questions. The idea of infinity is one of them. What constitutes being alive is another.

Young children see almost everything in the world as alive in one way or another. This "animism" pervades the child's thinking until the development of concepts that help draw the line between the alive and the not-alive. Childhood animism has two faces: it makes the world friendly and understandable, but it can make it frightening as well. Emerging from animism is more than a chapter in the intellectual development of the child—it is a struggle against the insecurities that come from not knowing what objects can act independently and potentially antagonistically. Children spend a great deal of energy trying to get such matters under control, and thus it is not surprising that they are disturbed when a computer behaves halfway between a person and a thing.

For the child for whom little seems under total control, toys and simple machines are reassuring exceptions. Dolls, soldiers, wind-up toys—all of these "come alive," but only at the child's command. Computer toys that talk, cheat, and win are not so compliant. Yet they have a "holding power." In part it is the holding power of the feared. Children love roller coasters and horror movies, but much of the time on the ride and in the theater may be spent with closed eyes. We are drawn to what frightens us, we play with what disturbs us, in part to try to reassert our control over it.

Laura is six years old, a beautiful child from suburban Boston. Her family calls her "Princess." I have interviewed several other six-year-olds from her neighborhood. Most of them seem street-wise. Laura is an innocent. She watches very little television, some *Sesame Street,* and her favorite, *Mister Rogers' Neighborhood,* which she likes because "there is magic and Mr. Rogers is very kind." She has no mechanical toys, "nothing that winds up or has batteries," she tells me, "just dolls and storybooks." As we chat, sprawled on the floor of my office, she remarks that she has never played with a tape recorder or a typewriter, and she gingerly tries mine out. And yet, when she is presented with the computer toys—Simon, Merlin, and Speak and Spell—she has no reticence. "My mother has a microwave like this," is her first comment about the touch-sensitive controls on Merlin, the toy that plays tic-tac-toe.

Laura begins her play session calmly. She quickly checks out the toys and has definite opinions. The toys have "minds," says Laura, but they are not alive, because "they don't have a brain—they know how to do things with minds." Laura says this in a tone that suggests disbelief that anyone could think otherwise. Of all the things she has ever met before, she thinks that Merlin is most like "a machine, a clock." And the thing that Laura says is most special about clocks is that "they don't do anything by themselves." When I ask Laura if her alarm clock "remembers" when to wake her up, she is firm about the answer. "No, you set it. And then it does it. But not by itself."

As Laura plays she becomes less composed. Merlin's "tic-tac-toe mind" turns out to be a formidable opponent. "How does he win so much? It tries to make me lose." Laura is completely engrossed. She doesn't look up. My presence is forgotten. I ask her if she thinks Merlin could lose if it made a mistake. Her "Yes" is almost inaudible. She is not sure at all. Laura begins to turn Merlin off between games, a ritual whose intent seems to be to weaken the toy. Her efforts are in vain: Merlin continues to win. After five minutes of this frustration, she puts Merlin aside and picks up Speak and Spell, a toy that can talk. Laura spells out her name on its keyboard. The toy obediently calls out the letters and displays them on a small screen: "L-A-U-R-A."* She seems satisfied and relaxes. This is going to be more reassuring than Merlin. Then Laura puts Speak and Spell into "Say it" mode.

Speak and Spell has a button that turns it on and another that turns it off. It also has buttons for choosing among different possible play modes. In "Spell" mode, the toy calls out a word and waits for the child to spell it by pressing out letters on its keyboard. After the child has made a guess, the game offers congratulations or a second chance before it provides the correct spelling. In the "Hangman" game mode, the toy offers blank spaces and clue letters on the screen and invites the child to complete the secret word. And then there is "Say it" mode, designed for younger children who, like Laura, may not be able to spell much more than their names. In "Say it" mode the machine calls out the phrase "SAY IT" followed by one of the words in its several-hundred-word vocabulary: "SAY IT . . . HAPPY." "SAY IT . . . LOSE." "SAY IT . . . HOUSE." And the child is given a few seconds to repeat the word before being offered another one.

Not surprisingly, since this is the way of electrical objects, Speak and Spell is designed so that you can turn it off at will. You can turn it off without finishing the "Hangman" guessing game or without completing the spelling of a word in progress. But the first version of Speak and Spell that came on the American market had

---

* It has become almost a convention to capitalize the names of computer programs and of all "output" from computer programs. When I depart from convention it is because the program's authors have done so.

a "bug," a programming mistake: you can't turn it off while it is in its "Say it" mode. This mode offers ten words, ten "Say it" commands, and it brooks no interruption until the presentation of the ten words is finished. You cannot change modes, and you cannot turn the toy off.

When Speak and Spell is in "Say it" mode its program doesn't check to see whether the user has pressed "Off" before completing its ten-word cycle. Although the programming error is trivial, it was discovered only after it had been "burned into" the computer chip manufactured for the toy. Correcting the mistake was deemed too costly. And, besides, the problem didn't seem very serious.

The uninterruptible "Say it" cycle takes long enough so that within their first few sessions with Speak and Spell most children try to turn it off while it is in "Say it" mode and discover they cannot. In a small way, they are meeting a situation that is at the heart of almost every science fiction movie ever made about a computer. It is the story of the machine out of control. As far as the child can tell, this machine has developed a mind of its own.

Halfway through the cycle, Laura wants to turn "Say it" off and get back to spelling her name. She presses the "Off" button. She persists, pressing it again and again, then trying several other buttons. "Why isn't this thing coming off?" She tries four or five buttons in a row, then all of them at once. Now Laura is panicked. She puts one of her hands on as many buttons as it will cover. She tries both of her hands. The machine goes on until it is done. Laura is quite upset.

The "Say it" bug contradicts our most basic expectation of a machine. When you turn the switch to "Off," machines stop. The cliché response to people's fears about computers "taking over" is that you can always "pull the plug." Laura's agitation is not unlike that of an adult who suddenly has reason to doubt the cliché.

Children can be frightened by the "Say it" bug, but at the same time they find it compelling. Once they discover the bug, they make it happen again and again. It gives them a chance to play with the machine as alive, out of control.

When Paul, seven, discovers the "Say it" bug, he is startled, but he doesn't say anything. His first reaction is to put Speak and Spell down on the ground. Then, kneeling above the toy but keeping some distance, he presses "Say it" again. This time, Paul presses all of its buttons in turn and then uses the palms of his hands, trying to press all of its buttons at the same time, trying to make it stop. The toy remains unobedient, but when its ten words have come to an end it stops unexpectedly. Paul puts the Speak and Spell in "Say it" mode again, but this time, just as it is demanding its fourth word, Paul turns it over, opens its back cover, and removes its batteries. Paul has found the way to "pull the plug." A group of children gather round. Most have run into the "Say it" bug, but no one had thought of batteries. There is much excitement. The children take turns doing Paul's trick. They put the toy in "Say it" mode and then take out the batteries, all the while shrieking their delight about "killing the Speak and Spell." The children allow the toy its most autonomous behavior, and then, when it is most like a living thing, they kill it.

The children are not only killing the Speak and Spell, they are also bringing it back to life. Somewhat older children play with more sophisticated computers in similar ways. As I have said, they delight in "crashing" the system, in overloading it or getting it into a state where it will not be able to function, and then they "bring it up" again.

In the first computer-rich elementary-school classroom I studied, there quickly grew up a community of experts at crashing and reviving the computer, skills that demanded considerable sophistication. This group of ten-and eleven-year-old experts didn't crash the system to inconvenience the teachers or the other students. They crashed the system in order to watch it go down and have an occasion to bring it up. After a few weeks of incessant crashes and virtuoso resuscitations, Peter and John, the two most skilled experts, developed a new variant on the crash/revive routine. They wrote a computer program that simulated a crash. This program made the computer appear ready for the "log in" command needed to "wake up" its operating system. But when someone went through the procedure of logging in, the screen would go blank, the system apparently dead. This would give the authors of the "pseudocrash" program an opportunity to do their "magic"—to type in a few characters and revive the machine.

At the time I was struck by the dramatic and witty flair of these fifth-grade "pseudocrashers." They seemed quite extraordinary. But in the years that followed, I saw that this episode was typical. Sooner or later, wherever there is a computer complex enough to make mastering its operating system a challenge, there develops the culture of the crash and the appearance of some variant of a pseudocrash program.

I ask a four-year-old named Ralph to draw a picture of something "not alive." He takes a large piece of paper and concentrates on weaving a small, dense mesh of lines in the middle of the sheet with a black crayon. And then he asks me to write out the name of the picture for him: Spider. Ralph looks up and announces, "Spiders are not alive." "Why?" I ask. He replies, "Because you can kill them."

Ralph has observed that spiders and ants can be stepped on, killed without hesitation, and to Ralph this makes them less alive to the point where he is willing to say they are not alive. But, of course, he contradicts himself, because you can't kill something that doesn't live. The tension in his answer shows him aware of the insect's marginal status as a living thing, a marginality that gives "permission" to experiment with the taboo on killing.

Speak and Spell in its "Say it" mode is also on the border. It is not alive, but seems to act willfully, of its own accord. Like the "marginal" insects, it can be an occasion for what seems an almost ritual exploration of life and death: pulling out the batteries and putting them back again. Appreciating the emotional charge of this ritual brings a more complicated and paradoxical picture of what is at stake when a child thinks about whether or not a computer is alive. Seeing the computer as alive adds to the emotion of killing it. But the relationship goes both ways: the excitement of killing the toy, of crashing the program, is itself an inducement to seeing the computational object as alive. It is exciting to play with the idea of life and death, and it is exciting to feel responded to by a "living" machine. Adults are not exempt from this excitement. Some who would instantly reject the suggestion that computers are alive are drawn into behaving toward a computer as though it were alive. Some philosophical stances are taken in action.

In the early 1970s, computer scientist Joseph Weizenbaum wrote what by now must be the most widely quoted computer program in history. This was the ELIZA program, which was "taught" to speak English and "make conversation" by playing the role of a psychotherapist, an extremely clever twist.[4] The project of making a computer program that can enter into dialogue on all possible subjects is far beyond anything that is technically possible at present. Some experts doubt that it can ever be done. But setting the context for a conversation with ELIZA in the consulting room solved a lot of problems. Certain psychotherapists use a technique of "mirroring" what their clients say to them. Thus, if the patient says, "I am having problems with my girlfriend," the therapist might say, "I understand that you are having problems with your girlfriend," or "Why do you tell me that you are having problems with your girlfriend?" This technique is convenient for ELIZA. It allows the program to make an acceptable response without knowing the meaning of what has been said.

The program is able to give its response by making a few grammatical substitutions: "YOU" for "I," "ARE" for "am," and then adding as a prefix a random selection from a list of stock phrases used in the technique of mirroring, such as "I UNDERSTAND THAT . . ." or "WHY DO YOU TELL ME THAT . . ." or "ARE YOU TELLING ME THAT . . ." So, for example, if you say to ELIZA, "I am happy," it will analyze the sentence as "I am" plus "X," transform "I am" into "YOU ARE," add a prefix such as "WHY DO YOU TELL ME THAT," and say, "WHY DO YOU TELL ME THAT YOU ARE HAPPY?" Some versions of ELIZA were made a little more varied and interesting by providing the program with lists of words that would trigger certain responses. The words "miserable," "unhappy," "sad," and "depressed" might trigger the program to use the stock phrase "I AM SORRY TO HEAR THAT" in the sentence that followed.

ELIZA was a "dumb" program. It could recognize the character strings that make up words, but it did not know the meaning of its communications or of those it received. To ELIZA, the string D-E-P-R-E-S-S-E-D called up one of a set of possible "boilerplate" prefixes, but the program did not have any further knowledge about what it *means* to be depressed.

Weizenbaum's students and colleagues who had access to ELIZA knew and understood the limitations on the program's abilities to know and understand. And yet, many of these very sophisticated users related to ELIZA as though it did understand, as though it were a person. With full knowledge that the program could not empathize with them, they confided in it, wanted to be alone with it.

As one becomes experienced with the ways of ELIZA, one can direct one's remarks either to "help" the program make seemingly pertinent responses or to provoke nonsense. Some people embark on an all-out effort to "psych out" the program, to understand its

structure in order to trick it and expose it as "mere machine."
Many more do the opposite. I spoke with people who told me of
feeling "let down" when they had cracked the code and lost the
illusion of mystery. I often saw people trying to protect their relationships with ELIZA by avoiding situations that would provoke
the program into making a predictable response. They didn't ask
questions that they knew would "confuse" the program, that would
make it "talk nonsense." And they went out of their way to ask
questions in a form that they believed would provoke a lifelike
response. People wanted to maintain the illusion that ELIZA was
able to respond to them.* Children are often more direct in expressing their desire to breathe life into their machines. Lucy, five,
is the youngest child in her day-care group. She is plump, small
for her age, teased by the other children. She badly needs a friend.
On the first day I come to work with the children in her group,
Lucy discovers my Speak and Spell. They become inseparable.
That evening she convinces her mother to buy her one of her own.
It becomes her constant companion. Soon she has worked out a
special way of keeping it "alive."

Speak and Spell has a speaker but no microphone. The only
input it can receive is letters typed into its keyboard. But in fantasy
Lucy modifies her toy. She uses its speaker as her microphone. She
calls it Speak and Spell's "ear," and talks to it. First she speaks
softly, "What do I have to spell to you?" And then, more insistently,
"What should I spell?" Now screaming, "Tell me!" At this point
and always at this point (for this is a sequence I watched many
times) Lucy presses the "Spell" button and the toy speaks. This

---

* Variants of ELIZA have other rules that make them seem more intelligent than they are.
For example, a program can count the negatives typed into it and, if they go over a critical
number, inquire as to why the "client" is being so negative. It can count the number of times
that the words "mother" and "father" are typed at it, and, if there are frequent "fathers"
and no "mothers" in the client's typed communications, it can ask, "WHY DON'T YOU EVER
SPEAK ABOUT YOUR MOTHER?"

The following is an example of "coaxing" the program into a lifelike response. This
version of ELIZA has the rule: if you use the words "no" or "not" more than three times in
a row, it will accuse you of being negative.

Person: You are not a person.
ELIZA: WHY DO YOU SAY THAT I AM NOT A PERSON?
Person: Because you are not.
ELIZA: ARE YOU TELLING ME THAT BECAUSE I AM NOT?
Person: No.
ELIZA: WHY ARE YOU BEING SO NEGATIVE?

time it says, "SPELL . . . GIVE." Lucy settles back, obviously content: she has gotten the toy to address her. Her favorite way of interacting with the toy is to put it in "Say it" mode and to go into "Say it" mode herself, injecting her own "Say it" in the few seconds between the machine's "SAY IT" and its pronouncing the word it "wishes" to have said. So the dialogue between Lucy and Speak and Spell goes like this: Speak and Spell: "SAY IT . . ." Lucy: "Say it . . ." Speak and Spell: ". . . LOSE." Lucy: "That's right, you're very good."

The other children boss Lucy around, and now she too has someone to bully. Lucy wants to give the toy an awareness of her. She wants to give it consciousness and a psychology. She describes Speak and Spell as "a little alive." She wants it to be.

In the child's animistic world, objects can have the power of active agents, with unknown, perhaps sinister intentions. Laura was simply afraid, but with Lucy we see a first strategy for how children deal with the situation. They play with and manipulate objects to get a sense of control over their powers. Lucy wants Speak and Spell to be alive, and an important part of wanting it to be alive is then to be in a position to bring it under control.

Paul used this strategy when he entered into cycles of putting Speak and Spell in "Say it" mode and pulling out its batteries. But this strategy can bring you only so far. Children often seem to have infinite patience for taking apart and putting back together, for doing and undoing. But there is a limit. Eventually something has to change within them to bring fears under control. One possibility: repress what threatens. For example, the child "forgets" the terrors of infinity. Another: weave intricate associative threads that join what is frightening with what is not.

When the young child sees clouds moving across the sky, the clouds may seem alive and independent, perhaps dangerous. But if one sees clouds as fleecy lambs, a metaphorical chain begins to neutralize the fear. The cloud may still be thought of as alive, but it is no longer terrifying. Repression and neutralization through metaphor are possible strategies, but there is another. Faced with the moving clouds, the child can theorize about their movement in such a way that the clouds cease to be alive. "Cloud movement" becomes differentiated from the kind of movement that makes things alive, because the clouds move only if they are "pushed" by the wind, and what can't move without a push from the outside is not alive. Children develop theoretical constructs that separate the motion of clouds from the motion of people and animals so that eventually the fear of living clouds disappears. If things seem uncomfortably on the border between the alive and the not-alive, use logic to redefine the boundaries so that things fall more comfortably into place. If it scares you, make a theory.[5]

Children construct theories that will help them situate the computer in the world of living and not-living things and neutralize what seems threatening about it. How do children come to define the ideas of life, thinking, and feeling in a way that takes account of what computers can do?

A New Disorder: "Are Smart Machines Alive?"

In the discussion of the children on the beach, Robert said that he thought Merlin was alive. Long before computers appeared, children held unorthodox views about what things were alive just as they held unorthodox views about why rocks rolled down slopes. When, in the 1920s, Piaget explored what children think is alive, he noted that children at the age of those on the beach frequently thought objects such as clouds or rivers to be alive. So it is surely to be expected that some children should think of computer objects, which are in many ways more lifelike than clouds or rivers, as alive. But when we compare children's ideas about the "aliveness" of computer objects to their ideas about the objects that surrounded the children Piaget studied, we see important differences, differences that again reflect the computer's status as an object somewhere between the worlds of psychology and physics.*

Piaget argues that children develop the concept of life by making finer and finer distinctions about the kind of activity that is evidence of life. In particular, the notion of life is built on progressive refinement of their concept of motion.[6] At age six, a child might see a rolling stone, a river, and a bicycle as alive for the same

---

* I introduced toys—some traditional and some electronic—to groups of children and to individuals and observed their spontaneous reactions. To engage further conversation I asked questions in Piaget's style and also used several techniques wherein I gave the children something to do, asking them to sort pictures of objects into piles of "alive" and "not alive," or asking them to draw something alive and not alive. This chapter is based on work with over two hundred children. A description of the methods used and quantitative data can be found in "Children's Psychological Discourse: Methods and Data Summary."

reason: "they go." By age eight, the same child might have learned to make a distinction between spontaneous movement (movement that the object can generate by itself) and movement imposed by an outside agent. This allows "the alive" to be restricted to things that seem to move of their own accord: a dog, of course, but also the sun, the rain, a cloud. An object drops out of the category of alive when the child discovers an outside force that accounts for its motion. So, at eight, the river may still be alive, because the child cannot yet account for its motion as coming from "outside of itself," but the stone and the bicycle are not alive, because the child can.

Cars and other motorized vehicles challenge this classification scheme, but children can adapt "pushing from without" to include the "push" that comes from starting a motor. Children distinguish those mobile things that move by themselves from those that move at the command of a living entity. It is not until eleven or twelve that they confine the concept of life to plants and animals, when the idea that internally generated motion confers life is refined by ideas about growth (things are alive if they grow) and other life activities such as breathing or metabolism.*

At different stages in a child's development, trees could be alive because their branches wave, then not alive because they stay in the same place, and, finally, alive again because they grow or because sap flows in them—a form of internally generated motion. The motion theory leads to misclassifications: the stationary trees that are not alive, the moving clouds that are. But these misclassifications are not consequential for children. Children can climb a tree and swing from its branches whether or not they think the tree is alive. And concepts such as metabolism that would make trees alive are far from children's everyday concerns. The motion theory is satisfying even though it does not always lead to the correct conclu-

---

* This is the story as Piaget told it. When one looks at the details of his data, and at subsequent research, including my own, one sees that some qualification is needed: the majority of responses of children do refer to motion in the strict sense of moving from A to B, but at all stages there are some responses that refer to motion in an extended sense, as physical activity: the "kettle boils," the "top spins." My purpose here is to contrast all such physical criteria, including the occasional reference to biology—"coming out of eggs," "being born"—with a very different kind evoked by computational objects. From this perspective, the difference between strict motion and physical activity is not relevant, and so I use the phrase "motion theory" in a generalized sense, to cover all references to physical as opposed to psychological criteria in talking about what is alive.

sions. And it is a good theory to grow with—it grows in complexity and differentiation with the child's development of increasingly complex and differentiated ideas about the physical world.

Children build their theories of what is alive and what is not alive as they build all other theories. They use the things around them: toys, people, technology, the natural environment; a rapidly running stream, the wind that dies down and starts up again, the jerky movements of a wind-up toy—these are objects to think with, to build with. The motion theory for distinguishing the living from the not-living corresponds to the world of objects that surrounds children: animate objects—people and animals who act and interact on their own—and all the other objects, pretty well inert.

But this orderly situation has changed with the coming of the computer. Children are now confronted with highly interactive objects that talk, teach, play, and win.[7] Children are not always sure whether these are alive or not alive, but it is clear, even to the youngest child, that movement is not the key to the puzzle. Children perceive the relevant criteria not as physical or mechanical, but as psychological: Are their electronic games aware, are they conscious, do they have feelings, do they play fair, or do they cheat?

Children use a psychological discourse to talk about other things than computers. One five-year-old told me that a cloud is alive "because it gets sad. It cries when it rains." Another five-year-old said, "The sun is alive because it has smiles. People paint smiles on the sun." But if an eight-year-old argues that clouds or the sun are alive, the reasons given are almost always related to their motion—their way of moving across the sky and the fact that they seem to do so of their own accord. By contrast, as children become older and more sophisticated their arguments about the computer's aliveness become focused on increasingly refined psychological distinctions. The motion theory of life can be adapted to take account of the automobile, but it is much harder for it to adapt to computer toys that do not move but are unrelentingly active. The child faces the computer with its lifelike properties: it talks, it wins at games, it knows facts. At the same time, the machine has properties that make it seem not alive. This creates a predicament. The computer provokes children to find ways either to deny it the status of a living being or to grant it a special kind of life. In the process it forces them to think about how machine minds and human minds are different and so enters into the development of psychological reasoning. It enters into thinking about mind: about computers' minds, other people's minds, and one's own mind.

The Construction of the Psychological

I studied over two hundred children from age four to fourteen, exploring how they interacted with and spoke about computer objects, from hand-held electronic toys and games to video games and personal computers.[8] Some care is needed to pin down exactly what is new. It is not a simple matter of children thinking that computers are alive. Children disagree and discuss the question with interest.

Elvira, four, says that Speak and Spell is alive "because it has a talking voice in it." Ingrid at five: "It's alive—it talks." Randall, an eight-year-old, says with an air of confidence and authority, "Things that talk are alive." Kelley, six, gives an answer with a different twist. She looks closely at the seven-by-ten-inch Speak and Spell and pronounces, "It's alive—there's a man inside who can talk." But eight-year-old Adam disagrees with five-year-old Lucy, who is sure that Speak and Spell is alive "because it talks." "OK, so it talks, but it's not really thinking of what it's saying. It's not alive." Adam's reply would have been a conversation stopper for most adults, but Lucy is not intimidated: "You can't talk if you don't think, Adam. That's why babies can't talk. They don't know how to think good enough yet." What is new is that psychological principles are used to argue both sides of the question.

Piaget too reported that children occasionally used "talking" as a reason for believing something to be alive, but reference to talking in his protocols was so isolated, so occasional, and so undeveloped that he dismissed it as not an essential part of children's construction of a theory of aliveness.* For the children I studied, "talking"

---

* "The child will add to its spontaneous ideas various adventitious definitions: to live is to speak, or to be warm, or to have blood, etc. But all the children who gave these secondary definitions were also able to give the usual answers, all being simply juxtaposed together, so that it was possible to neglect these various secondary notions whose completely individual character clearly showed them to be the result of chance conversations overheard, etc." Jean Piaget, *The Child's Conception of the World* (Totowa, N.J.: Littlefield, Adams, 1975), pp. 195–96.

was not isolated at all. When today's child confronts a computer toy, talking is part of a larger set of attributes used to construct the notion of alive/not alive. These attributes are psychological, and as the child grows in sophistication they are used in increasingly sophisticated ways.

There is room for debate about whether what children say when you question them about if and why something is alive accurately reflects what features they are really using to decide the answer.[9] A child's verbal answer may be determined by what is easiest to say or by an attempt to guess what kind of answer the questioner expects. One does not have to resolve this debate about the Piagetian method in order to see that something changes when we go from traditional objects to computational ones. The most frequent pattern I found was that children who had consistently placed traditional objects into the categories of alive and not alive on the basis of physical activity, usually by relegating the stationary to the status of the nonliving, used psychological reasoning when they came to a computer toy.* The arguments children use most frequently to discuss whether a computer is alive do not refer to the computer as a physical entity but to the computer as a psychological entity, to ways in which it seems or does not seem to be like a human being in the qualities of its "mind."[10] In addition to talking and consciousness, the most common psychological attributes that children mentioned in discussing the question of the computer's aliveness were intelligence, feelings, and morality.

Ron, nine, counts Merlin, the toy that plays tic-tac-toe, as alive because "it is a very smart toy." Sam, seven, says Speak and Spell is alive because "it thinks. It spells better than me." Ed, at five, says that Big Trak, a miniature tank that traces out whatever pattern of motion and firing of its guns its user programs into it, is alive because "it remembers." Stuart, at eight, agrees: "It knows just what you tell it to do. Sometimes I even forget and it remembers." This is a striking example of the shift from the motion theory. Even for a computer toy like Big Trak that does move and, for a

---

* One object fit into the pattern in a special way: an alarm clock. The alarm clock can be seen as a traditional mechanical object or as a primitive computer. It has visible moving hands and an invisible memory. Children answer with both a psychological and a physical discourse to the question, Are alarm clocks alive? Yes: "The hands move." "They wake you." No: "If you don't set them they don't *know* what to do."

toy, moves with more than usual autonomy, what strikes Ed and Stuart is its psychology: it "remembers," it "knows."

Children, particularly the younger ones under six, refer to possession of feelings as a reason for counting a computer toy as alive. Trina is five, and, like many of the other very young children I interviewed, she is sure that the *Star Wars* robots, R2D2 and C3PO, are alive: "Yes, they are alive. You can tell. R2D2 loves C3PO." Following the spectacular popularity of R2D2, a "droid" who makes sounds of affection, gentle chiding, and vulnerable disappointment, toy manufacturers all over the world rushed to make the new electronic playmates as ingratiatingly noisy as possible. For example, Simon is shaped like a flying saucer whose top surface is covered by four differently colored quadrants. These quadrants light up in a pattern that the player is asked to repeat. If you make a mistake, Simon emits a sound of clear displeasure. Merlin too makes a "happy sound" if you win and gives you "raspberries" if you lose. Children associate these sounds with feelings and then use the idea that the toys have emotions to argue that they are alive. Marilyn, seven, of Merlin: "You see, it's happy now. It made a happy sound." Norm, six, of Simon: "It makes it hard for you. But then when you can't do it, it's sad."

In the category of morals, the most common life-giving attribute is cheating. On the beach, Robert became frustrated when Merlin would not let him win the same way twice, an experience of machine unpredictability unknown in a child's world of conventional wind-up toys, toy trucks, dolls, and soldiers. This led Robert to complain, "Merlin is a cheating machine. And if you cheat, you're alive." For other children, usually somewhat younger, the accusation that the computer cheats does not have to do with unpredictability, but with the machine's all-too-predictable triumphs. "It wins all the time. It's not fair."

Children's views about what is alive emerge from reflection about the nature of objects and from the quality of their interactions with them. The children who are concerned with the computer's cheating have entered into "social relationships" with the machine in which they get competitive, angry, and even vindictive. When children find themselves treating the machine as though it were alive, scolding it, wanting to get back at it, this itself can feel like evidence in support of giving it some status as a living thing.

Lyndon is seven years old. He is angry with Merlin, which has been trouncing him at tic-tac-toe for fifteen minutes straight. "It's not fair. It's too tricky. It's cheating, because it wins all the time." Kelley, six, his "girlfriend" and sometime tic-tac-toe partner, is equally convinced that Merlin's steady triumphs are breaking the rules. "It cheats. It's not nice to win all the time." Kelley confides to me that sometimes she "cheats back" so that she can beat Merlin. She does this by taking two turns in a row. "But when I do it," she is quick to insist, "it is not breaking the rules. It's just to make things even." At six, righting a moral balance is not cheating.

Alex, another six-year-old, agrees. Like Lyndon and Kelley, Alex is used to playing tic-tac-toe with other children who make frequent mistakes and with adults who do not allow the game to go on for too long without letting him win. Merlin is clearly a different breed. After ten minutes of steady losses to Merlin, Alex is angry. "He cheats. It's not fair." And Alex falls back on Kelley's strategy. He begins to take two turns in a row, doesn't give Merlin a chance. Alex is jubilant. "Here I won. I tricked him. I touched two circles so he couldn't win me." Emboldened by victory, Alex goes back to playing it straight, and Merlin goes back to winning. With this new round of losses, Alex accuses the "innocent" Merlin of having done unto him what he has just done to it. He accuses Merlin of making a series of moves without giving him a chance. "Merlin saw my move, but he didn't light up a square for me. He doesn't let me light up." Alex turns on the toy with a moral indignation that was conspicuously absent in his view of his own behavior. "Oh, I see what you are doing, you stinky thing. Cheating. You're not letting me win—because when I push the button and I went, you take away my turn, you make it your turn. It makes you win."

I have been watching the Merlin–Alex match closely. Alex now turns to me looking a little embarrassed. Even at six, he seems to feel awkward bawling out a small plastic object that looks like a telephone receiver. "He always takes one of my squares and makes it one of his squares so then he wins and that is why the thing goes 'ya-ya.'" (Here he is imitating the noise that Merlin makes when it wins.) For Alex, the "ya-ya" is Merlin's contemptuous gloat, even though the manufacturers intended the sound as an expression of sympathy. The toy is not fair. "I am trying to figure out how it does it. Maybe he does it when he makes his wires get very hot." When I ask him if Merlin is alive, Alex has no doubts. "Oh, yes, this is not a regular toy. It is very mean."

One must ask if this psychological reasoning about the computer is due to unfamiliarity with the machine—to a first shock when faced with its anthropomorphic behavior. It is not. The children I have cited so far were meeting computer toys for the first time. But when children get used to the toys, the language they use to talk about them becomes more, not less, psychological. The more contact children have with computational objects, the more nuanced and elaborated this psychological language becomes. And children who have developed an elaborated psychological discourse about the computer use it in talking about other things.

For example, a child without computer experience may answer the question whether a television set is alive by referring to its physical properties. Arlene, at seven, says, "Yes, TV pictures are alive, they move," and Harold, nine, equally sure, declares, "No, the television just sits there. Not alive. Definitely not alive. The people on the television, they're the ones who are alive." Contrast these remarks with the perspective of Anne, who at nine has already done quite a bit of programming. Anne's ideas about whether television sets are alive have a different cast. We are discussing computers, and I ask her if she thinks they are alive. She frames her answer by comparing computers and television. "The television set isn't alive. It doesn't make up its picture. It only passes it on." A person, she explains, might have to tell a computer how to make a picture, but the picture doesn't exist in the world before the machine gets involved: "The computer has to know how to do it. To make it up." This reasoning leads her to a special kind of verdict for the computer: "It's sort of alive."

When a child explains the descent of a rolling stone by its wish to get to the bottom of the hill, the child is falling back on a psychological idea—the wish—because the physical idea—gravity—is not yet sufficiently developed. Physical phenomena cannot yet be explained in physical terms. As the child develops, this psychological discourse will be undermined from two sides. There will be growing sophistication about which domains are appropriately described in psychological terms—the behavior of rocks will not be among these.[11] And there will be growing sophistication about how to think about physical causality. Computers, however, don't easily fit into the category of physical objects whose behavior is to be described in physical terms. The psychological discourse about them becomes more pervasive and more nuanced with age and sophistication.

For example, in an elementary-school classroom where all children are given as much opportunity as they want to work with the computer, the most frequent answer to my question "Are computers alive?" is a variant of Anne's "sort of." And the reasons given for this ambivalence are overwhelmingly psychological: the machines are sort of alive because they think but don't feel, because they learn but can't decide what to learn, because they cheat but don't know they are cheating. For these children, the answer to my question is not a simple yes or no, it is complicated, and their answers are informed by their ability to think about psychology in increasingly nuanced ways.

Some children think computers are alive, some think they are not, others settle on "sort of." But to the extent that they debate the question in terms of the machine's psychological attributes they are getting practice in thinking about, talking about, and defending their ideas about the psychological. As the world of traditional objects serves as material for a child's construction of the physical, the computer serves as a stimulus to the construction of the psychological.

The computer presence is not the only new element contributing to this construction. Children are more than ever the subjects and objects of psychological thinking by parents and teachers, counselors and psychotherapists. Children hear a psychological language on television, especially on the soap operas many of them watch after school. Such influences lead them to "talk psychology" with each other as well. The impact of the computer on all of this cannot be easily isolated. But we can say with confidence that the culture that grows up around computational objects embeds the machines in a discourse about psychology.

The development of a psychological discourse about computers is plainly visible when we look at how children think about two specific questions raised by the computer's lifelike nature: whether computers cheat and where computers come from. Both are windows onto the development of an idea of psychology as distinct from biology or behavior.

Cheating Machines

When the youngest children talk about whether a machine can cheat, they comment on whether it has the appropriate body parts that would enable it to cheat. Older children comment on what they believe to be its behavior: cheating is as cheating does. It is only later, when the concept of the psychological is refined, that the notion of cheating demands being in a particular psychological state: cheating presupposes intention to cheat and perhaps the freedom of choice to do so or not.

In the first stage, "to cheat" requires a physical action of a sort that only a person can do. Megan, at five: "Merlin can't cheat, because it doesn't have hands." Tony, at six, has a similar theory based on a direct comparison between what he needs in order to cheat and Merlin's equipment: "Computers can't cheat, because they don't have eyes."

The second stage is behaviorist and no longer tied to human anatomy. Barry, eight, thinks that Merlin is "very tricky": "If a person went to get a piece of paper or something, Merlin could press real quick. That would be the way he cheats." Merlin clearly has his own way of "pressing." Visible physical action and "hands" are not necessary to it.

Robert, the eight-year-old who got into the argument about whether "knowing is part of cheating," fits into this stage-two description. After accusing Merlin of cheating, Robert took the familiar revenge on the toy: taking two turns in a row in order to win. "I can cheat it," he explains, "but I can't cheat it from the inside like he can. When I cheat, even in my best way, everyone can see. It's on the outside." When Merlin cheats—that is, when it unexpectedly returns to its strong, winning strategy—it doesn't "show." Not only doesn't Merlin need hands to cheat, but the toy turns deficiencies into advantage: lack of hands means that Merlin can cheat "from the inside."

In a third stage, children's idea of what is necessary to play a game like tic-tac-toe depends not on body parts or the ability to act, but on mental states. It is a fully psychological stage. Eight-year-old Fanny had a particularly pretty way of expressing this: "To play tic-tac-toe, you don't need a brain. You need a mind." If computers can't cheat, it is because they are not autonomous or because they are not self-aware. Jeff, at ten, puts it this way: "Sometimes I play checkers with my father and he takes a long time between moves and I forget he hasn't gone and I go twice. But that's not cheating. You can't cheat if you do it by accident. So let's say that Merlin's batteries were real low and his brain got mixed up and he took two turns. It wouldn't be cheating, because he wouldn't know." We saw how Jenny, at six, echoed Jeff's thought: "Knowing is part of cheating." Her comment dramatizes that there is never a simple relationship between ages and stages. She is six years old, but her thinking is already fully psychological. But there are some general patterns. By around eight, most children have moved from the first, "physicalist" stage to the second, "behaviorist" one. And by eleven, all the children I spoke with were discussing the question of cheating in terms of self-consciousness and intention.

During the first two stages children are divided on whether computers can cheat, although when children are looking for direct physical analogies between how they cheat and how an electronic toy might do so, they find it hard to get evidence. Merlin, for example, simply doesn't have enough body parts to cheat. But sometimes, particularly when they are angry with a toy, children find a way to attribute the missing part to the machine. So when Tony announced that "computers can't cheat, because they don't have eyes," one of his classmates disagreed: "Merlin wins all the time. He cheats. He does have little eyes. Tiny eyes. You just can't see them."

By contrast, in "behavioristic" stage two, children are able to argue that Merlin cheats because they grant it the ability to press buttons and follow moves even without hands or eyes. But stage-two children also argue that Merlin is unable to cheat, usually by referring to the machine's lack of autonomy: "It can't press by itself." In stage three, cheating demands intent to cheat, and for most children this seems beyond the range of a toy like Merlin.

But children at stage three who have experience with more complex computers have no trouble imagining a computer "programmed to cheat" at tic-tac-toe and other games—that is, a computer programmed to go twice in a row or to ignore its opponent's moves. Sometimes the child's reasoning becomes more complicated. One thirteen-year-old who regularly played chess with "Boris," a small chess-playing computer, said he preferred playing with people because "chess with Boris is like chess with somebody who is cheating. He can have all the most famous, all the best chess games right there to look at—I mean, they are inside of him. I can read about them, but I can't remember them all, not every move. I don't know if this is how he works, but it's like in between every move he could read all the chess books in the world."[12]

"Where Do Little Computers Come From?"

When younger children think about the origins of computers, they know how to talk only about the physical computer: was it born or was it made in a factory? They say that a computer toy is not alive because it doesn't have a mother, it doesn't come out of an egg, it is not born. When the child's psychological culture is not differentiated enough, not strong enough, to capture a global conviction that the computer ought not to be counted as alive, a biological argument is there to fall back on. But older children consider the origin of the computer's functions rather than its physical existence—not the origin of the machine itself but of the mind of the machine.*

Ronnie, six, on the question of origins: "The Merlin is not alive, because it doesn't cry when it comes out. It doesn't have a mother." Joe, seven, speaking of the omniscient computer on *Star Trek:* "It's not born. It's made." Barney, eight: "Alive things have babies." Alan, five, on Speak and Spell: "Not alive. It spells better than a grownup . . . but not alive. It could be if it came out of an egg, but it doesn't." Daniel, also five, in Alan's kindergarten class and equally involved in a project to hatch baby chicks: "Live things come out of eggs. Sometimes out of mothers. They come out like babies." Three weeks later, I run into Daniel in the school playground. He walks up to me and says without preface, "If you are a tree you don't have to come out of an egg."

As their ideas about psychology become more refined, children begin to think in terms of the origins of the machine's mind. Rona, eight, commenting on the computer that she saw at the Boston Science Museum: "Computers know a lot. They have the answers to questions. And when they play games, they try to beat you. But they aren't alive. People make them in factories. They don't have a family. They have a maker."

The maker can work in a factory, or the maker may operate from a more exalted position. Arthur, eight, is from a devout Catholic family and has often been told that he himself has a creator.

---

* At early stages, when their ideas about motion are still undifferentiated, children often settle for a similar fallback on the biological when they consider the aliveness of "traditional" objects, although it is the motion theory that will develop, become dominant, and ultimately lead back to the biological concepts of growth and metabolic activity.

But robots aren't in this category. He uses a different language from Rona, but he gets across a similar idea: robots aren't alive, because they don't have a creator. "They have a maker. But it's not the same as God doing it."

Tom, age seven, says about Merlin: "The computer is smart, pretty smart. But it gets its ideas from people. People tell it everything. They put ideas into the machine." He is thinking about the origins not of the physical but of the psychological machine. And these origins come from a program. Adam, at eight, says, "Simon is happy when it wins. Very sad when it loses. It makes noises to show it. But it's not alive. It does it all with a cassette. It is programmed to make those sounds. They put in this cassette. You can have a computer or a robot that has feelings, but it's not alive. You have to program it, you have to put in this special 'feelings cassette.'"

Tom and Adam are prepared to grant the computer all elements of human psychology. They allow that computers have intelligence and feelings. But the machine differs from people and is not alive in that its intelligence and feelings come from "the outside." In all of this talk about the machine's origins, children are struggling to develop the idea of an "outside push" for psychological activity much as they struggle to develop the distinction between inside and outside pushes for physical motion. In the case of computer toys, children can grab onto something concrete, a machine part, which helps them in this effort: batteries. Computer toys may be smart, triumphant in victory, irritated in defeat, but for some children they are not alive because all of this comes from batteries.

Batteries have become some of the most frustrating objects in children's lives. When their toys don't work and are brought tearfully to an adult, the response that comes back most often is "batteries," the mysterious batteries that grownups buy and take charge of. For many children, batteries are both an essential object and part of the "don't touch" world. What are batteries to computers? Alice, a five-year-old, said, "They're like their food."

Tucker, six, has had a discouraging session with Merlin. He has chosen to play a "magic square" game in which, he explains to me, "You have to figure out the secret combination of numbers that the machine has in its head." After nine minutes of typing, Tucker is still unsuccessful. "Merlin has me beat." I suggest going on to tic-tac-toe, thinking that it might be easier for him, and Tucker agrees.

But after a few tied games his frustration again gets the upper hand, and he becomes really angry with Merlin for making him feel stupid ("You better give me an easy one or I'll hate you") and for cheating ("He can do it when you're not looking, he can do it like if you go out of the room to go to the bathroom or something"). To Tucker, this toy clearly has a psychology, it has motivation, capacities, even malicious intent. But when I ask Tucker, "Do you think Merlin is alive?" the answer comes back immediately, "No. It's the batteries." The answer surprised me, but it pointed toward a tension that is common in adult responses to computers: anthropomorphize the machines but don't grant them the dignity of life.

The question of the computer's origin is always fueled by another question—sometimes explicit and sometimes not. How are computers different from people? The eggs, makers, batteries, and programs, each in a different way, allows the computer and the human to be differentiated from one another. The batteries for Tucker are like the cassette for Adam. They allow him to grant the computer a psychology and yet assert a difference between computers and people. The computer is like us to the point of being conscious, but it is not alive because its power comes from an external agency. In the end Tucker joins with Tom and Adam: computers are like people in their psychology but not like people in their origins.

Children frequently come to this position. But it is not stable. It is unsatisfying because it leaves the essential difference between computers and people tied to something that happened in the past, almost as though the computers' mind and the children's minds are alike and they differ only in their parents.

Older children find a way out by making finer distinctions about what people share and do not share with the psychological machine. Younger children throw together such undifferentiated observations as that the computer toy is happy, it is smart, it cheats, it gets angry. Older children make distinctions within the domain of the psychological. For example, they draw a line across it. They comfortably manipulate such ideas as "It thinks like a person but it doesn't feel" with a conviction that the line between the cognitive and the affective is firm and important.

With the splitting of the psychological, it is no longer that something has a psychology or does not. By developing a distinct idea of the cognitive, children have found a way to grant to the computer that aspect of psychology which they feel compelled to acknowledge by virtue of what the machines do, while reserving other aspects of the psychological for human beings. At nine, ten, and eleven, children no longer rely exclusively on physical differences or the origins of the machine to draw a line between computers and people. The cognitive/affective distinction allows children to settle down with what feels to them a more satisfying way of capturing what is different between people and machines. Katy, eleven, after a year of experience with computer programming says that "people can make computers intelligent, you just have to find out about how people think and put it in the machine," but emotions are a different matter. For Katy, the kinds of thinking the computer can do are the kinds that "all people do the same. So you can't give computers feelings, because everybody has different feelings."

For the older children I studied, reference to the line between thought and feeling often stood behind the assertion that computers are not alive and not like people. But it is by no means the only line that children draw across mental life in the course of coming to terms with the computer's nature. Discussion of computer cheating led to refined ideas about intentions and awareness—people can cheat because they intend to; computers cannot. Discussion about the computer's origins led to distinctions between free will and autonomy as opposed to programming and predetermination —people think their own ideas, computer ideas are "put in" by their makers. This distinction often leads children to another, this time between rote thinking, which computers can do, and originality, which is a human prerogative. Finally, discussion about how computers think at all led to the distinction between brain and mind. All of these distinctions, thought and feeling in the context of the computer's aliveness, intentionality and lack of awareness in the context of the computer's morals, free will and programmed thought in the context of the computer's origins, are elements of how the computer enters into what I have called "the construction of the psychological," the child's increasingly nuanced way of thinking about mental life.

In the children's distinctions we hear "child versions" of how adults talk when they debate issues of computers and mind. When the artificial intelligence community collectively disagrees with

John Searle, the philosopher most associated with the position that thought is uniquely a product of the human brain, they are insisting on Laura's distinction between brain and mind: Merlin and Simon "don't have a brain. They know how to do things with minds." Craig and Greg, the children on the beach who took it upon themselves to disabuse Robert of his illusions about what was behind Merlin's "cheating," join with philosopher Daniel Dennett in attributing the machine's limitations to its lack of intentionality: events happen, but they are not part of a system of purposes. And the children like Katy who argue that computers are different because they can't have feelings join with Joseph Weizenbaum, who draws a line between the computer's ability to calculate and the human's capacity for reason and understanding. The child's version: the human is the emotional. The adult's version: the human is the unprogrammable.[13]

Not all adult positions are prefigured by children. For example, the children I studied took the question of the computer's aliveness quite seriously as a subject for discussion. It was not dismissed with the "adult" response, "it's just a machine." This may change as the conventional "ready-made" answer becomes something that children more frequently overhear. And I heard only one child say, as many adults do, that computers and people are not different because human minds are also "programmed." On some points, children seem firmly committed to asserting a difference between people and machines. On others, they grant to the machine what adults most tenaciously hold onto as something it could never be.

Nowhere is this more evident than in the discussion of consciousness. There are disputes among the very youngest children about whether the computer knows it is cheating. It acts, but is it aware of its actions? Piaget reports that the idea of consciousness evolves side by side with the idea of life. When children ascribe life to inanimate objects, generally speaking, they ascribe consciousness too; when "life" becomes identified with "the biological," consciousness becomes a property only of animals. With computational objects the pattern is very different. Many children allow the machine to be conscious long after they emphatically deny it life. Tucker, who denied it life because of its batteries, is a good example of what this split looks like, although he is only six.

For Tucker, the not-alive machine has consciousness and malicious intent. Adults, of course, hold onto the fact that computers are not self-aware as a sign of their fundamental "otherness." In fact, later we shall see that, at least for some within the artificial intelligence community, computer consciousness has become the ultimate criterion for deciding when one should judge the computer intelligent enough to deserve to be treated as alive.

The children take a different view. The idea of an artificial consciousness is not what impresses them. They may be the first generation to grow up with such a radical split between the concepts of consciousness and life, the first generation to believe that human beings are not alone as aware intelligences. The child's splitting of consciousness and life may be a case where instead of thinking in terms of adult ideas "filtering down" to children, it makes more sense to think of children's resolutions prefiguring new positions for the computer culture to come.

Computers in the Culture of Living Things

Much of my discussion has been about what children say. Some children talk about computers as alive and, more important, the reasons they use to argue one way or another are different from those they use to discuss traditional objects. This leads to the formulation of a simple conclusion: when children discuss computers, psychological features replace physical ones as the fundamental criterion for aliveness, a difference that might be summed up with the mnemonic: "motion gives way to emotion." But the picture of children deciding that computers are alive because of a single feature is too static. It ignores the fact that children sometimes seem to *want* the computer to be alive or not alive, to be like people or unlike people. The child's judgment is embedded in feelings and wishes. Any simple formulation also ignores the cultural discourse growing up around computers.

Remember Ralph, the five-year-old who thought spiders are not alive "because you can kill them." The statement is paradoxical. "You can kill them" is logically a reason for thinking something alive rather than the other way around. But it is easy to imagine how Ralph's reversal might have come about. An original idea of being alive might be built on a criterion of movement or of similarity to people. But Ralph became aware that living things are more than members of a logical category. They are embedded in a discourse about ethics and morality; there are rules about what you should and should not do to them. The child hears that killing is wrong. Whether or not any given object is surrounded by this ethical discourse enters into the child's decision as to whether or not the object is alive. Ethics becomes a criterion for aliveness, just as whether something is alive becomes a criterion for whether an ethical discourse is appropriate to it. So, as children observe behavior in the world (a world in which bugs, spiders, and caterpillars are often treated as though they were not alive), what people are reluctant and not reluctant to kill enters into children's ideas about what is alive, not alive, and how to talk about it all. These ideas are determined through an interplay of different kinds of considerations: emotional, logical, physical, moral. There is no simple causal chain. There are fields of influence.

A culture grows up around spiders that places them in a world of not-quite-living things. And a culture is in the process of growing up around computers that surrounds them with a discourse of almost-life.[14] At the risk of putting it too simply: Ralph was convinced that spiders are not alive, in part because it is all right to kill them. In two computer-rich schools I have studied, children became biased toward seeing the machines as "sort of" alive because in these cultures it becomes taboo to kill them, to "crash" them, to interrupt programs running on them. The Austen School, discussed in more detail in Chapter 3, ran an experimental program in which every child had almost unlimited access to personal computers. There fourth graders discuss whether the machines prefer running simpler programs ("It's easier for them," "They hardly have to do any work") or more complicated ones ("They feel proud," "It's like they are showing what they can do"). They talk about the morality of pulling the plug, and develop a complex etiquette of when and how a computer should be shut off ("I think it's not right to turn the computer off when a program is running. It's in the middle of its thinking. I think it wouldn't like it. It wouldn't be fair"). They talk about whether the machines know how pretty their displays are. They fantasize about what the machines do at night. These children know that the machines are not alive in the sense that people are alive. But the machines are talked about and thought about with a discourse appropriate to living things.

Children are drawn into thinking psychologically about the computer because of its behavior. But there is another incitement to a psychological discourse about the machine: its opacity. In dealing with traditional objects, growing up out of animism meant entering a world in which things are explained in mechanical terms. Physics becomes the framework for understanding objects. The bicycle is understood in terms of its pedals and gears, the wind-up car in terms of its springs. Children try to use the same kind of reasoning with computer toys and computers. They try to understand how these work in physical terms. But this turns out not to be so simple.

Computer toys are for the most part sealed, but even if one takes off the plastic back and breaks inside, all that the most persistently curious child finds is a chip or two, some batteries, and some wire. Physically, these objects are opaque. They are frustrating. During my interviews, this frustration sometimes showed itself through a touching reaction: after trying unsuccessfully to figure out what was happening inside a computer toy, children would develop a sudden and marked interest in my tape recorder, specifically a fascination with the visible, understandable physical motion of the tape capstans. They would spontaneously offer sober mini-lectures on how my tape recorder "works," on how its wheels turned and its tape moved.

This is one common response to intellectual frustration: talk about something else. Another is to find an answer to one's question that will put a dead stop to further inquiry. In this spirit, children sometimes fix on the largest and most "everyday" object they find inside their computer toys: the batteries. For me, the certain tone of five-year-olds announcing that batteries account for the behavior of the most prized of their playthings has come to symbolize the cognitive dead-end effects of opaque computational objects in children's worlds. Ultimately, the idea of batteries is not satisfying for the children, either. There is nowhere they can go with it, nothing more to say about it. But children do not lack intellectual curiosity or inventiveness. They turn to a way of understanding where there is more to say—that is, a psychological way of understanding. One nine-year-old, Tessa, made this point succinctly in a comment about the chips she had seen when her computer was being serviced: "It's very small, but that doesn't matter. It doesn't matter how little it is, it only matters how much it can remember." The physical object is dismissed. The psychological object is now the center of attention and elaboration.

The Psychological Machine

A long tradition of Western science has drawn a line between the worlds of physics and psychology and has tried to take the laws of motion of matter as the fundamental handle for grasping the things it found in the world. Piaget's account of how children sorted out the question of alive/not alive in the world of "traditional" objects showed them conforming to this way of thinking. They tried to use motion as the primary concept with which to figure out whether dogs, trees, and clouds were more like the paradigmatically inanimate sticks and stones or more like the paradigmatically animate people. But Tessa's summary of what "matters" when you try to understand a computational object ("that it remembers") and the discussion about the intentions of Merlin cheating at tic-tac-toe ("does it know?") don't conform. This discourse is psychological, not physical. Using it to talk about computers is having an effect on how children think about people.

Traditionally, children came to define what was special about people in contrast to their nearest neighbors, their pet dogs, cats, and horses.[15] Pets have desires, but what stands out dramatically about people is how smart they are, their gifts of speech and reason. Computers upset the traditional scenario. First, they upset the distinction between things and people; it can no longer be simply the physical as opposed to the psychological. The computer too seems to have a psychology—it is a thing that is not quite a thing, a mind that is not quite a mind. And then they upset the way children perceive their "nearest neighbors."

What is special about people must be what makes them different from computers. This cannot be reason, intelligence; computers too are seen as "smart." The Aristotelian definition of "man" as a "rational animal" (powerful even for children because it defined people in contrast with the animals) gives way to different kinds of distinctions, made possible by children's developing ability to manipulate psychological ideas.

The most frequently expressed of the new distinctions uses emotions to draw a line between computers and people. This line is not drawn by the younger children who often see the computers as expressing emotion and cite this as a reason to declare them alive and like people. But older children use emotion to argue for the opposite conclusion. Computers are able to have a kind of life, but what makes people unique is the kind of life computers don't have: an emotional life. Computers have psychologies, but psychology comes to mean two different things. Machines are intelligent, but they don't love or hate. They don't have emotions.* One might say a view of people as "rational animals" has given way to a new idea of "emotional machines."

Emotion is the psychological quality most frequently used to separate the human from the machine. But it is not the only one. David, twelve, a sophisticated programmer, used a concrete language to express a more nuanced set of qualities: "When there are computers who are just as smart as people, the computers will do a lot of the jobs, but there will still be things for the people to do. They will run the restaurants, taste the food, and they will be the ones who will love each other, have families and love each other. I guess they'll still be the only ones who go to church."

My story about computers and children's theory building has had two main themes: computers and the construction of the notion of alive, and computers and the construction of what is special about the "human." In the first case children's way of sorting out the question of life becomes more psychological. And in the second case what seems special about being a person becomes less dependent on intellect and more dependent on emotion.

There is an element in all of this that many will find surprising and reassuring. Children's adaptation to the computer contrasts with a prevalent fear that involvement with computers inevitably leads to a more mechanical way of thinking about psychology, perhaps even to a mechanized view of people. Faced with a machine, children, at least, seem to resist seeing people as like it: they see people as essentially what it is not.

In the seventeenth century a rationalist science produced a model for thinking about people and nature no less orderly, no less impersonal, than that which the computer has come to symbolize. Newton's image of planets lawfully traveling in their orbits

---

* The child's construction of the emotional too follows the now-familiar pattern of moving from physical to psychological criteria. When the youngest children talk about the computer's feelings, they refer to physical signs: to the machine's noises, to imagined changes in the machine's innards. Megan, five, put this idea nicely when she said, "When Merlin is happy, its wires boil over." By ten or eleven, the machine's feelings, like its thoughts, are described in purely psychological terms.

was taken up as the true image of nature, as the ideal for the governance of states and the working of the human mind. What was most human was reason. There was a reaction to this view: sensibility and spontaneity were declared more important than logic, the heart more human than the mind.

Children too have a romantic reaction. They respond to the rational, logical nature of the computer by valuing in themselves what is most unlike it. Our culture found it difficult to accept the idea, often associated with Piaget, of the child as "little scientist." It seemed too cold. We are more comfortable with Rousseau's image of the child as free and spontaneous. We like the idea of the Romantic child, valuing the spontaneous and the "unprogrammable." And yet, there is something disturbing about the child defining self in opposition to the machine.

In their reaction to nineteenth-century science and technology, the Romantics split passion from reason, the sensuous from the analytic. T. S. Eliot, reflecting on the loss of the ability to integrate "states of mind and feeling," called it the "dissociation of sensibility." [16] Children growing up in a computational culture face a similar danger. Their easy acceptance of the idea that computers closely resemble people in their "thinking" and differ only in their lack of "feeling" supports a dichotomized view of human psychology.

Thought and feeling are inseparable. When they are torn from their complex relationship with each other and improperly defined as mutually exclusive, the cognitive can become mere logical process, the cold, dry, and lifeless, and the affective is reduced to the visceral, the primitive, and the unanalyzable. The child's sharpened distinction between intellect and emotion can easily lead to a shallow and sentimental way of thinking about "feelings." Without dismissing fears about computers leading to mechanical views of mind, I see another danger, captured by Eliot's idea of "dissociation" as well as by the more contemporary image of a generation taking the mix of mysticism, Zen, and romanticism that is the message of Yoda and the Force as what distinguishes the human in the world of the robots.

CHAPTER 2

Video Games and
Computer Holding Power

I watch a thirteen-year-old girl in a small family café in New York City's Little Italy. Four electronic games lined up near the door clash with the murals of Italian seacoasts. The child too seems out of place. She is angry and abusive to the café owner when he asks her if she would like something to eat. "Get the fuck away from me. I'm fucking playing your fucking games." The man shrugs, apparently used to the abuse of thirteen-year-olds.

The girl is playing Asteroids. A spaceship under her control is being bombarded by an asteroids shower. There are separate control buttons for steering, accelerating, and decelerating the spaceship and for firing its rocket guns against threatening asteroids and enemy ships. The player must keep up a steady stream of missiles as she maneuvers the ship. The finger on the "Fire" button must maintain a rapid staccato, an action that is tense and tiring.

The girl is hunched over the console. When the tension momentarily lets up, she looks up and says, "I hate this game." And when the game is over she wrings her hands, complaining that her fingers hurt. For all of this, she plays every day "to keep up my strength." She neither claims nor manifests enjoyment in any simple sense. One is inclined to say she is more "possessed" by the game than playing it.

The children playing with Merlin, Simon, Big Trak, and Speak and Spell at the shore—discussing whether their computer games could really cheat—were displaying that combination of innocence and profundity which leads many of us to believe in Piaget's model of "the child as philosopher." The scene on the beach had an aura of charming solemnity. The scene in the café, like that in thousands of arcades and in millions of homes, is more violent. Somewhat older children—from around nine or ten on—are in a relationship to the machine that seems driven, almost evoking an image of addiction. Children musing about objects and their nature has given way to children in contest. Reflection has given way to domination, ranking, testing, proving oneself. Metaphysics has given way to mastery.

For the girl in the café, mastery of her game was urgent and tense. There is the sense of a force at work, a "holding power" whose roots are aggressive, passionate, and eroticized.

There has been controversy about video games from the days of Space Invaders and Asteroids, from the time that the games' holding power provoked people who saw it as a sign of addiction to become alarmed. The controversy intensified as it became clear that more than a "games craze" was involved. This was not the Hula-Hoop of the 1980s. By 1982 people spent more money, quarter by quarter, on video games than they spent on movies and records combined. And although the peak of excitement about the games may have passed with their novelty, video games have become part of the cultural landscape.

Not all of the arguments against video games can be taken at face value, for the debate is charged with feelings about a lot more than the games themselves. Protest against video games carries a message about how people feel about computers in general. In the past decade, and without people having had anything to do or say about it, computers have entered almost every aspect of daily life. By 1983 the computer had become so much and so active a part of the everyday that *Time* magazine chose it to fill the role usually given to a Man or Woman of the Year. Only one other gift of science has been so universally recognized as marking a new era of human life. That was atomic energy.

It is an understatement to say that people are ambivalent about the growing computer presence: we like new conveniences (automated bank tellers, faster supermarket lines), but on the eve of a new era we, by definition, do not know where we are. The changes have been rapid and disquieting. We are ill at ease even with our children, who are so much at ease with a technology that many of us approach at arm's length. They take it for granted. To them it is not a new technology but a fact of life. They come home from school and casually report that they are "learning programming." The comment evokes mixed feelings. Parents want their children to have every advantage, but this new expertise estranges them. It seems to threaten a new kind of generation gap that feels deep and difficult to bridge. And so, for many people, the video game debate is a place to express a more general ambivalence: the first time anybody asked their opinion about computers was when a new games arcade applied for a license in their community or when the owner of a small neighborhood business wanted to put a game or two into a store. It is a chance to say, "No, let's wait. Let's look at this whole thing more closely." It feels like a chance to buy time against more than a video game. It feels like a chance to buy time against a new way of life.

Video games are a window onto a new kind of intimacy with machines that is characteristic of the nascent computer culture. The special relationship that players form with video games has elements that are common to interactions with other kinds of computers. The holding power of video games, their almost hypnotic fascination, is computer holding power. The experiences of video game players help us to understand this holding power and something else as well. At the heart of the computer culture is the idea of constructed, "rule-governed" worlds. I use the video game to begin a discussion of the computer culture as a culture of rules and simulation.

The Myth of "Mindless" Addiction

Those who fear the games often compare them to television. Game players almost never make this analogy.* When they try to describe the games in terms of other things, the comparison is more likely to be with sports, sex, or meditation. Television is something you watch. Video games are something you do, some-

---

* I have been studying video games since 1980, both in arcades and in homes. Whenever possible, participant observation and conversations with players in the game setting were followed up by interviews in a quieter setting. This chapter is based on over one hundred hours of field research and on interviews (ranging from one to four hours) with thirty game players.

thing you do to your head, a world that you enter, and, to a certain extent, they are something you "become." The widespread analogy with television is understandable. But analogies between the two screens ignore the most important element behind the games' seduction: video games are interactive computer microworlds.

Using analogies with television or with drugs, the popular debate about video games is filled with images of game players caught in a "mindless addiction." Half of this description is certainly wrong. There is nothing mindless about mastering a video game. The games demand skills that are complex and differentiated. Some of them begin to constitute a socialization into the computer culture: you interact with a program, you learn how to learn what it can do, you get used to assimilating large amounts of information about structure and strategy by interacting with a dynamic screen display. And when one game is mastered, there is thinking about how to generalize strategies to other games. There is learning how to learn.

Consider Pac-Man, the first game to be acknowledged as part of the national culture. On the screen there is a maze that contains four monsters and the familiar yellow Pac-Man figure. Also scattered in the maze are pellets of food, represented as little dots. The player controls Pac-Man, or, as children usually express it, "You are Pac-Man." Your job is to eat the food and avoid being eaten by the monsters. Doing so involves quick turns and good coordination. But even more important is strategy, figuring out the rules that govern the behavior of Pac-Man and his pursuing monsters.

Pac-Man needs to make quick decisions: eat this dot or flee that monster. His decisions are made more complicated by another factor: in the maze are four energy cookies. For a short period after eating a cookie, Pac-Man can turn the tables on the monsters and eat them. A master player shifts constantly between offensive and defensive strategies: when to go for a dot or a cookie and when simply to stay out of the monsters' way. In addition, there are elements of bluff and trickery. Each monster has a different personality and can be more or less easily thrown off the trail by sudden reversals of direction.

Pac-Man shares with chess strategies that depend on executing standard sequences of moves. A well-informed Pac-Man player has a repertoire of these "patterns," picked up from other players, from books, and from personal discovery. But just as you can't play chess by rote, the same is true of a video game like Pac-Man, in which being off by a split second can throw you outside your pattern. Then you have to improvise, relying on your coordination and understanding of general principles of the game—for example, the differences in the monsters' behavior and the "safe places" to hide out in the maze. But you always have to think faster than the monsters move, and this means that, in order for you to play successfully, the general principles, like the patterns, have to be more than memorized. It's more than thinking—in a way it is beyond thinking. The hand learns what to do and does it automatically, just as the hand "knows" after playing chord X on the piano to go directly and inexorably to chord Y.

People who have never played video games often think that success at them is like winning at a Las Vegas–style "one-arm bandit"; people who have played one game and given up acknowledge that they require "hand–eye coordination," often adding that this is something that children, but not they, possess. But success at video games involves much more. Working out your game strategy involves a process of deciphering the logic of the game, of understanding the intent of the game's designer, of achieving a "meeting of the minds" with the program. The video games reflect the computer within—in their animated graphics, in the rhythm they impose, in the kind of strategic thinking that they require. This "computational specificity" becomes clear when you contrast the games with their "grandparent," pinball.

Computational Specificity

In some ways video games are reminiscent of pinball. You stand at them, reacting to a moving object by manipulating buttons and levers. Scores pile up. You try to do better. But there are important differences, differences that go back to how the games are made.

Making a new pinball game required designing and constructing new physical devices, a process that took time, tools, and mechanics. The video game—the characters on its screen, their behavior, the way they respond to a player's actions—is made of logic; that is, of a program of tens of thousands of computer instructions. The new "logic technology" has made possible an explosion in the freedom of game designers to search for ways to capture the attention, the imagination, and the coins of players. If a designer wants to change the game, for example, to put a new monster on the screen, he or she doesn't have to "make" a monster, but simply has to write a program that will trace out the monster's shape. To have the new monster engage in a chase requires another program. Pinball games were constrained by mechanical limitations, ultimately by the physical laws that govern the motion of a small metal ball. The video world knows no such bounds. Objects fly, spin, accelerate, change shape and color, disappear and reappear. Their behavior, like the behavior of anything created by a computer program, is limited only by the programmer's imagination. The objects in a video game are representations of objects. And a representation of a ball, unlike a real one, never need obey the laws of gravity unless its programmer wants it to.

The liberation of the video game from the "real world" allows more than freedom for the designer's imagination. It allows the games to become a more perfect expression of the player's actions. A pinball machine has levers that can rust. It is tilted to a particular slant on a particular floor. It is a mechanism, with a weight, a certain balance. It vibrates differently depending on the noise level around it. The video game has no moving "parts." Its graphics display is electronic, impervious to its surround. It is always the same, reacting almost instantaneously.

Watch pinball players at their game: they kick, they shake and thrust their hips, gently at first, then violently urge the machine to one side or another. Controlling the two bottom flippers by means of two buttons is the only movement in the game that feels discrete or precise. The rest is more like a dance. You have to feel how far you can go without tilting the machine. There is no indicator, no "tilt gauge" to show you the state of things—that is, nothing until it is too late. The physical pinball machine—the legs it stands on as well as its posts and flippers—are part of the game. The video game is different: here all of the action is in a programmed world, an abstract space. In an important sense, it is a space where the physical machine and the physical player do not exist. It is not easy for pinball players to describe their feelings of what makes the game respond. Some describe it as a "conversation": there is a sense of give and take. But although it has become cliché to speak of the video game as "interactive," players describe the experience of being with one as less like talking with a person and more like inhabiting someone else's mind. Conversation gives way to fusion. In pinball you act on the ball. In Pac-Man you are the mouth.

Jarish and the Computer Within the Game

By the time Jarish was five he already thought of himself as small for his age, small and very nearsighted and very different. In certain ways he likes being different: "Like my name, it's special, my parents just made it up. Other names come from something . . . my name doesn't come from anything." But being different also had its price; different didn't always feel better. Games became a way to mark different as better; pinball became a favorite and something at which he could be best.

Now Jarish is twelve, and two years ago pinball gave way to video games. His initials are up on almost all of the machines in the arcade closest to his home. He works at a game until he gets the highest score of anybody around, often having to stand on a stool to play. "You know," Jarish remarks, "they really should put little steps on the games. Getting to see the screen can really be a problem."

The old-fashioned pinball machines have no memory. However high your score one day, the machine treats you next time with the same neutral indifference it gives the clumsiest of beginners. And it certainly does not inform anyone else how well you did. Arcade-game manufacturers were quick to see the advantage of using the computers within the games to remember the names—or at least the initials—of the top players who have used it since its memory was last cleared. The players whose names are up on the screens of a game in "their" arcade form a competitive community, and one of mutual recognition. Jarish is pleased: "Everyone knows my initials."

The amnesia of the pinball machine meant more than an inability to let players leave a trace of their prowess. No matter how high your score, you play your next ball on the same game. The video game's computer power makes it possible for the game to respond to the level of the player's skill. When you finish one round, another round, faster and more complex, awaits you.

Jarish was immediately impressed by this difference, enthusiastic about the increasing violence of the tests on successive rounds (in video talk known as "screens" because when you finish a round the screen usually changes, presenting to you an increasingly worthy opponent). "It's great, the pace speeds up, the monsters usually get smarter or whatever, chasing you. Usually, they start chasing you closer." By comparison, pinball "is fun but it belongs to the real world . . . it's always the same." Jarish describes his favorite video games as "crazy and weird," not of the real world.

> I have a favorite where there's this little rocket ship and different colors and there is this dark layout. And you have this violet ray, so that you and all your clothes are changed purple and violet, that's so neat, and you go around destroying the birds of the son of Satan and then there are whole packs of hounds and stuff, and you have to go around destroying them. And after every couple of screens, you meet the devil himself and you have to go and shoot him with your laser. If you don't hit the devil after a little while he starts spouting fire, and then he gets bigger and bigger and his face takes up the whole screen, and then there's this little missile base, that is you, trying to destroy him, and this big face is coming at you, growing, starting to fill up the whole screen. It's hilarious.

Jarish dreams about designing his own video games. He knows that this medium can satisfy his taste for excitement. Shift from one memory segment to another, and the whole world can change.

> Like if you are being chased by a little dog, that would start to get boring after a while, but if like it changes screens and then you have your army of cats, let's say [here Jarish laughs, really enjoying himself], and the dog is chasing the cats, you can shoot the dog or something and it could change into something else. It never has to be the same thing all the time.

Most adults describe the "stories" of video games as cute or funny but basically irrelevant to their play, saying that they like to play a particular game to work on a specific "skill." Children identify more directly with the games' characters as they are chased, besieged, or, as in the case of Jarish's favorite game, Robotron, saving the last family on earth. This game assumes that 1984 has passed uneventfully but that one hundred years later, in 2084, science has almost destroyed humankind. Jarish explains how: "The scientists have perfected the robotron, which are these ingenious robots who go around, they're supposed to be helping human-ity, but they have a short circuit and they go around trying to destroy the last family on earth, and you have this laser and you have to go and destroy the robots and save the last family." Jarish feels himself completely in the game: "Yeah, sometimes I think of myself as the kid of the family. I really care."

The intensity of Jarish's involvement has a price. Outside the world of the games he says "you feel sort of cut off. When I play the game, I start getting into it, and you start taking the role of the person . . . and then the game ends. And you have just put all of your energy into it. It doesn't make me angry, more like depressed. You walk out of the arcade and it's a different world. Nothing that you can control."

Talking about Robotron evokes Jarish's own feelings about being out of control. "A lot of the kids have girlfriends. I feel left out. I don't have any best friends. It's not my fault. It's my size. Everybody thinks of me as a little kid." Jarish also feels little power in his family. His parents were divorced, his father remarried and then divorced again. Now he is with someone new. As when "the game ends," as when "you walk out of the arcade," there is a feeling of being "cut off." Each change in his family means the start of something new where old investments seem lost. Jarish says that when he feels angry he plays Robotron. There he can really con-centrate, feel in charge.

When Jarish goes into an arcade he looks for the craziest, most out-of-control game he can find, "let's say a million little birds coming down and you have to fire your laser all over the place and in crazy different scenes," and then he sets out to discover its strat-egies, its "secrets," to find a way of bringing it under control. For Jarish knows that despite the complexity of the games, there is program behind, there are rules. There is the computer that Jarish mythologizes as the dream machine that can make anything pos-sible and as the rule machine that makes everything that is crazy ultimately controllable.

For Jarish, the fact that a video game "has a computer inside" is of great importance. He feels himself to be a child of the computer generation. *Star Wars* was the hit movie of his eighth year; "com-puter special effects" were something he thought about before he ever saw a computer. "Comic strip" does not mean *Superman,* but tales of androids and robot brains, all of which assume, as he does, that "artificial intelligence" will become a fact of life. Jarish believes that scientists can do anything, but if you can do anything, something can always go wrong. He sees nothing improbable about the computer-out-of-control Robotron scenario. In his image of his own future he too will become a powerful person capable of anything by mastering the computer. Indeed, just as pinball gave way to video games for Jarish, video games are starting to give way to the computer. His interest in computers started when he began to think about ways to change video games, mostly to make them more complicated.

> I would like to change games to make them crazier, like if you were in a two-player game, shooting another guy. I'd make it so like you'd fire these little weird rockets and then your friend could, let's say, press a button, and the rocket would turn into a bunch of, let's say, ants, and they'd fall around everything and you'd have little crater holes and missile silos coming out of the ground.

In science class Jarish dreams about how to use the "boring things we are learning" as materials for the video games he dreams of someday being able to make. "Like why a ball would move and why it goes faster. You might need to use this stuff to make a video game . . . that comes into my mind very often." But between knowing the physics and using it for a game there is, of course, a major step: programming. "Programming is what I need to know," says Jarish. It's how you get to the "real secrets."

After he became involved with video games Jarish saved his money and bought a small personal computer that he uses to play games at home and to experiment with programming. But Jarish dreams of bigger things.

> My biggest interest would be having a terminal. Like one that you can connect to any computer. That would be incredible. My friend has an Apple. She can attach it to a giant computer. It cost about a million dollars. If you can get into different computers you could get the different codes about the computers and different languages and things about it, and take games from them—you know, like games that you couldn't find anywhere else—and transfer them to your own computer, and

change the games into anything you like. That would be really terrific. That's the stuff I'd like to do.

For now, Jarish finds games programs in computer magazines and types them into the computer, making small changes in the games, sometimes on purpose to suit his taste, more often by accident when he makes a typo. An object of current delight is a chase game that he modified to make a custom fit for his younger brother. "The program used to have Martians chasing the character, but after my brother heard the song 'Valley Girls' on the radio I changed the Martians to Valley Girls." But when he made this change, something unexpected happened:

> . . . the screen changed to fifty million different things. It was fantastic. And it made this snow effect that's coming down all over the place. And I figured out how to change one of the screens to make it do different things when you eat the treasures. When you eat the treasure you leave this trail, and usually in this game the trail is just dots, but I erased this one line in the program so now it makes these crazy things.

Jarish feels cheated when manufacturers put the games in cartridges so that he has no access to the underlying program. He can't change them the way he can when he finds a game program in a magazine and types it into his own computer.

> There are so many great games and they're really protected. They're trying to not let people copy them. It's really frustrating, because there are so many exciting things you can do with a game. It has nothing to do with—I mean forget the moneymaking part [here Jarish is referring to an earlier part of our conversation in which he fantasized about "changing Pac-Man and making it better and making a million dollars"], it's for just having fun.

Jarish doesn't yet know enough about programming to really make his own game, but he is in the process of teaching himself and is encouraged by events like his accidental snow effect. The possibilities seem limitless if such marvelous things can happen by chance. "In computers there is always that random thing, that neat thing that you are going to find out. And you keep at it, trying to find these neat things. Video games showed me what you could do with computers, what you could program. They show you what you can do. It's really wonderful."

To Joust and Beyond

In sports the player is held by the power of total concentration on action, the sense of melding body and mind. The television spectator's body is out of the picture. Here the sense of immersion is through imagination and identification.

The entertainment industry has long believed that the highest payoffs would come from offering the public media that combine action and imaginative identification. The manufacturers of pinball machines try to introduce a missing imaginative component by naming games to suggest exciting stories (you are controlling a pinball, but you are the "Black Knight") and by the equally limited conceit of painted flashy pictures of monsters, pirates, and sexy ladies on the machine's surfaces.

Finally, however, the only objects to identify with in the pinball game are the shiny steel ball and a pair of flippers. A Disneyland ride tries to introduce the feeling of action: watching a space lift-off on television, you are entirely on the "outside." In a Disney spaceship ride you are ushered into a simulated space cabin, you hear the rockets roar, you feel vibration in the seat. But, for all of this, there is nothing for you to do except use your imagination. In the end, the Disney ride is more passive than participatory drama. Once again, designers try, but the media resists.

But Jarish was able to enter the video game microworld through both doors. The polarization between action and imaginative identification breaks down in the presence of the computer: with the computer behind them the video games provide imaginative worlds into which people enter as participants. Other kinds of microworlds—television, sports, Disney rides, pinball—might offer the holding power of action, of imaginative identification, of losing oneself in a world outside of the habitual. You can find elements of what makes a computer microworld powerful in other things. But the computer can bring it together, and video games were the first place where the culture as a whole, rather than just the culture of computer programmers, got to experience how powerful this is.

Video games began in the computer culture, at one of the places, in fact, where the computer culture itself got started. The first video game was Space War, built at MIT in the early 1960s. The screen shows two spaceships, each under the control of one of two players. The ships can be maneuvered and can fire missiles at each other. When Space War was first built, visiting computer scientists were amazed by its dynamic, interactive screen graphics—the kind of graphics display that twenty years later would be commonplace in shopping malls. At that time, however, the cost and size of the computer required for Space War made it impossible to move it beyond the research environments of such places as MIT.

Ten years later, microtechnology allowed Nolan Bushnell, who had himself been an MIT undergraduate and a Space War enthusiast, to surprise the world with Pong. Compared with Space War its action was extremely limited: a blip—a square ball (easier to make than a round one)—bounced backward and forward across the screen in a crudely simulated Ping-Pong. But, unlike Space War, which you could play only by having access to a large computer facility, Pong could be made generally available. Bushnell founded a company he called Atari, which manufactured Pong in a box smaller than a pinball machine. Soon it was everywhere. You could play it in movie theaters and bars. You could buy a version of it to play on your television set. Pong was a novelty, but it set the stage for the arrival of another game, one that had already taken Japan by storm. This was Space Invaders, the game that launched the video game culture.

It took another ten years for video games to catch up with the complexity of the original Space War. A game like Joust, a favorite of Jarish's, is of a generation of games that has begun to move beyond. Space War had a recognizable "generic" spaceship, but, with neither color nor detail, it was less a spaceship than a spaceship ideogram. Just like the square ball in Pong, the spaceship was there to serve as a "marker." In Joust, knights duel on flying ostriches, using medieval lances. The player controls his or her ostrich with a joystick. A tug on the stick causes an ostrich that has been trotting along the land to begin to fly, movements of the stick to left or right cause the ostrich to travel in either direction or to reverse direction in midair, digging its heels into the ground before trotting off the other way.

Technological advances have enabled designers to create games that provide visually appealing situations and demand a diverse and challenging set of skills. But the ambition is to have the appeal of Disneyland, pinball, and a Tolkien novel all at once. Games like Joust do not offer the imaginative identification with a character and a situation that literature does. The knights in Joust owe their appeal to associations the player makes with fantasies about medieval combat that have been sparked through other media. And even the graphically "advanced" Joust lacks the degree of individual characterization one has come to expect in animated cartoons.

Designers are starting to break out of these limitations. New generations of computer graphics will allow game characters to have more realistic gestures and facial expressions. New programming techniques offer the hope of creating characters who have more specific and interesting personalities than the monsters in Pacman so that players' interactions with them may feel more like a social encounter and less like controlling a pinball. A computerized game of poker, for example, could create players who are individual and idiosyncratic. Some might easily fall for bluffs, others could try to bluff but betray themselves by facial expression, yet others allow themselves to be charmed by attractive opponents.

In the late 1970s Woody Allen wrote a classic short story about Kugelmass, a shy middle-aged professor who longs for romance.[1] A great magician comes to his aid. The magician has a box in which you place yourself and a book, open to any page. With a magic incantation you are instantly transported into that book. Kugelmass chooses *Madame Bovary* and has an affair with Emma in the relative safety of the pages before she meets Rodolphe and the competition gets too rough.

Woody Allen fantasized the interactive novel. Video game designers plan to implement it, perhaps less voluptuously, by putting the player in control of a character who lives not in a maze but in a piece of literature. Already there is a game in which the player takes the role of a character, Jen, who is also the hero of the movie *The Dark Crystal*. The Jen of the game faces the same situation as the Jen of the movie. The world is in peril; he must find the magic crystal that will save it. The Jen of the game will wander through a landscape identical in its topography and inhabitants to that of the movie. But the player behind the game-Jen has a choice of how to proceed. You can follow in the footsteps of the movie character, or you can take an altogether different route, meeting different characters, different dangers, different challenges.

Certainly, "playing" *The Dark Crystal* is still a lot more like a game of Pong than a collaboration with Flaubert. But primitive though it is, it provides an image of one direction in which games microworlds could go. It is a direction that makes us ask whether it is accurate to call such things "games" at all.

As this book is published, traditional film images, stored on video disks, are replacing animated computer graphics. With such systems, easily indexed by computer, a given command—for example, "Enter this room" in response to the screen image of a room—can invoke the film image of what is in it. There are "tours" of cities where you are in the picture, "driving" your car through the streets, deciding what buildings to enter. Where things will go is hard to imagine: "movies" and "talkies" were, too. But once you let your imagination work and then let it run a little wild (as wild, for example, as the programmers who made the first Space War) the possibilities are intriguing. You are Scarlett O'Hara, opening the door to Tara. You are Rhett Butler, deciding to stay rather than leave.

In circles where people are trying to invent the future of interactive media there seems to be a great divide. Will the player of the games of the future be in a more complex world than is offered by today's games, but still in a world that is created by someone else? Or will the player be the designer of his or her own game? In other words, will players continue to be "users" of someone else's program or will they be programmers in their own right? Will they be able to create new characters and change the rules of the game? Both strategies are being pursued, and surely both will bear fruit. One leads to an image of an interactive *Gone With the Wind*, the other to children building computer worlds as today's children build ferris wheels with Tinkertoys.

When Jarish began to talk about his new enthusiasm for the computer he offered a touching statement of his loyalty to video games even as he sensed it being threatened: "I love the computer, but I love video games, and whatever happens I will always love them." Unlike pinball, promised Jarish, these would never be abandoned. The breathy commitment was sincere, but should we take Jarish at his own word? It is difficult to imagine him playing anything like Pac-Man or Joust when he is thirty. What is possible is that he might be exploring interactive computer microworlds that erase the line between playing a game and writing a program, much as they erase the line between playing a game and making a movie.

Games, Gnomes, and Computer Culture

When today's child stands in front of a video game, there is contact between the physical child and the physical machine. But there is another contact as well: between the child's culture and a culture of simulation. Unlike the worlds of pinball machines or sports or literature, the computers within them make video games "rule-driven." This was certainly a big part of what appealed to Jarish, who knew that behind each game there was a program that held the key to what he called "the secrets." Video games offer a chance to live in simulated, rule-governed worlds. They bring this kind of experience into the child's culture and serve as a bridge to the larger computer culture beyond. They are not the only agent to do so. Reinforcements come from surprising quarters. Children come to the video games from a culture increasingly marked by the logic of simulation.

Recall the dogs and cats of Jarish's imaginary computer game. Animals are unusual images for him. More typically, his fantasies are populated by gnomes, wizards, and magic-users. When I was a child I knew about gnomes and wizards and spells from reading stories. Jarish knows about such things in a different way—he lives them. Most weeks are punctuated with marathon sessions of Dungeons and Dragons, a fantasy game where you create a character from medieval lore by rolling dice to determine its properties; among these are its level of charisma, its ability to use magic, its strength and dexterity. These qualities will be tested as you use your character to explore an intricate universe where there are monsters, adventures, wars, treasures, and a lot of hand-to-hand combat. Unlike the real world, the game universe always conforms to rules. There is violence, murder, and theft, but the rules for what can happen and how to handle it are precise. The charts and tables that allow you to design worlds and play characters form a small library: "For a kid today," says Jarish, "it's very hard. You have to get the money together for four or five or seven books. Very thick books. Like about fifteen dollars each." Jarish boasts of having read them all. He has become a master of this lore, an expert at manipulating the rules.

There are no computers in the dungeons. But these constructed worlds are permeated with the spirit of a computer program. Their constraints are those imposed by rule systems, not by physical reality or moral considerations. Time might go backward, people might have superhuman powers, everything is possible. What is required is consistency.

In the early 1970s, fantasy gaming grew from cult to culture in the worlds around computer programmers. They found an affinity between the aesthetic of building a large complex program, with its treelike structure, its subprograms and sub-subprograms, and working one's way through a highly structured, constructed world of mazes and magic and secret, hidden rooms.[2] They played the fantasy games, used their considerable talents to build ever more complex dungeons, and began to translate the idea into their own medium. Soon fantasy games with complex underground universes began to appear on large computer systems. Adventure was the first of these game programs. In it players explore the labyrinth of Colossal Cave, fighting monsters, hoarding treasure, picking up and discarding tools, food, spells, and other supplies as they go.

Other games followed, and as personal computers became more powerful, with memories that could hold the large data bases the games required, fantasy games spread to home systems. By the late 1970s, Adventure-like games were a staple item in the program libraries of most home computer owners, and the Dungeon games played "live" had spread from the computer culture to the culture at large. College students all over the country were absorbed in role-playing fantasy games and soon their younger brothers and sisters caught on. Dungeons and Dragons, a game that most adults find too complicated to contemplate, with its rule books, contingency tables, and mathematical formulas, became a best-seller among sixth and seventh graders.

Jarish compares Dungeons and Dragons, "D and D," to "regular" fantasy, the kind where you say, "You be Nancy Drew and I'll be a Hardy Boy and let's go off and solve a mystery." For him the big difference is in the greater "reality" of the D and D simulation.

> In D and D there is so much in the world. It's so big. There is an incredible amount of data. If you, say, you're playing Hardy Boys, there is only a certain level that you can go to—like you can't really go up to somebody and, you know, interrogate them, or say that you're with the Secret Service and tell them that they have to give you information. I mean, they wouldn't even have the information. You can't go that far with it. You know you have to stop at a certain point, whereas in D and D you can just

go on, and you can bypass those limits. The game is just in your head, but from that it almost transfers to be real. So that you can go and really imagine, picture yourself going through this cave, and then, all of a sudden, this thing, glorping all over the wall and dropping down on you, and you can throw a spell at it or something. You could almost imagine that.

Jarish is sure that D and D has more detail, is more complete, than Hardy Boys or pirates or cowboys. Beyond that, he is uncertain whether D and D is more real than reality. He hedges the question. "In D and D there's always a stopping point, in reality I guess it sort of happened." But he is not really sure. After reading seven D and D books "about twenty times each" he certainly knows more about the structure of dungeon universes than he does about any moment in history. He knows more about the behavior of magic users than about any person who ever lived. What he learns in social-studies class about real history is pale in contrast to what he experiences in D and D. "I mean," says Jarish, "in D and D there is so much data."

Jarish designs medieval dungeons and he devours science fiction. His dungeon worlds are meticulously drawn out on graph paper to scale with predetermined decision rules on how to respond to any player's actions. For him science-fiction worlds are of the same breed: the author is designing a future as Jarish designs a dungeon.

The computer programmers who felt such affinity for rule-driven fantasy games were as taken with science fiction as is Jarish, and somehow it all seemed to go together. A science-fiction writer is allowed to postulate time machines, intergalactic travel, or mental telepathy, but cannot do it arbitrarily. A planet can have any atmosphere, but its inhabitants must be adapted to it. The author must make every attempt to acknowledge the planet's atmospheric peculiarities when he or she designs the planet's life forms. You can postulate anything, but once the rules of the system have been defined they must be adhered to scrupulously. Such are the rules for creating "rule-governed worlds." They are known to every computer programmer and are now being passed on as cultural knowledge to a generation of children. The aesthetic of rule-governed worlds is passed on through Dungeons and Dragons and science fiction before most children ever meet a computer.

This is the culture that Jarish and his peers bring to their first encounter with a video game. It is not just the games' TV screens that make them seem like old friends. Here is another world where everything is possible but where nothing is arbitrary. Ultimately there are programs that stand behind the action. They can be deciphered; children speak of learning their secrets, recognizing them as worlds of complex behavior that in the end are rule-driven —like science fiction, like D and D, and, as they are starting to learn, like computers.

Losing Oneself in a Simulated World

If there is a danger here, it is not the danger of mindless play but of infatuation with the challenge of simulated worlds. In the right circumstances, some people come to prefer them to the real. This danger is not specific to games; it reflects one of the ways in which the games are a microcosm of computation. Computers offer the possibility of creating and working within artificial worlds, whether to simulate the behavior of economies, political systems, or imaginary subatomic particles. Like Narcissus and his reflection, people who work with computers can easily fall in love with the worlds they have constructed or with their performances in the worlds created for them by others. Involvement with simulated worlds affects relationships with the real one.

For Jarish, Dungeons and Dragons is clearly superior to games where you take roles or make up a story freely as you go along. As he sees it, Dungeons and Dragons has more data and feels more real. But he has lost something in his structured, data-rich games, both in video games and in role-playing fantasy games like Dungeons and Dragons.

Video games encourage identification with characters—from science fiction, or sports, or war stories—but leave little room for playing their roles. For example, the screen that children face when they play Asteroids does not look very different from that which confronted Han Solo in *The Empire Strikes Back* as he rode through the meteor shower with the panache that marked him as the greatest space pilot in the galaxy. This allows a very immediate kind of identification with Solo—the video simulations put you "in the place" of the spaceship pilot or the missile commander or the adventurer in the Tolkien world. But you are not allowed to play the part. Dungeons and Dragons allows much more of the personal role-playing that is missing from the video game. Yet it provides it in a way that is custom made for the computer generation: you identify with an alter ego as you play your role in the dungeon, but the process of play is mathematical and procedural. Beyond the fantasy, there are always the rules.

In all of this, something is missing, something that is abundantly present in the open-ended role playing that children offer each other when one says "You be the Mommy and I'll be the Daddy." The variations on this game are endless, the characters change with the issues on the children's minds and with the heroes and heroines of their culture: "You be Annie Oakley and I'll be Buffalo Bill." "You be Roy Rogers and I'll be Dale Evans." "You be Superman and I'll be Lois Lane." In this kind of play children have to learn to put themselves in the place of another person, to imagine what is going on inside someone else's head. There are no rules, there is empathy. There are no dice to roll, there is understanding, recognition, negotiation, and confrontation with others.

Children do not face an either/or choice. A child can play video games and Dungeons and Dragons and Hardy Boys. But in reality there is only so much time. Doing some things precludes others. And, even more important, an individual develops a style. In this case, there is good reason to think that a generation develops a style.

In Jarish we see such a stylistic preference. The Dungeons and Dragons way of thinking, with its thick books of rules, seems more exciting and more challenging than history or real life or fantasy play where the rules are less clear.

Altered States

When you play a video game you enter into the world of the programmers who made it. You have to do more than identify with a character on the screen. You must act for it. Identification through action has a special kind of hold. Like playing a sport, it puts people into a highly focused, and highly charged state of mind.[3] For many people, what is being pursued in the video game is not just a score, but an altered state.

The pilot of a race car does not dare to take his attention off the road. The imperative of total concentration is part of the high.

Video games demand this same level of attention. They can give people the feeling of being close to the edge because, as in a dangerous situation, there is no time for rest and the consequences of wandering attention feel dire. With pinball, a false move can be recuperated. The machine can be shaken, the ball repositioned. In a video game, the program has no tolerance for error, no margin of safety. Players experience their every movement as instantly translated into game action. The game is relentless in its demand that all other time stop and in its demand that the player take full responsibility for every act, a point that players often sum up by the phrase "One false move and you're dead."

Executives, accountants, and surgeons stand behind the junior-high-schoolers in games arcades. For people under pressure total concentration is a form of relaxation.

Marty is a twenty-nine-year-old economist who works for a large Manhattan bank. He is a nervous, wound-up man. "I'm a real worrier. A real 'type A person.' That's me." He says he plays the game because he needs "to have something to do which is so hard that I can't think of anything else." The games force him into another mental space where the thoughts and the cares of his day cannot intrude. For many years, Marty used transcendental meditation to relax. Now he uses video games.

> For me this is the same thing. It fills your mind. I can be peaceful. No decisions. I wasn't that good at keeping up the concentration for the TM. Thoughts kept breaking in. This is better. There is no way to think about anything but the game or it's all over. One false move or one false thought and you're dead. It makes my wife nervous to watch me play. She says I look so intense. She's afraid I'll have a heart attack. But when I play, inside I am cool. You have to be. You have to think about the patterns, the strategy. You wall the world out.

Marty used to play pinball, but, like TM, it was not sufficiently "coercive." In pinball, you can rest between sets, you can choose when to release your next ball. In Asteroids, the first game that Marty got hooked on, the pace is never yours. The rhythm of the game belongs to the machine, the program decides. When the play picks up, Asteroids pounds out a beat that stands between a pulse and a drum. "It's its heartbeat," says the twelve-year-old player standing next to Marty in the arcade. "It's what you have to play to." There is no time for pause. You play to the relentless pulse of a machine heart.

Video games allow Marty to feel swept away and in control, to have complete power and yet lose himself in something outside. The games combine a feeling of omnipotence and possession— they are a place for manipulation and surrender. When Marty practiced TM, he felt it as "time out." Asteroids gave him more of a sense of achievement. It is a world where you are "lost," yet you have clear goals. "Unlike in the meditation, when I play games I feel that I've achieved something. I am getting good at something —in fact, I am always getting better. I love watching that score go up."

The games require total concentration—to which he attributes their "meditative" qualities—at the same time as they provide a stage for excellence. You get to do what achievement-oriented people like to do: get better. And yet, in their own way, they are also "time out." Marty calls it "meditation with macho": "It's the relaxation of forcing you to withdraw from the rat race, yet they give you a score that reassures you that you are a winner."

Roger is a fifty-year-old businessman who seeks out video games to achieve the state of mind that he gets into when he skis. He plays a game until that point where "the strategies are part of you," where he feels like an extension of the game or the game is an extension of him. Roger compares the feeling to being in touch with an unconscious self: "When I play the games I don't think. My fingers think. As in skiing, you know the terrain, you feel the terrain. My mind is clear. Things pass through it. I make connections. They say it's mindless, but for me it's liberating. I am in control of the game, but mind is free. The way I see it, I'm not wasting my quarters. It's cheaper than psychoanalysis."

To master a video game, conscious playing is not enough. You have to "think with your fingers." As in sports, mental and physical action have to come together. An athlete thinks with the body. You feel the skis as part of you, you know their relationship to surrounding space, objects, and obstacles in the direct way that you feel your body in space. Call it "muscle memory," call it "flow," call it "trusting your instincts"—the experience of feeling a continuity between mind and body is part of the inner game of any well-played sport. Skilled video game players experience this immediacy of knowing their game with more than their head, and the experience is exhilarating.

David is a lawyer in his midthirties. When he watches television, he says he is relaxed, lost in someone else's world. When he plays video games, he experiences another kind of relaxation, the relaxation of being on the line. He feels "totally focused, totally concentrated." And yet David, like Marty and Roger, indeed like all successful players of video games, describes the sense in which the highest degree of focus and concentration comes from a letting go of both. David talks about playing best when he is not "directed."

> Well, it's almost, at the risk of sounding, uh, ridiculous, if you will, it's almost a Zen type of thing . . . where I can direct myself totally but not feel directed at all. You're totally absorbed and it is all happening there. You know what you are supposed to do. There's no external confusion, there's no conflicting goals, there's none of the complexities that the rest of the world is filled with. It's so simple. You either get through this little maze so that the creature doesn't swallow you up or you don't. And if you can focus your attention on that, and if you can really learn what you're supposed to do, then you really are in relationship with the game.

Being in relationship with the game means getting recentered on yourself. Every day before going home David stops off at his favorite arcade and plays for an hour or two. At first he says that he does it to unwind, but then he decides that "unwind" is the wrong word.

> It's not so much unwind as it is that I can sort of cleanse myself in a sense, in a very strange sense. Now I'm done with the day, and I go there, and I play these games, and I've found myself again. And then I can start on something new. Because if I go right home, I won't be prepared to talk to my wife. All day I give people advice about their lives, about their divorces, just little pieces of advice. It's very fragmented. It's like being a psychologist, but I don't get to hear it in the full way that a psychologist would. Just little fragments. A lot is going on for my wife now. She is expecting this baby and she needs to talk. I need to be able to communicate with her. And after I play the games I'm prepared to realize that I'm in the middle of the whole picture

instead of just being on the outside looking in. OK, because when I play it is my picture. When I'm at work it's not really my picture. When I get home it is my picture again. And after I play I can go back and share me. So, sometimes the games are a preparation for getting out and being aggressive in the rest of my life, and sometimes they are there for, um, getting back into my own video game.

Metaphysical Machines

The emotional power of video games draws heavily on the computer power within that supports a simulated world and a meditative environment, what David called a place for "recentering." But the power of the games draws on other aspects of the computer as well, some of them resonant with children's fascination with computer toys as "metaphysical machines." As a computational object, the video game holds out two promises. The first is a touch of infinity—the promise of a game that never stops.

Most video games give you three chances: three "men," three "ships," three "missiles." Novice players get wiped out in seconds. And three chances to play for several seconds doesn't add up to very much time. The new player dreams of actually being able to shoot the invader or capture the monster or steer the ship. The new player dreams of a respectable score, and imagines that this will feel like "winning." But when the game skill becomes second nature, when the scores reach the hundreds of thousands, then it becomes clear that in a video game there is nothing except gaining more time, and, for some players, the idea that but for their growing fatigue, their "human limitations," the game could go on forever.

When you face a game of pinball, there is a clearly demarcated point when the game is over. You may have achieved a high score, you may win a free game. A video game presents no such moment. Mastery of one level of the game, one "screen," presents another screen, more difficult in its patterns or with the same task to do but at a faster rate. Some games give you an extra "man," an extra character to play as a bonus if you succeed with a particularly difficult move, but another character comes to the same thing: more time. The game will go on as long as you have a character to play. Everyone knows that the game is going to end "sometime," but sometime is potentially infinite.

Recall Matthew, the five-year-old who was frightened by the idea that a computer program could go on forever—frightened and also fascinated. Things that give a sense of contact with the infinite are held apart as privileged. They become charged with emotion. They are often imbued with religious feeling. The feeling can be evoked by a sunset, a mountain, the sea. It can be evoked by mathematical experiences, the idea of the infinite sequence of decimals of pi, the sight of two mirrors reflecting each other. And these feelings are evoked by the computer and by the experience of a game that need never stop.

The games hold out a related promise, also tied to the computer's presence within them. This is the promise of perfection.

Perfect Mirrors

Jimmy is fourteen years old, and he has made his play into an intensely private ritual. He plays at home, alone, and only one game, an "old game," Space Invaders. His manner of playing is disciplined and methodical. "I have my strategy and that's that. Once you have your strategy, then you just have to be perfect in doing it." Jimmy doesn't think of the game in terms of losing or winning. "For me the game is to see how long I can be perfect. Every day I try to be perfect for ten minutes longer."

Outside of the Space Invaders world, Jimmy is not perfect. Jimmy has a birth defect that has left him with an awkward gait and slightly slurred speech. He does not like the way he sounds. He has not made peace with his body. He fears that people are noticing him, "thinking that I am ugly. I especially hate being around girls." And he feels at war with his mind. "I'm usually thinking crazy things, like I don't even want to tell you what I'm thinking. Let's just say it's crazy." But Space Invaders puts him in an altered state. The game is itself perfect in its consistent response. It will deliver this perfection to the deserving player, to the player who is uncompromising in his or her concentration on the game. When Jimmy plays he feels himself becoming "perfect" and calm. "I don't, can't think of my crazy things. It's my discipline. I guess you might say I'm obsessed."

Jimmy's physical disabilities make his case dramatic, but what stands out in his relationship with Space Invaders—doing something that serves as a measuring stick for "perfection"—is not unique to him or to video games. Different people use different yardsticks. Some use their bodies as a material much as Jimmy uses his game, "playing with" their appearance, their dress, and their weight. Cara, for example, is a slightly overweight fourteen-year-old girl who defines her "discipline" as eating ten fewer calories every day, with many of the same feelings about it as Jimmy has about demanding ten more minutes each day from Space Invaders. There is the same desire to control the inside through action on the outside. Such efforts in control have a positive side. With them can come an enhanced sense of autonomy, self-esteem, a sense of being the "actor" in one's life. But with every powerful and manipulable medium that we use to feel more in control—our bodies, our money, our games—the medium can get out of control.

Most people don't become addicted to video games just as most people who diet don't become anorexic. But when they use these powerful materials to measure themselves, they are at risk. And, of course, some people come to the material more vulnerable than others. The greater the anxiety about being out of control, the greater the seduction of a material that offers the promise of perfect response. The body offers this kind of promise. So many fewer calories will cause so many pounds to drop. Part of the "holding power" of any diet is the sense of involvement with the process itself. People go on diets to improve their appearance. They begin regimens of exercise for the same reason. But the experience of molding the body, the experience of its response, its malleability, can take over. Similarly, the experience of a game that makes an instantaneous and exact response to your touch, or of a computer that is itself always consistent in its response, can take over. It becomes gripping, independent of anything that you are trying to "do" with it in an instrumental sense.

Itself seemingly perfect, the computer evokes anxiety about one's own perfectibility. There is pressure from a machine that leaves no one and no other thing to blame. It is hard to walk away from the perfect mirror, from the perfect test. It is hard to walk away from a video game on which you could do better next time, it is hard to walk away from a computer program with an undiscovered "bug," it is hard to walk away from an unproofread text on the screen of a word processor. Any computer promises you that if *you* do it right, it will do it right and right away.

People who try out video games and say they hate them, or who actively dislike their first experience with computer programming, are often responding to this same promise. Not everyone wants to be around the perfect mirror. Some people dislike what they experience as the precision, the unforgivingness of mathematics. Instead of being intrigued or reassured by the idea of there being a "right answer" in their first arithmetic class, they found it intolerable. It was felt as a pressure, as a taunt, as a put-down. Mechanical objects (they work if you handle them right, they don't work if you handle them wrong) evoke the same anxieties. And when these people (in our culture, often women) meet the computer the problem is taken to a higher order. Here is a machine that goes beyond all others in its promise to reflect human competence. It is not always welcome. For some, its challenge may be felt as an alien contest. For others as a long-awaited chance to finally test one's worth.

Perfect Contests

David, the lawyer who used the games to "recenter," who saw them as a kind of Zen, knows that he looks successful in the eyes of the world, but he feels unsatisfied, at war with his work. He would like to be in control of things and fantasizes himself a warrior, a hero, an explorer. He would like to test himself against danger, against the elements, against an unexplored terrain. He chose law as a career and specialized in litigation, hoping that the adversary world of the courtroom would provide the thrill of hand-to-hand combat. But the reality of his job is very different.

> There is no way I can challenge anybody in a pure mental challenge. Where you can really say, "This is it. This is me and this is you." I can go into court and I can think of myself as fighting like that, one on one, but there is always some other factor. He's got one set of facts and I've got another set of facts. I'm always constrained by those things.

In a video game there is no place to hide, no excuses of chance or accident. For someone like David, searching for the sense of urgency that comes from real danger, this is crucial to the games' seduction. It is a place where there is "pure you."

David's hours in the arcade are part of his search for the perfect contest. It is a place in which to stand alone, "It's you against it." But it is a fixed entity. "So ultimately," says David, "it's you against you. My life is bound up in external constraints. With the games I face only myself. If I do well, it is pure me. If I do poorly . . . there's nothing else I can blame for a failure or an unsatisfying experience with a video game. There's no little person changing it. Playing the game is an assertion, completely pure individual competition."

His medium offers a pure test. Unlike boxing, or golf, or tennis, there will be no change of partners, no new referee. David doesn't like the "realm-of-infinite-possibilities kind of game." He describes chess negatively as the kind of game where "you make a move and the other person responds, and the other person can respond in any one of, well, in any one of a thousand ways." David wants a different kind of game, a game where the set of circumstances is going to be the same every time. The video games with their programmed responses are made to measure. Shoot the opponent from a certain distance and you get so many points. Move a little closer and you explode. With practice, the performance rules become transparent. David likes video games when they can serve as the perfect mirror, the perfect measure of who he is. "I want the game as simple as it can be . . . not really simple, but fixed. Like how many times can I bounce the ball against the wall within the next twenty seconds? When I say 'simple,' what I mean is fixed, invariant. A true test in that respect."

He doesn't like it when random elements are programmed into video games. For he relies on the game's invariant nature to give him a measure of his state of mind. If he's calm and centered he'll do well. If he is tense, diffused, anxious, he'll do poorly. "The better I do at a game, the better I feel—not because I feel good for winning, but because I know that I am in a good state. It's not just what the games do for me, it's what they show me about what was there to begin with." Beyond this, they are a preparation for life. "It has to do with testing yourself; it has to do with the idea that basic training will make a man out of you, with the idea that you have never lived unless you've lived close to the edge. The games are that simple, 'close to the edge,' but they are not threatening. Do you understand? It's a peculiar sort of feeling."

David fears that all his life he has shied away from testing how hard and far he could push himself. "It's the thing of the moment that suits me for right now. . . . I'm growing up. I've been married a year and now we're expecting a baby." He wants reassurance that he can handle things. The games are his test.

David is deeply involved with video games. He has woven them into his most personal concerns. But it is not among adults that the weave is most dense. Although they play video games and work with the computer, they grew up in a culture built without these machines. Young people are building their generation's culture now; video games and computers are among their materials. Growing up with a technology is a special kind of experience. Although mastering new things is important throughout life, there is a time in growing up when identity becomes almost synonymous with it. Today's young people meet the games at that time. The games are not a reminder of a feeling of control over challenge. They are a primary source for developing it.

In the next chapters I turn to children who are doing more with computers than using them for games. These children are working with computer systems that turn the machines into a medium for self-expression. We shall see a child programming an animated scene of a space shuttle that is in no sense a simulation. The excitement here is not in the process of deciphering the program, but of making it in a highly personalized way.

I introduced this chapter by speaking of the games as a window onto the culture of computation. But when you play a video game you are a player in a game programmed by someone else. When children begin to do their own programming, they are not deciphering somebody else's mystery. They become players in their own game, makers of their own mysteries, and enter into a new relationship with the computer, one in which they begin to experience it as a kind of second self.

CHAPTER 3

Child Programmers:
The First Generation

Consider Robin, a four-year-old with blond hair and a pinafore, standing in front of a computer console, typing at its keyboard. She is a student at a nursery school that is introducing computers to very young children. She is playing a game that allows her to build stick figures by commanding the computer to make components appear and move into a desired position. The machine responds to Robin's commands and tells her when it does not understand an instruction. Many people find this scene disturbing. First, Robin is "plugged into" a machine. We speak of television as a "plug-in drug," but perhaps the very passivity of what we do with television reassures us. We are concerned about children glued to screens, but, despite what we have heard of Marshall McLuhan and the idea that "the medium is the message," the passivity of television encourages many of us to situate our sense of its impact at the level of the content of television programming.[1] Is it violent or sexually suggestive? Is it educational? But Robin is not "watching" anything on the computer. She is manipulating— perhaps more problematic, *interacting with*—a complex technological medium. And the degree and intensity of her involvement suggests that (like the children at the video games) it is the medium itself and not the content of a particular program that produces the more powerful effect. But beyond any specific fear, so young a child at a computer conflicts with our ideal image of childhood. The "natural" child is out of doors; machines are indoors. The natural child runs free; machines control and constrain. Machines and children don't go together.[2]

Something else feels discordant, and that is the nature of Robin's interaction with the computer. She is not manipulating the machine by turning knobs or pressing buttons. She is writing messages to it by spelling out instructions letter by letter. Her painfully slow typing seems laborious to adults, but she carries on with an absorption that makes it clear that time has lost its meaning for her. Computers bring writing within the scope of what very young children can do. It is far easier to press keys on a keyboard than to control a pencil. Electronic keyboards can be made sensitive to the lightest touch; more important, they permit instant erasure. The computer is a forgiving writing instrument, much easier to use than even an electric typewriter.

That a four-year-old or a three-year-old might learn to make a fire poses a real physical danger, but it does not call anything about childhood into question. We find it easy to accept, indeed we are proud, when children develop physical skills or the ability to manipulate concrete materials earlier than we expect. But a basic change in the child's manipulation of symbolic materials threatens something deep. Central to our notion of childhood is the idea that children of Robin's age and younger speak but do not write.

Many people are excited by the possibility that writing may be brought within the range of capabilities of very young children. But others seem to feel that setting a four-year-old to writing does violence to a natural process of unfolding. For them, what is most disturbing about Robin is not her relationship to the machine, but her relationship to writing, to the abstract, to the symbolic. Opening the question of children and writing provokes a reaction whose force recalls that evoked by Freud's challenge to the sexual innocence of the child.

In the eighteenth century, Jean-Jacques Rousseau associated writing with moral danger in the most direct way.[3] He saw the passage from nature to culture as the end of a community of free, spontaneous communication. Writing marked the point of rupture. In Rousseau's mind, this story of loss of community and communication projects itself onto the life of each individual. Each growing up is a loss of innocence and immediacy, and the act of writing symbolizes that the loss has taken place. To a certain extent, each of us reenacts the fall. Our first marks of pen on paper retrace the introduction of a barrier between ourselves and other people. Childhood, innocence, is the state of not writing.

The computer has become the new cultural symbol of the things that Rousseau feared from the pen: loss of direct contact with other people, the construction of a private world, a flight from real things to their representations. With programming, as for so many other things, the computer presence takes what was already a concern and gives it new form and new degree. If our ideas about childhood are called into question by child writers, what of child programmers? If childhood innocence is eroded by writing, how much more so by programming?

What happens when young children, grade-school children, become programmers?[4] Faced with the reality of child experts who have appropriated the computers that dot grade schools and junior highs across the country, there is talk of a "computer generation" and of a new generation gap.

Sarah, a thirty-five-year-old lawyer and mother of three, feels an unbridgeable gap between herself and her son, and she alternates between agitation and resignation:

> I could have learned that "new math." I could understand, respect my son if his values turn out to be different than mine. I mean, I think I could handle the kinds of things that came up between parents and kids in the sixties. I would have talked to my son; I would have tried to understand. But my ten-year-old is into programming, into computers, and I feel that this makes his mind work in a whole different way.

Do computers change the way children think? Do they open children's minds or do they dangerously narrow their experience, making their thinking more linear and less intuitive? There is a temptation to look for a universal, isolable effect, the sort that still eludes experts on the effect of television.

The problem here is the search for a universal effect. I have found that different children are touched in remarkably different ways by their experience with the computer. However, by looking closely at how individual children appropriate the computer we can build ways to think about how the computer enters into development, and we begin to get some answers to our questions. In a sense, I turn the usual question around: instead of asking what the computer does to children I ask what children, and more important, what different kinds of children make of the computer.

A Setting for Diversity

I observed child programmers in a variety of school settings. In most schools there was one or perhaps two computers per grade. In a few, every classroom had at least one computer. And in one special situation, every child had unlimited computer access. The children I observed programmed in a number of languages, including BASIC, PILOT, and Logo.[5] In every setting it was apparent that computers had brought something new into the classroom. In every classroom there were some children who were particularly excited about programming, who shared ideas with other child programmers, who began to build an intellectual community. These children often found themselves in an unusual situation: in this domain they became experts, even more expert than their teachers. In many classrooms this spontaneous emergence of intellectual community was limited to a particular kind of child, typically boys with strong interests in math or electronics or other things technical. This does not mean that other children did not learn to program. In fact, in several of the classrooms they were required to do so. But they did so in the spirit of trying to do well in a school activity and of trying to conform to a set of expectations imposed from without. What was remarkable in the school where there was unlimited computer access was the range of children who became seriously involved with the computer. In this environment, where the computer experience was relatively free from curricular expectations, children developed highly individualized approaches to programming that provided a window onto larger issues of intellectual style and personality.

A private school that I shall call Austen, with children from preschool through fourth grade, was the site of a broadly conceived research project involving the design of a special computer, the training of a group of teachers, and a research program to study the children's progress. All the children at Austen had access to computers, and a group of about fifty third and fourth graders were offered a more intensive experience. Fifteen of them, chosen for the diversity of their backgrounds, interests, and talents, were studied in depth. The school itself had a long tradition of open classrooms and flexible scheduling, which facilitated the integration of computers into classroom life. At almost any time of the day I saw children, working alone or in groups, at small personal computers scattered throughout the school.

At Austen, programming was not treated as a "school subject." The children had liberal access to the machines, to program as they wished. The general ferment of activity that resulted was so great that teachers could not closely monitor the children or impose an "official" way of doing things even if they had wanted to. And in this case, there was also an explicit commitment to encouraging the children to appropriate the project as their own.

This is not a school that "brought in some computers," but a school that created conditions for the growth of a computer culture. The intention was to simulate a future where computers would be everyday objects in the life of the child.

The Austen School used the Logo computer language. It is embedded in a philosophy of education described in *Mindstorms* by Seymour Papert, the mathematician and educator most associated with the development of Logo. Papert stresses noncompetitive learning and the use of the computer as a tool for intellectual development.

Two of Papert's images capture his ideas about computers and education. One is "the computer as pencil"—that is, that computers should be as available and accessible to children as pencils and should be used for as broad a range of activities, "for scribbling as well as for writing, doodling as well as drawing, for illicit notes as well as for official classroom assignments."[6]

Papert's second image is "the computer as mathland." The most natural way to learn to speak French is the way French children do, by speaking French to French-speaking people. By analogy, the most natural way to learn a mathematical language is through conversation with a mathematical speaking entity, and this is the computer. The child programs the computer. In "teaching" the machine, the child learns to speak its language and manipulate formal and mathematical systems. Papert calls this kind of natural learning "Piagetian" learning—learning that happens spontaneously when people are in contact with the right materials. One of the most striking things about the Austen project was the way in which the creation of a child programming culture created new relationships between students, teachers, and curriculum.*

Commonplace assumptions about what happens in schools did not hold true for the computer-rich Austen classrooms: that teachers know more than students, that teachers are more interested than students, and that it is the teacher's job to design artful ways to motivate children to learn things that would not come naturally to them.

Such assumptions are called into question when children are in passionate relationships with the learning material and when that material allows for its own natural exploration. An example may help to make the point. It is fairly clear that children playing video games show improved hand–eye coordination and learn how to decode the rules behind each game's structure. Imagine a situation in which teachers tried to "teach" children video games in order to work on these skills. The idea seems foolish because we know that children learn these games although they come with virtually no instructions. Children dive into their exploration. They watch others play, they figure it out for themselves. It is much like this with interactive computers. Children can learn a great deal without being taught. Many children move beyond their teachers in their degree of interest and even their expertise. In these cases teachers take on the role of guides to what is very much a new territory for them as well as for their students.†

A Children's Computer Culture

When children learn to program, one of their favorite areas of work is computer graphics—programming the machine to place displays on the screen. The Logo graphics system available at Aus-

---

* I followed the Austen project from its inception, spoke to the teachers during their training, and then when the machines were in place observed and interviewed the students and had access to the results of the psychological tests—Rorschach, WISC (IQ), Locus of Control —that had been administered to the fifteen children selected for special study. The study of the Austen students was a collaborative effort with Seymour Papert and John Berlow.

† Of course, some students respond less enthusiastically, less successfully. This chapter describes children who did get involved, in order to discuss the relationships between programming and personality. The phenomena discussed in this chapter could happen because a sufficient number of children became deeply involved to constitute a "subculture" that developed a degree of autonomy and that attracted very different kinds of children.

ten was relatively powerful. It provided thirty-two computational objects called sprites that appear on the screen when commanded to do so. Each sprite has a number. When called by its number and given a color and shape, it comes onto the screen with that shape and color: a red truck, a blue ball, a green airplane. Children can manipulate one sprite at a time, several of them, or all of them at once, depending on the effect they want to achieve. The sprites can take predefined shapes, such as trucks and airplanes, or they can be given new shapes designed on a special grid, a sprite "scratchpad." They can be given a speed and a direction and be set in motion. The direction is usually specified in terms of a heading from 0 to 360, where 0 would point the sprite due north, 90 would point it due east, 180 south, 270 west, and 360 north again.

At the time the system was introduced, the teachers thought the manipulation of headings would be too complex for second graders because it involves the concept of angles, so these children were introduced to the commands for making sprites appear, giving them shapes and colors, and placing them on the screen, but not for setting them in motion. Motion would be saved for later grades.

The curriculum held for two weeks. That is, it held until one second grader, Gary, caught on to the fact that something exciting was happening on the older children's screens, and knew enough to pick up the trick from a proud and talkative third grader. In one sense, the teachers were right: Gary didn't understand that what he was dealing with were "angles." He didn't have to. He wanted to make the computer do something, and he found a way to assimilate the concept of angle to something he already knew— secret codes. "The sprites have secret codes, like 10, 100, 55. And if you give them their codes they go in different directions. I've taught the code to fourteen second graders," he confided to a visitor. "We're sort of keeping it a secret. The teachers don't know. We haven't figured out all the codes yet, but we're working on it." Two weeks later, Gary and his friends were still cracking the code. "We're still not sure about the big numbers" (sprites interpret 361 as 1, one full revolution plus 1), but they were feeling very pleased with themselves.

Gary's discovery, not the only one of its kind, contributed to creating a general pattern at Austen. Students felt that computer knowledge belonged to them and not only to the teachers. Once knowledge had become forbidden fruit, once appropriation of it had become a personal challenge, teachers could no longer maintain their position as the rationers of "curricular materials." In a setting like Austen, ideas about programming travel the way ideas travel in active, dynamic cultures. They sweep through, carried by children who discover something, often by chance, through playful exploration of the machine.

Gary and his fellow decoders finally presented their discoveries to the authorities with pride of authorship. At Austen programming tricks and completed programs are valued—they are traded and they become gifts. In traditional school settings, finished book reports are presented to teachers who try to instill a sense of the class as community by asking the children to read them aloud to the group. In the context of children and programming projects, the sharing usually happens naturally. Children can't do much with each other's book reports, but they can do a great deal with each other's programs. Another child's program can be changed, new features can be added, it can be personalized. (One child can figure out how to get the computer to engage in a "dialogue," but a second child can change the script; one child can figure out how to write a program that will display an animated drawing of a rocket going to the moon, but a second child can build on it and have the rocket orbit once it gets there.) Most objects can't be given away and kept at the same time. But computer programs are easily shared, copied from one child's personal storage disk or cassette to that of another. As the child experiences it, the originator of the program gets to be famous. And other people get to build on his or her ideas.

Anne, an artistic fourth grader, had originated a program in which birds made of sprites fly across the sky and disappear behind clouds. One morning as we spoke, she glanced around the classroom. Five of the eight computers within view had objects disappearing, melting, and fading into other colors. "It's like a game of telephone," she said. "You start it, but then it changes. But you can always sort of see part of your original idea. And people know that you were the first."

At Austen we are faced with the growth of an intellectual community that we do not normally see among schoolchildren. What makes the community most special is that it includes children with a wide range of personalities, interests, and learning styles who express their differences through their styles of programming.

Jeff and Kevin

Jeff, a fourth grader, has a reputation as one of the school's computer experts. He is meticulous in his study habits, does superlative work in all subjects. His teachers were not surprised to see him excelling in programming. Jeff approaches the machine with determination and the need to be in control, the way he approaches both his schoolwork and his extracurricular activities. He likes to be, and often is, chairman of student committees. At the moment, his preoccupation with computers is intense: "They're the biggest thing in my life right now." He speaks very fast, and when he talks about his programs he speaks even faster, tending to monologue. He answers a question about what his program does by tossing off lines of computer code that for him seem to come as naturally as English. His typing is expert—he does not look at the code as it appears on the screen. He conveys the feeling that he is speaking directly to an entity inside. "When I program I put myself in the place of the sprite. And I make it do things."

Jeff is the author of one of the first space-shuttle programs. He does it, as he does most other things, by making a plan. There will be a rocket, boosters, a trip through the stars, a landing. He conceives the program globally; then he breaks it up into manageable pieces. "I wrote out the parts on a big piece of cardboard. I saw the whole thing in my mind just in one night, and I couldn't wait to come to school to make it work." Computer scientists will recognize this global "top-down," "divide-and-conquer" strategy as "good programming style." And we all recognize in Jeff someone who conforms to our stereotype of a "computer person" or an engineer —someone who would be good with machines, good at science, someone organized, who approaches the world of things with confidence and sure intent, with the determination to make it work.

Kevin is a very different sort of child. Where Jeff is precise in all of his actions, Kevin is dreamy and impressionistic. Where Jeff tends to try to impose his ideas on other children, Kevin's warmth, easygoing nature, and interest in others make him popular. Meetings with Kevin were often interrupted by his being called out to rehearse for a school play. The play was *Cinderella,* and he had been given the role of Prince Charming. Kevin comes from a military family; his father and grandfather were both in the Air Force. But Kevin has no intention of following in their footsteps. "I don't want to be an army man. I don't want to be a fighting man. You can get killed." Kevin doesn't like fighting or competition in general. "You can avoid fights. I never get anybody mad—I mean, I try not to."

Jeff has been playing with machines all his life—Tinkertoys, motors, bikes—but Kevin has never played with machines. He likes stories, he likes to read, he is proud of knowing the names of "a lot of different trees." He is artistic and introspective. When Jeff is asked questions about his activities, about what he thinks is fun, he answers in terms of how to do them right and how well he does them. He talks about video games by describing his strategy breakthroughs on the new version of Space Invaders: "Much harder, much trickier than the first one." By contrast, Kevin talks about experiences in terms of how they make him feel. Video games make him feel nervous, he says. "The computer is better," he adds. "It's easier. You get more relaxed. You're not being bombarded with stuff all the time."

Kevin too is making a space scene. But the way he goes about it is not at all like Jeff's approach. Jeff doesn't care too much about the detail of the form of his rocket ship; what is important is getting a complex system to work together as a whole. But Kevin cares more about the aesthetics of the graphics. He spends a lot of time on the shape of his rocket. He abandons his original idea ("It didn't look right against the stars") but continues to "doodle" with the scratchpad shape-maker. He works without plan, experimenting, throwing different shapes onto the screen. He frequently stands back to inspect his work, looking at it from different angles, finally settling on a red shape against a black night—a streamlined, futuristic design. He is excited and calls over two friends. One admires the red on the black. The other says that the red shape "looks like fire." Jeff happens to pass Kevin's machine on the way to lunch and automatically checks out its screen, since he is always looking for new tricks to add to his toolkit for building programs. He shrugs. "That's been done." Nothing new there, nothing technically different, just a red blob.

Everyone goes away and Kevin continues, now completely taken up by the idea that the red looks like fire. He decides to make the ship white so that a red shape can be red fire "at the bottom." A long time is spent making the new red fireball, finding ways to give it spikes. And a long time is spent adding detail to the now white ship. With the change of color, new possibilities emerge: "More things will show up on it." Insignias, stripes, windows, and the project about which Kevin is most enthusiastic: "It can have a little seat for the astronaut." When Jeff programs he puts himself in the place of the sprite; he thinks of himself as an abstract computational object. Kevin says that, as he works, "I think of myself as the man inside the rocket ship. I daydream about it. I'd like to go to the moon."

By the next day Kevin has a rocket with red fire at the bottom. "Now I guess I should make it move . . . moving and wings . . . it should have moving and wings." The wings turn out to be easy, just some more experimenting with the scratchpad. But he is less certain about how to get the moving right.

Kevin knows how to write programs, but his programs emerge —he is not concerned with imposing his will on the machine. He is concerned primarily with creating exciting visual effects and allows himself to be led by the effects he produces. Since he lets his plans change as new ideas turn up, his work has not been systematic. And he often loses track of things. Kevin has lovingly worked on creating the rocket, the flare, and a background of twinkling stars. Now he wants the stars to stay in place and the rocket and the flare to move through them together.

It is easy to set sprites in motion: just command them to an initial position and give them a speed and a direction. But Kevin's rocket and red flare are two separate objects (each shape is carried by a different sprite) and they have to be commanded to move together at the same speed, even though they will be starting from different places. To do this successfully, you have to think about coordinates and you have to make sure that the objects are identified differently so that code for commanding their movement can be addressed to each of them independently. Without a master plan Kevin gets confused about the code numbers he has assigned to the different parts of his program, and the flare doesn't stay with the rocket but flies off with the stars. It takes a lot of time to get the flare and the ship back together. When Jeff makes a mistake, he is annoyed, calls himself "stupid," and rushes to correct his technical error. But when Kevin makes an error, although it frustrates him he doesn't seem to resent it. He sometimes throws his arms up in exasperation: "Oh no, oh no. What did I do?" His fascination with his effect keeps him at it.

In correcting his error, Kevin explores the system, discovering new special effects as he goes along. In fact, the "mistake" leads him to a new idea: the flare shouldn't go off with the stars but should drop off the rocket, "and then the rocket could float in the stars." More experimenting, trying out of different colors, with different placements of the ship and the flare. He adds a moon, some planets. He tries out different trajectories for the rocket ship, different headings, and different speeds; more mistakes, more standing back and admiring his evolving canvas. By the end of the week Kevin too has programmed a space scene.

Styles of Mastery

Jeff and Kevin represent cultural extremes. Some children are at home with the manipulation of formal objects, while others develop their ideas more impressionistically, with language or visual images, with attention to such hard-to-formalize aspects of the world as feeling, color, sound, and personal rapport. Scientific and technical fields are usually seen as the natural home for people like Jeff; the arts and humanities seem to belong to the Kevins.

Watching Kevin and Jeff programming the same computer shows us two very different children succeeding at the same thing —and here it must be said that Kevin not only succeeded in creating a space scene, but, like Jeff, he learned a great deal about computer programming and mathematics, about manipulating angles, shapes, rates, and coordinates. But although succeeding at the same thing, they are not doing it the same way. Each child developed a distinctive style of mastery—styles that can be called hard and soft mastery.[7]

Hard mastery is the imposition of will over the machine through the implementation of a plan. A program is the instrument of premeditated control. Getting the program to work is more like getting "to say one's piece" than allowing ideas to emerge in the give-and-take of conversation. The details of the specific program obviously need to be "debugged"—there has to be room for change, for some degree of flexibility in order to get it right—but the goal is always getting the program to realize the plan.

Soft mastery is more interactive. Kevin is like a painter who stands back between brushstrokes, looks at the canvas, and only from this contemplation decides what to do next. Hard mastery is the mastery of the planner, the engineer, soft mastery is the mastery of the artist: try this, wait for a response, try something else, let the overall shape emerge from an interaction with the medium. It is more like a conversation than a monologue.

Hard and soft mastery recalls anthropologist Claude Lévi-Strauss' discussion of the scientist and the *bricoleur*.[8] Lévi-Strauss used the term *bricolage*, tinkering, to make a distinction between Western science and the science of preliterate societies. The former is a science of the abstract, the latter is a science of the concrete. Like the *bricoleur*, the soft master works with a set of concrete elements. While the hard master thinks in terms of global abstractions, the soft master works on a problem by arranging and rearranging these elements, working through new combinations. Although the *bricoleur* works with a closed set of materials, the results of combining elements can lead to new and surprising results.

Mastery and Personality

Computer programming is usually thought of as an activity that imposes its style on the programmer. And that style is usually presumed to be closer to Jeff and his structured, "planner's" approach than to Kevin and his open, interactive one. In practice, computer programming allows for radical differences in style. And looking more closely at Jeff and Kevin makes it apparent that a style of dealing with the computer is of a piece with other things about the person—his or her way of facing the world, of coping with problems, of defending against what is felt as dangerous.* Programming style is an expression of personality style.

For example, the hard masters tend to see the world as something to be brought under control. They place little stock in fate. In child's terms, they don't believe much in a rabbit's foot or a lucky day. Jeff is popular and sociable, but he likes to be committee chairman, the one who controls the meeting. From the earliest ages

---

* Not all computer systems, not all computer languages offer a material that is flexible enough for differences in style to be expressed. A language such as BASIC does not make it easy to achieve successful results through a variety of programming styles. This does not make BASIC any less adequate as a computer language. It means that it provides a less malleable material for different styles of use. In the Austen School the conditions were right for a wide variety of children to form very different relationships with programming. The environment allowed freedom to experiment, and the computer system was designed to go further than most in allowing for a diversity of approaches.

most of these children have preferred to operate on the manipul-able—on blocks, on Tinkertoys, on mechanisms. It is not surpris-ing that the "hards" sometimes have more difficulty with the give-and-take of the playground. When your needs for control are too great, relationships with people become tense and strained. The computer offers a "next-best" gratification. The Tinkertoy is inert. The computer is responsive. Some children even feel that when they master it they are dominating something that "fights back." It is not surprising that hard masters take avidly to the computer. It is also not surprising that their style of working with the computer emphasizes the imposition of will.

The soft masters are more likely to see the world as something they need to accommodate to, something beyond their direct con-trol. In general, these children have played not with model trains and Erector sets but with toy soldiers or with dolls. They have taken the props (cowboy hats, guns, and grownup clothes for dress-up) from the adult world and used them in fantasy play with other children. In doing so, they have learned how to negotiate, compromise, empathize. They tend to feel more impinged upon, more reactive. As we have seen, this accommodating style is ex-pressed in their relational attitude toward programming as well as in their relationships with people.

Very young children find the computer evocative because it seems to stand betwixt and between the world of alive and not alive. The sprite, the computational object that is there to com-mand on the screen, is also evocative. It stands between the world of physical objects and the world of abstract ideas. Ambivalent in its nature, it is taken up differently by the hard and soft masters, the hard masters treating it more like an abstract entity—a Newtonian particle—the soft masters treating it more as a physical object: a dab of paint, a building block, a cardboard cut-out.

Jeff sees the system of Logo sprites as a formal system, some-thing apart from his everyday life. He identifies with an abstract piece of it. He objectified the sprite, saw it as a thing apart, and then put himself in its place in order to command its actions. Jeff said, "I'm a sprite in there." The soft master identifies differently. Kevin did not objectify the sprite, he did not become the abstract thing—he took who he feels himself to be and entered a new world of make-believe. He said, "I'm me in there, driving the spaceship."

Identification is not for an instrumental purpose, but in the service of fantasy.

Psychologist David Shapiro has used the idea of "neurotic styles" to capture what each of us intuitively knows about him- or herself: we are the same person whether we are solving an intellectual problem or sorting out a personal difficulty. And, indeed, the blocks we run into, the ways we achieve or avoid success in the cognitive and affective domains, often take us aback by their similarity. The use of clinical categories to describe these styles reflects the fact that when we look at human psychology there is a continuum between what we see as ill and what we see as normal. The underlying processes are the same for everyone; some simply suffer from them more than others. Thus we come to understand ourselves better by knowing what we would be like if the stresses of life led us to a breaking point. At that breaking point, our "neurotic style" would be transformed into a disabling symptom. At that point, the style "takes over," severely limiting our ability to cope with reality. Before that point, a neurotic style is simply a way of approaching the world and of defending oneself against what is painful.

Shapiro describes an obsessive-compulsive style in terms that recall the relationship of the hard masters with their machines. He speaks of the obsessive-compulsives' intense and sharply focused attention and their interest in technical details. Like Jeff who was interested in only one thing when he looked at the other children's programs (was there any new technical stuff?), Shapiro's prototypical obsessive-compulsive may listen to a recording with the keenest interest in the equipment "but hardly hear . . . the music."[9]

On the other hand, Shapiro describes a hysterical style in terms that recall the soft master. When obsessive-compulsives are asked a question, they give a sharp and detailed technical answer. Hysterics respond with impressions; their interest is global: ". . . many times in connection with the mathematics problems on an intelligence test, hysterical subjects are unable to reproduce the processes by which they arrived at their answers . . . even if the answers are correct."[10]

Our approach to the world is profoundly marked by the ways we defend ourselves. Different personality styles rely on a characteristic set of defense mechanisms. Shapiro's "obsessives" rely on selective inattention, rigidity, and radical simplification. They tend to see things in black and white. In their emotional lives the "hard masters" are practiced in creating reductive models of the complex. In their intellectual lives they do so as well. In many ways, the hard masters' black and white representations of everyday life (Jeff talks about the friends he loves and the former friends he hates) are similar to their formalized representations of objects. Objectifying and identifying with a sprite or a pulley or a Newtonian particle—all of these useful simplifications for doing science and for dealing with formal systems—fit in with a tendency to simplify people and events. Both come easily. But, of course, Jeff's style of objectifying and identifying with objects—with the gear of the bicycle, the sprite on the screen—is easier and more natural for some people than for others.

The "softs," Shapiro's hysterics, deal with pain by forgetting it or through an impressionistic blurring of sharp lines. They often have particular trouble and indeed balk at the very idea of what they see as "reductive identification." Not for them the reduction of the world into black and white or the simplification of reality through abstraction. They can't identify with abstract particles, they can only identify with other persons. Not only are the softs less practiced in formal representation, but for them such representations can feel threatening.

In all of this, the computer acts as a Rorschach, allowing the expression of what is already there. But it does more than allow the expression of personality. It is a constructive as well as a projective medium. For example, it allows "softs" such as Kevin to operate in a domain of machines and formal systems that has been thought to be the exclusive cultural preserve of the "hards." For the first time Kevin could march into a mathematical world with hysterical colors flying full mast.

Mastery and Gender

I have used boys as examples in order to describe hard and soft mastery without reference to gender. But now it is time to state what might be anticipated by many readers: girls tend to be soft masters, while the hard masters are overwhelmingly male. At Austen, girls are trying to forge relationships with the computer that bypass objectivity altogether. They tend to see computational objects as sensuous and tactile and relate to the computer's formal system not as a set of unforgiving "rules," but as a language for communicating with, negotiating with, a behaving, psychological entity.

There are many reasons why we are not surprised that girls tend to be soft masters. In our culture girls are taught the characteristics of soft mastery—negotiation, compromise, give-and-take—as psychological virtues, while models of male behavior stress decisiveness and the imposition of will. Boys and girls are encouraged to adopt these stances in the world of people. It is not surprising that they show up when children deal with the world of things. The girl child plays with dolls, imagined not as objects to command but as children to nurture. When the boy unwraps his birthday presents they are most likely to be Tinkertoys, blocks, Erector sets—all of which put him in the role of builder.

Thinking in terms of dolls and Erector sets, like talking about teaching negotiation and control, suggests that gender differentiation is a product of the social construction that determines what toys and what models of correct behavior are given to children of each sex. Psychoanalytic thought suggests many ways in which far earlier processes could have their role to play; styles of mastery may also be rooted in the child's earliest experiences. One school of thought, usually referred to as "object relations theory," is particularly rich in images that suggest a relation between styles of mastery and gender differences.

It portrays the infant beginning life in a closely bonded relationship with the mother, one in which boundaries between self and other are not clear. Nor does the child experience a separation between the self and the outer world.[11] The gradual development of a consciousness of separate existence begins with a separation from the mother. It is fraught with conflict. On the one hand, there is a desire to return to the comfort of the lost state of oneness. On the other hand, there is the pleasure of autonomy, of acting on independent desire. Slowly the infant develops the sense of an "objective" reality "out there" and separate from the self. Recently, there has been serious consideration of the ways in which this process may take on a sense of gender. Since our earliest and most compelling experiences of merging are with the mother, experiences where boundaries are not clear become something "female." Differentiation and delineation, first worked through in a separation from the mother, are marked as "not-mother," not-female.

Up to this point the experiences are common to girls and boys.

But at the Oedipal stage, there is a fork in the road. The boy is involved in a fantasized romance with the mother. The father steps in to break it up and, in doing so, strikes another blow against fusional relationships. It is also another chance to see the pressure for separation as male. This is reinforced by the fact that this time the boy gives up the idea of a romance with the mother through identifying himself with his father. Thus, for the boy, separation from the mother is more brutal, because in a certain sense it happens twice: first in the loss of the original bonded relationship, then again at the point of the Oedipal struggle.

Since separation from the mother made possible the first experiences of the world as "out there," we might call it the discovery of the "objective." Because the boy goes through this separation twice, for him objectivity becomes more highly charged. Boys feel a greater desire for it: the objective, distanced relationship feels like safe, approved ground. There is more of a taboo on the fusional, along with a correspondingly greater fear of giving in to its forbidden pleasures. According to this theory the girl is less driven to objectivity because she is allowed to maintain more elements of the old fusional relationship with the mother, and, correspondingly, it is easier for her to play with the pleasures of closeness with other objects as well.[12]

Anne and Mary

In the eyes of a true hard programmer like Jeff, his classmate Anne, also nine, is an enigma. On the one hand, she hardly seems serious about the computer. She is willing to spend days creating shimmering patterns on the screen in a kind of "moiré effect" and she doesn't seem to care whether she gets her visual effects with what Jeff would classify as technically uninteresting "tricks" or with what he would see as "really interesting" methods. Jeff knows that all the children anthropomorphize the computer to a certain extent; everyone says things like "My program knows how to do this" or "You have to tell the computer what speed you want the sprites to go," but Anne carries anthropomorphizing to what, to Jeff, seems like extreme lengths. For example, she insists on calling the computer "he," with the explanation "It doesn't seem right to call it an it." All the same, this doesn't keep her from getting down to serious programming. She has made some technical inventions, and Jeff and the other male hard masters recognize that if they want to keep abreast of the state of the art at Austen they must pay attention to what Anne is doing. And Anne knows how to take advantage of her achievements. She analogizes the spread of programming ideas to the game of telephone and enjoys seeing versions of her ideas on half a dozen screens. "They didn't copy me exactly, but I can recognize my idea." Jeff's grudging acknowledgment of Anne's "not quite serious" accomplishments seems almost a microcosm of reactions to competent women in society as a whole. There, as at Austen, there is appreciation, incomprehension, and ambivalence.

When Jeff talks with the other male experts about the computer, they usually talk "shop" about technical details. Anne, on the other hand, likes to discuss her strong views about the machine's psychology. She has no doubt that computers have psychologies: they "think," as people do, although they "can't really have emotions." Nevertheless, the computer might have preferences. "He would like it if you did a pretty program." When it comes to technical things, she assumes the computer has an aesthetic: "I don't know if he would rather have the program be very complicated or very simple."

Anne thinks about whether the computer is alive. She says that the computer is "certainly not alive like a cat," but it is "sort of alive," it has "alive things." Her evidence comes from the machine's responsive behavior. As she types her instructions into the machine, she comments, "You see, this computer is close to being alive because he does what you are saying."

This remark is reminiscent of the talk among the somewhat younger children who were preoccupied with sorting out the computer's status as a living or a not living thing. There is, however, a difference. For the younger children, these questions have a certain theoretical urgency. For Anne, they are both less urgent and part of a practical philosophy: she has woven this way of seeing the computer into her style of technical mastery.

Anne wants to know how her programs work and to understand her failures when they don't. But she draws the line between understanding and not understanding in a way that is different from most of the hard-master boys at a similar degree of competence. For them, a program (like anything else built out of the elements of a formal system) is either right or wrong. Programs that are correct in their general structure are not "really correct" until the small errors, the bugs, are removed. For a hard programmer like Jeff, the bugs are there to ferret out. Anne, on the other hand, makes no demand that her programs be perfect. To a certain degree, although to put it too flatly would be an exaggeration, when she programs the computer she treats it as a person. People can be understood only incompletely: because of their complexity, you can expect to understand them only enough to get along, as well as possible for maintaining the kind of relationship you want. And when you want people to do something, you don't insist that it be done exactly as you want it, but only "near enough." Anne allows a certain amount of negotiation with the computer about just what should be an acceptable program. For her, the machine is enough alive to deserve a compromise.

This "negotiating" and "relational" style is pervasive in Anne's work but is more easily described by an example from her classmate Mary, another soft-mastery programmer and an even stauncher lobbyist for the use of personal pronouns to refer to computers. Mary differs strikingly from Anne in having a soft style that is verbal where Anne's is consistently visual.

Mary wanted to add a few lines of dialogue to the end of a game program. Her original idea was that the computer would ask the player, "Do you want to play another game?" If the player typed "Yes," a new game would start. If the player typed "No," the machine would print out the final score and "exit" the program—that is, put the machine back into a state where it is ready for anything, back to "top level." She writes a program that has two steps, captured in the following English-language rendition of the relevant Logo instructions:

> *If what-the-user-types is "Yes," start a new game.*
>
> *If what-the-user-types is "No," print score and stop.*

As instructions to an intelligent person, these two statements are unambiguous. Not so as instructions to a computer. The program "runs," but not quite as Mary originally planned. The answer "Yes" produces the "right" behavior, a new game. But in order to get the final score and exit, it is necessary to type "No" twice. Mary knew this meant there was an "error," but she liked this bug. She saw the behavior as a humanlike quirk.

What was behind the quirk? The computer is a serial machine; it executes each instruction independently. It gets up to the first instruction that tells it to wait until the user types something. If this something is "Yes," a new game is started up. If the user doesn't type "Yes," if, for example, he or she types "No," the computer does nothing except pass on to the next instruction without "re-membering" what has come before. The second instruction, like the first, tells the computer to wait until the user has typed something. And if this something is "No," to print the score and stop.

Now the role of the two "Nos" is clear. A single "No" will leave the computer trying to obey the second instruction—that is, waiting for the user to type something. There are ways of fixing this bug, but what is important here is the difference in attitude between a programmer like Jeff, who would not rest until he fixed it, and a programmer like Mary, who could figure out how to fix it but decides not to. Mary *likes* this bug because it makes the machine appear to have more of a personality. It lets you feel closer to it. As Mary puts it, "He will not take no for an answer" unless you really insist. She allows the computer its idiosyncrasies and happily goes on to another program.

Mary's work is marked by her interest in language. Anne's is equally marked by her hobby, painting. She uses visual materials to create strategies for feeling "close to the machine."

Anne had become an expert at writing programs to produce visual effects of appearance and disappearance. In one, a flock of birds flies through the sky, disappears at the horizon and reappears some other place and time. If all the birds are the same color, such as red, then disappearance and appearance could be produced by the commands "SETCOLOR :INVISIBLE" to get rid of them and "SETCOLOR :RED" to make them appear. But since Anne wants the birds to have different colors, the problem of the birds reappearing with their original color is more complicated.

There is a classical method for getting this done: get the program to "store away" each bird's original color before changing that color to "invisible," and then to recall the color when the birds are to reappear. This method calls for an algebraic style of thinking. You have to think about variables and use a variable for each bird—for example, letting A equal the color of the first bird, B the color of the second bird, and so on. Anne will use this kind of method when she has to, but she prefers another kind, a method of her own invention that has a different feel.

She likes to feel that she is there among her birds, manipulating them much in the way she can manipulate physical materials. When you want to hide something on a canvas, you paint it out, you cover it with something that looks like the background. This is Anne's solution. She lets each bird keep its color, but she makes her program "hide it" by placing a screen over it. She designs a sprite that will screen the bird when she doesn't want it seen, a sky-colored screen that makes it disappear. Just as the computer can be programmed to make a bird-shaped object on the screen, it can be programmed to make an opaque sky-colored square act as a screen.

Anne is programming a computer, but she is thinking like a painter. She is not thinking about sprites and variables. She is thinking about birds and screens. Anne's way of making birds appear and disappear doesn't make things technically easy. On the contrary, to maintain her programming aesthetic requires technical sophistication and ingenuity.*

For example, how does the program "know" where the bird is so as to place the screen on it? Anne attaches the screen to the bird when the bird is created, instead of putting it on later. The screen is on top of the bird at all times and moves with the bird wherever it goes. Thus she has invented a new kind of object, a "screened bird." When Anne wants the bird to be seen, the screen is given the "invisible" color, so the bird, whatever its color, shows right through it. When she wants the bird to disappear, the screen is given the color of the sky. The problem of the multiplicity of bird colors is solved. A bird can have any color. But the screens need

---

* The idea of a screened bird makes unusual use of a feature of the Logo system where moving objects are built out of screen sprites, each of which can be thought of as a mobile frame about half an inch square. On each sprite you can draw a picture. Large objects such as Jeff and Kevin's rocket ships are made by placing sprites side by side to make a large picture. Anne's birds are small enough to be drawn on a single sprite. Her innovation consisted of using two sprites (one for the screen, one for the bird) and placing them one on top of the other so that they occupy the same space, rather than side by side. To make them move together as a single object, she applied the techniques Jeff and Kevin used for keeping their compound objects together, but instead of thinking of the compound objects as a way of getting more size, Anne thinks of them as a way of getting more complexity of behavior.

only two colors, invisible or sky blue. A bird gets to keep its color at all times. It is only the color of its screen that changes. The problem of remembering the color of a particular bird and reassigning it at a particular time has been bypassed.

Anne's bird program is particularly ingenious, but its programming style is characteristic of many of the girls in her class. Most of the boys seem driven by the pleasures of mastering and manipulating a formal system: for them, the operations, the programming instructions, are what it is all about. For Anne, pleasure comes from being able to put herself into the space of the birds. Her method of manipulating screens and birds allows her to feel that these objects are close, not distant and untouchable things that need designation by variables. The ambivalence of the computational sprite—an object at once physical and abstract—allows it to be picked up differently by hards and softs. Anne responds to the sprites as physical objects. Her work with them is intimate and direct. The formal operations need to be mastered, but they are not what drive her.

No one would find Anne's relation to the birds and the screens surprising if it were in the context of painting or making collages with scraps of this and that. There we expect to find "closeness to the object." But finding a sensual aesthetic in the development of a computer program surprises us. We tend to think of programming as the manipulation of a formal system which, like the objects for scientific inquiry, is "out there" to be operated on as something radically split from the self.

Gender and Science

Evelyn Keller has coined the phrase "the genderization of science." She argues that what our culture defines as the scientific stance toward the world corresponds to the kind of relationships with the object world that most men (if we follow psychoanalytic theories of development) would be expected to find most comfortable.[13] It is a relationship that cuts off subject from object.

Scientific objects are placed in a "space" psychologically far away from the world of everyday life, from the world of emotion and relationships. Men seem able, willing, and invested in constructing these separate "objective" worlds, which they can visit as neutral observers. In this way the scientific tradition that takes objectivity as its hallmark is also defined as a male preserve. Taking it from the other side, we can see why men would be drawn to this construction of science. Men are highly invested in objective relationships with the world. Their earliest experiences have left them with a sense of the fusional as taboo, as something to be defended against. Science, which represents itself as revealing a reality in which subject and object are radically separated, is reassuring. We can also see why women might experience a conflict between this construction of science and what feels like "their way" of dealing with the world, a way that leaves more room for continuous relationships between self and other. Keller adds that the presentation of science as an extreme form of objective thinking has been reinforced by the way in which male scientists traditionally write and speak about their work. A characterization of science that appears to "gratify particular emotional needs" may "give rise to a self-selection of scientists—a self-selection which would in turn lead to a perpetuation of that characterization."[14]

In Anne's classroom, nine- and ten-year-old girls are just beginning to program. The fact that they relate to computational objects differently from boys raises the question of whether with growing expertise they will maintain their style or whether we are simply seeing them at an early stage before they become "recuperated" into a more objective computational culture. In my observation, with greater experience soft masters, male and female, reap the benefits of their long explorations, so that they appear more decisive and more like "planners" when they program on familiar terrains. But the "negotiating" and "relational" style remains behind the appearance and resurfaces when they tackle something new.

Lorraine is the only woman on a large team working on the design of a new programming language. She expresses her sense of difference with some embarrassment.

> I know that the guys I work with think I am crazy. But we will be working on a big program and I'll have a dream about what the program feels like inside and somehow the dream will help me through.
>
> When I work on the system I know that to everybody else it looks like I'm doing what everyone else is doing, but I'm doing

that part with only a small part of my mind. The rest of me is imagining what the components feel like. It's like doing my pottery. . . . Keep this anonymous. I know this sounds stupid.

Shelley is a graduate student in computer science who corrects me sharply when I ask her when she got interested in electronics and machines. "Machines," she responds, "I am definitely not into machines." And she is even less involved with electronics:

My father was an electrician and he had all of these machines around. All of these wires, all of this stuff. And he taught my brothers all about it. But all I remember him telling me was, "Don't touch it, you'll get a shock." I hate machines. But I don't think of computers as machines. I think of moving pieces of language around. Not like making a poem, the way you would usually think of moving language around, more like making a piece of language sculpture.

These words are reminiscent of women in other scientific disciplines. Barbara McClintock, an eminent biologist, describes her work as an ongoing "conversation" with her materials, and she speaks of frustration with the way science is usually done: "If you'd only just let the materials speak to you . . ."[15] In an interview with her biographer, Evelyn Keller, McClintock described her studies of neurospora chromosomes (so small that others had been unable to identify them) in terms that recall Anne's relationship with the birds and the screens. "The more she worked with the chromosomes, the bigger they got, until finally, 'I wasn't outside, I was down there—I was part of the system.' . . . As 'part of the system' even the internal parts of the chromosomes become visible. 'I actually felt as if I were down there and these were my friends.' "[16]

Keller comments that McClintock's "fusion" with her objects of study is something experienced by male scientists. But perhaps McClintock was able to exploit this less distanced model of scientific thought, far from the way science was discussed in the 1950s, more fully, visibly, and less self-consciously, because she is a woman. This is surely the case for the girls in the Austen classrooms. Their artistic, interactive style is culturally sanctioned. Of course, with children, as in the larger world, the lines of division are not rigid. Some girls are hard masters and I purposely took a boy as the first case of a soft master—Kevin, who did not see the sprites as "outside" but who is right there with them, who imagines himself a traveler in the rocket ship, taking himself and his daydreams with him.

Children working with computers are a microcosm for the larger world of relations between gender and science. Jeff took the sprite as an object apart and in a world of its own. When he entered the sprite world, it was to command it better. Kevin used the sprite world to fantasize in. Anne does something more. She moves further in the direction I am calling "feminine," further in the direction of seeing herself as in the world of the sprite, further in the direction of seeing the sprite as sensuous rather than abstract. When Anne puts herself into the sprite world, she imagines herself to be a part of the system, playing with the birds and the screens as though they were tactile materials.

Science is usually defined in the terms of the hard masters: it is the place for the abstract, the domain for a clear and distinct separation between subject and object. If we accept this definition, the Austen classroom, with its male hard masters, is a microcosm of the male genderization of science. But what about Anne and Mary? What about the other girls like them who are exploring and mastering the computer? Should we not say that they too are "little scientists"? If we do, then we see at Austen not only a model of the male model that characterizes "official science," but a model of how women, when given a chance, can find another way to think and talk about the mastery not simply of machines but of formal systems. And here the computer may have a special role. It provides an entry to formal systems that is more accessible to women. It can be negotiated with, it can be responded to, it can be psychologized.

The computer sits on many borders; it is a formal system that can be taken up in a way that is not separate from the experience of the self. As such, it may evoke unconscious memories of objects that lie for the child in the uncertain zone between self and not-self. These are the objects, like Linus' baby blanket, the tattered rag doll, or the bit of silk from a first pillow, to which children remain attached even as they embark on the exploration of the world beyond the nursery. Psychoanalytic theorists call these objects "transitional" because they are thought to mediate between the child's closely bonded relationship with the mother and his or her capacity to develop relationships with other people who will be experienced as separate, autonomous beings.[17] They are experienced as an almost inseparable part of the infant and the first not-me possession. As the child grows, the actual objects are discarded, but the experience of them remains diffused in the intense experiencing throughout life of an intermediate space. Music and religious experience share with the early transitional objects the quality of being felt simultaneously from within and from without.[18] So do creative moments in science and mathematics.

The idea of "formality" in scientific thought implies a separateness from the fuzzy, imprecise flow of the rest of reality. But using a formal system creatively, and still more, inventing it, requires it to be interwoven with the scientist's most intuitive and metaphorical thinking. In other words, it has to be mastered in a soft form.

So, in addition to suggesting a source of the computer's holding power, women's relationships with computational objects and the idea of the transitional object may illuminate the holding power of formal systems for people who are in the closest contact with them. Even for the hard masters, the "feminine" may be the glue that bonds.[19]

Mathematics for "Softs"

Many of us know mathematics only as an alien world designed by and for people different from us. The story of a third-grader named Ronnie may be a portent of how computers in children's lives can serve as a bridge across what we have come to accept as a two-culture divide. For Ronnie, as for the soft masters Anne and Kevin, building this bridge depends on the ability to identify physically with the sprites on the computer screen. The accessibility of the formal system depended on its having hooks in the world of the sensual.

Ronnie is eight years old and black; his family has recently moved to Boston from a rural town in South Carolina. He comes to school with a radio and dances to its beat. He climbs all over my colleague as he works with him at the computer. Ronnie is filled with stories—stories about his father's adventures as a policeman, about visits to his grandmother's farm down South, about the personalities of the baby chicks in his classroom. His favorite story is about the day his pet gerbil escaped, a story I get to hear many times, more elaborate, more embroidered, each time. The stories, like his physical closeness, are his way of making contact, of forging friendships, of drawing others into his life.

Ronnie is bright and energetic but he is doing badly in school. He has trouble with mathematics, with grammar, with spelling, with everything that smacks of being a formal system. In a way that is characteristic of the hysterical style described by Shapiro, he is impatient with anything that involves precise and inflexible rules, yet he enjoys his work with the computer although its rules are no less precise and inflexible. He is working with a program called "EXPLODE." In this program, the thirty-two Logo sprites are given the shape of colored balls and are stacked in the center of the screen—so that at the beginning you see only one sprite, the "one on top." The sprites are all assigned the same speed, but each has a different heading so that they move out in an expanding circle until a certain time has elapsed (the Logo system will also accept "time commands," for example to "wait 10 seconds"), at which point the circle implodes. The balls move back to the center, and the cycle repeats. The effect is a pulsating dance of color, to which Ronnie responds by dancing, too, and by making up little songs to accompany the pace of the explosion. But unlike the music on his radio, the beat of the computer dance can be modified. The pattern of the movement is determined by commands of speed and time. At speed forty, the speed at which the balls are set when he meets the program, the balls go halfway to the edge of the screen before falling back.

Ronnie has become very involved in the dance of the colored balls. He experiments with the different effects he can achieve by pressing the "home" key before the balls have come to the end of their travels. When he does this the balls travel a shorter distance and he is able to speed up the cycle. He carries this line of investigation to its limit. The effect is a multicolored pulse at the center of the screen. But finally Ronnie is dissatisfied with the new pulse effect, which he calls "drumbeat." He wants the dance to be "perfect," saying, "I dance perfect. I want them to dance perfect." At first, I don't understand. "Perfect" turns out to mean something very specific: "The balls should go right to the edge." He wants them to travel *exactly* to the outer reaches of the screen before falling back.

Ronnie has never heard the term "variable," and it would be

nearly impossible to explain it to him. But he has experimented enough to understand that to get the perfect dance he has to change the speed at which the balls fly out and the time of their flight before they return. So, without having the words to express precisely what he does, Ronnie works with two variables in order to control the spatial and temporal pattern of the explosion.

At first he does not know how to change the numbers that control speed and time. A speed of forty gets halfway to the edge. What would get all the way? Forty-one, thirty-nine, two thousand? All of these are tried and their effects intently observed. Nor does he know how to change the "time variable" that instructs the balls to fly out for a given number of seconds and then return to their starting place. Ronnie's mode of interaction with this program consists of trying different things, watching how they work out, dancing to the new rhythms, and then stepping back to make further attempts to make the patterns more satisfying by changing one or the other of the variables. Eventually, Ronnie brings the program under control. He has arrived at a combination of speed and time for the "perfect" explosion. Not only does he have a pair of numbers, but he has a principle. To make the tempo slower you increase the time, but in order to get the balls to go to the same place you have to decrease their speed. Understanding this relationship means that he can now get the tempo he wants and also get the balls to the edge of the screen. He can dance to the right beat and he can have the visual effect that matches the perfection of his dancing.

In the course of a long afternoon, Ronnie has learned how to work a little formal system, one that some people might learn in the section of the algebra curriculum called "rates, times, and distances." But Ronnie might never have gotten there, for the standard route to algebra lies through many hours of a different kind of activity: sitting still at a desk, filling numbers into squares, manipulating equations on paper. Some people like this kind of activity. Jeff, the master-planner computer expert, loves it—because it is structured, because of its fine detail, because it imposes an order by the manipulation of rules and the adherence to constraints. The difference between Ronnie and Kevin and a child like Jeff, who truly enjoys the experience of school math, is not simply one of "numerical ability." It is something more general, a difference of personality.

The conventional route to mathematics learning closes doors to many children whose chief way of relating to the world is through movement, intuition, visual impression, the power of words, or of a "beat."[20] In some small way that may prove important to our culture as a whole, computers can open some of these doors.

Tanya and a World of Words

The computer put Ronnie in contact with a mathematical experience. For Tanya, another black student, it mediated a first experience with writing.

Tanya's fifth-grade school record looks bleak: it reports that she can't spell, can't add or subtract, doesn't write. It gives no hint of what is most striking when you meet her: Tanya has a passionate interest in words and the music of speech. "I go by the word of the Lord, the word of the Bible. If you have the deep down Holy Ghost and you are speaking in the tongue which God has spoke through you, you harken to the word." As Tanya speaks, she wraps herself in a rich world of language. She speaks of apocalypse, salvation, and sin. "You think that just because you get burned by fire, that you know what fire is, but it ain't like that honey, because when you go to hell, you gonna burn, you gonna burn, you gonna burn . . ." The school language of readers and workbooks and sample sentences cannot compete with Tanya's flowing, tumbling discourse. She says "school is not a good place for my kind of words."

In fifth grade, her teachers, concerned that she had never written anything, tried to get her to "write" by asking her to say sentences about people she knew in order to make a "storybook." The teacher would recast each sentence to make it grammatical. Tanya, sensitive about ruining the now "perfect" sentence with her "ugly handwriting," would not even try to write out the sentence in her own hand. The teacher did the actual writing. Tanya drew a picture. The completed storybook project contains five sentences, each a teacher's representation of something Tanya said. A typical entry from the fifth-grade storybook reads, "Dr. Rose is my dentist. I was his first patient."

In creating the storybook, the teacher was trying to give Tanya instant "feedback," but what she heard was instant judgment. The storybook became a badge not of success but of failure, something less than "perfect." "Writing," then, was exposing oneself and being found wanting.

This is where Tanya was when she met the computer at the beginning of sixth grade. The computer room where Tanya worked contained four identical machines which Tanya personalized; she would only work with the computer she called "Peter."

> I thought the computer was gonna be like some little animal, some little tiny animal, you know, like these little toy animals. I thought it was gonna be one of those animals, you just pull a knob and it says something to you. I thought it would talk. Say hello.

From the very first day, Tanya wanted Peter to "talk" with her. She tried shouting at Peter, then used the keyboard as she was instructed, responding to the computer's error messages (YOU HAVEN'T TOLD ME HOW TO . . .) as cues to begin a dialogue: "Yes, I did tell you how to go forward 445, you fool. You are a fool. You know that. You are a fool."

Tanya's first program got Peter to "introduce" himself:

```
TO WHO
PRINT [MY NAME IS PETER]
END
```

The effect of this program is that whenever the word "WHO" is typed at the computer console, the machine will respond with "MY NAME IS PETER." The program delighted Tanya. She demonstrated it to everyone. But Tanya did not go very far with programming. As she was working on Peter's WHO program she made two discoveries that set her on another course. She discovered how to clear all text off the screen. And she discovered the delete key, the key that "erases" the last character that has been typed. For Tanya, the discoveries were as if magical: any letter could be deleted without trace or mess; anything written could be corrected, and then printed as tidily as a book. This girl who had never written before sat down at the computer and worked a whole hour on a single sentence until it was exactly to her liking. She ended up with a letter:

```
DORIS
DEAR DORIS HOW ARE YOU BEING UP IN NEW YORK. I HOPE I WILL
SEE YOU IN THE SUMMER. LOVE TANYA AND PETER.
```

From that beginning, Tanya's only activity with the computer was writing. More letters poured forth and then stories about relatives, about people she had once met, about classmates and teachers. Tanya wrote stories about classmates she had been afraid to speak to and the presentation of her letters became first acts of friendship.

Tanya's relationship with the computer showed the intensity of the most driven programmers and the most dedicated players of video games. She would be the first in and the last out in the periods assigned for her group to work with the computers. Tanya had a personal relationship with Peter. She introduced Peter to visitors with the WHO procedure, would say things like "Take good care of Peter" when she left for the day, and signed his name alongside hers at the bottom of completed letters. On one occasion when another student got into the computer room first and sat down at "her computer," Tanya threw a fit of temper. The teacher's declaration that the computers were identical simply fueled her rage. She did not want the computers to be identical. She wanted Peter to be special, different, more than a thing, if not quite a person.

What was cause and what effect? Did the power of Tanya's relationship with the computer come from her repressed desire to write or did the intensity and the pace of her learning to write come from the special emotional force of a relationship with a computer? In either case the computer mediated a transformation of Tanya's relationship with writing. When I saw her two years after the end of the research project that had given her access to Peter she was still writing, indeed she had come to define herself as a writer. Most of her writing is poetry. "I get my poems from looking at people," Tanya tells me as she reads me her "favorite part" of a birthday poem she has written for her mother.

> Cold in a rocking chair
> Watching Martin Luther King's memories go by.
> Sitting here yelling back and forth
> Like an old grandmother with a toothache
> You're bored stiff because no one's there to see your need.
> You're just rocking away like an old grandmother.

Most children learn to write with the most imperfect of media: their unformed handwriting. For most it does not seriously stand in their way. For Tanya it did. She is fiercely proud of her appearance. Her clothes are carefully chosen. Her hair is artfully arranged, usually with ribbons, barrettes, and braids, changing styles from day to day. She has very clear ideas about what is beautiful and what is ugly. She saw her handwriting as ugly and unacceptable. It made writing unacceptable.

The computer offered her a product that looked "so clean and neat" that it was unquestionably right, a feeling of rightness she had never known at school, where she was always painfully aware of her deficiencies, ashamed of them, and, above all, afraid of being discovered.

Tanya saw writing as telling Peter to write. She put the computer in the role of a child and she became the teacher and the parent.

> You tell a child to go to the store and it might, but the child will say, "Ma, you didn't tell me how to get to the store. I don't know how to get there." That's the way it is with computers. Like teaching a child. But when you teach a child you remember it too. When you are with a computer you know the whole time what you are saying. You have it inside your ear. When you are using your fingers to be with Peter, using emotions with the computer.

Tanya identified with Peter's learning. It was hers. She heard it inside her "ears," felt it in her "fingers" and "emotions."

Tanya continued to grow as a writer after the computer was no longer available to her because she had developed a strong enough idea of herself as a writer to find means of practicing her art without Peter. She has developed a stylized calligraphy that makes her own handwriting more acceptable to her. And she often persuades a teacher to take dictation, but now, on the model of Peter, the teacher is not permitted to make "corrections."

When Tanya anthropomorphized Peter she created a demiperson, a "little animal" that could play the role the teacher had played when she made the storybook. The teacher wrote down what she said. So would Peter. But unlike the first teacher, Peter was a perfect scribe. He gave Tanya the possibility of creating something not ugly, but he allowed her to do it by herself, without humiliating corrections. It was in gratitude that Tanya signed her computer stories "written by Tanya and Peter." The computer was a gentle collaborator. It allowed Tanya to disassociate writing from painful self-exposure and freed her to use writing for self-expression, indeed for self-creation.

As Tanya graduates, the school library accepts her gift of a volume of her poems. For Tanya, the presence of her book in the library marks her first relationship with a larger culture, one that begins with the school and extends beyond it. In other cases, children use the computer in an effort to break out of more limited kinds of isolation.

Computers and Cultural Divides

Children like Kevin and Ronnie tend to be afraid of technical objects and develop negative relationships with science and mathematics. As they grow older, they become more defensive. An early computer experience might make a difference. Unlike arithmetic and school math drill, the computer offers a glimpse into the aesthetic dimension of mathematics and science. And, unlike arithmetic and school math, it provides an expressive medium to which soft masters are drawn. Whether or not they go on to excel in computational, mathematical, or scientific studies is an open question. But they have a point of entry, and they will not be disfranchised in a world where computers are increasingly part of everyday life. They will not feel that all of that belongs to other kinds of people.

Walls are breaking down on the other side as well. In the year that I followed his progress, Jeff had a master plan—making a video game that involved several rockets, missiles firing lasers, consequent explosions, and the disintegration of an enemy ship. Jeff kept the structure in mind as he sought ways to achieve particular effects, assimilating what he needed to know (for example, about Cartesian coordinates and their implementation on the computer) to realize a not-yet-completed part of the whole.

The standard by which Jeff judged his work was whether or not it incorporated "new stuff"—that is to say, technically interesting material that could increase his range of control over the machine. Between two of my visits, Jeff modified the "explosion" part of his space shuttle program. In the first version there was a rocket, a flash, and then nothing. In the revised version, there was the rocket, the flash, and a moment of disintegration before the pieces of the rocket flew off and there was nothing left. It was very dramatic and beautiful. I told him so. He found the compliment difficult to accept. The change was not fundamental. "It only made it look better. It's nothing new." To Jeff, aesthetics don't count for much—remember his shrug as he passed by Kevin's space scene. And yet, when Jeff improved his explosion, he received what was perhaps his first compliment for doing something aesthetically pleasing. Although he didn't accept it easily, indeed hardly at all, in the end he looked pleased. Jeff doesn't draw, or paint, or play an instrument. For him, the computer experience may spark an appreciation of other ways of knowing the world, because for the first time he can feel himself a participant in them. Programming, in this case hard programming, can bring him closer to "softer" pursuits in the arts.

In this situation Jeff's experience depended on my coming in "from the outside." But analogous situations emerge from the natural interaction of children with each other. Ralph is the star athlete of his school in suburban Boston; he is captain of two teams. Even at eleven he has a clearly developed sense of himself as a "macho man." He has little to say and nothing to do with Michael, a small, bespectacled boy in his class who is known as the "math whiz." Or rather, Michael is politely known as the math whiz. To Ralph, he is a "nerd": not good at sports, no "personality," a loser. What does interest Ralph are video games. And when computers —with their screens, their graphics, their movement, their sound effects—came into his school, Ralph was taken with the idea of creating his own video game, a football match using his own favorite plays. Ralph has lots of ideas for the game, but to get them on the computer he needs the help of an expert; he needs Michael. At Ralph's initiative, the two boys start to work together. Michael, for his part, has always admired Ralph, but he has never before worked on an intellectual problem with another person, "except maybe the teacher, but nobody else in this class really is into math the way I am." He is happy for the chance. Ralph takes him out on the playing field "to show him some moves" that need to be incorporated into the video game. Michael in turn shows Ralph his most secret programming tricks. The game becomes increasingly complicated. The two boys fantasize about someday "selling it to Atari and making a lot of money." They start to have lunch together, to talk. It turns out that Michael does have something to offer, and not just programming tips. Ralph tells me, "This guy is really into science fiction. I mean he knows everything about science fiction. All the *Star Treks*. And even better stuff. He is giving me all of the really good stuff to read." They don't become close friends—Ralph still has his world, and Michael doesn't fit into it; Michael still has his math, and Ralph isn't really interested—but they talk, they go to a science-fiction-movie marathon, they work on their game.

Stanley and Ben are in the same fifth-grade class and have been together at school since first grade. They are friends at a distance, but belong to two different worlds. Stanley is another math whiz and always has been. He is the child of academics and describes himself in terms of his technical interests. He has been fixing radios since he was five, is deeply interested in electronics and circuitry. He wants to be a patent lawyer when he grows up, and his reasons are "technology-driven." "You get to learn the latest stuff about machines and about computers, stuff you would need to know anyway." Ben is in the "other" culture, a dancer. When school is over he is off to dancing lessons or rehearsals. At eleven years old he is already a professional.

Stanley and Ben developed a collaboration that closely paralleled Ralph and Michael's, in this case to produce a program that would choreograph a dance of sprites on the screen. Each collaborator brought to the task something the other did not have. Ben brought his sense of form, of movement, and his already well-stocked repertoire of dance routines. But to translate these for the computer required Stanley and his repertoire of programming tricks.

It is striking, and it is sad, that elementary-school classrooms seem to be microcosms for the kind of "splitting" that divides the adult culture. Walk into these classes and you see the humanists and the scientists, the artists and the mathematicians, the physical types and the intellectual types. All too often, you see them having very little to do with one another.

What really matters is not what choreography rubbed off on Stanley or the mathematics that rubbed off on Ben, what sports knowledge rubbed off on Michael or the programming that rubbed off on Ralph. What matters was that each child came, if only a little, to appreciate another aesthetic. Michael and Stanley took several steps beyond Jeff's "nothing new" reaction to Kevin's space shuttle. Ralph and Ben saw that mathematics could be personally relevant. When projected onto a future in which computers will be everyday objects in the lives of most children, these interactions could be a portent of new understandings in our culture.

Getting Stuck

The lives of all the children we have met so far seem to have been enhanced by their contact with computers. But for some children the computer seems to close as well as open doors. Jeff said the computer was "the most important thing in my life right now," but it was not the only thing. There are, however, children whose involvement with computers becomes consuming, almost exclusive. There is a narrowing of focus, a decreasing degree of participation in other activities.

Henry is such a child. He was having a difficult time before he met computers and learned to program. The computer did not create a problem where none existed, but he is an example of a kind of child for whom the computer may reinforce patterns of isolation and help lock a child into a world of getting lost in things at the expense of the development of relationships with other people.

The Austen School has two students who have taken on public identities as computer "whizzes." Jeff, whom we have already met, is one of them; Henry is the other. Henry spends a lot of time comparing himself to Jeff, whom he considers his rival. Henry is a small, unathletic child. He is awkward, tense, and self-absorbed. Whenever he came upon MIT visitors it was with an agenda. Without even saying hello, he would request some piece of technical information, something that "Jeff doesn't know." When we began to teach him about how to use x and y coordinates in his graphics programming, he commented, "Oh yeah, I saw Jeff do that. If I could do that I could do anything." His sense of being in competition went beyond his relationship with his primary rival. He defined himself and everyone he knew in terms of their place in a pecking order. He saw himself as the best in computers, and he was going to do everything to keep this place. He knew that the other students saw him as an expert, and he enjoyed the attention. He liked being in the limelight.

Henry knows that the limelight depends on his staying in a position of clear superiority by discovering programming techniques;

in the social world of the school he has nothing else. He shores up his position by trying to control the dissemination of ideas. For example, he credits himself with having discovered the Logo instruction that changes the design of the blank-space character. This creates a dramatic patterned effect by repeating the chosen design in every empty space on the screen—including the spaces between words and at the ends of incomplete lines.* The discovery made him famous, but he has regrets. He reproached himself several times for having told other children about his discovery, saying, "It's really spreading around, but we are trying to hold it down." "We" refers to the small group of experts that Henry considers worthy of this knowledge. They can appreciate it. He divides the culture of Austen programmers into "us" and "them." The best discoveries are somehow violated if they are put into the hands of the "thems" who can't appreciate their technical ingenuity but who use them simply to achieve pleasing visual effects.

Henry's growing-up toys were machines—an old air conditioner, discarded radios, tape recorders, broken blenders—which he patiently disassembled and put back together. He never found other people to talk to about his discoveries and grew up pretty much alone. Alone, he made inventions. He claimed to be inventing things all the time, but when we visited he was particularly excited about two of them. One would give him access to free games of Asteroids; the second, he hoped, might make him a millionaire.

Henry told us about the Asteroids invention. He says he is such a good customer at the game arcade that the owner offered him a free game one day as he was making his rounds to open the machines and collect the coins. Henry says he watched the owner initiate a free game by pushing a lever inside the machine. The image of the lever stuck in his mind. One day while playing with some pacemaker magnets that a friend's cardiologist father had given him, he noticed that an attracted paper clip itself became magnetized. If magnets worked like this, couldn't he use a magnet on the "outside" to pull the "inside" Asteroids lever? The metal casing around the game wouldn't be an impediment. To his mind, it would only help him out.

---

* An apparently "empty" screen is actually filled with invisible "space" characters, the character invoked by pressing the space bar on the keyboard. So if this character is changed to have a visible form—and this is what Henry discovered how to do—the blank parts of the screen instantly fill up with a tiling effect caused by the repetition of the new form.

It is hard to tell if there really is an Asteroids invention. What is important is that Henry's fantasies are about making mechanical things that will allow him to "win" or triumph. The second invention was more obviously fanciful. This is one that he would like to patent because he thinks it will make him rich. He calls it a "gear rater." It is a Rube Goldberg device for making a superfast bicycle with many parts, many gears, many ropes and pulleys. It is a new kind of *dérailleur* which, it seems, would work by creating energy. You pedal the same amount, but you go faster.

These inventions and others were never very far from Henry's mind. Questions about what he thought or what he felt were answered with new anecdotes about building something or taking something apart. These technical descriptions are monologues, and, whatever the subject matter, Henry doesn't pause to check out the state of his listener. He speaks in a rapid staccato, punctuating his stories with machine sound effects: *brrr, crkkk, prrrt*. His hand gestures are sharp and geometric. He uses them to indicate quantity, position.

Henry dreams of becoming an "electronics person." This fantasy includes "building a person out of lights," a person made of wires and circuits. "I would work with the electronics and wires and control things. I have a kit of little circuits now and I can control them." It often seems that Henry would rather control or ignore people than deal with them directly, just as he would rather control or ignore his feelings than deal with them directly. When the conversation turns to things that make him anxious, he retreats into stories about his machines, his inventions. Machine sounds (like his *brrr*s and *crkkk*s) substitute for talking about how he feels.*

Henry was awkward with us, on the playground, and in conversation with other children. He was rude, or embarrassed, or withdrawn. Not surprisingly, it was at the computer that he relaxed. Here he was in complete control. He typed rapidly, pronounced

---

* Henry's Rorschach showed a higher than usual proportion of machine images, often embedded in a story that made it clear that he controlled them. Mechanical forms were imposed on the blots even where their shape and size did not suggest them. This imposition of "inappropriate" forms is some measure of Henry's need to see things in terms of controllable objects. In the Rorschach, as in conversation, a tense moment would lead to a retreat into stories about his machines, his inventions, the gear rater, the Asteroids machine, ideas for space travel machines. Again, as in conversation, machine sounds substituted for talking about how the cards made him feel. Like the Rorschach, Henry's performance on the locus of control test also suggests a very strong need to feel that events will not happen to him but that he will make them occur.

every letter, number, and space of the Logo code he composed. His programs were very long, very involved, and written in a way only he could understand. When people try to make their programs understandable, they divide them into "subprocedures" (smaller programs that serve the larger program) and name them in ways that indicate their function. Henry's style was to bypass this kind of technique in order to create a labyrinth of code. Making them esoteric made them private. Making them private made him sole owner and helped him to keep his advantage over the other children. Making them complicated, often unnecessarily complicated, also made them seem "harder," not just to the other children but, to a certain degree, to himself. He enjoyed whatever increased his sense of dealing with terribly complex and arcane things. Whenever he could, he increased the "automaticity" of the computer, he tried to make it even more "alive." For example, he wrote a special-purpose program to give him quick access to the editor. He enjoyed adding the extra level of complexity to the system. He seemed to want to confer as much as possible a sense of autonomous existence on the computer. This gave him an empowering sense of control.

For the hard master the keynotes of programming are abstraction, imposition of will, and clarity. For the soft they are negotiation and identification with the object. Henry has a hybrid style, In many ways he is like a hard master. He revels in technical detail, he takes pleasure in imposing his will over the machine. But, for him, the keynote of programming is not clarity but magic. Jeff wants his programs to be clear so that he can share them and be famous. Henry wants his programs to be impressive but mysterious. The goal is the creation of a private world. He expresses this clearly in his labyrinthine code. He expresses it clearly, if less obviously, in his relationship with powerful programming ideas. Both Jeff and Henry asked us to explain the use of Cartesian coordinates. Jeff was looking for an understanding and illumination. Henry was looking for a magical spell. What most pleases Jeff is the effect that unfolds following a process whose logic he has set up and worked to make transparent. The discovery for which Henry is proudest, his transformation of the blank character, produces an instantaneous and dramatic effect. Its source of power is buried deep and hidden within the machine. When he gives his command, he is releasing a force, invoking his personal, magical power.

When hard masters meet the idea of "structured programming," using nested subprocedures to give programs a transparent, hierarchical structure, they are excited. They have found a tool that meets their ends. The softs are more resistant. They use structured programming as a technique, but they don't particularly like it. It takes away from the immediacy of the relationship. Like the soft master, Henry's pleasure in programming is tied to that sense of immediacy. He has none of the hard master's distanced stance toward his creation. Like the soft master, he is right in there with the sprites. Indeed, Henry's way of identifying with the computer goes far beyond anything that we have seen soft masters do. Beyond identifying with the sprites, Henry actually identifies with the computer. People and powerful emotions are threats. Seeing oneself and others as controllable machines is a way to be safe. Recall Henry's fantasy of building a person out of lights, a person he could control.

Henry didn't like talking about feelings and claimed not to remember any dreams about the computer. But one morning, after a long interview, he volunteered a dream in which he had to match wits with an evil rival, equally skilled in the mysteries of the machine. He came to the school one night, and all the windows were broken and all the computers except one were gone. He gave the instruction "TELL BACKGROUND SETCOLOR :BLACK," an instruction that dramatically leaves colored shapes luminescent in black space, and the message "YOU ARE GOING TO DIE" appeared on the screen. Then a riddle appeared that forced him to "match knowledge about computers" with the man who stole them. Henry won, got the computers back, and got to take one home. "Then I became a hero at the school." The dream was about mastery, mystery, danger, and winning the admiration of others for solving a puzzle on which life and death depend.

It is interesting to compare Henry's dream with one related by Kevin, the artistic soft master. Kevin's dream involved the same instruction to turn the background color of the display screen to black, but, in contrast to Henry's dream, there was no danger, no threat, no matching of wits. The dream was simply about the computer wanting its turn to give instructions, consistent with Kevin's "conversational" style of negotiating with the machine. The computer appeared to Kevin with a broad smile on its face. It spoke to him: "TELL BACKGROUND SETCOLOR :BLACK." It was not clear whose background was changed by the command.

In general, the presence of computers does not lead children to think of people as machines. But Henry shows us the psychological context in which this fear is most real.

Just as for Jeff and Kevin, Henry's style of relating to the computer is illuminated by a comparison with a clinical category, in this case, the idea of a schizoid style. This style has its roots in infancy and early childhood. It has its roots in a crisis not of sexuality but of what psychoanalyst Erik Erikson called basic trust: the fundamental confidence that there is a constant and a caring other, that "when I cry I will be fed." In the absence of this trust, the process of differentiation of the self from the mother is fraught with conflict. The child grows up with an impaired sense of self. There is a feeling of emptiness and a desperate need for other people to give a sense of being there.

The lack of trust that causes the problem blocks its solution. Not developing and internalizing a good and trusted image of the mother creates later difficulties in relating to anybody in an intimate way. The early experience of love rejected is transformed into rage against the other who frustrates and terror of the other to whom one is so vulnerable. There is fear of relationship, fear of being rejected, and, since one feels like nothing, fear of being swallowed up.

This is the description of a paradox: a terror of intimacy and a terror of being alone. When people are caught in this position they use a range of strategies. In their fear of intimacy, they flee toward not feeling—being depersonalized, frozen, numb, split off, lost in abstraction, lost in battles of ideas and great principles. In their fear of being alone, they desperately seek validation in the eyes of others. They want to be admired. But since they do not feel themselves to be true selves, the only way to gain admiration is by manipulating appearances, by magic. This is Henry's paradox and these are his strategies.

A culture expresses its essential conflicts in its dominant psychopathologies.[21] Hysteria, its origins in sexual repression, was the neurosis of Freud's time. A repressed thought finds its expression in a physical symptom: a paralyzed limb speaks for an unacceptable wish. In the later twentieth century, cases of hysteria have virtually disappeared. Indeed, clinicians report that their patients rarely suffer from a clear symptom of any kind. What they are suffering from is that sense of feeling empty, of feeling nothing, of not being able to relate. Schizoid process has taken the place of the classical neuroses.

Machines come into this picture in two ways. One can come to see oneself as a machine—this provides protection from feeling, invulnerability to the threat of being swallowed up. And one can turn to the world of machines for relationship. With the computer, both possibilities are enhanced. There is a "mind machine" and therefore more sophisticated machine models with which one can identify. And the computer, reactive and interactive, offers companionship without the threat of human intimacy.

Henry was involved in a private world of machines before Austen ever got its first computer. What difference did the computer make for Henry, and what difference will it make for him as he grows up? The answers to such questions are complex. When Henry was absorbed in his world of broken air conditioners and largely imaginary inventions, he was completely alone. He had no one to talk to about them; there was no one to listen. The machines reinforced his isolation, his living in a private world. But as computers and programming began to be the center of his inner life he had something to share, to engage others with. He became part of a community of other young people who are captured by the computer. So in a certain sense the computer brought him out into the world of people.

But there is another way of looking at the role that the computer is playing in Henry's development. Henry was lonely in the world of old machines and imaginary inventions. He received little reward or encouragement. Social pressures were pushing him toward other things. He was resistant, to be sure—he needed his machines because they kept him safe from social involvements that felt threatening. But adolescence is just around the corner for him, and with its changes Henry may be able to move beyond his safe machine world to experiment with the less predictable and controllable world of people. But at the same time some of the pressure to do so has been removed. His teachers are pleased with him, his parents are pleased with him, he can turn his computer skills into a lifetime career. There exists a waiting culture of master programmers that he can join—a culture that may reinforce and reward his exclusive involvement with the machine. The interactivity of the computer may make him feel less alone, even as he spends more and more of his time programming alone. There is a chance that the computer will keep him lost in the world of things.

Most children of Henry's age are involved with mastery, with testing their competency. But here, as at every age, most children strike a balance—the need for mastery of skills and concrete materials is tempered with the desire to do things with people where the results are never as clear. The computer is a powerful medium for playing out the intense desire to win that is at the center of Henry's preoccupation. The danger is that its challenge will be so seductive that he will play and replay winning to the exclusion of more complex satisfactions beyond it.

CHAPTER 4

Adolescence and Identity: Finding Yourself in the Machine

The concerns of the youngest children were metaphysical. These "child philosophers" were from four to eight years old, a time when children are forging fundamental categories to make sense of the world. They were intrigued by the nature of computers and computer toys and how they were like and unlike other things. The children were reflective. Most of them were eager to talk about the attributes, capacities, and personalities of the machines, and got into spontaneous arguments about whether computers felt, thought, cheated, knew. Putting very young children together with computers encourages a rich and continual philosophizing.

The interest in sorting out the nature of the machine, and in using computer nature for thinking about human nature, continues with older children, but these questions are less pressing. At eight, nine, and ten years old, children are preoccupied not by metaphysics but by the need to master.

These school-age children's primary interest in computers is in what they can do with them. This stage is dominated by action, not reflection. The hards and the softs, the girls and the boys, are looking for challenges to meet: to beat a game, to produce startling visual effects. Their interests are to make, to do, to master.[1]

With adolescence, there is a return to reflection, but this time reflection is insistently about the self. The questions of the first stage, What is this machine?, and of the second, What can I do with it?, give way to Who am I?

Adolescence is an often confusing time when there is a need to come to terms with a suddenly maturing body and new social pressures. It is a time of introspection and of trying to fit oneself into increasingly complex relationships. And it is a time when young people are able to bring a widening range of cognitive skills and cultural materials to bear on their reflections about who they are. It is a time of conscious self-creation: adolescents "try on" ideas about politics, religion, and psychology to test and develop emergent ideas of self.[2]

Adolescents use many different kinds of materials to construct their sense of identity. They use their relationships with clothing, with records, with causes. There is an obvious way in which computers can become part of this process: they can become a way of life. Some young people start to see themselves and are seen by others as "computer people," experts at the technical aspects of computation. They spend most of their time programming computers, and a computer center or a computer club can become the focus of their social life. But most adolescents don't take this route. They integrate their computer experience into their developing identities in ways that have nothing to do with becoming computer experts. They use programming as a canvas for personal expression and then as a context for working through personal concerns. They use the computer as a constructive as well as a projective medium.

We began to see examples of "working through" in elementary-school-age children. In the course of learning to program they are grappling with issues that go beyond mastery and competence. Computer programming helps shape their feelings about what kind of person they are (Am I somebody who is afraid of machines and technical things? Am I somebody who can create something beautiful?) Their style of working with the machine expresses something of who they are, giving them a chance to see themselves in the mirror of the medium. At the same time, they can use the experience as an occasion to experiment with who they are not. By this I mean experimenting with a part of the self that is not dominant—indeed, with a style of being that may pose a threat.

Ethan is a fifth grader in a San Francisco public school. His untidiness goes beyond a messy desk and room. He is overweight and unkempt. He is impulsive and often feels out of control: "I tell myself I am going to go on a diet. But then I will see some candy and I will eat it and then eat a whole box of cookies too." As I watch him program, something interesting emerges. Ethan is expert with the system, and he is very smart. He can hold a lot of code "in his head." He programs by "making a mess." The programs are complicated, unstructured. Instructions weave around like strands of spaghetti. And then he cleans them up by turning the out of control, sloppy programs into models of hierarchical, modularized structured programming. "When I program, I like to make a mess and then I like to make it clean." In programming Ethan is clearly playing with issues that go beyond "cognitive style," that put him in touch with far deeper emotional material.

It is characteristic of fourth and fifth graders that this process of working through happens but is not particularly reflected upon. By contrast, with the beginning of adolescence experiences with the computer are often made into elements for explicit reflection about themselves.

Children in the sixth grade of a school I shall call the Jefferson Middle School were given opportunities to program in Logo. The program was a government-funded collaborative project carried out by a local school committee and researchers from MIT. The researchers followed the children's progress and kept files of their work, noting their attitudes toward the computer, their interactions with each other and the teachers. Sixteen children with a diverse range of backgrounds and interests were selected for closer study. Two years after the beginning of their computer experience, I went back to the school and carried out a series of interviews with each of them.*

The computers used in this project were different from those used at Austen. At Jefferson, children were able to create sharp black-and-white line drawings, including geometric figures like triangles, squares, and polygons, as well as complex and rather beau-

* I also was able to study the computer culture that had grown up at Jefferson in the two years that computers had been present there. This was enough time for there to have developed a rich tradition of computer "stories," computer jokes, computer etiquette, and computer rituals. I visited classrooms and the after-school computer club, talked with teachers and administrators. In addition to the follow-up of the original computer experiment, there were also a three-month study of a new fourth-grade classroom and close observation of five students in that class, chosen for the diversity of their intellectual and personal styles.

tiful spirals and figures such as faces, houses, and street scenes. Where the primary computational objects at Austen were the sprites, here children gave commands to a "turtle." This is a triangular-shaped penpoint that responds to commands to move around the screen and leaves a trace as it goes. It can be told to move a hundred steps and turn ninety degrees with the commands "FORWARD 100 RIGHT 90." Thus the turtle becomes the instrument for a kind of TV screen doodling. (A precomputer generation will remember the feeling of making line drawings with Etch-A-Sketch.)

Programming begins when sequences of commands to the turtle are defined, named, and stored away in the computer's memory. For example, a program to make a square might read:

```
TO SQUARE
FORWARD 100
RIGHT 90
FORWARD 100
RIGHT 90
FORWARD 100
RIGHT 90
FORWARD 100
END
```

This program can then be called upon to build up more complex patterns. So, for example, a program to draw a house might be constructed out of five subprocedures: a large square for the body of the house, a triangle for the roof, smaller squares for windows, a small rectangle for a door, and an even smaller rectangle for a chimney. Defining the "superprocedure"—the "master program" —for the house is a more complicated job than just calling up its parts out of memory. The parts need to be placed in the right relationships to each other. For example, when the turtle has gotten up to drawing the two small windows, it has to finish one, then take its "PEN UP" and move to the exact place where the second window is to be drawn, and it must begin this drawing in the proper orientation.[3]

The grade-school children in the previous chapter are caught up with the challenge of the computer. When they work with a graphics system like Logo they typically pursue projects—making a space scene, a "movie" of a car going around a racetrack, programming a video game. Whatever personal issues are being worked out are being worked out through what they are doing on the screen. When younger children work with computers, less is immediately visible. First or second graders spend hours tracing lines on the screen and writing a variety of little programs. They are happy to be exploring, to be learning the ways of the new thing. They are involved with the question of how they are like and not like it. So too in adolescence: what is on the screen reveals only a small part of what is going on in the relationship with the computer.

Deborah and the Machine as Microworld

Deborah is thirteen, blond, round-faced, sweet-looking, poised between innocence and sophistication. Her hair is cut in a tousled "shag" style that she picked out of a magazine. She is wearing a Western fringed jacket that she proudly announces she chose herself. After we have been talking for several days she tells me she wants to show me "the best thing I have done all year." It is a beautiful drawing of a horse that she says her art teacher wants to frame and hang in the art room. She is on a diet and solemnly sips a Diet Pepsi as she watches me eat the lunch of the day offered by the school cafeteria: a peanut-butter-and-jelly sandwich and ice cream.

Deborah first encountered the computer two years ago, in sixth grade. Her teachers remember her at that time as withdrawn, frightened, and explosive. When teased by the other children for being overweight ("They used to call me Fatso"), she would break into a tearful rage. She had little self-confidence. When she was asked to do something on her own she would become petulant or tune out ("My father calls it going onto Channel Thirteen"). The explosions, the petulance, and the Channel Thirteens were frequent. Deborah describes her eleven-year-old self as dependent and unhappy, a child who could not control her tears or her temper.

She was the youngest of three children, the baby of her family. Her family's efforts to compensate her for a history of childhood illnesses exaggerated her "baby" position. Other people were always doing things for her, buying her clothes for her, telling her that she was not yet old enough to do the things that she most wanted to do—baby-sit, be in charge of going to the Laundromat, stay over at a friend's house, choose her own hairstyle and clothes.

Everybody else in the family had responsibilities. Things they had to do. I was the baby. My parents used to treat me like I was a little four-year-old. Like they used to buy my clothes, little pants with big strawberries on them. My mother would say, "Oh, aren't these perfect for school?" Everyone would say, "Oh, Deborah, she can't do anything. She can't bring the clothes down to the dryer. It's down in the cellar. She'll be scared. She'll get hurt. The basket's too heavy for her with the wet, damp clothes and the wet dungarees," and my mother would get my sister or brother to do it and they'd always give me a hard time, saying, "Deborah is Mommy's little pet."

I didn't do anything by myself. I wouldn't do anything by myself. I got my mother to go down to the store for me, got my brother and sister to go places with me, to get me this or get me that. Like I'd say to my sister, "Can I have that shirt you have," and I'd make her give it to me. And I'd say things like that to other kids too. I was really bad about my friends. I couldn't do nothing without them. I had to always be with them. And when I wasn't with them, I'd be yelling at my mother and making my house a rotten place, getting everyone into fights. I got into fights in school too. I was very bad. All the teachers hated me in sixth grade.

Me and this other girl, Tessa, we used to be awful when we were in sixth grade. We'd go behind the stage curtains and we'd rip things down and we'd hide in the closet and we used to skip classes. One time we went down to the gym, and you know that big curtain down there, well, that was shut, and we hid behind it. And this kid, he came up and he grabbed me from behind. I peed in my pants. I had it all over the floor and I was so embarrassed. I was so ashamed. That was really my worst day. I had to get Miss Bryan to wash out my things. I was in my gym shorts all day. I wanted to run away.

Dependent on others and with an image of herself as sick, weak, and fat, Deborah had little sense of her own boundaries and no confidence in her ability to say no, to exert control. By eleven, she was already involved with a crowd that was smoking, drinking, using drugs. Toward the end of that year Deborah was introduced to programming computers in Logo, which, as we have seen, is specifically designed to be accessible to children. Deborah was shown how to draw pictures on a screen by giving commands to the "turtle."

At the beginning of Deborah's participation in the computer project, she spent most of her time trying to get as much of the teacher's presence and attention as possible. She refused, as might be expected, to do anything on her own. And she measured any effort that she did make against the progress of the other children. She always found herself lacking, and this made her want more and more help from others.

Children experience making computer graphics—including dynamic "special effects"—as a source of great power. For Deborah, the sense of power was not liberating, it was threatening. A breakthrough came when she had the idea of restricting the commands she could give to the turtle. She made a rule that she would allow herself only one turning command—a right turn of thirty degrees. Deborah describes her decision as arbitrary ("One day I just decided to do it, and I picked out thirty degrees"), but this world turned out to be extraordinarily rich. By repeating rotations of RIGHT 30 it is possible to make 90-degree right turns, "about-face" 180-degree turns, and 120-degree turns, all useful maneuvers for making geometrical shapes.

Once she had her rule, Deborah got down to serious work. She drew flowers and rabbits and stars and abstract designs, everything built up from right turns of thirty degrees. "I really liked my rule. It was neat. It was hard. I had to figure everything out. I thought about it all the time. I was the only one who had a rule." Suddenly she found herself, perhaps for the first time, in a situation simple enough for her to feel in control, yet varied enough to allow for creative exploration. Weeks later, Deborah was the master of her restricted world and she began to dare to come out of it to experiment with a less restricted geometry. Her mathematical learning had taken a leap forward.

In building her world, Deborah built an environment in which she could be successful. She had never been successful at anything before—not in school, where she was considered below average in all her subjects, and not at home, where she was not allowed to act independently and was afraid to try. The thirty-degrees world was an environment in which a girl who thought of herself as a loser got a first taste of what it was like to be a winner.

> One time the teacher, he showed a movie that this guy did about computers and how to make stars with them, and then I tried. But of course I made them with the thirty degrees. I made the star and I got a letter from the person who made the movie, saying that it was a really hard thing to do and that he was really proud. I still got the letter in my book.

The thirty-degrees world provided more than a first taste of success. Deborah first knew the computer as something apparently uncontrollable. She was afraid to press its keys without asking the teacher to stand by, because whenever she got an "error message" from the machine she reacted as though the machine were "yelling at her" and she started to cry. Later, she saw the computer as something she could control—indeed, as a part of her mind that she could examine, reflect on, manipulate.

> When you program a computer, there is a little piece of your mind and now it's a little piece of the computer's mind . . . and now you can see it. I mean, the computer can be just like you if you program it to be, your thoughts, your pictures, your feelings, your ideas, not everything, but a lot of things. And you can see the things you think and change them around.
> Sometimes I would go down there, and like if I had a fight with the kids it would be good to go down and really sort of have a conversation with it. Like you could, um, make it talk to you if you programmed it right. I mean it wasn't really talking, but it was like talking. I would get all tense and just want to get away, just want to get away so I would go down to where the computers were, I would sneak away. I couldn't wait until computer classes could start every day. I would tell it what had just went on with my friends, all the really bad things. It made me a lot happier than when I came in. You could talk to it. Say you drew pictures in it. You get your feelings into that picture, and it just makes you happier. If it's just on a piece of paper, it's not the same. With the computer it's different. It's somebody there. It's having something that you make your own things on. I liked it because I could put my feelings into it.

Before she met the computer Deborah didn't think about her problems in terms of control. Of course she knew people who did not break things or cut classes or stuff themselves with candy until they were sick. She saw herself as different not because they had resources for self-control that she didn't, but because they were that way "by nature." They were good, she was bad. This kind of global characterization gave her no way to think about how to be better. She needed a world apart in which to build a new set of distinctions that she could then transfer to her way of thinking about herself and others. The computer provided this world. It gave her categories more useful than good or bad: things could be in or out of control. With the new distinction came a new way to think about her problems: I am in trouble because I have no rules. I am not in control. And I should be. I can be. The thirty-degrees world not only suggested that control was the issue, it presented a strategy for dealing with one's lack of control: make a rule, make a safe place, experiment within it.

Control has remained a central issue for Deborah. It is the thing she thinks about most: controlling her temper, her eating, her smoking.

> You program yourself how to be. In sixth grade I got really upset, and I started drinking and smoking. I don't even know why I did it. A lot of kids would say, "Oh, you're a chicken." And I'd say, "I am not," and I'd gulp down the beer. I didn't even want it. But I didn't know a thing to do.
>
> Then I started to make rules. The thirty degrees was for the computer, but these are for me. Like today I will not do this thing. Don't eat candy for lunch. If you're angry, hold it in and scream after school. Or I make a rule for two days. Like I'm gonna really work, try hard, I'm gonna do good on my English tests. I won't have a cigarette. Since the computer isn't around now, I take a pencil and draw.

This conversation takes place as Deborah is about to graduate from eighth grade. She no longer has easy access to the computer. The experimental program for her grade had come to an end. Although the computer remains in her school, to use it she would have to compete against a crowd of computer whizzes who monopolize its time. She chooses not to compete. Drawing has in some measure replaced graphics programming for her, but she has moved on with some wistfulness: "When I just wanted a cigarette it would have been good to be able to go down to the computer instead of picking up a pencil. It is more there with you. And it's funny, even though I did it such a long time ago, it still reminds me of making rules and keeping to them, of being independent."

Computers also represent a threat to independence. You can get hooked on them.

> I liked the computer because I put my feelings in it. But you can't get too hung up on it, because everything else can get screwed up. You just want to do it all day. Once, I was making this really hard picture on the computer and I didn't want to go to class because I was too into it, too involved with getting it just right.

Deborah warms to her subject. I ask her if she ever feels too involved with other things. She hesitates a long time. Finally there is a slow "Yes, maybe with my drawing a little," but then there is an even slower "No. It is different with drawing. It is more so with the computer. It's like somebody's there." This is something I often hear about the holding power of the computer. I hear it from children and from adults. Many people are lonely and isolated, but when they have a computer around it can feel like somebody is always there, always ready, always responsive, but without the responsibility of having to deal with another person. The computer offers a unique mixture of being alone and yet not feeling alone.

Deborah says that she stopped using the computer because access became too difficult. But there is more to it than that. She is withdrawing from something that served its purpose but that she senses as a danger.

> I could start to get bad grades again because I started thinking of the computer all the time. That could screw me up pretty bad. I didn't like getting help from teachers no more 'cause I got so used to people helping me that I couldn't do things on my own. And I could get myself stuck like that with the computer. It would be the same thing. You get so used to it that it's always there, like the teacher helping you. You couldn't do without it.

Deborah's images of what can happen to people with computers come too close to the dependent place where she began. She is not about to go back.

Deborah used the computer to build a safe environment that allowed her to experiment with something new. The way Deborah used her experience of the machine as an "experience-to-think-with" was unique to her. But using the machine for world-building was something I discovered again and again among children her age.

Bruce and the Mirror in the Machine

It is eighth-grade lunch period. The boys' side of the school cafeteria is a sea of blue jeans, Oxford shirts, and windbreakers. Bruce floats out upon it: love beads, open-necked velour sweater, aviator sunglasses pushed up high on his forehead. Bruce at fifteen sees himself as creative, artistic, an individualist. His recollections of childhood include a golden age when he was six and seven, a time when he most felt how different he and his family were from everything around. At that time they lived not in the city but in Glendale, described by Bruce as a "gross suburb." The gross suburb was the backdrop for a clear, marvelous sense of feeling special.

> I hated Glendale with a passion. Everyone was alike. When one kid got a three-speed bike, everyone would get three-speed bikes. And then of course I did not ride a bike. Then they would get ten-speed bikes. I just use bicycles as an example. They were into other things in the same way. Like sports. And I'm not, not at all, into sports. My father was never really into sports—he is more of an artistic person. And so that kind of rubbed off. He wasn't the type of father who would take me out to the lawn and say, "Let's play baseball." I thought my family was the least alike to everybody in Glendale because my father was a college professor. We had a big house, and at night all these people would drive up and they'd come in the house and we'd turn out the lights. Everyone in the town would wonder what we were doing in there. My dad had switched from just being an English professor to running a film center, and every night he would show a movie in the house. I would come home after school, and in the evening my father would have massive movie parties and there would be twenty-seven college kids staying there all night, sitting and talking and drinking. I would really love these parties and the movies. I would come down in my little pajamas at two

o'clock in the morning and say, "What are you doing?" People would be playing guitars and sitting around. I loved it. We were really different.

Even now, the thing I hate most is the idea of being typical. My father came out of a typical—well, he lived in a suburb outside of Washington and he lived a sort of typical, *Leave It to Beaver* life. You know, like "Come on, Bill, let's go over and play baseball in the backyard." And then he rebelled and now he's living a life that's similar to mine, with going to parties and whatnot. An artistic crowd. He doesn't want to be a typical middle-aged father. When we get angry at each other, he says, "Typical teenager" to me and I say, "Typical middle-aged father" to him.

Bruce acts in a local children's theater, and the week of our interviews is tense for him. He has tried out for a part in a summer production of *Peter and the Wolf* and has just been called back for a second audition. First he is nervous about the audition, then about its outcome. Two weeks later Bruce catches me in the hall to tell me that he has gotten the part. "I'm so relieved. The worst thing about these acting tryouts is that everything is out of your control." As with Deborah, control is on Bruce's mind.

I have a lot in common with my father. . . . We both have chaos. Emotionally, we tend to act, not think, be fatalistic, because when you're in a really chaotic state it's easier to say, "Well, yes, however it turns out, it was meant to be that way." I'm a slob in my way of thinking, in how I keep my things. Both my father and I would like to have a little order. That's where my mother comes in. My mother pretty much is the order, and that might be one of the reasons my father married my mother. I think it's the same reason that I think it's good that my parents are a bit protective of me, even though I sometimes complain about it. Like, I like it that we have dinner together every night. I wonder if my father and I were ever alone—I wonder what would happen. I think all hell would break loose. We once went to a wedding without my mother, and we both got really drunk. It was really funny. It was also scary. We both ended up doing a lot of things without thinking. Hoping for luck. Being disorganized. But I would love to have control. I would absolutely love to have control. I know that you're here because you care about what happened with the kids who had the computers. And I really have to tell you that that was the first thing I really loved about them. I mean, you command them. However you want. I remember loving that idea of giving commands.

While he was growing up Bruce found a way to have control. He found it in his toys. He liked toy cars and really loved a set of homemade puppets. With these, he gave the commands. But the less passive toys were threatening—like a toy robot he got when he was five.

I had this robot. A frightening robot. I really hated this thing with a passion. It would start walking. It had a big metal box on it, and all of a sudden the doors would open up and guns would shoot out and it would close its doors and keep on walking and every so often the eyes would light up—it was a horrid thing. Then the batteries would run out and it would go slower and slower and you never knew when . . . and then it would fall over. I remember looking at it, watching it walk around shooting things, and I remember hating it. I remember having my grandmother put it away for three years and then getting it again. I guess it was a pretty expensive thing, so they just kept it for me. And then I know that when I got it back I would make it walk off tables. I still hated it. I would make it start from high places and it would do its horrible things and then I would have it fall off—that kind of thing. It was weird. I never did that sort of thing with other toys, I was never violent or tried to hurt other toys. But this robot, though, it was such a frightening image. It would shoot out, it would break down. You never knew when it would do what. I didn't like them [battery-operated toys], I didn't like the way they started going slower and slower and you couldn't help it, couldn't do anything about it. For me, batteries always meant that the toy couldn't be exactly trusted. I had great fun a few years ago. I dissected batteries. Yeah. I took them apart. I always hated them.
  I never was much with machines. Not really machine phobia, more like awkwardness. I always feel that I'm going to break this. That kind of thing. Not really able to interact with it. When my father was showing films at the house he taught me how to thread the projector. But I always used to get nervous that I would do something wrong, that the machine would break—you never knew when it would break, it's flaky like our toaster—and it would be my fault. The first thing I even remember, literally

my first memory, was when I broke a typewriter when I was like three. My parents were always typing. I said, "What's this?" and I pushed the typewriter off the table. They were really upset.

Bruce and Deborah are both unsure of finding the inner resources to exert self-control. This issue dominated their lives before they ever came near a computer; it is not surprising that it became a major theme in their interactions with it. Bruce and Deborah are contrasting cases of what "microworld" construction can be about. Even though their concerns are similar, what they do with the computer is at opposite extremes. Deborah uses the computer as an emotional medium to "play with the other side," to play with a small world of control and constraint. What she got from the experience is clear: by restricting herself she put herself in a position to experience what it is like to exert a greater degree of control than she had ever known. Her experience did not change her into "somebody else." She still feels that her actions are determined more from without than from within. But she had an important experience of feeling what it is like to be "the other kind of person" and learned to integrate some of their ways of coping.

Bruce took the same computer and used it, not to "play with what he wasn't," but to externalize what he felt himself to be, a chaotic person. Deborah worked hard to create order in her computer world. Bruce worked no less hard to maintain disorder in his. He consistently rejected orderly programming practices even though he was aware of these techniques and knew that ignoring them would cause him inconvenience. He would refuse to take notes about what he did, or would leave them lying around the classroom, perpetually "lost." Perhaps most saliently, the subject matter of Bruce's programs was at the other extreme from Deborah's. Deborah's careful, planned, rule-governed shapes were exercises in restraint. They enforced a demand for total understanding of how they were built. For Bruce, the goal seemed to be to produce as much wild, uncontrolled, and not always explicable movement as possible: one of his favorite programs created triangles that spun in complicated and confusing counterrotations.

Both used the computer to create a microworld, as other children create them with drawing materials or dolls or toy soldiers. The child who begins to draw by taking up a pencil and asking for a ruler in order to draw "perfect" stick figures, and the child who starts out by applying color in broad, sweeping strokes, the child who arranges dolls in a neat circle and has them all sit down to afternoon tea, and the child who lines up toy soldiers in opposing camps for a battle—in each case there is projection that reveals something about how the child is thinking, feeling, and organizing experience. In all of these cases the world the child creates, of rules or disorder, peace or violence, reflects back an image of who that child is or perhaps wants to be. Such images can help people move toward greater insight about conflicts, problems, and ways of thinking.

But Bruce comes to the computer with a conflicted emotional agenda. He needs not only to put his own disorder into the situation but also to vanquish any sense of the computer as autonomous. The computer must be chaotic—it reflects his inner life—but it can have no life of its own. In order to reassure himself about this, Bruce goes to extremes. For example, the computer comes with aids for editing programs that make it easy to insert a new instruction in the proper place in the body of the program. Bruce would rather retype the whole program than use the automatic device. In the middle of "wasting" a half hour struggling with typing that he knew was unnecessary, Bruce was not upset. He used the moment to reassert his individuality. When he noticed raised eyebrows he would simply say, "Leave me alone, it's my funeral."

Many young programmers who share Bruce's interest in visual effects and love for the spectacular like to produce screen effects that computer scientists call "artifacts." The "straight" route to computer graphics puts shapes onto the screen and sometimes sets them in motion under the logical control of a program. The overall result is often surprising. For example, superimposed shapes can produce illusions of dimensionality. But the surprise is in the mind and the eye of the viewer. Each detail on the screen can be traced back in an intelligible way to the instructions in the program. But sometimes the reign of logic breaks down. In the system Bruce was working on, the computer's display can put up only a certain number of lines. As long as a program instructs the system to put up fewer lines, things proceed smoothly and predictably. But when the critical number is exceeded, the computer shows symptoms of "overload"—for example, a strobelike flickering on the screen. Many children are delighted when they first encounter this kind of effect and work hard to exploit this "unofficial" unprogrammed behavior of the computer. It adds to the machine's "magic." Not Bruce. For him all artifacts were anathema: they recalled the robot taking off on its own. He didn't want anything going on behind his back.

Bruce wants the machine to be predictable in spite of his most unpredictable programming. He would like it to be as different from the unpredictability and the variety of people as possible.

> I think of the computer as being perfect. People are imperfect, and that's the difference. As of now, when you put things into a computer you pretty much know what it is going to do. With people you never know. That's the point. It could be that some-day they could make it so that you would not know what the computer is going to do. It would all get too complicated to know. One of the first movies I remember was Kubrick's *2001*. Wow! HAL in *2001* and my robot that I kept trying to destroy by making it walk off the table—I never thought of them to-gether. HAL was certainly unpredictable, and he was supposed to have feelings.

Bruce was reassured by his experience with Logo programming. He was able to see the computer as "perfect," by which he meant that it did only what it was told. He found a style of working with it that gave it no chance for surprises. Some people not only delight in artifacts, but eventually even develop an aesthetic of program-ming that puts a value on the surprising, the counterintuitive. For them, programming is a way of walking on the threshold of the machine's mysteries, pushing it to its limit as an "unpredictable system." But this demands a tolerance for the machine as lifelike, as "magic," as surprising. Bruce had none. Against his sense of inner chaos, the world of things was reassuring only if predictable.

Bruce liked the computer insofar as he could see it as at his total command. This is what attracted him to the machine. But then the computer has to be kept in line. For Bruce, concessions to the machine's ability to carry out complex functions or, even worse, to produce artifactual effects outside his control seemed to confer too much "personhood" on it. His response to the threat of what we might call the computer's "automaticity" illustrates its power to reflect the programmer's personality.

Bruce expresses who he is in his spontaneous behavior with the computer. He also has worked out a set of abstractly formulated beliefs about computers and people. He has an ideology about "what it is to be a person." A person refuses dictated order. A person is not predictable. A person is emotional. In the sense that the computer is perfect, to be human is to be not-perfect. It is to be not-computer. Bruce fears that somehow computers in their perfection might be a threat to the nonperfection of people. He sees the machines as undermining the things that he and his father most value: unpredictability and variety.

> What I really hate about computers is that they might cut down on the variety of people. I have seen some footage that frightened me. It was on *Nova* a few years ago. They showed a clip from a Kawasaki promotional film. It was all robotized, with all these giant computer arms building motorcycles. All of these identical things. And there were no human workers in the plant. If that happens all over the world, that means that humans won't do that kind of work. I like the idea of variety in people. Some people like to do mechanical work, and I would hate to think that a certain kind of work would be cut out by anything. The idea that computers might cut down on the variety of things that people could do—that's the thing that bothers me.

When I asked Bruce to look back on his whole experience with the computer and tell me what he thought he had gotten out of it, he said, "The very best thing was I loved doing things on my own. Making things that nobody else has ever made. Nobody could have ever done that exact same thing."

Deborah wants more than anything else to be like other people, and she uses her experience with the computer to bring out qualities she might share with them. Bruce wants to be as different as possible from everyone else. He uses the computer to underscore this difference, as a mirror for his own uniqueness. He tells me, "When I saw what I did with the computer, I used to laugh. I could see what a nut I was." Externalization onto a canvas is a way of seeing who you are.

The difference between Deborah and Bruce is not only a matter of psychology, but of the different worlds they live in. Reality for Deborah is protecting herself from drink, drugs, and sex—and their consequences. Her mother may be protective, but she can't protect her in the social world outside. Deborah's difficulties in asserting control place her at risk, and she knows it. In self-defense, in the machine she found an aid for making rules.

Deborah's family is poor. Bruce's is relatively well off. Deborah's father does odd jobs. Bruce's father is a teacher and writer. In Bruce's world the threats are not those of the street, not threats on the person, but threats on a felt sense of personhood. He worries about the computer coming too close:

> I think I believe that maybe someday they could give computers feelings. But I would think more of the human race if it didn't happen. We'd be like gods if we could create something that had feelings. It would be something that would be a clone of who we are. I think it would be very hard to do this, but two thousand years ago they didn't think we could do the things we do now. But I think it would be different from the things we do now. Much worse. Putting the feelings into the computers would be much worse. It would be like the apocalypse.

Reflecting on the computer experience leads Bruce into an elaborate theory of what constitutes order in the cosmos.

> To me the Frankenstein story is the apocalypse . . . Being able to create. The test-tube baby always sickened me. But at least the test-tube baby, it's not really all that synthetic. I mean there were still people. But the whole idea of computers having feelings, I could not stand that. It is possible for it to happen, but I hope it doesn't. If there are enough people like me it won't. I think that human beings were meant to be the things with feelings. There are natural things, animals and humans, they can have the right to have feelings. I believe that God made us, animals and natural things.

Here Bruce is struck by a very personal image of what is so bad about the "feeling computer." Such a computer could share in an experience that constitutes one of his most intimate bonds with his father: "I mean, could you just see a computer watching a movie, saying, 'Well, no, this isn't very good'? I hate it. It makes me cringe."

Thinking Through

The story of Narcissus is usually read as a warning against self-love. Narcissus saw his image in the water and fell to his death because of his desire to touch it, to be closer to its beauty. But there is another way to understand the story. Narcissus fell in love with what appeared to him to be another. This image of that other person fascinated him because it objectified a sense of beauty of which he had felt only a vague inner sense.

Mirrors, literal and metaphorical, play an important role in human development. In literature, music, visual art, or computer programming, they allow us to see ourselves from the outside, and to objectify aspects of ourselves we had perceived only from within. Bruce was referring to this when he said, "I could see what I was doing on the computer and I could see what a nut I was." Deborah came even closer to this idea: "When you program a computer there is a little piece of your mind, and now it's a little piece of the computer's mind. And now you can see it."

Infants are fascinated by their reflections as they grope toward a sense of their bodies as coherent wholes. With puberty, there is an assault on the sense of coherence of the body and the mind. There is new growth, new desire, new feelings. As adolescents we return to our mirrors; in programming, Deborah and Bruce found powerful ones. Some children become far more explicit than they about seeing the computer as a mirror of the mind. These are children who make explicit use of computational metaphors to think about themselves. Looking at the detail of how they do so provides a vantage point for understanding something that goes beyond the stories of individual children. It helps us to understand how computer metaphors can turn into a new popular psychology for the culture at large.

Carla is a fifth grader who has been working with the computer for five months. I visit her classroom on an unusual day. Her teacher is out sick, and a substitute teacher is taking over. Unsure of the children's normal routine, the new teacher gives them an unaccustomed chance to sit around and talk about the computers, to compare notes on their experiences. Since the class has thirty-five children, they break up into smaller groups to pursue their conversation. In one circle of twelve, the discussion turns to whether or not computers are alive. Someone in the circle says, "No, they are not alive, because they are programmed," a comment that is met by mumbles of approval—almost everyone finds this a very good answer. Everyone, that is, except Carla, a quiet girl who usually does not take a stand against any consensus. "Well, I don't know if they are alive. They certainly are not completely alive, but I don't think it has to do with that they're programmed. We are all programmed."

I talk to Carla for a long time. Her family is poor. They are very religious, very observant Catholics. She is the youngest of six children, her parents are in their fifties. Carla's life is filled with complex rules. There are rules of religion, rules of demeanor, rules about whom you can and cannot play with. There are rules for dress: all of her clothes are rank-ordered in terms of their "goodness" so that she can wear the "worst" ones to school and wear them out before proceeding to the next in line. When children are learning to program, one of the things that most delights them is naming the programs. When Carla wrote her first computer program, she called it CLOTHES. The idea of executing steps in a procedure was not new to her. It was how she was made to organize her closet, and to a certain extent, it was how she thought about her life. She answered questions about what she liked to do, what she did after school, and who her friends were, with the rules for what games she is allowed to play, how late she is allowed to stay out, and whom she is allowed to play with. It is not surprising that her encounter with the computer, with its step-wise procedures, was familiar and could be integrated into her way of talking about herself. "I think that I am programmed like the computer. Other kids in the school aren't as programmed as me. They have to do things, but they don't have to do them in order. My mother did my programming. And the Pope. Well, not really, the priest did it. But the Pope did his."

Here Carla breaks out in nervous giggles. She has clearly said something that to her feels like a very bad thing to say, and she looks at me somewhat warily. I don't say anything, and she continues, looking nervous. Finally I say, "Well, I guess that can be sort of rough—all those rules." Her reply astounds me: "Well, you know, you can change the program. Once you know how, you can change the program. I can't do it now, but that doesn't mean that I won't be able to someday." For Carla, experiencing herself as programmed is not to see herself in a situation of total constraint. It expresses a hope that somehow the program—and her life— might be changed.

Dennis has just begun high school. He is fourteen and preoccupied with the ways in which he is like and unlike his father. His father is a political-science professor, very successful, intellectual, intense. Dennis feels he is like his father. "The other kids don't think I'm much fun. I guess I turn everything into a brains contest." But he also admires his father. "He really is the smartest person." Dennis is concerned with what there is about him that is "real," what is his "true identity," and what is changeable, accidental (and here he uses a computer expression), "artifactual." Is he like his father in some fundamental way? Will he be like that for the rest of his life?

Dennis started to program computers when he was ten. He got involved with them by hanging around the computer center of a large university that accepted "tourists" on the system, and, indeed, his precocity won him the role of favored guest. Recently, he has found that thinking about levels of programming languages offers a way to think about his personal problem. Each computer comes with its own specific "machine language." This is a fixed characteristic. Dennis explains to me that it is part of the "hardwiring" of the system. He thinks of this as the computer's "real identity." But most programmers do not communicate with the machine by "talking to it" in its machine language, since this would be cumbersome. They communicate with it in a "high-level language" of which Logo is just one example (BASIC, FORTRAN, COBOL, PASCAL, and LISP are others). The machine accepts the high-level language and translates it back into the machine-language commands that are in direct communication with its hardware.

A computer that plays master chess may have the same machine-language identity as a computer that runs a robot arm on an airplane assembly line or passes messages between branch offices of a bank. Yet these machines have different behaviors that are defined in the programming of the high-level language. These behaviors, which Dennis thinks of as "psychologies," can be changed, reprogrammed. When you are interacting with a particular computer, the most salient thing about it seems to be its behavior, its way of interacting with you, but, as Dennis points out, "that's just because you only know enough to get involved with it at that level. That's your problem, not the computer's. It's not part of the computer's 'core identity.' "

Dennis began to elaborate a model of himself in which he distinguished between his machine language—his "core machine"—and high-level programs written on top of it. He decided that he and his father had different machine languages. They were two very different machines, "like an IBM and a DEC. We are fundamentally, fundamentally different." But, Dennis explained, clever programming, "neat hacking, really neat hacking," had been able to get these two very differently structured machines to behave similarly. This way of thinking landed Dennis in a more comfortable spot. All of the similarities between his behavior and that of his father, similarities that he didn't like and wanted to be able to change, were on the level of a higher-order language that was reprogrammable. The machine analogy left him with an optimism not unlike Carla's. The trick was to find a way to do the reprogramming.

Dennis has never read Freud or any of the American "neo-Freudians" who considerably softened Freud's notions of the determining power of the unconscious when they put forward a notion of an autonomous ego that the individual could feel to be a "center," a "self."[4] But as I listened to him pondering reprogramming strategies for himself, I thought to myself that here was a boy who had rediscovered the notion of a "conflict-free" zone of the ego: a platform to stand on, a zone of mental functioning that is not determined, that is open to change.

Carla's analogies and Dennis' theorizing are not isolated examples of what happens when people meet up with computers. They are taking first steps towards playing with the idea of mind as machine, personality as program. This kind of play with computation and models of the self is very much a part of what the adult world is doing with computers. It is not confined to the experts. It happens among college students taking their first programming course, among people buying personal computer systems for their homes, among people whose contact with computers was initially "just for business," to handle tax returns, to help them run a small company, or to do word processing. It is also part of children's computer experience. It is implicit in the musings of very small children. It is implicit in the anthropomorphization of the machine by the third, fourth and fifth graders who are more deeply committed to mastering it. And it becomes increasingly explicit as adolescence unfolds.

George, a college sophomore, was lethargic, depressed, unable to focus his attention on anything that required him to take an initiative. He was failing most of his courses, did little else during his day but watch television soap operas. He didn't spend time with friends, and he had nearly broken off contact with his family. He was particularly anxious about the prospect of any contact with his father, a successful physician. George had always admired his father, wanted to please him and grow up to be like him. As a freshman George did not have to choose a major, and he did very well —so well, in fact, that he felt he would be able to handle premedical studies. At the end of his freshman year he declared his major to be biology, a subject in which he had always excelled, and he spent the summer sailing with his parents. He came back the following fall filled with expectations—only to find himself in a state of debilitating depression.

Shortly after I met him, George began to take an introductory course in biostatistics required of all biology majors. He quickly became absorbed not in the course itself, but in the intricacies of the computer system that handled the statistical material. George became deeply immersed in computer programming.

In his depression, George's attention span was short. Correcting an error, in a biology experiment or in an English paper, seemed overwhelming because making a change implied starting over, rethinking the whole, like when a tower of blocks falls down for a child. Programming had a different "feel." The "feel" as he described it was that he "could go into the program and deal with the thing that is wrong with it, deal directly with the rotten part. I could fix up the problems but leave things basically intact." He enjoyed the sense of being able to deal in an isolated way with a specific error and see an immediate result. Moreover, he was able to carry out experiments with his programs that seemed (although sometimes he admitted that this might be an illusion) to provide information about how well things were going. He felt himself to be the recipient of continual feedback on his progress. And he could initiate the process that would get that information back to him. In the course of a few months George started to build on this experience.

First, he was able to use his successes in programming to restore his confidence that he could finish a task. He completed a series of small programming projects; when each one was done he brought the printout of the program to sessions with his psychotherapist. They were symbols of hope, symbols that he could find a way back. Second, programming was the first thing he had ever done that was not "required" of him. He did it for his own pleasure. He could have easily passed the statistics course by learning a few "cookbook rules" on how to feed data into a preprogrammed package, but instead he turned himself into a programming wizard. He discovered a talent and he found that he could pursue it wholeheartedly without outside pressure. But what is most relevant here is that George took a concept from programming and used it as a metaphor for thinking about his mind, his problems, and their possible solution.

Programs are instructions to a computer that tell it literally what to do, what steps to take, what procedures to follow. Their broad outlines can be planned in advance, but they hardly ever come out "perfect" on a first pass. A detail doesn't work or there can be unforeseen interactions among segments of the program that were designed independently from each other. These are the program's "bugs." Programmers learn to think about what ails their products without recourse to the formula "the program is wrong." The program is basically sound; it simply needs to be debugged. Debugging is the search for errors that can be identified and isolated. And once isolated they can be dealt with in a "local" way.[5]

George began to think about his mind in terms of a program, and of working his way out of his depression in terms of debugging. His whole life had not been bad. The foundation seemed solid.

> When I began psychotherapy, I began to read Freud. I thought that it might help. I read some in high school and it seemed pretty interesting. I think that in terms of all the "Freudian stuff," the basic things, I think I had a very good start. Very good basic programming with my mother and father. But there is a bug. Not really fundamental. I started to feel that my father would be disappointed in me if I didn't become a doctor. I started to feel it because I wanted to be like him. I mean I think he is a really tremendous person. But he never said so. And this past week I called him and asked him straight out and he said that he really didn't feel that way.

George went on to say that he must be stuck in a loop, a vicious programming circle where all paths lead back to the same unproductive starting point. George used the image to get a handle on his experience. It was a place to start talking about the cycle of frustration in which he felt trapped, a frustration born out of misunderstanding and too great a desire to please through emulation.

How far the debugging metaphor can go is another question. In learning situations, the notion can be liberating. It allows you to stop thinking of right or wrong and to start thinking of "fix it." For George it gave a sense of optimism, a belief that once he had identified emulation of his father as a central problem he could get on with the business of living. But the metaphor also has serious deficiencies. The notion that painful emotional states—depression, inability to act, anxiety—are the result of purely local bugs ignores the complex and resistant structures behind the symptom. The "local fix" may work in only a limited way: symptoms may shift or reappear, underlying problems persist. When behavioral therapists "reprogram" one phobia or compulsion, it is sometimes replaced by another.

Psychoanalytic ideas are a powerful language for self-reference, for marking the significant dates, the significant events and relationships in one's life. We live in a "psychoanalytic culture," which has little to do with how many people have been psychoanalyzed, are in therapy, or even have read Freud. A set of concepts that offer guides for what is important in thinking about the self, for what is useful in thinking about personal experiences, has filtered out into the culture as a whole: repression, the unconscious, the superego, the Oedipal struggle with the father. In everyday conversation, when people talk about their problems, they make reference to these.

George, like Dennis and Carla, had stumbled on another language for self-reference, a computational language. They have not picked up their ideas through the diffusion of theories about mind as program. Their ideas have been sparked by interaction with the machine itself. The computer is enough like a mind to make analogies between the self and programs seem plausible.

They are not concerned with whether computers might one day be like people; instead they are struck with the idea that their minds have something in common with the "mind" of the computer before them. Whether or not computer scientists ever create an artificial intelligence that can think like a person, computers change the way people think—especially about themselves.

PART II

THE NEW COMPUTER CULTURES: THE MECHANIZATION OF THE MIND

CHAPTER 5

Personal Computers
with Personal Meanings

Children use the computer in their process of world and identity construction. They use it for the development of fundamental conceptual categories, as a medium for the practice of mastery, and as a malleable material for helping forge their sense of themselves. The computer is a particularly rich and varied tool for serving so wide a range of purposes. It enters into children's process of becoming and into the development of their personalities and ways of looking at the world. It finds many points of attachment with the process of growing up. Children in a computer culture are touched by the technology in ways that set them apart from the generations that have come before.

Adults are more settled. In the worst of cases, they are locked into roles, afraid of the new, and protective of the familiar. Even when they are open to change, established ways of thinking act as a braking force on the continual questioning so characteristic of children. Family and work responsibilities and the very real constraints of social class can make it too risky to cast doubt on certainties. But there are events and objects that cause the taken-for-granted to be wrestled with anew. The computer is one of these provocations to reflection. Among a wide range of adults, getting involved with computers opens up long-closed questions. It can stimulate them to reconsider ideas about themselves and can provide a basis for thinking about large and puzzling philosophical issues.

Of course, this doesn't happen for everyone. Some people are intimidated by computers and keep their distance. Others see them merely "as a tool" and assimilate them into their nine-to-five life. But within the world of home computer owners, within the world of virtuoso programmers known as "hackers," and within the world of artificial intelligence experts, a community dedicated to the enterprise of building "thinking machines" and computational theories of mind, people have taken up the computer in ways that signal the development of something new. The "something new" takes many different forms. A relationship with a computer can influence people's conceptions of themselves, their jobs, their relationships with other people, and with their ways of thinking about social processes. It can be the basis for new aesthetic values, new rituals, new philosophy, new cultural forms.[1]

In this chapter on personal computer owners I put the emphasis on these developments by focusing on the role of the computer as a catalyst of culture formation. What joined the first generation of personal computer owners into a culture was not only that they used the same hardware, read the same magazines, and attended similarly organized users' groups, but also, as I learned, something else. They shared a quality of relationship with the computer, an aesthetic of using the computer for transparent understanding. In this chapter I show how, despite important changes in personal computers themselves, in the kinds of people who are buying them, and the uses to which they are being put, this issue of transparent understanding remains an important theme for a new generation's relationship with their machines.

The Birth of a Personal Computer Culture

In 1975 the popular symbol of "the computer" was the IBM card, a fragile object—"Do not fold, spindle, or bend"—an object that was to be fed into a large machine owned by a bank, a corporation, a research institution. As this book goes to press, another image dominates public awareness: a person, intense and concentrated, hunched over the keyboard of a small computer with an interactive screen display.

In 1975 the most common complaints about the computer were about billing errors ("the computer did it") and lost airplane reservations ("the computer is down"). The threat from the computer was the threat from the impersonal system that knew you only as a number. Now the threat seems all too personal, captured in the fear that a child or a spouse will get "hooked" and become addicted to a machine.

Nineteen seventy-five was a watershed year. Until then the number of people who kept a personally owned computer in their homes could not have exceeded a few score. Then quite suddenly things changed. A small company named MITS announced a kit for $420 containing everything one would need to build a small computer. It was called the Altair, and it started a revolution. Within a year thousands of people had bought the Altair or the spate of products that quickly followed to fill the growing demand for kits, for parts, and for ready-made small machines. Within a year thousands of people had joined computer clubs and subscribed to personal computer magazines. Within five years the number had climbed into the millions.

From the beginning, most promotional literature and popular accounts of home computer use emphasized the instrumental: how computers could teach French or help with financial planning and taxes. But from the beginning it was clear that this utilitarian rhetoric was not the source of the real excitement. I spoke at length to members of that first generation of personal computer owners, the people who bought and built small computers in the late 1970s.* Some justified their purchase of a personal computer by referring to a specific job—monitoring a home heating system, keeping records for a small business, establishing an inventory for a kitchen or a toolroom—but in most cases they also described a point at which their sense of engagement with the computer had shifted to the noninstrumental. They spoke about "cognitive play" and "puzzle

---

* I began my study of personal computer owners in 1978 with a questionnaire survey answered by ninety-five New England home computer owners (their names had been drawn from the roster of a home computer club and the subscription list of a personal computer magazine). I interviewed twenty-seven of these original respondents, and in 1978–79 I interviewed another thirty-three home computer owners drawn from other sources in Boston, New York, and San Francisco. By 1981 the technology available for home use had grown sophisticated and foolproof enough to attract people without technical backgrounds. I interviewed a second group of thirty East Coast home computer owners who had just bought their machines. In addition to the home computer owners with whom I had extended conversations (usually visiting them in their homes) I attended meetings of personal computer clubs and users' group meetings. (Users' groups are special associations that form within personal computer clubs which bring together the "users" of that particular kind of machine.)

solving," about the "beauty of understanding a system at many levels of complexity." They described what they did with their computers with phrases such as "building another room in my mind." Once people actually had a computer in their home, the most interesting thing about it became the computer itself, not for what it might do, but for how it made them feel.

We saw that computers can broaden children's sense of their talents and possibilities. Computers can do something of the same sort for adults who have more entrenched ideas about what they can and cannot do, their aptitudes and ineptitudes. Many people think of themselves as incapable of doing anything technical or mathematical, and learn from their interactions with a personal computer that this simply isn't true.

One high-school French teacher who describes himself as "having a love affair with a TRS-80" explains: "After Sputnik, when I was in grade school and then in junior high, there was all that fuss, all the kids who were good in math got to be in special classes. Rockets were going up, men trying to go to the moon. Decisions about things. Scientists seemed to be in charge of all that." For him, learning to program has a symbolic meaning, making him feel that he has crossed a line to become a member of a technical culture from which he had previously felt excluded. A more complex example of the computer changing one's self-conception is illustrated by Barry, who has always thought of himself as a "technical person," but who was "scared out of real science."

Barry went to college for two years, hoping to be an engineer, then he dropped out and went to technical school. He has a job calibrating and repairing electronic equipment for a large research laboratory, and he likes his job because it gives him "a chance to work on a lot of different machines." But he came to it with the feeling of having failed, of not being "analytic or theoretical": "I always had a great deal of difficulty with mathematics in college, which is why I never became an engineer. I just could not seem to discipline my mind enough to break mathematics down to its component parts, and then put it all together. I could never grasp what was really important in science." Five years before I met him, Barry bought a programmable calculator and started "fooling around with it and with numbers the way I had never been able to fool around before." He says that "it seemed natural to start to work with computers as soon as I could." To hear him tell it, numbers stopped being "theoretical," they became concrete, practical, and playful, something at which he could tinker.

> I'll pick up the calculator, and if I don't know how to do a problem I'll play with the calculator a few minutes or a few hours and figure it out. It's not so much that the calculator does a particular calculation, but you do so many, have so much contact with the numbers and the results and how it all comes out, that you start to see things differently. The numbers are in your fingers.

The calculator and the computer made numbers seem concrete. "They put mathematics in my hands and I'm good with my hands."

Barry says that he doesn't think of engineering as a pipe dream, nor does he think of what he is learning with the computer as something that could make it real. In terms of his career, nothing has changed, but in a more private sphere a great deal has changed. Working with the computer has made Barry reconsider himself.

> I really couldn't tell you what sort of things I'm going to be doing with my computer in six months. It used to be that I could tell you exactly what I would be thinking about in six months. But the thing with this, with the computer, is that the deeper you get into it, there is no way an individual can say what he'll be thinking in six months, what I'm going to be doing. But I honestly feel that it's going to be great. And that's one hell of a thing.

Barry's world has always been divided into the people who think they know what they'll be doing in six months and people who don't. Barry has crossed this line, and now he has started to call other lines into question, the lines he has always used to "mark off" what was off-limits to him. In school, his inability to do the kind of mathematics he respected made him lose respect for himself as a student. The computer put mathematics into a form he could relate to. More important than the mathematics he has mastered, he has come to see himself as a learner.*

---

* To some extent, hobbies have always played this kind of role. But the way people talk about buying a personal computer makes it clear that unlike the case for many hobbies they have tried in the past—stereo, carpentry, model railroading—it makes them feel a part of something that is growing and that the society at large really cares about. It can mean new feelings of empowerment; it can mean crossing a frontier that separates tinkering from real technology.

These issues recall those that came up when I discussed adolescents, identity, and computers. But Barry and the other home computer owners I shall be speaking of here are adults. They have the whole computer—the hardware and the electronics, as well as the program—to work with. And, most important, as adults they live in many worlds—worlds not just of play and learning, but of work and productivity. They bring new pressures and greater complexity to their relationships with their machines.

The computer is Janus-like—it has two faces. Marx spoke of a distinction between tools and machines.[2] Tools are extensions of their users; machines impose their own rhythm, their rules, on the people who work with them, to the point where it is no longer clear who or what is being used. We work to the rhythms of machines— physical machines or the bureaucratic machinery of corporate structures, the "system." We work at rhythms that we do not experience as our own. What is most striking in the story of the revolution that began with the Altair personal computer is that for many people the computer at home becomes a tool that compensates for the ravages of the machine at work.

Like Barry, most of those who bought or built the first generation of personal computers were "technical people." And, like Barry, most worked in the electronics industry. Many of them were computer programmers. Unlike Barry, however, most were dissatisfied with their jobs.

In the course of the last decades programmers have watched their opportunities to exercise their expertise in a spontaneous way being taken away. Those who are old enough remember the time when things were different as a kind of golden age, an age when a programmer was a skilled artisan who was given a problem and asked to conceive of and craft a solution. For those who are young, the memory of such times remains alive in the collective mythology of the shop. Today, programs are written on a kind of assembly line. The professional programmer works as part of a large team and is in touch with only a small part of the problem being worked on.[3] Thus programmers are particularly sensitive to the fragmentation of knowledge and the lack of a feeling of wholeness in work to which so many of us are subject. And when these "proletarian programmers" buy home computers they bring this sensitivity to their hobby. When those I interviewed spoke of their home computers they spoke of the sense of power that came from having full knowledge of the system, of the "feeling of control when I work in a safe environment of my own creation." They spoke of how good it felt to work with "whole problems."

In many ways Carl is typical of the first generation of personal computer owners: thirty-five, college educated. He had worked as a programmer for over eleven years when his company "made the switch" to structured programming: "good for business, death for the joy of the work." He has recently built a small computer system for his home, and he devotes much of his leisure to programming it. Although Carl works all day with computers, what he does with his home system is not more of the same.

Carl has thought a great deal about what he calls his "mental ecology." At work he sees himself as only one small part of a process he cannot understand or control. "Like they say, I'm just a cog." He thinks about the need to put different kinds of thinking in balance, and about how his home computer can help.

> If you never or rarely get to finish things at work, if your job is basically to make little pieces and it's somebody else's job to make them fit into a whole, then working with a computer at home can give you an experience of getting it all together. You do the whole thing—building up from machine code to finished project. It makes you feel in balance.

Personal Computers and Personal Politics

When personal computers were first introduced they were most accessible to people like Carl whose work experiences prepared them to use the machines (with the early models this took considerable technical expertise) and gave them a desire to exploit the machines' potential for creating worlds of transparency and intelligibility. There is something else notable about the introduction of personal computers: they came on the scene at a time of dashed hopes for making politics open and participatory. Personal computers were small, individually owned, and when linked through networks over telephone lines they could be used to bring people together. Everything was in place for the development of a politically charged culture around them.[4]

The computer clubs that sprang up all over the country were imbued with excitement not only about the computers themselves, but about new kinds of social relationships people believed would follow in their wake. Of course there was talk about new hardware, new ideas for programming and circuit design. But there was also talk about the rebirth of ideas from the sixties, in which, instead of food cooperatives, there would be "knowledge cooperatives"; instead of encounter groups, computer networks; and instead of relying on friends and neighbors to know what was happening, there would be "community memories" and electronic bulletin boards. Computers, long a symbol of depersonalization, were recast as "tools for conviviality" and "dream machines." Computers, long a symbol of the power of the "big"—big corporations, big institutions, big money—began to acquire an image as instruments for decentralization, community, and personal autonomy.

Personal computers have entered the American consciousness as a new variation on the Horatio Alger story—the story of Steve Jobs and Steve Wozniak beginning with a machine in a garage and turning it into the Apple computer corporation. But in the late 1970s another mythology was also born, as resonant of the 1960s as Horatio Alger was of an earlier period: build a cottage industry that will allow you to work out of your home, to have more personal autonomy, more time for family and the out-of-doors.

Hannah worked as a programmer in a large corporation for ten years before starting her own software consulting company specializing in educational programs for personal computers. To her, nothing is more depressing than working on a tiny piece of a problem. In her old job, "most of the time I didn't even know what the problem was. With my computer at home I do everything. I get to see all my kinds of thinking. Most important, I have more control over my time, I can spend more of it with my family."

CoEvolution Quarterly, Mother Jones, Runner's World, and *Byte* magazines lie together on Hannah's coffee table. The tableau was not unusual. In the years after they first appeared, people tied personal computers into aspirations for ecology: decentralized technology would mean less waste because people would attend electronic meetings and conferences, do more work out of their homes, and save on transportation and energy costs. Personal computers fueled aspirations for alternative education: schools would become obsolete as computers brought an individualized curriculum into the home. Personal computers became symbols of hope for a new populism in which citizens would band together to run information resources and local government.

When in the 1960s social critic Ivan Illich searched for an image of how people could have direct access to each other—for learning, for teaching, for bypassing traditional hierarchies—he came up with a giant telephone directory and switchboard. A decade later, personal computers linked on networks provided new technical images to support such aspirations.

There was talk of harnessing computer power for networks and "knowledge co-ops." Some people joined with others to try to make it happen. Most did not. The more usual way in which the machine became associated with anti-establishment politics was due to a vague sense that the computer in the basement, living room, or kitchen was a window onto a future where relationships with all technology would be more immediate, where people would understand how things work, and where dependence on big government, big corporations, and big machines would end. But this vague sense did not come only from the idea that the small, personally owned computer could be of practical help in creating new political networks and decentralized information resources. Something else, less instrumental, more subjective, was at work. As the first-generation personal computer culture grew, a particular style of working with the machine evolved, and the style itself was used as a political metaphor. People imagined a computer-rich future by generalizing from their special style of relationship with home computers, a style which, as we shall see, was characterized by transparency, simplicity, and a sense of control.

For some people the railroad signifies progress; for others it signifies the rape of nature. But either way, if you want to use the railroad, you have only one choice. You buy a ticket, get on the train, and let it take you to your destination. This is not true of every technology, and with the computer it is not the case at all. Deborah's carefully planned-out stars and rectangles were very different from Bruce's whirling, out-of-control spirals. What was different was not just the product, but the way in which the actual experience of using the machine offered a way to think about who one is and who one would like to be.

The men and women I am writing about here also used the computer as an "object-to-think-with." But here the computer experience was used to think about more than oneself. It was used to think about society, politics, and education. A particular experience of the machine—only one of the experiences that the machine offers—became a building block for a culture whose values centered around clarity, transparency, and involvement with the whole. Images of computational transparency were used to suggest political worlds where relations of power would not be veiled, where people might control their destinies, where work would facilitate a rich intellectual life. Relationships with a computer became the depository of longings for a better, simpler, and more coherent life. Understandings in the realm of personal computers were contrasted with more diffuse understandings elsewhere.

Wayne is around fifty and has always worked as a salesman in electronics. He bought his computer on an impulse, but it soon became a preoccupation. He taught himself to program, mobilized friends to teach him about hardware, became a devoted member of his local computer society and a smaller users' group. Within the space of a few months, Wayne had joined a subculture: he had learned a new language, felt himself to be the holder of esoteric knowledge, and several nights a week were taken up with sharing its collective rituals. What Wayne wants out of his computer is a perfect illustration of what I mean by computational "transparency": Wayne wants to know "exactly how things work" and expresses sharp frustration at gaps in his ability to follow the system through. "I can't really follow the continuum. . . . There is a big gap in my own mind from the idea that an electrical circuit can be on or off to the binary number system, and again from there on to the BASIC language. I've got to understand all of that."

Wayne's desire to understand his system from the and/or gates through the flipflops, the machine language, the assembler and up, carried the emotional intensity of long-standing political frustration.

> People used to understand more about how things work. We live in a world where we don't understand how anything works. I live in an economy, and I don't understand how things happen in it. I watch the energy crisis, I don't understand why things are happening that way. . . . I don't want that to happen with the computer.

In the computer, Wayne saw a chance to develop a depth of understanding that eluded him elsewhere. And then he took his hoped-for relationship with the machine as a standard for other things. Just as the computer is available to understanding, so should the political world: "Politics is a system, complex to be sure, but a system all the same. If people understand something as complicated as a computer, they will demand greater understanding of other things."

I heard many echoes of Wayne's sentiment. But this tone of "pleasing populism" in the early personal computer culture was not itself unproblematic. The satisfactions that the computer offers are essentially private. People will not change unresponsive government or intellectually deadening work through an involvement, however satisfying, with a computer in the den. They will not change the world of human relations by retreating into the world of things. There is a tension here. It would certainly be inappropriate to rejoice at the "holistic" relationships that personal computers offer if it turns out that they serve as a kind of opiate. One thing is certain: for the technical hobbyists of that first generation, part of what made the personal computer satisfying was that it felt like a compensation for dissatisfactions in the world of politics and the world of work.

Understanding how the computer can be used in this way requires that we step back and look once again at styles of programming. The "hard masters" among children demanded control. But here, for this community of adults, something new is added to the desire for control. Intellectual fragmentation at work and the complexity and smokescreens of political life create new pressures, and with them a desire to find transparent understanding *somewhere*. In contrasting hard and soft mastery, the issue was planning versus the pleasures of negotiation. Here another contrast is needed: risk versus reassurance.[5]

Risk and Reassurance

At Indianapolis, cars zoom by in the hands of master drivers highly tuned and sensitized to the machines' response. Yet many of these drivers end up in fatal crashes. By contrast, there is another kind of automotive mastery, where pride comes from detailed knowledge of cars to help insure family safety. There is mastery in the service of the desire to operate just on the edge of disaster, and there is mastery to feel safe. Cars can kill. Computers don't. But here too there are safe programmers and "racing-car" programmers, those who pursue risk and those who avoid it.

Risk and reassurance can be played out in programming because the computer presents two possibilities to the programmer: there is the "local simplicity" of the line-by-line program and there is the global complexity of the dynamic processes that can emerge when the program is run. Locally, each step in a program is easy to understand; its effects are well defined. But the evolution of the global pattern is not always graspable. As soon as a program reaches a certain level of logical complexity, its behavior is no longer predictable by its programmer in any simple sense. One is dealing with a system that surprises. Depending on how the programmer brings local simplicity and global complexity into focus, he or she will have a view of the machine as completely understandable and under control or as mysterious and unpredictable, even fraught with risk. By concentrating on the local, the line-by-line, you feel in control. By concentrating on the global, you see control slip away and can then feel the exhilaration of bringing it back.

In Carl, the programmer who feels like "just a cog" on the job, we have met someone who demands an understanding of the whole and a sense of total control when he works with his computer at home. By contrast, the "racing-car" programmers enjoy the sensation of playing with risk: the system might "crash" or behave in unexpected ways; some new relationship between parts of a program might trigger an unanticipated effect in the hardware of the machine.

We see the spirit of risky programming in Howard, now a university professor, who thinks of himself as a hacker. He uses the term "hacker" to identify himself with a subculture of programming virtuosos devoted to programming as an art in itself.

Howard described a fantasy in which he would walk up to any program and "fix it, bend it to my will." As he talked, he used the kind of hand gestures a stage magician makes toward the hat before he pulls out the rabbit. For Howard, what was most thrilling about the experience of programming was "walking down a narrow line," using his ability to make small changes to keep the whole under control while at the same time producing dramatic effects. He was always searching for ways to make a local fix, what he called "neat hacks"—changing some very small thing in a program that would have a powerful "and in the best case utterly counterintuitive" result for the system as a whole. His was a magician's fantasy because what he was looking for ideally was doing something small, like touching one key or typing one character, and having the whole system come alive.

Howard's fevered love of programming, which he describes as the feeling of "walking near the edge of a cliff," contrasts with Carl's approach, which is geared toward maintaining a safe place. Carl works on well-defined projects he chooses himself, projects whose beginning, middle, and end are all under his control. Carl is not interested in mystery, in magic, in local fixes; when he programs he likes the sure and the explainable, he likes to see the whole problem in all its detail. Howard works on large, "almost out-of-control" programs; Carl chooses well-defined, delimited ones. He describes his home projects as compensation for the alienation he feels on the job and says that he works most intensively on his home projects when he feels furthest away from "seeing how the whole thing fits together at work." Howard finds documentation a burdensome and unwelcome constraint; Carl enjoys it, he likes to have a clear, unambiguous record of what he has done. Indeed, much of his sense of power over the program derives from his feeling of mastery over its precise specifications. Howard and Carl may work at the same computer, but they approach it with different aesthetics, they are looking for different satisfactions.

This is illustrated by the computer language each prefers, the mode each uses to communicate his ideas and intentions to the machine. The computer can be thought of as a set of locations, each designated by a number. These locations are like different "addresses" within the machine. Each address contains a sequence of elements called bits. Each bit can be on or off. If the two states, on and off, are given the names of 0 and 1, then the sequence of elements in any location can be thought of as a number expressed with the digits 0 and 1.

Some simple operations are built into the computer. One is the ability to transfer information stored at the various addresses—for example, to move the contents of one address to another or to move the sum of the contents of two addresses to a third. Another kind of primitive operation involves taking the contents of a given location and treating them as instructions to be acted upon—that is, treating information within the machine as a program. These primitive operations built into the hardware are the machine's language. Machine-language programming consists of getting the computer to achieve increasingly complicated effects by stringing together the primitive operations. When you use only these to program you are in direct contact with the "bare machine." This does not mean that the contact is physical. You program in machine language by typing at a keyboard. The closeness of the contact is symbolic—you are talking the only language that the machine can "understand" directly. All instructions need to be designated with 0s and 1s; locations in the machine must be referenced by number. All other "higher-level" languages you might use will ultimately have to be translated back into these long strings of 0s and 1s. But when you use a high-level language you are not involved in that process of translation. It is done for you by a translation device that takes programs written in the high-level BASIC, or Logo, or PASCAL, or FORTRAN and puts them into machine language.

Howard will program only in high-level languages. They let him play with the computer without having to worry about the details of the hardware. Carl knows four high-level languages, and his home system allows him to use two of them, BASIC and PASCAL, but when he works at home he prefers to write in "assembly language," which is a way of programming one very small step up from machine language. In assembly-language programming, the programmer still has to think in terms of the machine's primitive operations, but is able to refer to them and to locations within the machine by using easier-to-remember names. For example, if the programmer is trying to add several numbers, he or she may refer to the location in which the sum will appear as "TOTAL" or "SUM" instead of referring to it by a number, like 0000000000100011. In common parlance, when programmers talk about "machine-language programming" they are usually talking about assembly language. With assembly language, you are still very close to the bare machine—only a few mnemonics away. Like a high-level language, an assembly language needs to be translated back to machine language. This is done using a translation program called an "assembler." People like Carl who enjoy contact with the bare machine and its logic often increase their contact by writing these translation programs themselves.

Carl does not justify his preference for assembly language in instrumental terms. He does not speak of how fast his assembly-language programs can run. His reasons are subjective: working in assembly language gives him the feeling of having direct contact with what is "really going on" in his computer. The safety he seeks is a symbolic safety, more like the kind that Deborah worked toward when she constructed her "thirty-degrees world." He wants to feel in close contact with machine logic; he wants the reassurance of step-by-step mastery. Howard thinks that this kind of contact is a "total waste of time." He doesn't even think of it as mastery of the computer. It is simply tagging along after its machine limitations. For Howard, programming is the enterprise of transcending these limitations. Programming as magic means programming as transformation.

In the high-level languages Howard prefers, the programmer no longer has to think in terms of locations or of machine-level operations, and there is no longer a transparent relationship between the steps written by the programmer and events taking place in the machine. The logic of high-level languages is adapted to how people think, not how the machine "thinks." For example, in the high-level language BASIC, an instruction might read "LET y = SIN X." In Logo, we saw the instructions "FORWARD 100" and "RIGHT 90" and "SETCOLOR :RED." These instructions are far from the 0s and 1s of machine locations. Just as an assembler stands between an assembly-language program and the machine language, a much more complex translator (some are called compilers, some are called interpreters) stands between a high-level-language program and the machine language. When you program in Logo or BASIC, the internal structure of the machine need never cross your mind. The compiler or interpreter takes care of it for you. High-level languages take the programmer away from contact with the bare machine. For Carl, this feels like a loss; for others, like Howard, a liberation. The differences are not simply of individual taste. Preferences in programming language and programming style are building blocks in the construction of computer cultures, in this case the culture of the first-generation hobbyist and the hacker.*

One might see the differences among computer cultures as

---

* High-level languages have another quality that makes them attractive in one way, yet less satisfying if you come to them with Carl's desire for transparency. Each of them is designed for a special kind of programming. For example, BASIC is designed for algebraic manipulations, COBOL is designed for manipulations such as sorting records in business applications. Programs of the kind for which the high-level language is specifically designed can be written more quickly and economically in it. But other kinds of programs might be cumbersome or even impossible. A car is a superior means of transportation if you know that you are going to be traveling paved roads. If you will be traveling up a mountain trail or across sand dunes, you might do better to have a horse. The computational analogy to the horse as a "general-purpose" aid to transportation is assembly language.

expressions of differences in the typical styles of their members' personalities. For example, the incipient hacker might spend time with other hackers because of shared personality traits such as a need to assert control that is so strong, so absolute, that it can be expressed only in relation to things. But once in their company, he or she becomes integrated into a community that amplifies whatever shared features of personality brought its members together. What might have begun as an expression of individual personality develops into a social reality.

Carl sought safety by making the computer a protected, intelligible world. In this he is typical, seeking what most first-generation hobbyists I met looked for in their machines. Sometimes they found it in assembly-language programming, which they described with such phrases as "I like the feeling of knowing I can optimize better than any dumb compiler" and "It makes me feel calm. Having control from the bottom level of the program and up makes me feel comfortable, safe, sort of at home." Sometimes they found it in relationships with the computer's hardware. Carl himself is deeply involved in a plan for revamping his home system's hardware. He built his system from "components"—a processor, a monitor, a keyboard, a printer. Such a component system needs to be connected with interface devices, usually a simple circuit. In Carl's case, each interface circuit needed only a few specialized and inexpensive chips. But Carl had a plan to use a separate microprocessor as an interface for each component. There was no need for a general-purpose microprocessor at each interface; it was "overkill" in terms of computer power. But the specialized chips that could do the job for less money could not satisfy his desire to build a transparent, maximally coherent system. To him, the special-purpose circuits were "black boxes" you couldn't see inside. By replacing the black boxes with separate, identical general-purpose microprocessors whose workings he understood, the system, at least in Carl's eyes, became uniform, intelligible, and elegant. Carl had conflicts about his project. He felt uncomfortable because he could not justify it "rationally." But from the perspective of Carl's subjective relationship with the technology, his rationale was clear. The "inexpensive" solution, a collection of opaque, ad hoc circuits, felt unintelligible. It felt like his relationship with the machine at work. His plans at home were dictated by the logic of psychological compensation rather than by the logic of material economy. Most important here was working in an environment where there were no black boxes and "things didn't change unless you want them to."

Of course, sometimes things did "change." The first generation of personal computers had problems. There were false starts and frustrations. There were bugs in the machines. But even if they couldn't be found, bugs became "known," "familiar," even reassuring. Joe owns a secondhand computer "with a lot of hardware problems." He likes to envision the relation of his program to specific actions taking place within the core of the computer, its central processing unit, the CPU. When Joe suspects a bug, he pulls out an oscilloscope and checks whether the CPU is doing what it should in response to a given instruction. He figures out what the signals should be doing and collects evidence for what is going wrong. He traps the bugs himself. Sometimes he fixes them. Mostly, he "just finds out what is going on." He says the bugs in his system "have become almost like friends. I turn on the machine and I check out my 'old friends,' and I swear, finding them there has a certain reassuring element."

What is reassuring here goes beyond predictability. Joe, like Carl, is looking for a direct relationship with the CPU, the "body" of the machine. If the "mind" of the computer is that part of computation which involves thinking in terms of high-level programs, then relating to the body of the computer means not only working on hardware, but also working with programs in a way that is as close as possible to the machine code, the language the "body" understands.

Not everyone is drawn to or could even tolerate the fastidious, meticulous work and record-keeping that so reassure Carl, Wayne, and Joe. The desire for this kind of understanding, the desire for an as-close-as-possible relation with the CPU, reflects individual personality. But it reflects other things as well. For many pioneers of the personal computer culture, this style of relating to the computer was "overdetermined" in the sense that a host of other, more general forces also came together and were expressed through it.

To begin with, it had an intellectual dimension. The first-generation personal computer owners were for the most part men who had always been interested in technical things and had a long history of involvement with computers. It has become a cliché to say of microcomputers that they follow the developments of larger computers with a ten-year delay. These people knew what was state-of-the-art and where the art was going. For them, the early personal computers seemed incredible, even awesome, because of their low cost and small size, but there were many things about them that seemed second-best—a collection of hand-me-down pieces, a collection of patches (in computer jargon the word is "kluges") dictated by arbitrary corporate decisions, by economic necessity, by the manufacturer's need to cover over past mistakes. The corner of the personal computer which they felt had the greatest intellectual integrity, which distilled the best ideas in computer science, was the CPU.

Whether or not they ever pull out an oscilloscope as Joe did and follow their machine-language programs step by step as its instructions pass through the CPU, getting close to the bare machine makes them feel in touch with what is most "pure" in the computer. They built a computer culture around a widely shared aesthetic of simplicity, intelligibility, control, and transparency. It is not surprising that for them, involvement with the "unspoiled" part of the machine holds the greatest satisfactions.

A second dimension is more directly psychological, related to the deep roots of computer "holding power." When children program the Logo turtle to make designs on the screen, or if they are using the small robot that has come to be known as a "floor turtle" to trace designs on paper on the floor, they are told to "think of themselves as the turtle." They are asked to "play turtle" and to make their design happen by instructing the turtle to do what they have to do in order to trace the same pattern with their bodies in space.

When you watch children learning to program in Logo, you watch children moving, tracing shapes, reflecting on what they have just done and trying to make the turtle make the same moves. The turtle has holding power because there is what Seymour Papert has called a "body syntonic" relationship between it and the programmer. When people become involved with the CPU, here too the relationship can be physical, although this is not as immediately apparent as when we look at children and turtles. Here too there is a body-to-body connection. The CPU's primary activity is moving something that is conceptually almost a physical object (a byte of information) in and out of something (a register) that is conceptually almost a physical place. The metaphor is spatial, concrete. One can imagine finding the bytes, examining them, doing something very simple to them, and passing them on. This kind of identification is a powerful source of computer holding power. People are able to identify physically with what is happening inside the machine. It makes the machine feel like a part of oneself. It encourages appropriation of the machine as a tool in Marx's sense —as an extension of the user.

Third, this relationship with the CPU as extension of self is all the more powerful because it is in contrast with the "other computer" that people know at work. There they relate not to the tool, but to the machine. I have noted that many members of the first generation of personal computer owners worked in the middle echelons of the computer industry. A bureaucracy stands between them and the computer; a bureaucracy schedules the computer, decides its up and down time, apportions the work for its software design, and decides on priorities and procedures for access to it. At work, when something goes wrong with the system it is usually the fault of an intermediary person, yet another "someone else" who deals with the machine, or it may be the fault of an intermediary in the machine itself, a compiler, an interpreter, an operating system; all of these are someone else's program. At home, what is savored is the opportunity to work directly with the CPU. When something does go wrong, it is between oneself and the bare machine.

When the early owners of home computers bought their machines, their software and hardware were in a state of disequilibrium. The CPU was elegant and transparent but the high-level languages available on the first small machines were opaque, arbitrary, and primitive. The interpreters and compilers that allowed them to run were designed to optimize what you could do on a small computer. They were designed to be practical, not to be understood. Everything was in place, then, for the first generation of personal computer owners to develop a relationship with the bare machine and to see it as a model for transparency and comprehensibility. Everything was in place for the technology to attract a group of people who had a particularly strong need to work through frustrated desires for that kind of transparent understanding. And everything was in place for them to use their relationships with personal computers as a metaphor for a new grassroots politics.

The Next Generation

Technical hobbyists dominated the early personal computer culture: they gave that early culture a certain coherency and supported one of its dominant themes, the computer as a way to counteract feelings of political alienation and discontent in the workplace. The people who are buying their first personal computer in the 1980s are buying a different machine than was available to the first generation of owners. They are not coming to the computer during a time of heightened political awareness. And for the most part, they are not technical people.

When the personal computers first appeared, nontechnical people were intimidated and kept their distance. "Computers" continued to be the electronic teller at the bank, the data-retrieval system at the office, the word processor on the secretary's desk. But increasingly, the computer became less compartmentalized. Millions of Americans brought them into their homes, encouraged by the increasing availability, reliability, and now portability of the machines, and encouraged, too, by their decreasing cost.[6]

Their interest is being elicited. They are inundated by articles in magazines and images on television telling them that they need a personal computer. And they believe it, even if they don't know why. Computers are being marketed by associating them with new, appealing images. For example, from the beginning, Apple had an image of being a counterculture computer. Its name and its logo suggest nature and simplicity. When IBM came into the field, it sensed the need for a strong symbol to break away from its Brooks Brothers image. Its promotions made an icon of antitechnological innocence into the trademark of its personal computer: the Charlie Chaplin tramp, Charlot with a rose.

Beyond being sold as an "antitechnology technology," personal computers are being presented as a technology for the young, the chic, the successful, who build their own companies and make their own schedules.

Onto such complex and ambivalent images manufacturers project more concrete promises as well: the machine will help Father with his finances, Mother with her writing, the children with their schoolwork. The machine is presented as a way of asserting status, a way of saying that this is someone who has not been left behind. Few purchases carry so much expectation. Even before the purchase is made, people start spending time "on the computer," because the decision to buy one carries the question "Which one?" It is unusual for people to come to a major purchase with so little prior knowledge. It is unusual for people to come to a major purchase with so little confidence in their own taste.

Just contemplating owning a personal computer means entering a new world of information to be gathered and assimilated and discussed. For most people, the portal to that new world is the personal computer store. Considering the purchase already means that one finds oneself in debates about 16K versus 64K, about disks versus tapes, about high resolution versus character graphics, about dot-matrix versus daisy-wheel printers.

There is something striking about these conversations. People seem to feel a pressure to have an opinion about all such matters. There is a reluctance to treat them as technical decisions to be left to a technical expert. Becoming fluent in this language, participating in this world, is part of what people are buying.

In the case of the technical hobbyists, the computer rarely served a truly instrumental function—the point of having the machine was the pleasure of working with it. For nontechnical users—and the typical home computer owner of the 1980s fits this description —the machines are used for a purpose: games, word processing, record keeping, reinforcing school learning. But here too, once they are in the home, personal computers get taken up in ways that signal the development of something beyond the practical and utilitarian. People buy an "instrumental computer," but they come to live with an intimate machine.

Carl built interface cards and programmed his computer in assembly language. The concerns of today's computer owner who uses the machine to play games or as a word processor appear to be far from his. And yet the language people use for talking about their personal computers, and the feelings the machines evoke, recall the first-generation hobbyists. In some cases the similarity comes through loud and clear, in others one has to listen carefully for it. But in either case, I have come to see Carl and his peers as more than members of a somewhat exotic and isolated subculture. They offer a window onto an aspect of how many of today's home computer owners relate to their machines.

David, the lawyer who found Zen in the video game, talks about buying a home computer to play games. What he says about their satisfactions is reminiscent of Carl's feelings about assembly language and Wayne's desire to "follow a whole system through." Like many of the first-generation owners, part of what the computer means to David is a chance to recapture the sixties. He complains about the conventionality of his life. He calls it "music you could play at anybody's wedding."

Like Wayne, David does not feel he is in a relationship with the world where he understands how things really work: "People don't build cars, people build transmissions or people build widgets that go inside the transmissions of cars. No one ever gets to see the whole thing that they've done." Like Carl, he is frustrated with not dealing with the whole on his job:

> After I'm done taking care of your divorce or some guy's criminal problem, that's the end of my involvement with that person. I can't have the follow-through to find out the end of the story, which could be that he went out and got arrested in Nevada and somebody else is representing him, or he lived happily ever after. I get fragments, always fragments of people's lives.

David likes the games because they form a transparent, completely knowable world. "It is a small one, maybe not a very important world, but you get to know it all the way":

> You win something for yourself. You lose something for yourself. You live out an existence. Even if it's just the existence of the character you are playing, you get to live it out in its entirety. You get to see the whole picture. There's nothing more to the game than what is there. There's nothing that you don't have control over.

David complains about not being closer to nature and dreams of moving toward "something more real." The irony, of course, is that for David a simulation, a computer game, is what comes to feel most real.

A forty-five-year-old editor named Gerald has similar feelings, in his case not about games but about using his new personal computer for word processing. Like David, Gerald comes from a nontechnical background and has always seen himself on the other side of a divide that separates him from people who are good at sciences, good at math, and "good with machines." He tells me that the computer has changed his life. He talks about an experience that first-generation owners called "coming to see all of your kinds of thinking."

Gerald quickly went beyond using ready-made word-processing programs. He learned to customize his system to suit his own needs. And as he modified his system, he modified his sense of not being able to work in domains that require precision and clear-cut decisions.

> As a kid in school, I was always interested in literature and history, the "soft subjects." But as soon as I hit high school I started to get really jealous of the science types. Not because I wanted to do it, but because you could be so sure of yourself. You had a right answer. You could go for the right answer, and if you got it, no discussion. I was so insecure. I always felt that that kind of certainty, the science certainty, would be great for me. But I thought it was beyond me. At my job as social science and philosophy editor, there is always ambiguity. The art is in the judgment call.
>
> I got a computer when they began to seem reliable, when you wouldn't be spending all of your time hunting after some genius to fix it, and I started to do programming right away. For me it's the first time that I have that feeling of knowing the right answer, of understanding everything that's happening. It's a real break from the rest of my "everything is relative" life.

Thus, when people today speak about the machines they have brought into their homes, their way of talking about them has many similarities with the discourse of the first-generation hobbyists. With David and Gerald we see a first: the computer is looked to as a medium of compensation for what is not found at work. There is a second: although the computers available and the population buying them have changed, there still seems to be the impulse to find a way to a sense of intimate understanding of the logic of the machine.

The first-generation home machines were easy to "open up," to peer into and experiment with, but the new machines tend to be closed "black boxes." They are built as a technology to be exploited, not explored. Manufacturers, now in the business of mass marketing to consumers not likely to be experts, are worried about warranties, guarantees, and parts replacement. Hardware comes in boxes marked "Do Not Open," "Not User Serviceable," "Warranty Is Void if Seal is Broken by Owner." And if you do open the box, you find that behind the physical inaccessibility of the hardware there is a new intellectual inaccessibility. The first personal systems were built up in a modular way. You could follow function through form. With mass production, with greater compression of function on single chips, intelligibility is sacrificed to ease and cost of fabrication.

At the same time that the hardware is growing more "opaque," a greater and more powerful variety of languages, operating systems, and other software is becoming available: text editors, file management programs, and debugging aids. Such systems give increased computing power. But the increased power does not lead to a sense of direct control where nothing stands between the programmer and the bare machine.

Despite all this, many people make active efforts to bypass the new features to get back to a more direct sense of contact.* As we have seen, the "direct-control" style does not necessarily depend on physical contact with the hardware. When you program in machine or assembly language, you are typing at a keyboard. The sense of physical relationship depends on symbolic contact.

Arthur, thirty-four, is an architect. He owns one of the most up-to-date personal computers on the market. He bought it "off the shelf" at a computer store and had it set up to do useful things. It has an elaborate word-processing system that he uses for writing proposals and reports, and it has a special program to do calculations necessary for his design work.

After one month Arthur started to teach himself to program. "I think of myself as a competent man. Programming seemed like something I would probably be good at." He learned BASIC and PASCAL and then wanted to do more. For him, this didn't mean learning other high-level languages or starting to work on larger or more complex programming projects or machines. Expansion was to be vertical, not horizontal. "Pretty soon programming in BASIC and PASCAL started to feel elusive. Like I wasn't in touch

---

* Indeed, part of the success of the Apple II computer seems to have been due to the fact that it was designed to make it easy for people who wanted to get at its "innards."

with where it was really happening. I wanted to get down there and play with the machine. I liked getting inside, changing things around, seeing that I really understood them."

Arthur became a master of "peeks" and "pokes." These are instructions in high-level languages that reach down to the level of the bare machine. Normally, when you work in a high-level language, you do not think in terms of machine events or actual locations in machine memory. But the "PEEK" instruction allows the programmer to look into a specific memory location and see what is happening in it. And the instruction "POKE" allows the programmer to act on a location, by inserting or "poking" a specific byte into it. These are ways of breaking out of the limitations set by the high-level language. Arthur was drawn to the CPU because he wanted to "get inside" and be able to "move things around." "This kind of programming is a real high, a very sexual thing. Sometimes I feel guilty when I do it for too long."

When people repair their bicycles, radios, or cars, when they build their own stereos, they are doing more than saving money. They are surrounding themselves with things they have put together, things they have made transparent to themselves. Bicycles, motorbikes, cars, and radios are one thing, but microprocessors, which cannot be taken apart, whose structures are microscopically etched on silicon chips, are another. Nevertheless, we have seen that many personal computer owners insist on treating their computers like bicycles. They labor to make the computer transparent. Professional computer scientists work to develop technology that does not demand technical knowledge of its user, to develop "human interfaces" that will make relating to computers more like holding a conversation and less like taking apart a bicycle. But, at least for now, many are unwilling to accept the computer as an entity whose underlying structure can safely be ignored. They demand some sense of understanding the machine. Of course, for different people what counts as understanding is different. For Arthur, it was directly linked to what the first-generation hobbyists searched for, the "body" of the machine. For someone like Doris, it is less direct.

Doris is a professor of history and has never felt comfortable around technical things. She was able to get good grades in math courses in school, but says, "I had no sense of really understanding the symbols I learned to push around." She bought a computer not out of any particular interest in the machine but because of an urgent deadline on a writing project and a friend who argued that she would write faster if she had one.

In Doris' first tentative probings of her word-processing system, she used a cookbook method, making lists of rules on cards she kept at her side. Little by little she found herself playing with the rules, seeking alternative ways of getting the same result: moving a paragraph, filing key words to use later in an index, and so on. A computer scientist looking at Doris might say that she is not "really" learning about the computer, because she is not programming or learning about the machine's internal structure. The computer scientist would be wrong. There is another reality: Doris is acquiring a sense of what it is like to work within a formal system.

The art of writing a program (like the one Doris uses for word processing) that must be accessible to the computationally unsophisticated, consists of designing an abstract, artificial world so that it feels like a familiar physical one. When you use a word-processing program you become familiar with an environment in which there are "places" analogous to files, "objects" analogous to sheets of paper, and "operations" analogous to copying, cutting, pasting, and filing.

The analogies with physical reality helped Doris get started. She could pretend that she was in the physical world with small differences: instead of using an in–out tray for temporary storage, she used a "place" called a buffer; instead of placing her text in a file, she gave an order for it to be placed there. But Doris soon discovered that the analogies with the "real" were not precise: what ruled here were the laws laid down by the programmer. Some simple operations produced results as if one were through the looking glass. If you give two documents the same name, one vanishes. If you display a document on your screen, it stays where it came from as well. Slowly, without any sense of a conscious break into a new way of thinking, Doris learned the ways of a formal system—she began to learn the peculiarities of a purely logical universe, one defined entirely by rules. And her pleasure in doing so came from her belief that this universe is in principle totally understandable. In this, although she does not program, Doris' relationship with the computer had much in common with what programming means to those who approach it in the spirit of the first-generation hobbyists.

Doris did more than get to know one constructed world. She was doing her writing on a general-purpose computer, rather than the much more restricted special-purpose word-processing machines that are common in business settings. This meant that she also got to work with other programs. She needed to use a separate program in order to prepare the disks on which her text is kept, to make "back-up" copies of her work, to rename files, and to combine them to make her chapters into a book manuscript. Her involvement with these many programs gave her a sense of accomplishment at being able to find her way around not one constructed world, nor, indeed, a number of them, but within a system of logical worlds whose unity is symbolized by the "operating system," the program that coordinates and gives access to the other programs in the system. At first, using the operating system felt to her like the symbol-pushing of her memories of school mathematics. But as time went on, its rules and hierarchy began to seem elegant, its patterns reassuring. Like Carl, Doris found pleasure in understanding a system in that especially complete way that does not ever happen in the "real" world. Doris' manipulations of the operating system, like Barry's manipulations of mathematics in his fingers, like Anne's painterly manipulations of the "sprites" in the Logo system, offer a tactile, "soft" access to a world of hard rules. The question of how this point of access can be transformed into fluency with other things scientific and mathematical is an open one. But a threshold has been crossed.

There is something else notable about Doris' relationship with her computer: she brought it into her life to write a book, but it brought her into a culture. Doris attends a users' group, she communicates regularly with the other faculty at her school who own her brand computer, she subscribes to two personal computer magazines, one that features news about her computer and another more general in scope. She is even beginning to think of herself as a particular kind of computer user, different from others. Although Doris does not program, she is clearly on one side of the divide separating the style of the "prototypical hacker" from that of the "prototypical hobbyist." She is interested not in magic, but in transparent understanding:

I have a friend whose son wants to be a computer wizard [the term used at her university for virtuoso programmers in the style of hackers]. For a while, I called on him whenever I had a problem. But I can't stand the way he works with the computer. He won't read the sections of the manual I show him. He sits down and starts typing. He never seems to know exactly what's going on, but somehow by instinct he finds a way to solve the problem. I can't stand it. I have stopped asking him for help.

Doris' style recalls the first generation of hobbyists, a style that puts a premium on transparent understanding. And she knows enough about what she enjoys in the machine to feel a sense of difference from her friend's son, the incipient hacker. Most people think of a computer as one thing for all people, and so, when they become aware of this kind of differentiation, it surprises them. Doris' initial reaction was to treat it as a matter of who knew more about the computer, and then as a manifestation of arrogance on the part of the young wizard. But something more is at work here.

Doris is beginning to get the idea that although she and the wizard use the same computer, she belongs to one culture and he to another.

Personal Computation and Personal Philosophy

In this chapter I have "tagged" two different styles of relating to the computer—one that focuses on magic, the other on transparency—by associating them with the culture of computer hackers and first-generation computer hobbyists. But these relational styles have a life of their own. They exist outside of these cultures. The story of Doris and her friend's son illustrates that now, within the personal computer culture, there are a multiplicity of styles.

These styles enter into programming and into the computer owner's feelings about what makes the machine consequential, what makes it satisfying and "beautiful." I discovered that they also find expression in something else as well: how individuals use the computer to think about other questions, among them "metaphysical" ones.

Children find in the question "Are computers alive?" a way to talk about the line between computers and people. Adults don't. Nonetheless, they are affected by the questions that stand behind the question: "What is life?" "What makes us special?" "How do computers challenge our definition of ourselves?" One way of getting adults to talk about these things is to ask not about "life" but about the possibility of machine intelligence. And here different styles of relating to the computer correspond to different kinds of answers.

Among the children at the Austen School it is Anne, the most advanced of the "soft" programmers, and Henry, the young hacker who put the highest value on magic, who are ready to ascribe to the computer a "sort of" life. In their own way, each tries to keep the computer mysterious. They do not try to understand it completely. Perhaps they even try not to understand it completely. Like the people who coaxed the ELIZA "psychotherapist" program into making lifelike responses, like Lucy who made Speak and Spell obey her spoken orders, they seem to have a stake in experiencing the machine as autonomous. By contrast, Jeff, a prime example of a "hard" style, found the question of the computer's life too "dumb" to discuss: computers were obviously not alive. This is not a simple matter of hard masters being more hard-headed. We saw that Jeff's style of programming has much in common with that of the first-generation hobbyists: it is an element in a coherent system of thinking about the computer as transparent and under control. As such, it shares nothing with the unpredictability of living things.

Adults express their ideas about what computers share with people not through opinions about machine aliveness but about machine intelligence. Committed to a notion of the computer as ultimately comprehensible in terms of its "specs," most first-generation hobbyists ruled the enterprise of artificial intelligence out of court: "How can you program something that can't be reduced to specs?"

Today people like Doris are drawn toward a relationship with the computer equally committed to keeping it unmysterious. And this often brings them to that same position: computers are too "mechanical" to have anything in common with mind or with life. What is powerful about the computer is placed in a different realm from the human mind. According to the aesthetic of what we might call the "pure" hobbyist culture, human intelligence has a quality of mystery. It is precisely what cannot be reduced to specs. It is precisely what cannot be meaningfully analogized with computational processes. One computer owner put it this way: "In a computer, no matter how fancy, all that is going on is GIGO, 'Garbage in and garbage out.' You can have all of these programs, you can even have them talking to each other, but in the end, you told them to do it. You can't have a spark of life in a computer. That spark of life in people, well, that must be God."

Other computer cultures—for example, the culture of artificial intelligence researchers or the hacker culture to which the "risk-taking" programmer Howard said he had once belonged—have very different computational aesthetics that can lead them in very different directions when they use what they know about computers to think about themselves. Recall that Howard's sense of real computer power is more like that of Henry and his mysterious inventions—for them it is somehow incompatible with specs. Far from finding artificial intelligence irrelevant, Howard sees it as an embodiment of what he finds most exciting about the computer: the way in which unpredictable and surprising complexity can emerge from local ideas. Howard believes that if you make the system complicated enough, the simultaneous operation of millions of interacting programs might be able to create in a machine "that sense of surprising oneself . . . that makes most people feel that they have free will, perhaps even . . . a soul." Someone like Carl sees computers as mechanical. Either people are the opposite or, if they are to be analogized with computers, the human psychology that emerges is resolutely mechanistic. People like Howard see the machine as complex and unpredictable. They want to see the machine as like the human and want to see the human as like the machine.

In the early days of personal computation, the world of the hobbyist came close to being a distinct and homogeneous computer culture. But as personal computers enter the lives of wider groups of people, this culture has been overwhelmed by centrifugal forces: an increasing diversity in who participates and why—and "participation" can come to mean no more collective activity than attendance at an occasional meeting. By contrast, the following chapter describes a group that has developed in conditions favorable to its growth as a culture: it shares a unity of place, lifestyle, and passion. It has developed its own rituals, language, myths, even its own literature. This is the culture of virtuoso programmers known as "hackers." Hackers are often described in the media as people whose involvement with computers has drawn them away from involvement with other people; in fact they are drawn away from people who don't belong to their world, but within it they form a tight web of relationships where the computer is the center of an all-embracing way of life.

CHAPTER 6

Hackers:
Loving the Machine for Itself

Every spring, MIT students hold an unusual contest. It has the form of a beauty pageant, but it is a contest to choose "the Ugliest Man on Campus." For several weeks, the students who think of themselves as most ugly parade around the main corridors of the Institute, wearing placards that announce their candidacy. They flaunt their pimples, their pasty complexions, their knobby knees, their thin, undeveloped bodies. They collect funds to support their campaigns. There is a vote. The proceeds of the campaign collections go to charity.

I spoke with the ex-student, now a professor at another university, who began the contest more than twenty years ago. He is proud of his contribution to MIT culture. "Everyone knows that engineers are ugly. To be at Harvard is to be a gentleman, to be sexy, to be desired. To be at MIT is to be a tool, a nerd, a person without a body. The contest just makes irony of the obvious."

Today's MIT students echo his words. They feel comfortable with a ritual that celebrates a denial of the body, yet at the same time some are upset by the contest. "It hits too close to home. I'm not ugly enough to compete, but I'm not pretty enough to be normal, to have a girlfriend, to know what to do at a party." Some are angry about it, and angry at me for noticing it. "I hate that goddamn contest. It gives the whole place a bad name. It makes me ashamed to be around." Some deny the importance of the whole thing. Others reproach me for being just a "humanist type," oversensitive. Don't I know it's "just a joke"? They point out that good-looking people sometimes compete, "trying to look ugly for a good cause." But most feel that although the contest is a joke it nevertheless expresses a truth. Some might call it the "social construction" of the engineer. These students see it more simply: an engineer is ugly in the eyes of the world, an alien to the sensual.[1]

The Social Construction of the Engineer

I probably do not have to say the obvious, that many MIT men are involved with and proud of the body and its pleasures. But there is, too, a widespread presence of what has to be described as self-loathing. This is more than the symptom of an individual malady; the illness is social. Our society accepts and defensively asserts the need for a severed connection between science and sensuality, between people who are good at dealing with things and people who are good at dealing with people.

This split in our culture has many social costs, of which the first and most poignant is paid by children, particularly the suffering of many gifted adolescents. MIT students talk about growing up in "all-American" schools. For example, Ron, a junior majoring in astronomy:

> I've always thought of myself as ugly, inept. All of the boys who had friends and were popular were into sports and didn't care about school. Or if they cared about school they were sort of good more or less at everything. But there I was. All alone, fixing used ham-radio equipment. And all of the other kids I knew who were into ham-radio stuff felt just as ugly as I did. We had a club in sixth grade. And we called it "the Gross Club." I'm not kidding. So don't expect me to be surprised to come to MIT and find that all the other loners, doing their math and science and thinking of themselves as losers, make themselves an ugly-man contest.

Ron's sense of himself as ugly is not supported in any way by his physical inheritance, although it is well supported by his grooming and gait. Muscles eventually take their form from the habitual posture of the body and set of the face. Ron's muscles express ambivalence, long felt, toward his body. He sees the power of his mind as a gift that brought him mastery over technology, but for which he has had to pay with shame and misery in the world of people.

The sense of a polarization between science and sensuality is made explicit by Burt, a sophomore majoring in chemical engineering:

> I think of the world as divided between flesh things and machine things. The flesh things have feelings, need you to know how to love them, to take risks, to let yourself go. You never know what to expect of them. And all the things that I was into when I was growing up, well, they were not those kinds of things. Math, you could get it perfect. Chemistry, you could get exactly the right values when you did your experiments. No risks. I guess I like perfection. I stay away from the flesh things. I think this makes me sort of a nonperson. I often don't feel like a flesh thing myself. I hang around machines, but I hate myself a lot of the time. In a way it's like masturbating. You can always satisfy yourself to perfection. With another person, who knows what might happen? You might get rejected. You might do it wrong. Too much risk. You can see why I'm not too pleased with the way my personality turned out.

The chances are that Ron and Burt will make an adaptation. They will emerge one day with diplomas and good job offers to be used as steppingstones to well-paid careers, to a sense of belonging in a social world that contains wives and children and the fabric of a supportive culture. But the transition from pariah to social integration is not easy; getting there is a struggle. Many feel the presence of a choice that can be put off, but that is always there. You are constantly coming to the fork in the road.

One path leads to what many MIT students call the "real world." The other leads to what Ron sees as a continuation of the Gross Club—an ever deeper commitment to ways of thinking and living that keep one apart from it. Those who take the second path flaunt their rejection of "normal" society by declaring, "We are the ugly men. You can keep your hypocrisy, your superficial values, your empty sense of achievement. We have something better and purer."

The struggle of the choice is described by Burt, who feels that he and his roommate are choosing opposite branches of the fork:

For me, MIT isn't the real world. It's sort of a joke around here, to talk of the Institute and to talk of the "real world." But it's not funny. I mean I think of it as a struggle. But my roommate— for him there was no struggle. All there was for him was the ninth floor of Technology Square. I mean where they keep the computers. No struggle at all. Intellectually, I mean when I tried to feel normal about it I always came back to feeling that he had a perfect right to live in any world he wanted to, but when I would see him—and I hardly ever saw him, because he more or less lived there, all nerdy and talking about "foobar, bletch, meta-bletch"—I really hated him. I mean I pitied him. But I can get like that myself. I was like that in high school. I hated him for giving up. I think that if you become obsessed with computers it makes it easy to give up trying to be a real person.

Burt's anger is not merely a feeling of the moment. It is persistent. He uses his roommate as a foil for his own struggle. It is a struggle to create a bridge between a world of things and a world of people. Like other students who talk about a split between their "people selves" and their "technology selves," Burt is trying to put things together. He wants to believe that intense relationships with technical things need not keep him from productive relationships with the larger culture and caring relationships with other people. In short, Burt wants to be an engineer and live in the real world.

Within every culture, even a culture that wears a collective badge of self-denigration, there is a hierarchy. At MIT, some science is uglier than other science. Some engineering is uglier than other engineering. Some kinds of self-absorption are more unsavory, perhaps even more dangerous than others. And contact with some machines is more contaminating than with others.

The Image of the Hacker

In the MIT culture it is computer science that occupies the role of the "out group," the ostracized of the ostracized.* Computer science becomes a projective screen for the insecurities and self-

---

* This is true although it is also the case that increasing numbers of MIT students want to major in electrical engineering and computer science. And the self-denigration of the computer scientists coexists with their sense of being a privileged elite. The situation I am describing is nothing if not paradoxical.

hate of others in the community. And many of the computer-science students accept this reflection of themselves as archetypical nerds, loners, and losers. On the MIT computer system that is considered to be the most advanced, the most state-of-the-art, the users are referred to as the "lusers." When you "log in" on the system to activate your account, you are given a "luser number" that identifies you to the computer and you are told how many other lusers are working along with you. How many other ugliest men.

Why are the computer-science students seen as the ugliest men or, when they are women, women who are somehow suspect? The self-image of engineering students is already low. Already they fear that quietly, insistently, in a way they do not understand but through paths they dimly suspect, the world of machines has cut them off from people, that they are the "kind of people" who demand perfection and are compelled by the controllable. The formal mechanical and mathematical systems they play with are the externalization of their taste. In the "computer person" they find someone who seems to have taken their taste and carried it to an extreme, someone who has taken their taste, already a source of tension, and transformed it into a perversion.

A fear about oneself is projected onto the perceived excesses of another. Such processes proceed by stereotyping, by mythologizing. In the case of seeing computation as ugly, as perversion, it is carried by taking a special community within the computer-science world and constructing the image of the "computer person" around it. At MIT, that community is known as "computer hackers." Elsewhere they are known as "computer wizards," "computer wheels," "computer freaks," or "computer addicts." Whatever the label, they are people for whom computers have become more than a job or an object of study, they have become a way of life.*

---

* My field research on the hacker culture included participant observation within the MIT hacker community, reading two years of "science-fiction-lovers mail," "human-nets mail," and systems messages as well as interviewing twenty-seven people who identified themselves as hackers, ex-hackers, and "on the way to becoming hackers." The hacker study also used a data-collection strategy made possible by the computer itself. When I began to study the world of programmers and hackers, I sent out a message describing my project on a nation-wide computer net, and said I would like to talk with anyone who was interested. On the computer system I was using, people could respond to my message when I was "off-line," that is, they could leave electronic mail for me in a "mailbox" file, or they could wait until I was "on-line," working at my terminal. The system has a feature which allows someone who

Engineers rationalize, indeed sometimes apologize for, the overintensity of their relationships with machines by describing them as tools, even as they express their identification by describing themselves as tools as well. The image of the machine as tool is reassuring because it defines a means–ends relationship. With our tools we forge things that can be used by other people. What is different for many hackers is that the means–ends relationship is dropped. The fascination is with the machine itself. Contact with the tool is its own reward. Most hackers are young men for whom at a very early age mastery became highly charged, emotional, colored by a particular desire for perfection, and focused on triumph over things. Their pleasure is in manipulating and mastering their chosen object, in proving themselves with it. It is not hard to understand why these few who "flaunt" the pleasures of the thing-in-itself become the objects for the projection of the nervousness of the many.

We saw the engineering student living with ambivalence, with the sense of being at a fork in the road. One direction leads to engineering being integrated into the everyday flow of relationships with people; the other leads to isolation and ever deeper immersion in the world of machines. Engineering students place great value on those things—books, movies, ideas—that connect their concerns with something larger. *Star Wars* was loved for the way it offered a bridge, even if superficial, between high technology and a romantic humanism. Robert Pirsig's *Zen and the Art of Motorcycle Maintenance* and Samuel Florman's *The Existential Pleasures of Engineering* are held in great regard.[2] These works achieved cult status because they describe how intense relationships with technical objects can lead to reflections on the philosophical concerns of the larger culture. They give courage to people like Burt that it is possible to be an engineer and live in the real world as well. By contrast, the hacker crystallizes an image of getting lost in the thing-in-itself.

One of the ways groups mark and protect their boundaries is through the use of language. Engineers develop a language of their own, a jargon. It is a source of pleasure, but also of alienation

---

wants to "speak" with another on-line user to flash a message onto his or her screen. Both parties can type at each other, sending messages back and forth. Over several years of working with this medium I received hundreds of letters and had many more brief and not-so-brief electronic correspondences.

from nonengineers: "I try not to use it [the jargon] in 'mixed company,' if you know what I mean," says one student. The hacker, however, is lost in the jargon of his machine and its programs. His machine is "intelligent." His machine is "psychological." It offers a language easily applied to people. He uses it in mixed company, and his refusal to talk of other things enrages his engineering colleagues who are struggling to assimilate, to find a language for moving into the real world. This rage helps to set the hacker off as so ugly that the others feel beautiful, at least for the moment, by comparison. The hacker is a threat because he comes to stand for cultural isolation in the enterprise of engineering.

Passion in Virtuosity

With the computer young people can find channels to a certain kind of virtuosity without passing through the filter of formal education. And a large research environment can benefit from an almost unlimited quantity of this virtuosity. Over the years at MIT there developed what was perceived by both sides as a fair trade. The hackers would supply virtuosity; in return they would be left free to construct their own way of life around one of the most powerful computer systems in the world. To understand what hackers do and how they do it, let us take a case in point: how the MIT hackers built the operating system that controls the computer on which the final draft of this book was typed.

When a company buys a computer, the machine comes with a large collection of programs called the operating system. These are the tools that enable the company's programmers to write special-purpose applications programs with vastly less effort and technical knowledge than would be necessary if they had to work with a bare machine. A simple example of what an operating system does is time-sharing, which allows many users to be served by the same computer in a way that seems to them to be simultaneous. In fact the computer is giving each user a quantum of time so short that he or she does not even notice and become jealous of the attention being paid to the others. This idea is simple, but bringing it about needs so much work that the job of making a time-sharing system of the professional quality of those supplied by a major manufacturer has probably not been carried out as many as a hundred times in the history of computation. The operating system is standard, and may not be optimal from the individual purchaser's point of view, but the purchaser of a computer has little choice but to accept the operating system offered on it. This system would have been constructed by a team of dozens or even hundreds of professionals and would represent the investment of many millions of dollars. To repeat the work and construct an operating system "to one's taste" is unthinkable.

When the Artificial Intelligence Laboratory at MIT obtained its first large computer it did the unthinkable almost without thinking. There had already grown up a community of gifted and totally dedicated young men, many of whom had dropped out of MIT academic programs in computer science in order to devote themselves more exclusively to computers. They were prepared to be on the job sixteen or eighteen hours a day, seven days a week; they lived and breathed and thought computers. More important for the story of the operating system they developed, they lived and breathed and thought the one computer that the lab had purchased. In record time they built what many considered to be the world's most advanced time-sharing operating system, and one to their taste: ITS. The letters stand for Incompatible Time Sharing, a joking reference to contrast it with the operating system that another, more professionally structured MIT laboratory had recently installed, the Compatible Time Sharing System, CTSS. CTSS was compatible with systems outside MIT to make it easier to run programs written by outsiders. CTSS was practical, but some felt that the system had achieved its practical advantage by compromising its power. ITS was written by people who loved the machine-in-itself. It sacrificed nothing.

ITS was built with little planning and certainly with no formal decisions about the "specs" of the system. It cost a fraction of what it would have cost to make such a system under "industry" conditions. Its development became a model for a mode of production different from the standard, a mode of production built on a passionate involvement with the object being produced. Loyalty was to the project, not to the management; there was no rigid hierarchy, no respect for power other than the power that someone could exert over the computer.

This hacker-style work is not confined to university settings. Industries have learned to profit from intense relationships with computers—some have become quite expert at capitalizing on in-house cultures of passionate virtuosity.

In *The Soul of a New Machine*, Tracy Kidder tells the story of how a new computer, the Eagle, was designed and built by people with uncommon devotion within the Data General Corporation. The book is written as an adventure story, indeed as a "cowboy tale" of a distinctly American variety. There are the "good guys"—the ones who are trying to build the machine. There are the "bad guys"—their rivals working on a competing machine in North Carolina. There is the struggle of the individual to "get back at" the authority of a corporation tempted to take the straight and conservative path when genius and vision offer another.

The word "Soul" in the title of the book is well chosen. It is what the group who created the machine devoted to the task. For the period of production they lived an almost monastic life. Other worldly cares and responsibilities dropped away. A religious leit-motif runs through Kidder's story of their dedicated labors where personal ego and personal reward had no place. What was impor-tant was winning. But this is a story in the real world. When the machine goes "out the door" to be marketed, the reality of that dedication is denied.

> The day after the formal announcement, Data General's famous sales force had been introduced to the computer in New York and elsewhere. At the end of the presentation for the sales per-sonnel in New York, the regional sales manager got up and gave his troops a pep talk. "What motivates people?" he asked. He answered his own question, saying, "Ego and the money to buy things that they and their families want." It was a different game now. Clearly, the machine no longer belonged to its makers.[3]

The Data General hackers created a successful new machine. The MIT hackers associated with ITS also wrote other influential programs and became an integral part of the intellectual life of the MIT Artificial Intelligence Laboratory. In short, hackers play a significant though controversial role in the history of computation. What sets them apart is that they work for the joy of the process, not for the product.

The Hacker Controversies

The roommate who so angered Burt by spending all his time on the ninth floor of Technology Square is following in the footsteps of the senior hackers, most of whom have gone on to other things, some of whom are still around, all of whom are mythologized. As the earlier hackers did in their time, Burt's roommate is finding that the computer allows him rapidly to attain a level of virtuosity that will make him indispensable. And as he moves closer to the center of hacker culture he is moving farther away from academic values, from acceptance of hierarchy, from the "day life" of most of the rest of the world. It is not surprising that he upsets a lot of people.

Indeed, hackers have become objects of criticism and controversy both within and outside the computer community. Their existence challenges assumptions about human motivation ("ego and money") somehow more forcefully because they are technologists than does the existence of priests or poets. People seem ready to accept that artists play with paint or clay, brush or chisel, with a certain disinterest in the final product. However, when an engineer adopts this stance toward his tools, it evokes anxieties about intellectual masturbation. Tools are made to be used, not played with. They should belong to work life, not to intimate life. Public controversies about hackers are fueled by the fact that hackers externalize widespread fears about machines and the dangers of too intimate relationships with them.

Many people first became aware of the existence of hackers in 1976 with the publication of Joseph Weizenbaum's *Computer Power and Human Reason*. The book's description of hollow-eyed young men glued to computer terminals is reminiscent of descriptions of opium addicts and compulsive gamblers:

> Wherever computer centers have become established, that is to say, in countless places in the United States, as well as in virtually all other industrial regions of the world, bright young men of disheveled appearance, often with sunken glowing eyes, can be seen sitting at computer consoles, their arms tensed, and waiting to fire, their fingers, already poised to strike at the buttons and keys on which their attention seems to be as riveted as a gambler's on the rolling dice. When not so transfixed, they often sit

at tables strewn with computer printouts over which they pore like possessed students of a cabalistic text. They work until they nearly drop, twenty, thirty hours at a time. Their food, if they arrange it, is brought to them: coffee, cokes, sandwiches. If possible they sleep on cots near the computer. But only for a few hours—then back to the console or the printouts. Their rumpled clothes, their unwashed and unshaven faces, and their uncombed hair all testify that they are oblivious to their bodies and to the world in which they move. They exist, at least when so engaged, only through and for the computers. These are computer bums, compulsive programmers. They are an international phenomenon.[4]

Hackers have been the centerpiece of numerous articles in the popular press expressing grave concern about the dangers of "computer addiction." The nature of this concern varies. There are fears that young people will fall victim to a new kind of addiction with druglike effects: withdrawal from society, narrowing of focus and life purpose, inability to function without a fix. Others fear the spread, via the computer, of characteristics of the "hacker mind." And hackers are almost universally represented as having a very undesirable frame of mind: they prefer machines to sex, they don't care about being productive.

Several years ago *Psychology Today* published an interchange called "The Hacker Papers."[5] It was a warning on the part of some, including some hackers, that hacking was dangerous and depleting, and a defense on the part of others that hacking was a creative outlet like any other. The article prompted a flood of electronic mail debating the question. Artificial intelligence scientist Marvin Minsky presented the strongest defense of the hackers. They are no different from other people seriously devoted to their work, he said. "Like poets and artists they are devoted to developing tools and techniques." And as for their alleged ineptness at social relationships, Minsky said that the hackers are superior to the psychologists who trivialize human beings in their rush to stereotype and classify.

In this polemical form the debate is, to say the least, flat and oversimplified. Hackers are caught up with their computers, often to the point where other things in their lives do drop out. But the metaphor of addiction evokes an image of a deadened mind, which does no justice to the hackers' experience of their work as alive and exciting. Minsky is right that hackers are intellectually serious people. But, on the other hand, Minsky contributes to flattening the issue by refusing to allow any difference between hackers, poets, and artists. There are differences between hackers and most poets. Indeed, Minsky might well be betraying the side of himself that is closest to the hacker when he tells us that he sees the essence of the work of a poet as developing tools and techniques. This might be true in some cases. But in many, perhaps most, the work of the poet includes exploring the complexities and ambiguities of areas of feeling where, we shall see, the hackers seek simplicities.

Both sides sell the hackers short by saying either that they are just like everyone else or that they are like nobody else except perhaps junkies or poets. A better understanding requires a closer look at hackers as individuals and as part of a culture that expresses and supports the psychological needs they bring to their relationships with computation.

Hackers live a paradox: this is a culture of "lusers" who see themselves as an elite. They are the holders of an esoteric knowledge, defenders of the purity of computation seen not as a means to an end but as an artist's material whose internal aesthetic must be protected. Most paradoxically, they live with a self-image as "lusers" at the same time as they define their relationship with the machine in terms of "winning." They are caught up in an intense need to master—to master perfectly—their medium. In this they are like the virtuoso pianist or the sculptor possessed by his or her materials. Hackers too are "inhabited" by their medium. They give themselves over to it and see it as the most complex, the most plastic, the most elusive and challenging of all. To win over computation is to win. Period.

Perfect Mastery

The issue of mastery has an important role in the development of each individual. For the developing child, there is a point, usually at the start of the school years, when mastery takes on a privileged, central role. It becomes the key to autonomy, to the growth of confidence in one's ability to move beyond the world of parents to the world of peers. Later, when adolescence begins, with new sexual pressures and new social demands from peers and parents, mastery can provide respite. The safe microworlds the child master has built—the microworlds of sports, chess, cars, literature, or mathematical expertise—can become places of escape. Most children use these havens as platforms from which to test the difficult waters of adolescence. They move out at their own pace. But for some the issues that arise during adolescence are so threatening that the safe place is never abandoned. Sexuality is too threatening to be embraced. Intimacy with other people is unpredictable to the point of being intolerable. As we grow up, we forge our identities by building on the last place in psychological development where we felt safe. As a result, many people come to define themselves in terms of competence, in terms of what they can control.

Pride in one's ability to master a medium is a positive thing. But if the sense of self becomes defined in terms of those things over which one can exert perfect control, the world of safe things becomes severely limited—because those things tend to be things, not people. Mastery can cease to be a growing force in individual development and take on another face. It becomes a way of masking fears about the self and the complexities of the world beyond. People can become trapped.

The computer supports growth and personal development. It also supports entrapment. Computers are not the only thing that can serve this role; people got "stuck" long before computers ever came on the scene. But computers do have some special qualities that make them particularly liable to become traps.

The adolescents who got stuck on ham-radio or fixing cars or playing chess could only with great difficulty take these worlds with them into adult careers. There was room for just so many radio repairmen or auto mechanics or chess masters. Parents, teachers, the educational system didn't support these hobbies—there was pressure to move beyond them, to "grow up." Not so for computer worlds: the gifted high-school programmer can go on to a college major in computer science and on again to lucrative adult work. Other factors in the computer's seduction, and these are the more important ones, have to do with the specificity of the computer as a medium to support the desire, the needs and in extreme cases the obsession for "perfect mastery."

With the computer you can set your own goals. Joe is twenty-three; he dropped out of computer science at Stanford in order to devote himself more fully to computers. The course work was not challenging enough; Joe needed to set his own goals in order to be able to continually surpass them. Now he is part of the support staff for one of MIT's large computer systems. His "official" job is rather undefined. He defines it as continually improving the system by adding features to it (improvements on its editor and mail and message programs) that test the limits of his knowledge. Joe describes himself as "stuck on winning" before he met computers. As a freshman at Stanford, he was stuck on the violin.

> I tried to do the same thing with the violin that I am doing now with the computers. But it really couldn't be the same thing. With a musical instrument, you are continually confronting the physical thing. The violin can only do so much, and your fingers can only do so much. You can work for years and not feel that you are making a real breakthrough. And you are constantly under the pressure of knowing your own limitations. I mean, I knew I was not great. I was obsessed—but I was not great. With programming, whatever you think of—and you are always thinking of something—it can be immediately translated into a challenge. That same night. You can set yourself up to do it in some really esoteric, unusual way. And you can make a deal with yourself that you won't be satisfied, that you won't eat or go out or do anything until you get it right. And then you can just do it. It's like a fix. I couldn't get that kind of fix with the violin. I could be obsessed, but I couldn't get the high.

With the computer as your medium there is no limit to how much you can flirt with losing in your pursuit of winning. There is no limit to the violence of the test.

In *The Right Stuff* Tom Wolfe tells the story of the Air Force test pilots who were chosen to be the first generation of astronauts.[6] As gripping as the story of Project Mercury is what the narrative reveals of the psychology of the test pilot. It is a psychology that demands that one constantly test the limits of the physically possible, push "the outer edge of the envelope": flying aircraft higher than they were designed to be flown, pushing them beyond their maximum intended speeds, pulling out of a dive with more acceleration than they were designed to tolerate. Always pushing, playing with the limits until the system failed, the limits of the technology were reached, and only having "the right stuff" could save a man's life. This is the stuff that lets you function as a superhuman when you have pushed yourself beyond the edge of the humanly and technically possible. Belief in "the right stuff" allowed a man to feel in control in situations that were set up in advance as situations where control would be lost.

The test pilots didn't put their psychologies away when they left the airfield, when they left their jobs. None of us does. Pushing the "outer edge of the envelope" was translated into rituals of "drinking and driving." They would drink until they were almost out of control and then race cars at speeds almost out of control. And when they survived, they would have further proof that they were the magical few who had the right stuff—which is what they needed to have the courage to go on.

People are not "addicted" to test piloting or race-car driving or computer programming. They are addicted to playing with the issue of control. And playing with it means constantly walking that narrow line between having it and losing it. Computer programming offers this kind of play, and it is a part of the hacker culture. MIT hackers call this "sport death"—pushing mind and body beyond their limits, punishing the body until it can barely support mind and then demanding more of the mind than you believe it could possibly deliver. Anthony, twenty years old, an MIT senior, is a computer hacker who is very aware of the pleasure and the perversion of sport death.

> Computer hacking is kind of masochistic. You see how far you can push your mind and body . . . women tend to be less self-destructive . . . hackers are somewhat self-destructive. They don't take care of their bodies and are in general flunking out. Burnout is common. Women are not so sport death; they are more balanced in their priorities. The essence of sport death is to see how far you can push things, to see how much you can get away with. I generally wait until I have to put in my maximum effort and then just totally burn out.

There are few women hackers. This is a male world. Though hackers would deny that theirs is a macho culture, the preoccupation with winning and of subjecting oneself to increasingly violent tests makes their world peculiarly male in spirit, peculiarly unfriendly to women. There is, too, a flight from relationship with people to relationship with the machine—a defensive maneuver more common to men than to women. The computer that is the partner in this relationship offers a particularly seductive refuge to someone who is having trouble dealing with people. It is active, reactive, it talks back. Many hackers first sought out such a refuge during early adolescence, when other people, their feelings, their demands, seemed particularly frightening. They found a refuge in the computer and never moved beyond. Alex is one of these.

Alex spends fifteen hours a day on the computer. "At least fifteen, maybe three for eating, usually a big pancake breakfast with the other guys after a night of hacking. Or sometimes we'll do a dinner in Chinatown at about one in the morning. Six for sleeping. I sleep from about nine in the morning to three, when I go over to the computer center."

> If you look at it from the outside, it looks like I spend most of my time alone. But that is not really true. First of all, there are the other hackers. We eat together a lot, we talk about the system. And then I spend a lot of time, I mean *a lot of time*, on electronic mail. Sometimes I think that electronic mail is more of an addiction for me than the computer is. I talk to people all over the country. When you type mail into the computer you feel you can say anything. A lot of it is just about the system, but sometimes it gets pretty personal. When you type into the machine you can go really fast. The touch is very sensitive. I don't even feel that I am typing. It feels much more like one of those Vulcan mind melds, you know, that Mr. Spock does on *Star Trek*. I am thinking it, and then there it is on the screen. I would say that I have a perfect interface with the machine . . . perfect for me. I feel totally telepathic with the computer. And it sort of generalizes so that I feel telepathic with the people I am sending mail to. I am glad I don't have to see them face to face. I wouldn't be as personal about myself. And the telepathy with the computer—well, I certainly don't think of it as a person there, but that doesn't mean that I don't *feel* it as a person there. Particularly since I have personalized my interface with the system to suit myself. So it's like being with another person, but not a strange person. Someone who knows just how I like things done.

The image of computer telepathy comes up often and not just among hackers. It is an important aspect of the holding power of the machine. And it is another reason why people who know computers come to fear them, why, as one architecture student put it, "I swore to myself that this semester I wouldn't touch the machine. It's like making a novena. Promising to give up something for God. But in this case I have promised myself to give it up for myself." He describes himself as "very involved with my work," but "I like to think of my work as 'out there.' And I am 'in here.' The thing with the computer is that you start to lose track of the ins and the outs."

The experience of losing track is captured by Alex's description of the computer as transparent to his thoughts. So much so that he is aware only of a flow of ideas from him to the machine. Programming can be a Zen-like experience. We have seen this quality as the power of the transitional object—the object that is felt as belonging simultaneously to the self and to the outside world. Such objects can evoke an "oceanic feeling" of fusion and oneness. And for Alex, the computer is this kind of object.

> Some people don't program straight from their mind. They still have to consciously think about all the intermediate steps between a thought and its expression on a computer in a computer language. I have basically assimilated the process to the point that the computer is like an extension of my mind. Maybe of my body. I see it but I don't consciously think about using it. I think about the design, not implementation. Once I know in my mind exactly what I want to do, I can express it on a computer without much further conscious effort.
>
> I usually don't even hear in my mind the words that I am typing. I think and type ideas expressed in LISP. My hands know which way to go. I think of an idea that I want to express and then I listen to how my hands are saying it. My hands are a really important source of feedback.

Alex's comments evoke the power of the transitional object. His remarks about when he eats and sleeps, about electronic mail, pancakes, and Chinese food touch on something else that makes getting stuck on computers much easier than getting stuck on mathematics or physics, the two things that hackers are most likely to suggest they would have done if they hadn't met the computer. This is the power of belonging to a group, in this case a cohesive and self-protecting computer culture. Most of these young men grew up as loners. Many of them describe a sense, as long as they can remember, of a difference between themselves and other people. Finally, they feel that they belong. Alex is very clear about this: "I always knew I was weird. I mean I didn't know why I was weird, but you could see from how other kids treated me that I must have had a big sign on me saying: 'Weird One—Fold, Bend, Spindle, and Mutilate this One.' "

Loneliness and Safety

Hackers don't live only with computers; they live in a culture that grows up around computers. The mathematics world that hackers might have joined would have left them alone much of the time. Of course, mathematicians get together, talk about their work, hold departmental colloquia and professional meetings, but the culture of mathematics is a culture of relative isolation. The hacker culture is a culture of loners who are never alone.

It is a culture of people who leave each other a great deal of psychological space. It is a culture of people who have grown up thinking of themselves as different, apart, and who have a commitment to what one hacker described as "an ethic of total toleration for anything that in the real world would be considered strange." Dress, personal appearance, personal hygiene, when you sleep and when you wake, what you eat, where you live, whom you frequent —there are no rules. But there is company.

The people who want to impose rules, the inhabitants of the "real world," are devalued, as is the "straight" computer-science community. They are in a means–end relationship with the computer. They want it to "run" their data, facilitate their experiments. The "straights" control the resources and pay the salaries, but they do not share a true allegiance to the machine. In academic departments, research laboratories, and industries where communities of scientists, engineers, and policy analysts become dependent on complex computer systems and thus on the hackers who maintain them, there is skirmish after skirmish. The hackers are always trying to "improve" the system. This can make the system less reliable as a tool for getting things done, because it is always changing. The hackers also make the system more complex, more "elegant" according to their aesthetic, which often makes it more difficult for other people to use. But the hackers have to keep changing and improving the system. They have built a cult of prowess that defines itself in terms of winning over ever more complex systems.

In most of these settings there is a standoff based on mutual dependency and a measure of mutual distrust. The researchers and administrators can push things only so far, because if the hackers don't get what they want, they will leave. The hacker wants to work on the best systems, but even if he has access to the most state-of-the-art computer he will remain in a work environment only if he feels it is a safe place, that is, an environment where he can work with relative autonomy.

David is a hacker at Stanford. He has moved around a lot looking for safety.

> I only really feel good around the computers at night. It used to be that the night culture got going because that was the time when the turnaround time on the system was fastest. Now the systems are so powerful that you hardly ever get that feeling of slowdown. If anything, you sometimes get it at night when all the hackers are on. But the night culture remains. Because that is when you are on the machine with your friends, with other people like you. Then it is a secure place where nobody can tell you what to do. And if somebody tries to, you can out-hack them —screw up their programs so that they are kept real busy trying to sort out what hit them. Then they come running to you asking for help and are not exactly in a position to boss you around.
>
> At night there is security. I feel safe from people who think they are smarter than me and from those who want to tell me what to do.

By the standards of the outside world, the hacker culture is tolerant. But it has its own codes and rituals; it provides a framework for living. For Nick, an MIT senior, it is home.

> Hacking is a safe lifestyle, but it's a lifestyle that once you're in it it's hard to get out of it again. Your whole life is amazingly clear. You hack, you talk to other people who hack, etc. There's a society associated with it, there's a culture associated with it, and there's a lifestyle associated with it. It's a whole world. It's always a retreat. There's always things to do, you're never alone.
>
> Deli-Haus, IHOP [a twenty-four-hour-service International House of Pancakes], eating Chinese food at one of the "officially

certified" Chinese restaurants—all of these are good, all-American things to do if you're a computer person. The lifestyle grew up from the things hackers did. They stayed up all night, so they always seemed to see the same people, ate at the same open-all-night-type places, they engaged in the same leisure activities, and they grew together, since they always lived together. Newcomers fall into it as if it were natural.

Being Special

Hackers do fall into the life as though it were natural. Its routines reassure. But it is set up to leave maximum room for people who have defined themselves for a long time, for as long as most of them can remember, as different. Alex makes this point very clear. "Since I was different, different enough so that I wasn't exactly going to fit in with 'the guys,' I guess I decided that I was really going to be different. Really different. I have always wanted to be very special. And when I hack, it is very important to me to have my own territory. I think true hackers all feel this way."

A large computer system is a complicated thing. It leaves plenty of room for territoriality, plenty of room for people who feel that carving out their own terrain and winning at what they are good at might be their only chance of being loved ("I certainly am not going to be loved for being the same as everybody else," Richard says as he points to his hair, a wild Afro that reaches down past his shoulders). And so the hacker culture is held together by mutual tolerance and respect for radical individualism. You can't be a real winner if you are the same as everybody else. Even on the computer system, only difference will make you indispensable. Indispensable means that "they" cannot get rid of you. And indispensable is at least a stand-in for love, as Nick explained:

> I feel a very strong need to be different. I have spent all my life set apart and have been taught that this is the right way to live. My dream, what I want to do, is to be a person that does something, discovers something, creates something, so that people will look at me and say, "Wow, this guy is really something special, let's love this guy." That is all I ever wanted. To be loved by everybody in the whole world.
>
> Hacking . . . it's another world. It was a place where I could make a name for myself because it was stuff that I was good at,

something I could do, something that makes me different—sets me apart. There are programs on the system right now that can't be fixed without my help, and that makes me happy. I don't know why I need this so bad.

His friend Anthony hacks on the same system, and shares his values. Nick talks about being unique in terms of being loved. For Anthony, being unique is the only way to give life meaning and purpose.

One thing that bugs me the most whenever I fly home: I look down and see all those houses and all those people who have never done anything that could not have been done by anyone else. That's a terrible thing. I would never want to be like that. It is important not to be common, because if you are your existence is meaningless because it makes no difference if you exist or not. So you must do something out of the ordinary like computer hacking to leave something behind you maybe even more than having kids will.

Computer hackers try to distinguish themselves both from the rest of the world and among themselves. A hacker comes in and he makes sure his personality is different from every other hacker's personality as much as possible even if it means becoming something he's not. Computer hackers have a great fear of drowning in the sea of humanity—all those blank faces. So they set themselves apart.

Sex and Romance: Getting Burned

The hacker culture appears to be made up of people who need to avoid complicated social situations, who for one reason or another got frightened off or hurt too badly by the risks and complexities of relationships. This impression comes in part from talking to hackers about their experiences growing up—of being misunderstood and even terrorized by other children, particularly in early adolescence. And it is something that hackers tell you if you ask, "What do you get out of hacking?" They talk about the high of working on complex machines, of being the best, of winning, of the companionship of the culture. And then there is an almost inevitable turn to a theme best summed up by the word "safety." First, there is safety from painful isolation. Most people escape isolation through relationships with other people. But if having control is always a necessity, this can seem too risky. Hacking is a way out of isolation without what many hackers refer to as "complicated" relationships with other people. "Complicated" can mean several things. It can be synonymous with "unpredictable," it can be synonymous with "risky." Hackers talk a lot about getting burned. And if you need to feel in total control, "getting burned" is one of the worst things that can possibly happen to you.

Anthony has "tried out" having girlfriends:

> Hacking is easy and safe and secure. I used to get into relationships that usually led to me getting burned in some way. It is easy to go out with people who are only interested in hacking because it is a safe and secure environment. It is safe from rejection if rejection is the act that is going to cause anguish. It is safe from getting involved.
>
> With a computer you can take nice little steps and you don't have to worry, because there is always someplace to come back to. With anything else you are less sure and you won't know if you like it before you try it. With a computer you know what is going on and you know everything is going to work out. So with computers you have confidence in yourself, and that is enough. With social interactions you have to have confidence that the rest of the world will be nice to you. You can't control how the rest of the world is going to react to you. But with computers you are in complete control, the rest of the world cannot affect you.

There is no such thing as the "average" way twenty-year-olds talk about romance. Most are struggling with establishing intimate relationships, efforts that bring painful rejections as well as pleasures. Certain themes do recur: self-doubt, realization that their knowledge of themselves and empathy with others need further development, worries about how much they are able to let go and get close to another person.

Most people talk about relationships by comparing them to other relationships, real or fantasized. Anthony compares relationships to the sense of accomplishment and control that you can get from a machine. This does not mean that he sees machines as a "substitute" for women. A better way to hear Anthony is by keeping in mind that his quest is for what can be controlled and mastered. He judges everything he meets according to this standard. He knows he is not getting a "substitute." But he is not sure that he can function in the worlds where you can get burned.

Sex and romance are desirable, but they are risky. "Sport death" is risky, too, but it is a special kind of risk where you assume all the risk yourself and are the only one responsible for saving the day. It is "safe risk." Anthony sees sex and romance as another, more disturbing kind.

> I haven't figured this sex thing out, but I don't think the important issue is control. It's bizarre. I don't understand it. A lot of the drives that cause hacking and sex are the same. They are both risk-taking activities and they both lend a sense of accomplishment. But hacking is safe in that you are in complete control of your computer world, and sex and relationships are risky in that the rest of the world has control.
>
> Hacking and sex do not fill the same needs. I think every hacker feels he is missing out on life. They say, "Oh, God, if only I could get a girlfriend I wouldn't be so miserable all the time." It's really a matter of time. If you want to do something to make yourself feel good and you want to share that with some people, hacking is a lot more of a sure bet than if you ask someone out on a date. There's a chance the other person doesn't have the same thing as you in mind, whereas the machine always has the same thing in mind. Sometimes I think I spend too much time with computers, because they might be pushing out other parts of my life like relationships. But I'm not sure yet. . . . A romance is a very controlling thing. It pushes computer hacking and a lot of other things I like to do out. I think computer hackers tend to get very strongly involved in relationships. This is because they are used to having this very close, clear, intimate relationship with the computer and they expect to have the same kind of relationship with a girl. They expect to understand the other person more than it is possible; they expect more control over the other person than is reasonable. People just don't work like computers.
>
> Computer hacking tends to be incompatible with romance. It's just that when you do something a lot you don't have much time for other things and you also get into this computer mind-set that is hard to break out of. Romance is not a safe kind of thing. Computer hacking is almost pure pleasure with very little risk. But it is not as fulfilling, because in the end you have just made a few lights blink. You only have so much energy. You can either spend it on computers or you can spend it on people.

It is poignant that Anthony begins by admitting that as far as sexual relationships go, control probably isn't the most important thing, but then he goes on to talk about sexual relationships almost entirely in terms of control. Anthony prefers the mysteries of complex systems because he can get to work decoding them. People, especially women, are a different matter.

Along with the fear of getting burned there is another, perhaps more fundamental issue at the heart of the hacker's relationship with sexuality: the insistent antisensuality of the hacker culture.

Antisensuality

Hackers are not alone in denying the sensual. But it is fair to say that the hacker culture crystallizes something problematic in engineers' relationships with what Burt called "the flesh things."

The sensual goes beyond the overtly sexual. There is sensuality in music, literature, art, and there are sensual relationships with the world of things: the musician caresses his or her instrument; its shape, its tonality, its touch, can be pleasing and exciting. But the prototypical hacker's taste in each of these realms tends not toward a sensual caress but toward an intellectual contact.

There is a strong music culture within the hacker community. Yet it is one where preference rarely moves out of the Baroque. The hacker's computational aesthetic with its emphasis on intricacy of structure carries over to musical taste. Musical hackers are intrigued by the contrapuntal complexity many see as "mathematical," by the purity of compositional forms that depend less obviously on tonal color and drama for their effect. Peter, a systems programmer at Carnegie Mellon University, says, "Beethoven is too emotional. He really didn't get into what you could create with the mathematics of the scale." Peter is passionate about music, but in his own way. He spends a lot of time playing an out-of-tune piano, practicing a technically excellent Bach.

Bill is a systems hacker in California who has invited me to see the harpsichord he is building. He shows me the half-finished product, and I ask to stay and watch him work on it. I am interested in how he goes about it and how he feels as he puts things together. I sit with him for many hours. He does not work in silence. Bach fugues are playing in the background. The record is scratchy, to me painfully so. The record player is a stereo, but Bill casually mentions that "every once in a while the left speaker sort of conks out" and the stereo is "transformed into a hi-fi—you know, circa 1956." To me, there is no high in the poor and painful fidelity of the sound. But Bill is not listening to the sound, he is listening to the "sense." He has analyzed these fugues before, has read Douglas Hofstadter's *Gödel, Escher, Bach,* and is listening for "recursive phenomena." The sound quality is irrelevant. This is an exercise in composition, structure, technique.

As I watch Bill work, my mind goes back to the only other person I knew who built a harpsichord. I met him many years before, a fellow graduate student who explained that he wanted to "get a feel for the texture of the medium" in which Bach worked. He was a friend. I wasn't interviewing him. I was simply drinking tea and reading as he worked on his harpsichord, but I remembered the expression "texture of the medium." Bill is making his harpsichord in a state of equal reverence for Bach, but his comments don't have to do with texture, they are about the intricacies of a system. "Bach wrote programs, you know—his structures are every bit as complicated as a really complex program. And this was his machine." Bach is a hacker colleague, and, to put it most flatly, Bill is checking out Bach's computer.

Bill's sensibility is not unusual in the computer world, where the preference for the formal extends from music to art. Escher was a favorite among computer people before *Gödel, Escher, Bach* captured a long-standing computer-culture aesthetic by making the point, well known to programmers, that Escher's prints of hands drawing each other or of stairs that continue to rise until they reach their starting point are recursive. These are "strange loops" whose power originates from the fact that they refer to themselves. When Bill makes a visit to Cambridge I interview him in my office. On the wall are several Japanese prints, line drawings with blushes of color, mere suggestions of place and feeling, and reproductions of two Monet paintings. Bill visits several times, and on the third visit he brings me an Escher print. "I thought you might like this," he tells me. "It gives you things to think about." I thank him for the gift, wondering to myself if he is giving me an "object-to-think-with" for my study of the hacker culture. This is not the case. Bill's gift is not that self-conscious. "I don't like your art," he tells me. "It doesn't have ideas."

Curt is a stranger to MIT who spends a term visiting the computer-science laboratory. He is a linguist who is interested in music. At first, he is excited by all the "music talk" in the laboratory, excited by the intensity of the interest, pleased that music is a bridge between himself and "technical" people he always thought of as so different. After a few months we speak again. Curt is frustrated and disappointed. The divide has not disappeared; it seems deeper than ever because it is no longer sustained by stereotypes about "humanists" and "engineers." Now it is connected to something concrete and important to him: his music.

> Of course I am held by the "form" of music. It's fundamental. But I also have the sense sometimes of becoming the music. Sometimes a note or a phrase will make a color or a feeling happen, some kind of knowledge that makes me feel close to the composer. Sometimes I hear instruments in different parts of my body, like feeling cellos in my chest. But I don't think that this kind of thing is what people around here are responding to. It's not that they don't talk about the "content" of music. It's that, in some very fundamental sense, I think they're not connecting to what I experience in the content—and that makes me feel pretty strange. I mean, their interest is so formal, but not in a musical sense. They want to "hack" counterpoint. They want to know the algorithm. But I don't think they want to know the music.

On another occasion, Curt talks more about his life inside the computer culture.

> The other night I invited some people over, some people from the lab and some of my other friends: a philosophy graduate student, a psychologist. The next day I was talking to them, and one of them said that he thought the lab people were amazingly smart, but had I ever noticed how few words they use? It's true. Everything is precise and nothing is left unspecified, but not much vocabulary. I was talking about this with another friend, and she said that Virginia Woolf had said that the only worthwhile conversations were those where no sentence was ever finished and everyone knew what was meant. That has to do with empathy, with a shared sense of understanding. And to me, it's a lack around here.

Curt's comments about language, precision, and intuition bring us to another aesthetic domain: literature. Engineers are devoted readers of science fiction. Why shouldn't they be? They feel participant. They are the ones who will design the spacecraft. In this computer culture, science fiction has a special place.

A science-fiction story is a microworld, isolated from all the assumptions of everyday reality, including assumptions about sexuality. In Barbarella's world, people make love by taking "transcendence pills." In Woody Allen's vision of the robotized future, people take sex breaks by jumping in and out of little ecstasy boxes. I distribute a questionnaire to a programming course for computer-science majors. One of the questions is: "What are some of your favorite books and can you say why?" A student answers: "Winning science fiction. In science fiction, you can start from scratch. It's like writing a program. Even in Logo programming, children can create worlds that operate by Aristotelian principles instead of Newtonian ones. No physical constraints. Make a whole new world with its own rules." As in the case of writing a program, the only imperative in science fiction is consistency. Once you write a microworld, in computer code or between the covers of a book, you have to obey its constraints. Hackers are drawn to making microworlds. They provide safety, elegance, controlled fantasy. Science fiction operates by their code. Another student answering the same question writes, "I like science fiction. I like watching the author making up rules and sticking to them. Even when it gets really hard to stay with them. It's a very disciplined form of writing."

Science fiction gets its complexity from the invention of worlds rather than the definition of character. While most traditional fiction takes everyday reality as its backdrop and develops its interest in the complexity of its human characters, science fiction characters tend to be more one-dimensional. They often are representative types with a stock "psychology." Mr. Spock will always be logical; Captain Kirk will always be smug and philosophical, the engineer Scotty will always be plodding and loyal. All of this is reassuring if you have a strong taste for consistency.

The Arpanet is a communication system that links all of the major computer centers in the United States. When the net was designed, the idea was that instantaneous mail and message-passing facilities would foster collaborative work among scholars at different centers. In fact things worked out differently. The Arpanet is mostly used for sending mail and messages. The messages can be sent "person to person," or they can be sent to many members of a community of people who declare themselves to have an interest in common. This community constitutes a "mailing list," a forum for ongoing conversations.

One of the largest of such mailing lists is the "science-fiction-lovers" list to which most hackers belong. Some of the conversations on it are technical. For example, there were long correspondences discussing engineering inconsistencies in the design of the set for the starship *Enterprise* in the first *Star Trek* movie. These discussed the incompatibility of the *Enterprise*'s docking system with the ship's overall structure and the foolishness of using round screens for the crew's video monitors. (It may have looked futuristic, but it was far from optimal: too much information would be lost.) But many of the interchanges are not about technical matters but about metaphysical ones. For example, what are the implications in *Star Trek* of "beaming down" crew members to the planets they wish to visit? The molecules that "reconstitute" them on the planet's surface are not the same ones that made them up originally. What new definitions of personhood would be required in a world where technology could make a copy of a person? If I can create a second me, which one of them is "I"? Are we both Sherry Turkle? And what if the second Sherry sets off on her own and has her own set of experiences, her own travels, her own friendships. Is "she" still "me"? Do I have proprietary rights over her by virtue of being her "nonartificial" originator?

Through these descriptions emerge the large outlines of the hacker culture: a culture of mastery, individualism, nonsensuality. It values complexity and risk in relationships with things, and seeks simplicity and safety in relationships with people. It delights in ambiguities in the technological domain—where most nonscientists expect to find things totally straightforward. On the other side, hackers try to avoid ambiguity in dealing with people, where the larger culture finds meaning in the half-defined and the merely suggested.

Something important is missing in this description: what it feels like to hack. If you are not an expert programmer, there is no way to share it directly. For me, two discoveries led to a better understanding of the hacker's experience.

The Game of Adventure

During my interview with Ron I expressed frustration at not knowing the "feel" of hacking. He came back with a plan of action, the same that was suggested to Tracy Kidder in the basement of Data General when he wanted to experience what draws someone into becoming a "Midnight Programmer." Ron typed some commands at his terminal and set me to playing the game of Adventure.

In Adventure the computer creates a complex underground world. You are in a clearing in the forest, standing before a house. It is up to you to find the grate which, if you open it correctly, will put you into Colossal Cave. The computer will move you through this world in response to the commands you type on the keyboard. Each time you move, a new message appears on the screen telling you where you are (a room, a dark tunnel, a maze, a passageway) and what objects and beings are there with you. At each point you must convey a two-word instruction saying what you want to do next. You can choose direction, and you can pick up things, drop things, open things, close things. In principle, you are trying to get the treasure, but even after months of playing, drawing maps, struggling with strategies, few players arrive. Most have been permanently stalled by dragons, trolls, snakes, hatchet-hurling dwarfs. Each of these adversaries can be conquered, but only through complicated strategies. The program will let you carry only so many things at a time, so if you face a rusty door you will probably decide to drop the water you are carrying, which might be useful later, but now will only make rust rustier, and go back to retrieve the oil can that you passed on the trail fourteen moves ago. On your way back to the oil, a path you can find only if you have been making a map as you proceed, you may be outwitted if you forget to bring something to carry it in. Finally, perhaps several hours later, if you are not skillful, you will have retraced your steps back to the rusty door.

Adventure is a window onto a way of experiencing the computer. The experience it gave me was of a far different order from what I had gotten from a beginning course in computer programming. There I learned to write simple instructions and got to watch the computer following them. Like most people, I came out of this with a vision of the machine and of programming as simple, controllable, linear. "The machine is dumb, just a giant calculator," the professor had said. "Programming is a straightforward act of mechanical regurgitation. Garbage in, garbage out."

Adventure has nothing in common with writing a simple program in an introductory course. But this just means that the course fails to give its students a sense of what programming is to its virtuosi. When systems get complex they become worlds that you can live in.

Imagine yourself at the computer. You are a systems programmer. A truly peculiar piece of behavior—a bug—has been reported by a fellow hacker. You have printed out the program on a stack of folded paper. It has twenty thousand lines of code. Somewhere in all that is the cause of the bug. How will you find it? It is like being lost in Colossal Cave. You come to a "place" in the cave. You don't see what you are looking for, but you see something that might be relevant later if you can remember where it was and find your way back to it. You debug your game by developing the skill of getting through the maze.

Cultures take their central experiences and play with them through fantasy, ritual, and art. When "winning" is at the center of cultural life, a game takes on this role. For the hacker, where what is most central is mastery over complexity, the game takes the form of a labyrinth.

The Hack

Adventure is a window onto the phenomenology of hacking, but the hacking experience has another component that goes beyond mastery of the labyrinth.

Remember Howard, whose magician's gesture symbolized his fantasy of walking up to any program and bending it to his will with a few deft strokes at the keyboard. I came to understand what he was looking for as a central organizing theme in the hacker culture. It is "The Hack." It is the holy grail. It is a concept that exists independently of the computer and can best be presented through an example using another technology complex enough to support its own version of hacking—and hackers.

In the 1960s, telephone hackers were called "phone freaks." One of the most famous was known as Captain Crunch, who took his name from a breakfast cereal. In every box there was a toy whistle, like the prize in Cracker Jacks. The whistle produced a 2600-cycle tone. A young man just entering the Air Force as a radio technician, Crunch was fascinated with electronics, circuitry, and winning. He was a hacker without a computer. He discovered that the Crunch whistle was a lock pick to one of the most complex closed systems ever designed. First you dial a long-distance telephone number. Then you blow the Crunch whistle. This disconnected the dialed conversation but kept the trunk open without further toll charge. From that point on, any number of calls could be dialed free.

Crunch experimented with the whistle for several years. His feats became more and more extraordinary, more and more legendary. His most mythologized "hack" became known as "the call around the world." Crunch sat in a room in California with two telephones. Using the whistle and his knowledge of international telephone circuitry and codes, he picked up the first phone and dialed the number of the second phone. The call started in California, went through Tokyo, India, Greece, Pretoria, London, New York, and back to California. The second telephone rang. He talked into phone number one and heard himself twenty seconds later on phone number two. Even this became boring and needed more embroidery. Winning means making the system and the challenge ever more complex. Finally there were four phones, and he called himself simultaneously around the world in two directions.

The hack became a myth and its replication a challenge. During my junior year in college I attended an open house at one of the undergraduate dorms at MIT, and several of the students boasted that they had set up something extraordinary on the third floor. They called it "Phineas Fogg." A small troop of technologically naïve Radcliffe students climbed up to the third floor and watched the by-now "classic" around-the-world demonstration, by this time done not with whistles but with "blue boxes" of circuitry. The demonstrators explained that the hack was not new, but that the size and reliability of the box was. Their achievement had been to miniaturize the hack. The telephone switching system was as complicated as any computer. It had taken them months to master it. The diagrams that covered their walls were not unlike the maps for the game of Adventure that would be covering those same walls ten years later. Intricate tunnels, unexpected connections. A world unto itself. They had been on a collective adventure: the exploration of a labyrinth. They had won out over complex mysteries.

Appreciating what made the call around the world a great hack is an exercise in hacker aesthetics. It has the quality of Howard's magician's gesture: a truly surprising result produced with a ridiculously simple means. Equally important: Crunch had not simply stumbled on a curiosity. The trick worked because Crunch had acquired an impressive amount of expertise about the telephone system. This is what made the trick a great hack, otherwise it would have been a very minor one. Mastery is of the essence everywhere within hacker culture. Third, the expertise was acquired unofficially and at the expense of a big system. The hacker is a person outside the system who is never excluded by its rules.

Great hacks, telephonic or computational, are mythologized much as Crunch was. The early hackers at MIT made an attempt to publish some of their most powerful techniques in a document called *Hackmem*. In a different culture this might have been the beginning of a journal, but it is not in the nature of the hacker culture to do anything so official or academic. Great hacks are passed along in more direct ways: as things you are shown, as something done to you. What did happen to the document was that it itself became part of myth. We catch a glimpse of it in a piece of hacker literature.

"Software Wars," by Stanford hacker Mark Crispin, was "published" on the science-fiction mailing list. Crispin takes the *Star Wars* plot, a battle between good and evil, and transforms it into a battle between good and evil computer cultures. The good is the hacker culture; the evil is the culture of the "straights," the administrators and "computer-as-tool" programmers who do not respect the magic of the machine. In "Software Wars" the two cultures are symbolized by their taste in programming languages. In principle, you can "say" the same things in different programming languages just as you can say the same things in French and in German, but the structure of the programming languages, like that of the natural languages, encourages different ways of thinking. To the eyes of the hacker, business languages, for example the IBM languages FORTRAN and COBOL, and the "scientific" language PASCAL have come to represent the uniformity of mass culture that buries the individual in the crowd. In "Software Wars" these appear as the languages appropriate to the totalitarian rule of "the Empire." LISP is the language of pleasure, of individuality, a language that facilitates a way of thinking where, as Douglas Hofstadter once remarked to me, "It is easy to live in the world of *Gödel, Escher,*

Bach. These MIT hackers lived inside of my book before I ever wrote it." For the hacker, the beauty of LISP is that it is fully recursive and self-referential, higher levels are built up from their own elements, like Escher's endlessly rising staircases and Bach's "endlessly rising fugue" that keeps going to a higher key until, seemingly inexplicably, it ends up exactly where it began.

The moral struggle in "Software Wars" centers around evildoers known as PASCALS, and the forces of good, the hackers, energized by the software equivalent of "The Force." This is The Hack, a magical flow of power and computer wizardry that turns the computer from a tool into an artistic medium.

As in *Star Wars,* "Software Wars" begins with the memory of a golden age. In this case it was a time when hackers weren't regimented by computer bureaucrats and engineers.

> Long ago and far away, the data processing galaxy was ruled by the sinister forces of the PASCAL Empire. Years ago, it had been the Hacking Republic, where all programming languages and programmers lived together in peace and harmony. The land of the Republic was patrolled by the Wizards, skilled in all forms of magic, who daily unveiled new miracles for the wonder of the citizens of the Republic. They drew their mystical powers from THE HACK, which was their succor in any difficulty.

The villain who put an end to all this was Daemon Feature. His name plays on several programming "puns," as does his method of doing evil, the entrapment of Wizards on "fencepost errors," a common programming bug.

> But the days of the Republic were numbered, for one of the wizards, Daemon Feature, fell in with the PASCALS, who brought in crooks and bletcherousness to the beleaguered Republic. Using methods both sinister and cunning, he managed to entrap most of the loyal Wizards in a fencepost error, where they were ruthlessly slaughtered. At last the Republic was proclaimed to have ended, and the Empire was established with Record Structure, the leader of the PASCALS, proclaimed Emperor. And the lot of programmers was unhappy.

Of course the programmers are unhappy. Their aesthetic has been submerged. When hackers are inspired and in creative tele-

pathy with the machine, it is as if they are inhabited by the medium, inspired by the muse. Their minds must be free to fly, to
invent, to surpass the limits. "Records" and "Structure" are spiritual death. It is time for the forces of life to enter: the hacker as
rebel, enemy of the establishment and conformity, defender of
idiosyncrasy, individuality, genius, and the cult of the individual.

Who can be the hero of a software soap opera? It must be someone who is trapped in a false identity. Someone who will, through
confrontation with a force greater than himself, The Hack, find
his true measure as a man. In "Software Wars," it is Fluke Software
Specialist. Fluke has been raised by his aunt and uncle, who "over
the years had established a prosperous, if unpretentious business,
supplying COBOL utilities for many of the settlements in this galaxy." Fluke does not know his true origins. The hacker-to-be is
doing the most "losing," spirit-deadening thing that a hacker—
born to be inspired by the interactive, breathing presence of a
computer beneath his fingers—could possibly do: he writes
COBOL programs on cards, on pieces of paper that he feeds into
the machine. Although Fluke's aunt and uncle have raised him as
their own, when he receives a message addressed to the mythologized hacker hero, Moby Foobar, they realize that his destiny is
elsewhere and that they must let him go. His aunt understands:
"You know, we can't keep him forever. He's just not destined for
COBOL. There's too much of his father in him." But his uncle
fears destiny: "Yes, that's what I'm worried about. For him. I'm
afraid he'll get involved in hacking like his father did."

"Software Wars" gets played out as the dramatic projection of
loves and hates, supports and threats to the hacker's universe.
There is a feared tribe of "users," the professors and graduate
students who believe the machine to be theirs (because their research funds pay for it), and who try to keep the hackers under
their boot. There is the power of The Hack, and its "darker side."
This is the aspect of hacking that has gripped Daemon Feature,
who has the power but uses it for evil.

And, of course, "Software Wars" has its reference to *Hackmem*.
Fluke finds Moby Foobar, who tells him of better days, speaks to
him of his father, and of The Hack.

Moby . . . paused, searching his memory, back to a time long
ago, ". . . Your father left me something to give to you." He

reached into the piles of paper and old, dusty manuals on the table, and withdrew a single binder. "This is HAKMEM, an elegant programming tool, of a more civilized age. With it, one skilled in The Hack could perform programming miracles, get better response time, and be invited to all the good parties. Here." He handed the HAKMEM to Fluke.

Fluke took it, and looked at its first page intently; strange it seemed, yet a feeling grew on him, as if he were looking at something far greater than he could comprehend. He was considered a good programmer, one of the best in the quadrant; but the HAKMEM took his breath away. "What is The Hack?" he asked finally.

"The Hack is that which is nearest and dearest to the hearts of all the Wizards. It is what gives the Wizard his power. The Hack is everywhere and is part of everything. Without The Hack, only crocks remain."

"The Hack!" gasped Fluke. He then pondered these words in silence. A whole new vision was before him; he saw things of beauty and elegance that he could not yet put into words . . .

Fluke captures enemy base by using the special magic power of LISP. When the time comes, he is inspired:

Fluke, remember The Hack. The Hack, Fluke. He could almost hear Moby's voice repeating this to him. But what could he do? He turned around to face his approaching foe, and attacked. LISP has base ROMAN to read and print Roman numerals.

The blow that Fluke has struck is recursive, a feature that uses itself to build itself. The ultimate weapon in this hacker tale is one that uses the same image of generation through self-generation that got Douglas Hofstadter to the weaving of his *Gödel, Escher, Bach* "Golden Braid."

The rebels had succeeded! And all the users tried the new operating system and pronounced it a winner. Instantly everything was converted to run on it. Almost immediately, a flood of new software appeared. . . . And the universe was again winning.

Mythologized in an elaborate oral and written tradition, the ideal of the hack suffuses the hacker culture. It embodies shared values and passions. And, of course, it is the centerpiece of hacker rituals.

Rites of Passage

Rituals of initiation bring novices, defined as being on the "outside" of a culture, and subject them to experiences designed to alter their identity. The novices emerge on the other side as different people, full members of the group. In some societies, rituals of initiation take the form of large collective festivals. In the hacker culture, the principal relationship is dyadic, between the individual and the computer. So the rites tend to be more private, although they are often followed by some collective expression: a Chinese banquet, a pancake breakfast. Certain experiences of an individual with a computer are invested by the group with the consequence of a passage.

Initiations into the hack are through mastery games that stand somewhere between playing Adventure and "phone freaking." For example, you log into the computer. Instead of finding your files you find yourself in another world. The challenge is to recover your files by finding your way through the computer's labyrinth. What you need to triumph is the force of "The Hack."

At MIT, hackers speak of a moment when they would accept someone new into their fellowship. It would be when an individual had developed enough mastery of the system to figure out how to triumph over one of several "hacker harassment" programs. For example, there is the "Cookie Monster" program. An experienced hacker sends a little beasty into the program of the novice. The recipient of the cookie invader finds a small creature starting to chomp away at the text written on his terminal's screen. He becomes a hacker when he can successfully battle the encroachment of the Cookie Monster.

The hacker culture has a code. These games are for testing the mettle of the novice or for playing among master hackers. They are not pranks to be played on others. This would be aggression, unfair play. When this happens (and sometimes it does), one or a group of the system masters sets traps for the aggressor, who is likely to find his or her own files garbled or chomped or hidden. An MIT hacker told me the tale of how many years ago he began to "hack" the files of a graduate student he had a crush on. To win her attention he set it up so that whenever she logged in and asked for a file, the Weizenbaum ELIZA program would be summoned in its stead.

Let's say she would ask for the file "foobar.3." The program would say to her, "Tell me more about why you feel that way about foobar.3." And if she typed ":help" (the standard way of asking for instructions to get you out of trouble on the system), instead of getting a menu of helping instructions, the machine would just come back with "Why do you feel you need help?" or "You seem to have a lot of strong feelings about help." I thought it was sort of funny. I guess I was pretty immature. But I got paid back and in kind. I spent two weeks of nights at the lab trying to ungarble my files.

Locked Doors

The mastery games and initiations test the ability to win over complexity and break out of confining situations. And we saw that hackers are drawn not only to winning over computers. Other complex systems have a similar appeal.

Many hackers are expert lock-pickers and carry their "picks" around with them on their key chains. Their pleasure is in "beating" the lock. They break, they enter, and then they leave. They are not after material goods, but after the thrill of triumph. Richard, an MIT hacker, had a summer job working at a large computer company with a conservative, corporate environment. At night, every desk and file drawer was locked. Every office door was locked. This was the kind of computer culture where people work nine to five. Richard, of course, was from another culture, where nothing is private and people work all night. At MIT, he had worked out a detailed time schedule for himself. "I discovered that I work best on a thirty-six-hour cycle. So I get myself into a thirty-six-hour cycle—twenty-four hours awake, twelve hours asleep. This is what maximizes my efficiency." Over the summer, largely to avoid overlap with the members of the day culture, whom he found alien in spirit, Richard went back onto "standard hacker time," sleeping during the day and working at night. And every night, alone in the building, he unlocked every office door. "They changed the locks. I opened them again. They changed the locks again. I never took anything, I'm not a thief. I just don't like a locked door."

A closed system is a challenge. A safe is there to be cracked. A mystery is there to be solved. It is the hacker's variant on the more widely understood cliché that Mount Everest is there to be climbed.

If you can't tolerate a locked door on a computer system, you are going to be an enemy of what is usually called "system security." "Security" comprises all of the features of a computer system that protect the information within the system and the privacy of its authorized users. A first level of protection simply controls access. To gain entrance to most computer systems, you need to be given an "account," which means that the system will receive you if you "log in" with your name. And then you need to be given a "password." When I log in as Turkle on the MIT MULTICS system, the computer asks me for my password. When I type it in, no characters appear on my screen. My secret name prevents outsiders from entering the system by using my name. But this is only first-level protection. Most computer systems control what files within the system I can have access to, and what I can do with them if I am allowed to see them.

Many different issues are tied up in the question of system security. In an academic computer facility, where computer power is being used for research and writing, keeping people out is justified most often by the claim that a little knowledge is a dangerous thing. If I can wander around a computer system I can do a lot of inadvertent damage. Second, there is the issue of privacy. On the ITS system at MIT I can look at, manipulate, and print any file of any user. I can also run a program called "SPY" to look in on what any other user of the system is doing at any moment. SPY was designed by hackers who don't believe in locked doors.

In nonacademic computer systems, security issues go beyond the fear of accidental damage and personal privacy. Files may contain confidential information about people, products, institutions, and events. The locked rooms that Richard broke open contained data that, from most people's point of view, deserved to be protected: corporate secrets and personnel files. But for Richard the fact that a door is locked is justification enough to open it.

Most assaults on computer-system security are not done by members of the culture of hackers I have been discussing. Indeed, the systems programmers I interviewed expressed dismay that their vocation has been tainted with the image of "computer crime." "It gives hacking a bad name." But the break-ins are often done by people who share the hacker's style of relating to the machine as a puzzle and who share their glorification of "the win." Many are done by high-school and college students who talk about the exercise the way they would about a good game of Dungeons and Dragons. They see the labyrinth. And they see the opportunity for something else. After they enter, they leave their mark, a trace that they were there. Usually this is a message to taunt the system's authorities who have tried to keep them out. They make the point that the system is not secure and sometimes add that they would be happy to be hired as consultants to work on the problem. Captain Crunch and several of his associates did end up working for the telephone company. The pattern of hack the system, leave a trace, get a little famous, and be recognized by the big guys has become part of the hacker myth.

For example, a group of four thirteen-year-old students at the Dalton School, an exclusive preparatory school on the Upper East Side of Manhattan, carried on an elaborate security-breaking hack through which they electronically entered the computer systems of twenty-one organizations in the United States and Canada. At one point, when their "victims" began to install new protection devices, the students became frustrated and decided to see how far they could go. They went quite far. One of their victims claimed they had erased about a fifth of its computer files. "This looks like what we used to do as kids—ring someone's doorbell and run around the block. Only it's a more sophisticated doorbell and a longer block."[7]

The media often portray the computer expert who breaks system security, if not as a hero, then at least as a genius. Many people are intimidated by computers. And don't like them much. When they hear about teenage boys who broke into a large computer system, turned it off for an hour, and left a message of triumph, they know that they have probably broken the law, but they are sympathetic.

The Dalton students had broken the law. But for many people, something about the sophistication of the doorbell, the length of the block, and the havoc they caused made the "Dalton Four" seem like heroes. In the two weeks after their story hit the newspapers, I interviewed a diverse group of New Yorkers on how they saw what had happened. A common reaction was to soften any criticism of the students with a heavy dose of admiration. One high-school science teacher commented, "They were just out to beat the system. We all are, in a way. It's natural." A businessman did not side with the companies that had lost money because of the hack, but with the students: "Myself, I hate those lousy computers. If a bunch of kids can get the better of them, so much the better." And another teacher felt that in some way the students were acting in her behalf: "Somebody's gotta demystify those computers. It looks like it'll be through a children's crusade."

People are deeply ambivalent toward computers. For many, they have replaced Ma Bell, or ITT, or even the CIA as the symbol of things too big, too complex, too impersonal. People use computerized bank tellers, find them convenient, but resent them as well. Going to the bank used to involve a relationship with a person who said hello, knew your name, and sometimes did you a favor. This is gone. People are also becoming increasingly aware that every time they use their credit card they are leaving an electronic trace of where they have been, of what they were doing. Computers are perceived as the medium for an automated intrusiveness and violation of privacy, and they are perceived as a medium of mystery. In the hacker, people see someone who holds a key to the mysteries and is willing to defy the establishment to open them; there is the fantasy of an electronic Robin Hood.

Building Straight from Your Mind

Anthony, the MIT student who hacks for sport death, also hacks to build. As a child, Anthony took clocks apart and "tried to put them back together in new ways—to make new kinds of clocks." There are limits to how far you can make the materials of a clock into something new, but programming presents no such limits. The rules need not respect the physical laws that constrain the real world. "When you are programming," Anthony tells me, "you just build straight from your mind." Anthony makes an association with parenting.

> Men can't have babies, and so they go have them on the machine. Women don't need the computer, they have them the other way. Why do you think people call ideas brainchildren? They are something you create that is entirely your own. I definitely feel paternal towards the programs I write. I defend them and want them to do good for the world. They are like little pieces of my mind. A chip off the old block. But the computer doesn't act like a kid, so the effect is limited.

The image of paternity is widespread among hackers. Nick hopes to leave behind some monuments.

> If you are a computer scientist, all your monuments, all the things you are proud of, are computer things. You protect your monuments. The computer is your world, your reality. When someone screws around with this they are messing with your universe.
>
> Hacking computers is not just intellectual, there are emotions. But the delicate emotions like empathy or sadness or loneliness have no place, because there is no application for them. The primitive emotions exist, like anger or fear. You get mad at the undefinable "they" who are sticking it to you.

Nick expresses love, intellectual excitement, and pride of author-ship. He also expresses sadness, a sense of loss, the fears of young men that the fork in the road no longer exists for them. Richard goes on a thirty-six-hour day. Anthony pushes himself to the limit of his physical strength. They justify these acts in the service of "maximization," but what is being maximized?

When Weizenbaum's description of the hollow-eyed program-mer became a *cause célèbre*, many hackers rose to their own defense: they were artists, they were masters, they were not different from other people intensely involved with their work. But there was another reaction as well: self-recognition. Many hackers are wor-ried. They feel in the grip of something powerful. They know they can control the computer, but they are less sure that they control themselves.

Anthony is afraid: "I have devoted so much of myself to the computer that all the humanity has drained out of me. You're just a device. I am afraid that by hacking I am draining myself of something I need to live—humanity or something."

There is fear as well as joy in fusion with the machine. Some people can't break away. "When you hack on a computer you are taking this risk that you won't finish for three days and you will forget about everything else that you have to do. You are taking a risk . . . only if you finish your project fast are you out, because you can't stop before your project is finished. You are trapped."

Artists become inhabited by their medium. The poet "makes" a poem, but the poem also "makes," and sometimes haunts, the poet.

There is no question that hackers are the artists of their medium. They too are possessed.

> *I control you.*
> *You're inside me.*
> *Might as well obey me*
> *Or I'll make you go away.*

This poem by a hacker is called "Punk Solipsist." The poem also speaks of "No more talking/No more thinking," and of other things that were left behind: "No more kneeling down to idols/No more feeling suicidal." The computer is there to wall out the pain of being with other people. You control and internalize it. It is you and not-you. Your anger at not being able to control ourself is transferred onto the machine.

In *The Empty Fortress*, Bruno Bettelheim tells the story of "Joey the Mechanical Boy," an autistic child who thought of himself as a machine run by other machines as a defense against the unpredictability of people. Bettelheim comments that Joey was particularly hard to work with, not because the child was more "difficult" than others at the Orthogenic School, but because Bettelheim and his colleagues were so uneasy around Joey—an expression of their feelings and fears about machines. In the Middle Ages, Bettelheim says,

> even Lucifer was viewed as a person, though a distorted one. What is entirely new in the machine age is that often neither savior nor destroyer is cast in man's image any more. The typical modern delusion is of being run by an influencing machine. . . . Just as the angels and saints of a deeply religious age help us to fathom what were man's greatest hopes at that time, and the devils which he trembled at most, so man's delusions in a machine world seem to be tokens of both our hopes and our fears of what machines may do for us, or to us.[8]

Bettelheim and his colleagues had a hard time getting close to Joey. "His delusions had an impact which we, accustomed to living with autistic children, had experienced with no other child. Our fascination was morbid, instead of the vital one so needed to reach him."[9]

Marvin Minsky's response to the popular fascination with hackers was to put the burden on the other side, on the "people hackers" who categorize others with psychological labels. For him, attempts to characterize the hacker are ill-intentioned. But for me these attempts are symptoms of a profound unease. I think that what was true of Bettelheim as he faced Joey is true of most of us as we try to comprehend the hacker in his relationship with the computer.

We are surrounded by machines. We depend on them. We are frightened by how powerful they have become. Our nuclear machines have the power to destroy the world. We are suspicious of the new "psychological machines" and fear the hacker's intimate relationship with his object. Its control over him is disturbing because we too feel controlled. We fear his sense of becoming a "device" because most of us, to one extent or another, have had that feeling. We fear his use of the machine as a safe companion because we, too, can feel its seduction.

Intimate involvements and identification with machines pose what Bettelheim calls "the unspoken anxiety of our age": "Do machines still serve our human purpose or are they cranking away by now without purpose? Even more unnerving: are they working away for their own ends which we no longer know or control?" [10]

CHAPTER 7

The New Philosophers
of Artificial Intelligence:
A Culture with Global Aspirations

For fifteen years, as long as the PDP-6 computer lived on the ninth floor of Technology Square, the sanctum sanctorum of MIT hackers, three gilt trophies stood on its console. This was the first computer to play chess well enough to enter a tournament and win —albeit in the novice class. Or rather, it was not the computer that won the tournament, it was a program written by Richard Greenblatt, one of MIT's most renowned hackers, a program known affectionately as MacHack. But MacHack's most famous game won it no trophies. It was a game to defend the honor of artificial intelligence.

In 1965 the Rand Corporation published a report by philosopher Hubert Dreyfus in which he compared artificial intelligence, usually referred to as "AI," to alchemy.[1] According to Dreyfus, AI was a fraud. Its seeming progress was illusion and would lead only to dead ends. For example, AI scientist Arthur Samuel had written a computer program that played checkers and improved its play by practice. It had gotten good enough to beat an American champion.[2] The AI community was enthusiastic about the accomplishment, but for Dreyfus it didn't mean much. He claimed that there is a technical difference between the kind of thinking needed for checkers and the kind needed for "real" human intelligence. Dreyfus compared citing such accomplishments as steps toward artificial intelligence to citing the fact that an ape climbed a tree as a step toward reaching the moon.

In 1957 Herbert Simon had predicted that within the decade a computer program would be chess champion of the world.[3] Prominent in Dreyfus' critique of AI was the fact that Simon's latest effort at a chess-playing program had been roundly beaten by a ten-year-old child. For Dreyfus, this was not a case of progress being slow; real chess, unlike checkers, required real human thinking, it required intuition, it couldn't be done digitally.

Given his position, Dreyfus could not refuse a challenge to play against MacHack. The game was a cliffhanger. Dreyfus lost, much to the glee of the AI community, which reported the match with a headline drawn from Dreyfus' original paper "Alchemy and Artificial Intelligence": "A Ten Year Old Can Beat the Machine— Dreyfus" and a subhead that read: "But the Machine Can Beat Dreyfus."[4]

Dreyfus stuck to his guns, claiming that nothing was proved by the fact that the computer beat him, a "rank amateur," and he still maintains that computers cannot play "real chess." As things stand today, Simon's prediction remains unfulfilled. Chess programs can beat most experts, but they do seem to be separated from the world championship by a barrier to whose crossing the AI community is no longer willing to give a date.

For a long time chess was prized by AI scientists as a test bed for ideas about creating intelligence.[5] The discipline had been characterized by one of its founders as the "enterprise of trying to make machines do things which would be considered intelligent if done by people." Chess was certainly considered intelligent when done by a person, the criterion for success seemed clear (winning over increasingly skilled opponents), and the knowledge required was sufficiently well defined to allow for experiments with different programming methodologies. AI scientists saw it as a problem on which to cut their theoretical teeth.

But the driving force of the science came from far greater ambitions than making a program perform brilliantly at chess or any other particular task. The real ambition is of mythic proportions: making a "general-purpose" intelligence, a mind. In a long tradition of romantic and mystical thought, life is breathed into dead or inanimate matter by a person with special powers. In the early 1950s there was a growing belief among a group of mathematicians of diverse interests that this fantasy could be brought down to earth. They would use the computer to build mind.

Where Descartes wrote in the most general terms of automata controlled by strings that could be pulled to produce an action at a distance, and Leibniz described mechanisms built of gears, this generation of mathematicians had a more abstract stuff out of which to build intelligence. This was the idea of program, the concept of an ordered set of procedures. Using this idea, Alan Turing, John von Neumann, Norbert Wiener, and Claude Shannon began to describe mechanisms that might allow machines to take the first steps toward playing chess or otherwise manifesting intelligence.

There is no simple way to fix the birth date of a new discipline, but many people use a conference held at Dartmouth College during the summer of 1956 as a reference point. Until then there had been influential theoretical papers written by people working in relative isolation. To Dartmouth came the men who would take the first practical steps toward translating these ideas into vigorous attacks on the problem of machine intelligence. After Dartmouth, things happened fast. A diverse group of researchers began to see themselves as a community committed to the idea of creating intelligent machines, and by the mid-1960s the enterprise was rolling in specialized artificial intelligence laboratories. The largest in the United States were at Carnegie Mellon, directed by Alan Newell and Herbert Simon; at MIT, directed by Marvin Minsky and Seymour Papert; and at Stanford, directed by John McCarthy. By the early 1970s, AI had all the trappings of an established academic field: international congresses, journals, textbooks, and course listings in the catalogues of most major universities.

In the congresses, journals, textbooks, and courses there is little discussion about where these scientists expect to go in the really long term. When asked, many take the position that the science is too young to justify speculation beyond the next decade. Others, and let me call theirs the "hard-core" AI position, are sure that eventually (whether this is in a few decades or a century is not seen as very important) machines will exceed human intelligence in all respects. For example, you have a disease and you want a diagnosis. Naturally you consult the best possible source. They assume that this will be a computer. Not a human doctor aided by a computer, but a computer. Or perhaps, given how sensitive people seem to be on the matter, a computer "aided" by a human doctor. Another scenario: you are an industrialist with a technical problem and you need a new synthetic material with specific properties. Today you hire chemists and physicists. In this imagined future you will address your needs to a computer. Indeed, some AI researchers go so far as to say that the industrialist of the future might "itself" be a computer, or, as Edward Fredkin of MIT puts it, "Artificial intelligence is the next step in evolution."

Against the backdrop of these aspirations the daily work of artificial intelligence laboratories seems mundane. Most of the work falls into one of two categories.[6] The first has come to be known as knowledge engineering or expert systems. Programs that serve as expert systems are essentially "mind programs"—they do things like play chess or advise a medical diagnostician. Here, sensory and motor interactions with the physical world are simple or nonexistent. The second category is industrial robotics. In practice, this has little in common with the image of robotics in science fiction. Indeed, most of what industrial robots are being made to do we scarcely think of as requiring intelligence when done by people. Most research is directed at having machines do what most people would consider "child's play"—for example, recognizing and picking up an object. When it comes to systems that deal directly with the world, the state-of-the-art in artificial intelligence is not adequate to get machines to do even the things that two-year-olds find easy.

For some leaders in the field the long-term "futuristic" goals and the daily research into "child's play" are not as far apart as they might appear. They make a technical argument captured in the remark that "AI knows more about playing chess than building mudpies." There is a widespread perception that the hard problems for AI are not imitating the sophisticated thought processes of the expert adult, but rather the naïve commonsense thinking of the child. If this problem could be cracked—if we could make machines do the simple things—the problems of sophisticated intelligence would quickly succumb. Sophisticated thinking is seen as an overlay on an elemental ability, shared by all human beings, that makes intelligence work.[7]

When AI speculates about what is simple and what is hard and how they are related, its concerns join with those of theoretical psychology. Early in the life of the discipline it became clear that the project of programming machines to be intelligent required thinking about a lot more than machines and programming. Old psychological questions came up again with new urgency. For example, is there a general mechanism of intelligence at work no matter what subject matter the intelligence is turned to, or are there many varieties of intelligence, so different that quite different programs would be needed to embody them?

The influence of the computer on how hackers and hobbyists saw their own psychologies was personal, and it stayed with the individual. But when the AI scientist talks about program, it is no longer as personal metaphor. Artificial intelligence has invaded the field of psychology.[8] As it has done so, it has built theories in which the idea of mind as program occupies center stage. And these theories have begun to move out beyond this computer culture to influence wider circles.

Psychoanalysis, with its idea of the unconscious, generated new ways to look at old questions in all fields of the humanities and social sciences. AI theories share with psychoanalysis the pretension to be a new interpretive metaphor for the culture as a whole. As in the case of psychoanalysis, AI is not monolithic. Rival schools pursue the fundamental ideas in different ways. But just as psychoanalytic theories all have something in common, the idea of the unconscious, in AI too there is a family resemblance: in one way or another all the theories use program as the prism through which to look at the human mind.

To convey the personal and cultural implications of this idea, I introduce a small number of people in AI whose ways of looking at the question of mind and program are starting to have an influence in the world beyond the academy.*

---

* The people I discuss in this chapter do not represent the AI community as a whole, but a subset characterized by a sense of the discipline as a theory of mind. This chapter is based on several years of observation of the life of the MIT AI Laboratory and on interviews with twenty-four senior scientists, graduate students, and young researchers in artificial intelligence, most of them at MIT. I chose to concentrate on the MIT setting for several reasons: because of its accessibility, because it has a history of working within the tradition of "AI as a theory of mind," because it is a good place to study the relationship between the AI enterprise and the hacker culture, discussed in the previous chapter. Outside of the MIT community I interviewed AI scientists from other universities and from the Xerox Palo Alto Research Center.

Programming as a Prism

In 1957 Herbert Simon made three other predictions. The second and third, somewhat more extravagant than computer as chess champion, were that within the same span of ten years a program would compose music of serious aesthetic value and would discover and prove an important mathematical theorem. The fourth prediction attracted little public attention: that within ten years programs would be the standard form for psychological theory. Just as after Newton the standard form for the laws of mechanics became the differential equation, the proper explanation of a psychological phenomenon would be a program that displayed this phenomenon.

In this last prediction, Simon was referring to a very specific relationship between program and theory that grew out of his work with Alan Newell.[9] They developed a paradigm for how to build computer models of how people think. These models set out to account for a particular piece of mental activity. The subject being studied is given a problem, often a brain teaser, for example a problem in "cryptarithmetic" where numbers are coded into letters and the code needs to be unscrambled. As the subject works on the problem, every move is recorded. Usually he or she is asked to talk while working. These remarks, along with eye movements and whatever other behavioral data can be collected, are noted and searched for clues about mental process. When the data collection is over, the long work begins of making a program that will simulate the solution process in every detail: not only the correct moves, but also the false starts and how they are undone, the pauses, the glance to recall a piece of information written on a corner of a worksheet, and the exclamations that punctuate the subject's progress.

In one famous Newell and Simon experiment, subjects are given the cryptarithmetic problem "SEND + MORE = MONEY." Each letter stands for a digit from zero to nine, and the subject's job is to break the code. Most people begin by scanning letters for a "foothold," a place to begin, and finally note that when you add two four-digit numbers you get either a four-digit number or a five-digit number beginning with one. So, MONEY must be a five-digit number beginning with one. This piece of information can be used to generate more. For example, we now know that S and M produce a "carry," so, since M is one, S must be nine. But stop, we can't be so sure. Perhaps S is eight and there has already been a carry from adding E and O. From here, several strategies are possible. Some people decide to eliminate one of the possibilities, for example S = 8 or S = 9, by working through each until it can be ruled out. Others try to follow several paths at once. A third approach, although not particularly helpful in this case, is to look for another "foothold" that might produce a less ambiguous result. Similar choices come up at every stage of solving the problem.

Since different people go about any such problem in different ways, each problem yields a collection of somewhat different programs. But Newell and Simon's theoretical assertion is that all of these individual programs have the same general form. And it is this general form that is said to characterize how people think, at least about problems of this kind. In practice, for the limited domain of "logical brain teasers," Newell and Simon have constructed programs that capture a large percentage, if not quite all, of the steps taken by human subjects. According to their model of how AI research should proceed, the strategy for the future is to increase the proportion of captured "steps" and to extend this kind of analysis into wider areas of mental activity.

To most people, cryptarithmetic feels "logical" and they are not surprised that it can be captured by a computer program. But AI also makes claims on areas of thinking that we feel are less formal —for example, the area of medical diagnosis.[10]

Physicians claim that a lot of what they do is intuitive. It is reasoning through the associations built up over years of practice. But when AI scientists work on the problem of medical diagnosis, their effort is to see the diagnostic process as a set of explicit procedures that can be captured in a program. AI experts attack the problem by interviewing a physician over the course of months, trying to pin down every aspect of how he or she makes decisions. They model the structure of that practical knowledge which "feels intuitive." The resulting program will, given the same information as the physician, usually come to the same conclusion. The process of writing such programs has a side effect. If the program "thinks" henceforth like the physician, the physician's thinking about his or her activity has been changed by collaboration in the making of the program. What once seemed intuitive to the physician has been shown to be formalizable.

At MIT's Artificial Intelligence Laboratory there are knowledge-engineering projects in a domain widely perceived as being even less subject to formalization, even further removed from "rules," than medical diagnosis. This is the domain of jazz improvisation. Here too the AI method follows from the assumption that what looks intuitive can be formalized, and that if you discover the right formalisms you can get a machine to do it.

As in the case of medical diagnosis, the AI scientist does not take the jazz player's feeling of "intuition at work" as an obstacle. But it is not ignored either. It is taken as something that itself has to be explained. Marvin Minsky, the principal investigator on the MIT jazz improvisation project, argues that the feeling is only to be expected. One of his famous sayings advises that if you want to understand any piece of intelligent behavior you should look for three algorithms. The choice of the number three is something of a joke, but what Minsky is saying is serious: the interaction of a small number of quite simple processes can create an impression of ungraspable complexity. One stone thrown into a pool of still water makes a "simple" and "intelligible" pattern—concentric circles going out from the point of entry of the stone. Two stones produce a more complex but still easily graspable pattern as the circles intersect. Three stones produce a disturbance of the water so complex that if you didn't know in advance how it was produced, it would take sophisticated analytic techniques to figure it out. The appearance of complexity does not rule out causal simplicity.

Ask different AI theorists what are the most important AI theories, and you get different answers. But what is common to all of them is an emphasis on a new way of knowing. The new way of knowing asks that you think about everything, especially all aspects of the mind, in computational terms, in terms of program and information processing. Freudian phenomena are not excluded. There is even a computational theory of what have come to be known as "Freudian slips."

In asserting the primacy of program, artificial intelligence is making a big claim, announcing itself, as psychoanalysis and Marxism had done, as a new way of understanding almost everything.*

---

* In this chapter and the next, I use the term "program" in a very broad sense to refer to a wide range of computational processes, in no way limited to serial programs written in standard programming languages.

In each case a central concept restructures understanding on a large scale: for the Freudian, the unconscious; for the Marxist, the relationship to the means of production. We saw that hackers valued programming as a thing in itself, but for the AI researcher, the idea of program has a transcendent value: it is taken as the key, the until now missing term, for unlocking intellectual mysteries.

Using Programs to Think About Freud

The idea that everyday mistakes are windows onto the unconscious has become part of our general culture. It colors the thinking of millions of people who do not know, still less accept, the technical details of Freud's work. Donald Norman, a psychologist who works within the AI tradition, has taken a new look at Freudian slips.[11]

Before doing graduate work in psychology, Norman studied electrical engineering at MIT. He went on to do research in the field of memory in the Harvard psychology department. "With electrical engineering and a lot of ideas about memory in my toolkit, I went on to a career in which I tried to put them all together," he says. "I saw myself then and I see myself now as someone who can bring computational ideas to 'card carrying' psychologists."* In recent years this vocation has included a computational look at a slice of psychology long appropriated by the Freudians. While Newell and Simon work at getting computers to emulate minds, Norman's perspective is to theorize about the mind as emulating a computer.

At first sight, says Norman, the kinds of slips that people make seem very different from the ones to which machines are vulnerable. People forget their umbrellas, pour ketchup instead of cream into their coffee, say the "wrong thing." Norman does not propose to construct a program that will instruct a machine to pour ketchup into coffee or replicate a particular subject's embarrassing mistakes, he does not program a machine to make human slips; he argues the other way: the kinds of slips people make are the kinds that machines make, and for similar reasons. His method is not experimental. He builds his model of what is behind the slip by

___
* This and all other quotations not marked by a raised reference number are drawn from personal interviews.

reflecting, as did Freud, on a collection of actual slips and interpreting them according to what he knows about how programs
might become "derailed" in a multiprocessing computer.

Take a slip from Freud's own collection. At the beginning of a
meeting the chairman stands up and says, "I declare this meeting
closed." For Freud it is obvious that the slip is a source of information about the real wishes of the chairman. Norman suggests
another way of looking at it. An analogy gives the flavor of Norman's thinking.[12] First think of the brain as a computer that contains information in something like a dictionary. In an ordinary
dictionary, the words "open" and "closed" are far apart. But when
information is stored in computers it is common to use a code in
which opposites are represented by the same symbol, with a simple
"bit" (or symbol) to indicate a negation. In other words, hot =
−cold, dry = −wet. In this computational dictionary, the words
"open" and "closed" are right next to each other, precisely because
they are so far apart in meaning. When somebody sits at a control
panel with many buttons, pushing button seven instead of button
eight does not seem to need much explanation. By the same token,
if you think of the mind storing things in its computational dictionary, substituting "closed" for "open" is easily justified. It needs no
recourse to the idea of emotional conflict. It can be accounted for
by the simple mechanics of how words and their meanings are
represented in a computer.

Norman believes that since the representations of knowledge
developed for computers are efficient and rational, the evolution
of human mental mechanisms is likely to have converged along
similar lines. He reads experimental evidence such as our tendency
to substitute a word for its opposite as confirmation of the idea
that computational coding is used in human memory and of the
more global proposition that the human mind can be best understood as an information-processing system.

Freud saw meaning behind every slip.[13] Sometimes the meaning
was obvious, sometimes it had to be traced through complex chains
of association and linguistic transformations. Norman's emphasis
on computational representation draws attention not to meaning
but to mechanism. There is a way to interpret his mechanism theory so that it does not necessarily conflict with Freud. Freud could
be right that slips have meaning. And he could be right about what
that meaning is. We could see Norman's mechanisms as simply

illuminating how the meanings get out in particular slips. So, for example, the "proximity" argument implies that substituting "closed" for "open" requires less deviation of the generative process than some other substitution. At the same time it does not exclude the Freudian claim that the switch reflects the chairman's ambivalence about the meeting. Similarly for the case of an airplane pilot who forgets to put down the landing gear: a Freudian explanation in terms of the pilot's "death wish" could still allow room for a computational explanation of this particular mechanism for how the wish was expressed in action.

But in the end Norman's computational and Freud's analytic perspective *do* conflict. A computational perspective suggests that when we understand the mechanisms of information storage and the programs that control our actions, we will come to see certain slips as likely, so likely that a Freudian search for meaning will be unnecessary and misguided. What used to be interpreted as sexually charged feelings becomes a bit of information lost or a program "derailed." Freudian slips become information-processing errors.

When we think of a mistake as "Freudian," this allows us to use it to put us in touch with our sexuality, our personal history, and our significant relationships. Psychoanalysis makes it clear that these will offer the clues to understanding our errors. Norman's view undermines the importance of such factors. They are not part of the processing problem.

In a "psychoanalytic culture," mistakes are not mistakes, they are the unconscious speaking its intentions. The Freudian theory asserts that no matter what we are doing, including mathematics or logic, our deepest motivations and desires are never very far away. Norman's theory, by appropriating things that have been associated with emotion, history, and sexuality into the realm of thought, leaves "pure feeling" isolated.

For Freud, thinking and feeling were inseparable. Not so for Norman, or for the children who respond to the computer's psychology by drawing a sharp line between intellect and emotion and choosing the latter as the essentially human. Paradoxically, the AI theorist who puts the focus on the cognitive joins the child in the dissociation of thought and feeling.

Marvin Minsky also sees Freudian slips through the prism of programs, and, like Norman, he believes that by reinterpreting them in this way he is coming to Freud's aid: Freud was a good observer, but he simply did not have the appropriate set of concepts with which to think through his theory.[14] He saw slips, but he had to think about them using the scientific language of his time. He was driven back to talking about hydraulic pressures when he wanted to specify mental mechanisms. And when these didn't seem appropriate, Freud resorted to literary images, for example that the "errors" are held back by censors—censors whose very name conveys their anthropomorphic properties. Norman believes that he can help Freud do better by pointing out the processes by which programs can become temporarily derailed; Minsky believes that he can help Freud do better by identifying in the operation of certain programs processes that function like censors, thus providing a more scientific model for something that Freud could refer to only in a loose, anthropomorphic way.

Even MacHack, Greenblatt's chess program, had a feature that fueled the AI theory of mistakes. Ironically, this feature was itself put into the program by mistake. For each move it had to make, MacHack was supposed to select its seven best moves according to limited criteria and then explore each of these moves in more depth. For a year or so Greenblatt and everyone else assumed that this was what his program was doing. But in fact the program was actually considering its six best moves along with the worst possible one. The bug took a long time to surface, because the program took a second look at these seven choices and on the second round it always recognized that the seventh, "worst" move would lead to disaster. So MacHack's secret dwelled silent within it.

After the error was discovered, Marvin Minsky described it in Freudian terms.

> So here you had a sort of demon inside the machine—a sort of self-destructive impulse of the worst kind, but it was always censored before it reached the machine's consciousness. This demon was always considering the worst. There are probably lots of people who are always doing that too, and who hardly ever do the worst thing they can think of. For me, the interesting question that this raised was that if you had some large complex program how would you ever be able to detect such a demon. . . . The brain also has a lot of bad thoughts that get censored by the good ones. It's only in Freudian slips—as Freud would say —that one can see that a person is considering some horrible

thought as well. The person himself may not even be aware of it on a conscious level. But a little "error information" can leak out in a moment of confusion.[15]

Minsky equated the program's mistake with what Freud might describe as a repressed desire to lose the game. In the process of translation by the AI scientist, Freud's meaning is changed. Self-destructiveness becomes split from passion; its presence is only a commentary on how well an intelligence is working.

Free Construction

The hacker culture is isolationist. The computer offers hackers a way to build walls between themselves and a world in which they do not feel comfortable. The culture of artificial intelligence is imperialistic. Here too there are walls that create a sense of being in a place apart. But this time the walls are felt as a fortress from which to conquer the world rather than as a protective shield to keep it at a safe distance.[16]

The first justification for AI's invasions and colonization of other disciplines' intellectual turf was a logic of necessity. The excursions into psychology and linguistics began as raids to acquire ideas that might be useful for building thinking machines. But the politics of "colonization" soon takes on a life of its own. The invaders come not only to carry off natural resources but to replace native "superstitions" with their "superior" world view. AI first declared the need for psychological theories that would work on machines. The next step was to see these alternatives as better—better because they can be "implemented," better because they are more "scientific."

Being in a colonizing discipline first demands and then encourages an attitude that might be called intellectual hubris. You need intellectual principles that are universal enough to give you the feeling that you have something to say about everything. The AI community had this in their idea of program. Furthermore, since you cannot master all the disciplines that you have designs on, you need confidence that your knowledge makes the "traditional wisdom" of these fields unworthy of serious consideration. Here too, the AI scientist feels that seeing things through a computational prism so fundamentally changes the rules of every game in the social and behavioral sciences that everything that came before is relegated to a period of intellectual immaturity. And finally you have to feel that nothing is beyond your intellectual reach if you are smart enough.

Most of the founders of AI were mathematicians who brought to the new field the mathematician's sense of the way to build theories: by pure thought. One might say that in moving into AI they set out to be mathematicians of the mind, they set out to construct by pure thought not only the theory of thought but the principles for the design of machines as capable of thought as they. The mathematician's culture insists that what one can do intellectually is limited only by imagination. The great mathematician David Hilbert said, "In mathematics there is no Ignorabimus." One need not submit to the ignominy of brute facts or to ignorance that cannot in principle be overcome by thinking hard enough.

This attitude is reinforced by the nature of programming. For many programmers, much of the excitement of the computer comes from freeing the mind from the constraints of matter. Recall the hacker who described programming as "building straight from the mind." What is most valued and most beautiful is what is most freely constructed. In the AI culture that has grown up around Minsky at MIT, the greatest pleasure is building worlds out of pure mind. And his students speak long and lovingly of their earliest experiences of doing this.

Danny Hillis, one of Minsky's students, describes being five years old and "drawing maps of imaginary countries, that's what I really loved to do."[17] Gerald Sussman, once a student of Minsky's, now himself a faculty member at the MIT Artificial Intelligence Laboratory, describes his "first real scientific theory" as a product of pure mind, of pure mental force.[18] As Sussman reconstructs the story now, someone gave him a pair of toy binoculars when he was four or five years old, and he observed ("as everyone does," he adds) that when you use the binoculars in the "right" way, things appear larger, but that objects appear smaller and more distant when they are used in reverse.

> I was really shaken by that—that you could turn them around
> and it worked both ways. Somehow that clicked with other things
> —like if you look in a mirror and see someone, they can see you.

I remember all of these things happened very fast. And all of a sudden I had this large collection of things and I suddenly realized that they were all the same thing.

From the binoculars, Sussman proceeded to develop a general point of view in which the idea of reversibility became a powerful tool for generating ideas. He describes how he decided that it must be possible to get a car to generate gasoline if you ran it backward. If gasoline can be consumed to generate motion, than you can consume motion to generate gasoline. It must be possible to invert the engine of the automobile as he inverted his toy binoculars.

Sussman came to see himself as someone who could "make up big ideas." More important, he came to associate making these leaps with a certain kind of feeling. He speaks of what it felt like to discover the reversibility theory: "It was a great thrill to have thought of it. And I can remember that there was this tremendous charge I got, and I decided I would spend the rest of my life looking for charges just like that one."

Sussman's "charges" do not necessarily follow upon external rewards or even external effect (no reverse motor ever produced any gasoline) but from experiencing his own inner conviction that he has understood something important. When we watch Sussman with his binoculars, we are watching Sussman the child developing the intellectual personality of Sussman the AI scientist. He already has the belief that what is most important is a universal idea—at four, reversibility, now computational structure. He already has the conviction that the most powerful theories do not come from what we are taught or even what we can make work, but are pure products of mind.

Artificial intelligence takes the hacker's aesthetic of free construction and turns it into a theory of the mind. The hacker speaks of programming as building from the mind. AI sees the mind as built from programming—and not only robot minds but the human mind itself. And, says AI "constructivism," there is something more. We construct our own minds: "mind building mind." This last notion is central. It influences the way people within the field speak about their own lives—they are fascinated with those experiences in which they felt themselves the builders of their own minds—and it influences their attitude toward childhood in general. They imbue it with an almost religious importance and are attracted by Piagetian ideas in which the child is seen as an autonomous builder of mind rather than as a recipient of "education."

When psychoanalysts talk about their lives we are not surprised to hear them dwell on the kinds of events their theory sees as most important—for example, conflicts with parents that are theorized as central to the playing out of the Oedipal drama. In a similar vein, AI scientists often dwell on those experiences which trained their minds as builders. Some involved building something—often against the advice of an authority. Danny Hillis has been building computers since he was five years old, then out of papier-mâché and imagination, now out of the most sophisticated materials. For him, a turning point in his confidence in himself as builder came with a magazine rack he made in sixth grade. A teacher, impressed by Hillis' success at making things, had suggested that he build a magazine rack for the school library. But when she saw his unconventional design (he describes the pieces as a jigsaw of "weird, very strange shapes") she pronounced it unworkable. His arguments were long, protracted, and bitter. The teacher could not be convinced. For Hillis, the story had a happy ending. A professional carpenter not only declared that his designs were workable, but added that they were amazing, "I don't see how you could have thought of them out of your head."

Another kind of "building" experience involved understanding an existing structure rather than making a new one. Gerald Sussman recalls his adventures with a broken-down radio when he was five years old. Sussman made it clear to me that this was a "real" radio—a traditional radio made of large, discrete parts. At five, he did not know enough electronics to understand how these parts worked individually or how to put them together so as to pick up speech and music, but his long, fascinated examination of the radio taught him a great deal.

> I had no idea what any of the parts did. Capacitors and resistors and parts I didn't know the names of: tubes that plugged in and things like that. What I did assimilate is that . . . the critical thing about this device was that it was made out of lots of pieces and that the pieces were connected in special patterns and that one can discover truth or something like that by looking through the patterns that connect this device.
>
> I never fixed the radio, but I remember that there would be

times when all of a sudden I would have this large number of
things that I had noticed about the radio and I would suddenly
realize something about how it all fit.

The adage states that the whole is greater than the sum of its
parts. In cybernetics, the whole is not just greater but more real.
From a cybernetic point of view, an early radio built of tubes and
a later one built of transistors are identical if their different parts
perform the same function and have the same interconnections:
the two collections of parts make up the same system. Sussman was
already beginning to learn to think in terms of the primacy of
system, treating the material parts as arbitrary and less real than
the system as a whole.

There are systems in nature as well as in artifacts like radios.
Minsky has forcefully argued that education should concentrate
on helping children appreciate them. For example, in a lecture on
"The Future of Artificial Intelligence," Minsky expressed the opinion that children should not dissect frogs.[19] In this there was no
humanitarian antivivisectionism. Minsky believes that children's
experiences provide models to be used throughout their lives. And
from Minsky's point of view, dissecting a frog does not provide
good ones. "The body," said Minsky to an enthusiastic audience of
MIT students, ". . . is a teleoperator for the brain." What is important about life is mind. And Minsky thinks it is obvious that understanding "mind" means understanding "structure and
subroutines," not the "bloody mess of organic matter." There is
nothing wrong with dissection per se. Anatomy is interesting for
itself. But for children at a formative age, in the process of putting
together models for seeing the world, it is a bad start, certainly a
very poor way to get to know about subroutines. "It would be far
better for the children to spend their time building with Tinkertoys." The Tinkertoys are better as "objects-to-think-with." At the
lecture, one of his enthusiastic colleagues added a telling frill. Children should have Tinkertoys even in the biology class; "what they
should be learning there is how to analyze complex systems—what
parts work together and how they go wrong."

A teacher can stand at a lectern and point out how the liver is
related to the stomach, but what children see in the viscera of the
frog does not suggest system. On the other hand, the structured
anatomy of the radio gave Sussman a model that allowed him to

see structure everywhere. AI scientists believe that the most important thing about people is that we are intelligent and as such closer than anything else in nature to pure program. So, for them, building a Tinkertoy structure, or building a magazine stand, or analyzing the parts and wholes of a radio are more relevant to understanding life than looking at the biology of a living thing.

Another Science of Self-Reflection

Artificial intelligence began with the goal of finding out how to program machines to do certain acts people do. This led AI scientists to thinking about how the human mind works, even if only because the human mind was the only model available, the only assurance that the very remarkable phenomenon we call mind is even possible. But beyond looking at the human mind in general, they turned to their own. It is easy to understand why. Indeed, it is scarcely conceivable that scientists could be engaged in developing the ideas that will make it possible for machines to emulate minds without wondering whether these ideas would explain their own minds as well.

There is long precedent for turning to one's own mind to build a general theory of mind. For Freud, his self-analysis, his technique for self-understanding was indissociable from the development of his general theory.

Within traditional science the line between subject and object is usually taken as sacred. But, like psychoanalysts, AI theorists often make a profession out of dissolving the line between "subjective" and "objective" reflection. "There's only one place to get ideas about intelligence, and that's from thinking about myself," says Roger Schank, an AI scientist at Yale.[20] "In the end I have just myself, and if it feels right that's what I have to trust," says Norman.

We saw Minsky and his students at work on a computer program designed to improvise jazz. The project was chosen not out of any sense that the world needs such a program, but because Minsky and several of his students are themselves improvisers. Minsky has made it clear that as far as he is concerned you can make a machine do only what you yourself know how to do. His method for building programs: engage in self-analytic activity.

In the early 1960s, Minsky worked with a student, Thomas

Evans, on an AI program that could pass the familiar visual-analogy tests: A is to B as C is to D, E, or F, where each letter stands for a geometric drawing. The reactions to the program were violent, not dissimilar to the early reactions to computer chess. The main objection: the computer was not doing "real" analogical thinking. Minsky discusses these objections in a way that asserts his commitment to finding the three algorithms behind what seems like intuition, and that asserts his commitment to self-reflection as a scientific method:

> It [the analogy program] irritated some people a lot. Rudolph Arnheim, who was a Gestalt psychologist, wrote an article in which he said that what the machine did was a bizarre travesty of what people really do. He felt that what they [people] do involves "intuitions" and Gestalt abilities to see form. He was typical of a lot of people who felt that if you could program something then the machine is not "really" doing it—that it really doesn't have a sense of analogy. I think that what it showed was that once one comes to grips with "intuitions" they turn into a lot of other things. I was convinced that the way the thing worked was pretty lifelike. Until one finds a logic for the kind of thing that Evans' program did, it looks like "intuition"—but that is really superficial.
>
> What we had done was to find a logic for this kind of problem solving. What we never did was to use a lot of statistical psychology to learn what some "average" person does when solving these problems. For a long time I had a rule in my laboratory that no psychological data was allowed.[21]

The "psychological data" Minsky wants to avoid are the results of experiments: "I had read a lot of that when I was in college and I felt that one couldn't learn very much by averaging a lot of people's responses." But his methodology was deeply psychological: think about yourself. And the reference point for the method was psychoanalysis: "What you had to do was something like what Freud did. Tom Evans and I asked ourselves, in depth, what we did to solve problems like this and that seemed to work out pretty well."

This sounds like simple introspection with all of its limitations. But AI theorists have several arguments for why it is more. First, they say that trying to capture one's thought processes in the form of a program forces you to confront objectively your initial idea of how you think you think. Once you have it in front of you it is not likely to seem adequate. But you do have a material on which you can work toward closer and closer approximations of something that will both "feel right" and "run"—that will produce the right results. Second, the idea of program offers a profusion of concepts for representing processes that naïve introspection fails to capture because the introspecting mind has an inadequate concept vocabulary for talking about process.

For many who come upon the AI culture for the first time, the place given to self-reflection in its method and its discourse comes as a surprise. In particular, the humanist's prejudice about the discipline creates an expectation that there will be an "objective" ideology in a science of mind that takes its central metaphors from a machine that has become a symbol of the logical, the scientific, the rational. But in fact, major sectors of the artificial intelligence community have given new life to the self-analytic method, and in doing so have developed a somewhat paradoxical identity as the cybernetic descendants of Freud.

Philosophy in Yet Another New Key

Psychoanalysis challenges the philosopher's attempt to give a logically coherent analysis of what is meant by such notions as "to believe" and "to know." In a psychoanalytic context, a statement such as "Smith believes the proposition 'P' " must always be explicated in a way that leaves open the possibility that Smith unconsciously also believes "not-P." Thus, psychoanalysis excludes any model of mind which demands that an individual's "knowledge" or "belief system" be consistent. Traditional logic cannot deal with "P" and "not-P" at the same time. Psychoanalysis requires that logic as the cement of mind be replaced by something more capable of dealing with elements of knowledge that struggle with one another.

The popular vision of a computer model stresses internal coherence and Spock-like logic. But Greenblatt's chess program was not internally coherent. That particular program, and the notion of program in general, allows internal conflicts and contradictions to be "transcended" when it comes time to act. In a program, coherent behavior can emerge from conflicting elements.

In the case of Greenblatt's program, the conflicts arose from an identifiable programming error that could be corrected. The error was an "accident." But, claim many AI experts, what might have been an accident in this program becomes inevitable as a program aspires to something like true intelligence.

In episode after episode of *Star Trek,* people have to outwit computers that have somehow gotten out of control. A strategy put to much use by the *Enterprise* crew is to trick the computer into considering a paradox and then stand by and watch the machine go up in smoke. The *Star Trek* writers miss a point that has become commonplace in AI: intelligent systems cannot avoid having internal contradictions and must know how to deal with them.

Thus, AI makes a demand on the philosophy of mind. Traditional logic will not suffice. It needs to be replaced by a logic that assumes inconsistency and then knows how to transcend it. Some go so far as to say that this new process logic must transcend the categories of truth and falsity as well. Roger Schank explains philosophers' attacks on artificial intelligence by the fact that AI is "competing for the same role in the study of man."

> We are very much modern-day philosophers. We're addressing the same questions that Aristotle addressed, and everybody else in between. We have a different method of doing it. That method can be summed up in one word: process. What we're saying is that the right approach to an analysis of events in the world is the process approach, seeing what the steps are, seeing what the inputs are, and providing algorithms to get from one place to another place, place A to place B.
>
> Philosophers have written tomes on the difference between knowing and believing. An AI person would have a lot less to say about that subject, but be a lot more coherent about it. In other words, the whole question of whether you really know or you really believe can be addressed in terms of what you do when you see the word "know." What do you do when you see the word "believe"? Under what circumstances? And when you reorient the question the way I just did, you change the question significantly. And this kind of change—well, in my judgment, that is what the philosophy of AI is all about.
>
> What I'm saying is, let's look at the old philosophical questions. Let's look at them in terms of what we do, in terms of how we approach and operate on these things rather than on truth. Truth is a nonmeaningful AI term, but truth is a key philosophical term.

One of Schank's students picks up this rhetoric as he tells me that he has "pretty much taken the semester off to study Douglas Hofstadter's *Gödel, Escher, Bach.*"

> It has always bothered me that the philosopher types think that they are the only ones who know how to think deeply. I mean to think deeply about philosophy. Science fiction thinks about philosophy. If you start from a world that is a complete blank and you can fill in all the details, which is what you do in science fiction, you are doing the same thing as Plato: creating a whole system. Make the minds in that system work however you want them to. In AI, we do that same kind of thing, but we take it one step further. We don't just fantasize about minds, we think about building them. With actor languages, and recursion, and multiprocessing, well, I think that the scientists have what it takes. I mean what it takes to think about the mind. We are the new philosophers. Not everybody can see it yet. But they are going to.

Between Science and Myth

Challenging the concept of truth, seeing oneself a new philosopher—these are not small things. These global aspirations are an expression of the pervasive intellectual hubris of AI, part of its sense of being an enterprise of mythic proportions.

From their earliest years, many people in the field have thought of themselves as creators of life—a robot in one's image.* Along with "building from the mind," their childhood reminiscences include frequent references to the fantasy of making a robot. For example, Don Norman says, "I have a dream to create my own robot. To give it my intelligence. To make it mine, my mind. To see myself in it. Ever since I was a kid." Roger Schank is listening to our conversation. "So who doesn't?" he interjects. "I have always wanted to make a mind. Create something like that. It is the most

---

* Several present-day AI researchers at MIT grew up with a family tradition that they are descendants of Rabbi Loew, the creator of the Golem, a humanlike figure made of clay into whom God's name breathed life. These scientists include Gerald Sussman, Marvin Minsky, and Joel Moses. Joel Moses reports that a number of other American scientists have considered themselves to be descendants of Rabbi Loew, including John von Neumann and Norbert Wiener.

exciting thing you could do. The most important thing anyone could do."

For Schank, thinking of the robots as mind led to challenging the notion of truth. For some, it leads to challenging the notion of life.

Gary Drescher, another graduate student at the MIT AI Laboratory, is struck by how our ideas about life have followed upon what our technology could not do.[22] "People used to think that moving on your own power was something only living things could do. But now we use the expression 'doing it on your own steam'— using the technological image to describe how people move or are motivated. Moving around no longer has to do with what is special to life. These things change."

Drescher believes that there is an ultimate criterion for life. It is what today's most sophisticated machines don't have: consciousness. "I give no privilege to biochemistry as being at the heart of life." As Drescher sees it, there will be artificial intelligences of increasing sophistication and as they develop to the point of consciousness there is no doubt they will be alive.

He is exceptional among his peers in his commitment to thinking about the ethical implications of robotics. "We have the right to create this life," he says, "but not the right to take our act lightly." He does not believe that God created humans, but he does believe that when people create a new consciousness they are acting as gods and have to deal with new ethical questions: in a society where human and artificial intelligences live together, what will be their respective rights, who will make their Ten Commandments?

Drescher has several proposals for the new ethics. Whereas Isaac Asimov's "Laws of Robotics" were originally written to protect people against the robots, Drescher proposes that we give equal protection to the machines.* Consciousness is life, and killing one is a new form of murder: "People always talk about pulling the plug on computers as though when it comes to that they will be saving

---

* Asimov's laws are:
  1. A robot may not injure a human being nor, through inaction, allow a human being to come to harm.
  2. A robot must obey the orders given it by human beings except when such orders would conflict with the First Law.
  3. A robot must protect its own existence as long as such protection does not conflict with the First or Second Law.

the world, performing the ultimate moral act. But that is science fiction. In real life, it will probably be the other way around. We are going to be creating consciousnesses, creating lives, and then people may simply want to pull the plug when one of these intelligences doesn't agree with them." People will want to kill the created lives. So, Drescher's first tenet for moral coexistence with the robots is "no consciousness without commitment, people's moral commitment to the life we have created."

When MIT's Edward Fredkin talks about AI as a natural step in evolution he is taking this kind of reasoning a step further.[23] Most of us feel a loyalty—sentimental, moral, or religious—to our species. But from a position of confidence about the artificial intelligences of the future, Fredkin casts a cold eye on our human limitations.

> We forget things, learning is incredibly slow and difficult. We try to teach something to somebody twenty times, and they still don't get it. If you did that to a computer, you'd have to complain and throw it out. . . .
> There is a popular view that the human mind is this fantastic thing that most of us are just barely using—5 or 10 percent of its capacity. If we could only unleash the whole human mind and all of its powers, we'd be supermen. Now my notion is that for an ordinary person to get along in society in a conventional way requires about 110 percent of the capacity of the human mind, causing breakdowns and trouble of various sorts. Basically, the human mind is not most like a god or most like a computer. It's most like the mind of a chimpanzee and most of what's there isn't designed for living in high society but for getting along in the jungle or out in the fields.[24]

We respond to aggression, to attraction, to threat in a "local," immediate way, the way an animal needs to. "We're tuned," says Fredkin, "to dealing with local not global situations, and our biggest problems turn up when global problems emerge." Politics, world famine, fending off the possibility of war—these call for the global thinking we are worst at. But we are in the process of creating entities that will do it far better than we.

> Humans are okay. I'm glad to be one. I like them in general, but they're only human. . . . The intellectual doesn't like the idea

of this machine doing it better than he does, but it's no different from the guy who was surpassed physically. . . . The mere idea that we have to be the best in the universe is kind of far-fetched. . . . The fact is, I think we'll be enormously happier once our niche has limits to it. We won't have to worry about carrying the burden of the universe on our shoulders as we do today. We can enjoy life as human beings without worrying about it. And I think that will be a great thing.

. . . Now with the AI coming along . . . if it were a slightly better human, then we'd disappear. But it's not going to be a slightly better human. It's going to be a completely, a totally different thing, which leaves us our niche. We'll still be the best creatures at being human on the whole planet. And you know what? We might enjoy it.[25]

Perhaps our species will follow the dinosaurs into extinction. Or perhaps our descendants will be content with a subordinate role. In either case, when the AI researcher considers all of this with equanimity, it reflects a very particular set of values. There is the habit of thinking on the largest possible scale, on the mythic scale. And there is the commitment to the idea that thinking is the most important thing in the world.

But will computers think?

Critics of artificial intelligence point to the very limited intellectual capacities of present-day machines. Dreyfus argued that these limitations are not simply reflections of the current state-of-the-art but reflections of fundamental technical roadblocks in AI. He named his book *What Computers Can't Do*.[26] In recent years, a different philosophical attack on AI has commanded particularly wide interest, I believe because it captures something that is close to the center of popular resistance to the idea that machine thinking could be like our own. Instead of getting into a debate about what computers can or cannot do, the philosopher John Searle argues that no matter what feats of intellect computers perform, the machines will never be thinking, they will only be simulating thought. According to Searle, there can be no "behavioral" criterion for granting to a machine the status of an intelligent being. In the language that has grown up within AI and philosophy for discussing such questions, Searle is saying that the Turing test doesn't prove anything.[27]

What has come to be known as the Turing test is a method

invented by the mathematician Alan Turing to cope with such questions as "What does it mean for a machine to be intelligent?" and "Can you define intelligence?"[28] Rather than provide answers in the abstract, Turing proposed a contest. You enter a room and see two terminals. One is connected to a computer and the other to a person who can speak through it from another room. You may type questions, assertions, insults, anything you wish, at either terminal, and you may do so for as long as you like. Your goal is to decide which of the terminals is connected to a computer and which to a person. In doing so you may assume that the person is trying his or her best to help you make the right decision—for example, not "acting mechanically" in order to confuse you. The machine, of course, is not under this constraint. If you give it a sum to add, it may well decide to take its time with it, as a person would, or to make a mistake, as a person might. If it did so, the machine would not be cheating. The rules of Turing's game dictate that its job is to simulate a person however it can.

Turing suggests that if under these circumstances you cannot decide which is the computer and which is the person, you will have to conclude that the machine is intelligent.

No machine exists today that could come even close to passing the Turing test. A program like ELIZA, the simulation of the psychotherapist, is able to sound as "smart" as it does only so long as its interlocutors confine their remarks to those appropriate within the boundaries of a therapy session. But if you say to ELIZA, "Let's discuss paths toward nuclear disarmament," you might well get the nonsense reply "WHY ARE YOU TELLING ME THAT YOUR MOTHER MAKES PATHS TOWARD NUCLEAR DISARMAMENT?" if you had introduced the word "mother" in your previous interchange.

When someone like Dreyfus attacks artificial intelligence on the grounds of "what computers can't do," he is implicitly accepting the legitimacy of the Turing test, although he would like to use it to prove machines are not intelligent rather than that they are. If you commit yourself to the idea that there will be something that the computer cannot do, some subject that the computer cannot adequately discuss, then, in the Turing situation, you would merely have to raise one of those subjects for the machine to be exposed.

But if instead of focusing on what machines can't do, you grant, at least for the sake of argument, the idea of a machine capable of meeting any specifications, you can still ask, "So what? Does this mean that it is thinking?" This is where Searle begins and thus makes the Turing test irrelevant to pursuing the question of the computer's relation to thought.

Centralized vs. Decentralized Minds

Searle asks us to imagine a situation in which a person simulates the operation of an AI computer. He calls it the "Chinese Room Experiment." The essential of the thought experiment is that Searle, who assures us that he does not know the Chinese language, asks us to imagine that he is locked in a room with stacks and stacks of paper, let us say index cards. He is given a story written in Chinese and then is passed slips of paper on which are written questions about the story, also in Chinese. Of course he doesn't know he has a story, and doesn't know that the slips of paper contain questions about the story. What he does know is that "clever programmers" have given him a set of rules for what to do with the little pieces of paper he is passed. The rules tell him how to match them up with other little pieces of paper that have Chinese characters on them, which he passes out of the room. The rules say such things as "The 'squiggle-squiggle' sign is to be followed by the 'squoggle-squoggle' sign."[29] He becomes extraordinarily skillful at following these rules, at manipulating the cards in his collection. We are to suppose that his instructions are sufficiently complete to enable him to "output" Chinese characters that are in fact the correct answers to the questions about the story.

All of this is set up for the sake of argument in order to ask one rhetorical question in plain English: Does the fact that he sends out the correct answers prove that he understands Chinese or the questions to which he gives the correct answers? To Searle the answer is obvious: No. The test would not prove that he understands Chinese. All that has been proved is that he is skilled at applying rules that clever programmers have given him that enable him to match little pieces of paper with other pieces of paper. He is acting as a digital computer and he understands nothing.

> ... I can pass the Turing test for understanding Chinese. But all the same I still don't understand a word of Chinese and neither does any other digital computer because all the com-

puter has is what I have: a formal program that attaches no
meaning, interpretation, or content to any of the symbols.

What this simple argument shows is that no formal program
by itself is sufficient for understanding, because it would always
be possible in principle for an agent to go through all the steps
in the program and still not have the relevant understanding.
And what works for Chinese would also work for other mental
phenomena. I could, for example, go through the steps of the
thirst-simulating program without feeling thirsty. The argument, also en passant, refutes the Turing test because it shows
that a system, namely me, could pass the Turing test without
having the appropriate mental states.[30]

When Searle published his argument, seventeen defenders of
artificial intelligence took up their word processors to refute him.
One of their arguments was particularly persistent, surfacing in
many different forms. Searle himself recognized it early and gave
it a name: "the systems reply." Essentially it argues that "while it is
true that the individual person who is locked in the room does not
understand the story, the fact is that he is merely part of a whole
system, and the system does understand the story."

Searle counterattacks with ingenuity. If the systems reply says
that the room as a whole understands, well, then, make the room
part of the man: ". . . imagine that the man internalizes the whole
system. Suppose he has a super memory and a super intelligence
so that he memorizes the instruction book and does all the calculations in his head. To get rid of the room, we can even suppose
he works outdoors."[31]

Now the "system" is part of the man, but Searle insists that nothing of consequence has changed: "since the man doesn't understand Chinese, and since there's nothing in the system that is not
in the man," there is still no way the system could understand
Chinese.

Actually I feel somewhat embarrassed to give even this answer
to the systems theory because the theory seems to me so implausible to start with. The idea is that while a person doesn't understand Chinese, somehow the conjunction of that person and bits
of paper might understand Chinese. It is not easy for me to
understand how someone who is not in the grip of an ideology
would find the idea at all plausible.[32]

When Searle speaks of ideology he is reflecting that what is at issue here is indeed the confrontation of two different intellectual cultures.

The AI scientists are saying that Searle is caught in an old philosophical trap. Descartes said, *"Cogito ergo sum."* The statement assumes and reinforces a presupposition that wherever there is thinking there must be an "I," a self, an agent. Only an "I" can think. Anyone who shares this point of view will share Searle's astonishment at the suggestion that a room and its contents (or, as Searle puts it, a "conjunction") could possibly think. When Searle looks for "thinking" he begins with a search for the "I." In the conjunction of the man and the papers there is only one candidate: the man. But Searle himself has defined the man in such a way as to exclude him from thinking, since he merely shuffles papers without knowing what they mean. Searle grants that the man is able to produce a simulation of thinking. But no thinking is taking place.

From the other side, from the AI scientists, the astonishment is no less. For them, the suggestion that there must be a thinking agent, an "I," in order for thinking to happen is, as Minsky likes to say, "prescientific." That is, it is prior to scientific models of mind. The AI scientist belongs to a culture deeply committed to a view that thought does not need a unitary agent who thinks. Farther on we shall see that this culture has now built up an arsenal of metaphors, images, and turns of thought to support this position. Their coherence is the coherence of a culture: a culture of system, of process, of simulation. "Indeed," quipped one of its recursively minded members, "it is more than a culture, it is a simulation of a culture."

The AI culture accepts the criterion of the Turing test: a perfect simulation of intelligence *is* intelligence. People who accept Searle's argument are asserting that for them there is an unbridgeable gulf between the simulated and the real.

Debates about what computers can or cannot be made to do ignore what is most essential to AI as a culture: not building machines but building a new paradigm for thinking about people, thought, and reality. Still less do they capture what most people feel uneasy about when they confront AI. For the moment, people's deepest concerns are not practical but philosophical. Whether or not AI can make robots with superhuman powers has material consequences of the first magnitude. But it is far away. What is here and now is the challenge of a new philosophy.

Searle sticks tenaciously to the primacy of things over process. He looks for a man in the room, for a neuron in the brain, for a self in the mind. His AI opponents stick just as tenaciously to the primacy of process over things. A system might be made of silicon, Tinkertoys, or fluids—this is irrelevant. As when Minsky discussed the frog and Sussman discussed his radio, it is the system that matters.

The drama of the confrontation between the two cultures is captured in a fundamental difference in perception. For Searle the proposition "a room thinks" is definitionally absurd. In the AI culture, the conviction that it cannot is an archaic belief. For them, the idea that an agent in the room must be "doing the thinking" is just a modern echo of the idea that there must be a "soul" in the pineal gland.

PART III

INTO A NEW AGE

CHAPTER 8

Thinking of Yourself as a Machine

When confronted with the AI vision of superintelligent computers of the future, computers that could serve as psychotherapists, judges, or physicians, many react with a force of feeling that surprises them. Some try to neutralize their discomfort by asserting the impossibility of artificial intelligence. Others insist that even if possible, it should not be allowed. The vehemence of response expresses our stake in maintaining the line between the natural and the artificial, between the human and the mechanical. Discussion about computers becomes charged with feelings about what is special about people: their creativity, their sensuality, their pain and pleasure. But paradoxically, when faced with a machine that shows any degree of "intelligence," many of these same people seem pulled toward treating the machine as though it were a person.

Jean is an airline ticket agent who uses a computer to make customer reservations. She first represented the computer as a neutral object—programmed, passive, completely under the control of its operators, threatening only in its impersonality. But then she moved on to more ambivalent descriptions.

Jean often confronts angry clients. The planes are overbooked; the computer has been programmed on the assumption that some people won't show, but occasionally everybody shows, and not everyone can go. Jean's excuse is, "The computer fouled up." I talk to her about what she means. Is this a "manner of speaking"? It is not. She seems to experience the computer as an autonomous entity that can act on its own behalf and is thus "blamable." This anthropomorphization has consequences. It means that when things go wrong Jean need not call the policies of her company into question or lay blame on fellow workers. The anthropomorphized machine gives her an out. She can sympathize with her inconvenienced clients without jeopardizing her relationship with co-workers or her security as a "company person."

The simplest force that makes the computer seem more than a machine among other machines is its behavior. Jean asked her computer questions and it gave her answers. She tells me that "of course people give the computer the flight schedules, they program them in so it will know the rules, but then it uses its own mind." Like the ELIZA program whose psychotherapeutic dialogue drew people into its "confidence," Jean's computer behaves in a way that encourages her to treat it as a person.

Jean's computer did not draw her into an explicitly metaphysical discourse about minds and machines. But like the child who argues about Merlin's cheating, she has taken a step toward allowing a continuity between the psychologies of machines and people.

Jean's anthropomorphization is naïve. She treats the computer as a black box, and she doesn't look inside. But computers encourage their anthropomorphization because of more than their behavior. In an important sense the computer is irreducible. It is hard to block the temptation to personify the computer by saying what it "really" is, hard to block the suggestion that the computer "thinks" by saying what it "really" does. It is hard to capture the computer by seeing it in terms of familiar objects or processes that existed before it was invented. The computer is not "like" anything else in any simple sense.

Anthropomorphization and Irreducibility

Airplanes come in all shapes and can be described in all sorts of ways, but there is no conceptual problem in stating what they do: they fly. There is no equally elegant, compelling, or satisfying way of defining the computer by its function. You can say "it computes," and the computer scientist can set up a conceptual frame of reference in order to define "the computable." But even then what has been isolated as "the essential computer" presents no easy analogies with other objects in the world (as the airplane does the bird), except, of course, for its analogies with people.

Some might say that no matter how complex the computational product—a medical diagnosis, a move in a chess game—"all the computer really does is add." In a certain sense this is true. But saying that a computer "decided to move the queen by adding" is a little bit like saying that Picasso "created *Guernica* by making brushstrokes." Reducing things to this level of "local" description gives no satisfying way to grasp the whole. When we talk about perception—for example, how we grasp visual images—there is a tension between the atomic and the gestalt. Do we build up the picture from discrete bits of information or do we grasp it as a whole? Similarly, in thinking about computers, there is a tension between the local simplicity of the individual "acts" that comprise a program and the global complexity that can emerge when it is run. When you talk about the overall behavior of the program, descriptions of local simplicities seem off the point, and the temptation is to see the machine as something that borders on life.

Computers are certainly not the only machines that evoke anthropomorphization. We often talk about machines, and even to machines, as though they were people. We complain that a car "wants to veer left." We park it on a slope and warn it to "stay put." But usually, when we "talk to technology," we know that any voluntary action we may have ascribed to a machine is really a series of unambiguously "mechanical" events. We know that the pressure of the emergency brake will prevent gravity from pulling a car down a hill. But when we play chess with a computer and say that the computer "decided" to move the queen, it is much harder to translate this decision into physical terms.

In the early nineteenth century, the exhibition of what was claimed to be a chess-playing automaton created a sensation.[1] The machine was a fake. Inside the chess-playing machine there was a chess-playing man. No one knew how to make a machine with the complexity of behavior that goes into playing even poor chess. No one knew what such a machine might be made of—wheels, gears, levers, strings, pipes with flowing liquids? And even if one knew what "parts" to use, what principles could guide their organization?

It is now possible to walk into a toy store and buy a chess-playing machine that probably plays a better game than the nineteenth-century man in the machine. We have computers programmed to play chess, but not because anyone found the right "parts" to use. Indeed, one might say that the breakthrough was the realization that any particular physical "part" is irrelevant. The physical parts of a computer mark states in a process. Most computers are made of electrical markers, but they don't have to be. A computer has been constructed out of Tinkertoy parts. It was made at MIT to dramatize that what is important about a computer is the machine's ability to embody a process, to specify a sequence of rules. In a very real sense, the chess machine and the Tinkertoy machine, like all computers, are not made of wood, or water, or silicon. They are made of logic. And thinking about the core of a machine as the exercise of logic leads people back to thinking of the computer as mind.

But despite these encouragements to personify computers, people have a stake in seeing themselves as different. They assert this difference, much as we saw children do. They speak of human love, sensuality, and emotion. They speak of the computer's lack of consciousness, originality, and intention. In the end, many sum up their sense of difference in the statement "Computers are programmed; people aren't," or "Computers only do what they are programmed to do, nothing more, nothing less." This last response has a history. It is associated with Lady Ada Lovelace, a friend and patroness of Charles Babbage, inventor of the "analytical engine," the first machine that deserves to be called a computer in the modern sense. In a memoir she wrote in 1842 she became the first person known to go on record with a variant of "Computers only do what you tell them to do."*

From the perspective of this model of a computer program—let us call it "the Lovelace model"—people listen with incredulity to the AI scientist who says that the human mind can be captured by program. They can't understand how anyone could think that his or her mind works that way. But AI ideas are moving out and capturing the popular imagination because the AI community has generated a set of ideas that undermine the Lovelace model of what it means to be programmed.[2] This chapter is about some of these ideas and how they are picked up by those who come into contact with them. People become sympathetic to the idea that

---

* Lovelace put it like this: "The analytical Engine has no pretensions whatever to originate anything. It can do whatever we know how to order it to perform."

machine intelligence has something to teach us about human intelligence, and even to the idea that the computer's psychology may be close to our own, when they are drawn into thinking that somehow Lovelace must be wrong—that in some sense computers must be able to do more than "what you tell them to do."

Beyond Lovelace

Jordan is a sculptor. Until recently he never had anything to do with computers, except for the one that dispenses cash at the bank. Jordan's relationship with computers changed when small chess-playing machines were introduced. Together with art, chess is his passion. He bought a chess machine and found it was good enough to give him an exciting game. Computers became more than undifferentiated "smart machines." Jordan wanted to know how this particular machine worked.

Our culture is rich in ways of thinking that answer Jordan's question in Lovelace style: for example, the chess machine plays by rules that have been programmed into it. To this Jordan's disappointed reaction was clear: computer chess has nothing to do with human chess. He was sure that he didn't play by consulting rules and he rejected the machine's intelligence despite its intelligent behavior: "It's not thinking, it's just rules."

Several months later Jordan changed his mind when he heard that his chess machine doesn't play by rules but by "heuristics," something that is ultimately a rule, but which feels like something else, more like what we call a "rule of thumb."

Since a chess program cannot check through and evaluate all the possibilities for each move, it relies on general guidelines, "heuristics," to pick out a few it will examine in depth. The idea that a program can have a degree of flexibility and imprecision gave Jordan the sense that it possesses something akin to what he calls "intuition." And with this, he could once again identify with the computer.

Jordan was able to see the chess computer as like him, as a "thinking thing," once he moved from seeing its program as rigidly serial—one fixed action after another—to thinking of it as multiple processes in interaction. More elaborated versions of this kind of representation allow AI scientists to see in the notion of "program" not what is most inhuman about machines but what computers and people must have in common. These "anti-Lovelace" representations figure in the writings of AI theoreticians. They have spread to their students and beyond. Recently, they have reached Hollywood. They are the representations that serve to break down people's resistance to seeing a continuity between computers and people.

Tron and a Society of Mind

I attend the Boston premiere of the Walt Disney movie *Tron*, advertised as "taking place inside of a computer." The film creates an "interior" computational landscape, and the hero, a hacker named Flynn, spends three-quarters of the film trapped there, prisoner within a system he has built. *Tron* shows the insides of a computer as a community of programs, each personified as an "actor" with a history, a personality, and a function within a complex political organization. We meet the inhabitants of this world at the time of a political crisis. A program called the Master Control Program, unaffectionately referred to throughout as the MCP, has assumed dictatorial powers. Brutal police programs are used to bring all other programs under control. There are skirmishes, battles, and finally, with Flynn's help, all-out warfare within the society.

When the film is over and the lights go on I see Marvin Minsky. Minsky has been charmed. "That was great," he says, "That's a whole lot better than bits! I am in the middle of writing a paper which proposes to outlaw the whole idea of bits. It's no way to think about what goes on inside of a computer."

When Minsky talks about "outlawing the whole idea of bits" he means changing the first image most people get of computers. It begins with the idea that the computer is made of electronic switches that are either on or off (these are the bits) and builds up to the Lovelace step-by-step model of a program. If you are trying to use the computer as a model of mind, the bit and Lovelace models are unsatisfying, just as thinking of "rules" was unsatisfying for Jordan trying to identify with his chess machine. I ask Minsky what he wants to put in place of the bits. He answers, with a look that makes it clear that the answer should be evident, "A society, of course, just like in *Tron*." "Society" is his mnemonic for multiple, simultaneously interacting programs within a complex computer system. In the *Tron* landscape Minsky has found an image, how-ever fanciful, for what he has in mind.

The image of the computer as a "bit machine" and the image of the computer as a society of programs are not irreconcilable. Any computer has the bits that Minsky wants to outlaw, but the question here is at what level we choose to understand things. It has often been suggested that the relationship of bits to program is analogous to that of brain to mind. In the "brain" there are physical things—neurons, synapses, electrical impulses. In the "mind" there are images, concepts, ideas, language, and thought. Similarly, within the computer there are physical things (the bits), and then, at the level of "mind," there are programs.

In some sense, the activity of the neurons must be the physical manifestation of the same events we experience as thoughts and images, but usually the detail of how this happens is irrelevant for using one's mind: for feeling, thinking, communicating. On the other hand, in the case of neurological disorder, priorities change. Then it becomes important to find someone who knows how to probe, stimulate, and record the activity of the physical brain.

In a computer, different levels of understanding are appropriate at different times. The repairman focuses his attention on bits, but if you want to think of mind as computer, you are not likely to be drawn to the level of on/off switches or Lovelace models. You are more likely to be swept into the world of *Tron*.

Tron does more than assert the primacy of software over hardware, of program over electrical circuit. Its presentation of a computer system as an unruly society is in dramatic contrast with the linear model of programming. Even if the members of the *Tron* society had been produced by Lovelacian programming, their interaction leads to the playing out of an unpredictable drama.[3]

The idea of a computer system as a "society" of competing programs is one of several key ideas from the AI community that challenge the image of the computer as following step-by-step instructions in a literal-minded way and make it easier for people to think of mind as machine. Another one of these is that the computer is capable of "learning." In that case, you don't have to tell the computer everything it needs to know; you have to tell it how to learn. And yet another, which combines these two, is an idea that I will refer to as "emergence": you don't have to tell the computer everything it needs to know; you have to arrange for it to obtain—by being told or by learning—the elements out of which something nonprogrammed can "emerge."*

In the 1950s, research began on the theory of random networks, inspired by the impression that neurons in the brain are randomly connected and by the hope that intelligence might emerge from this disorder as a phenomenon of critical mass. And also in the 1950s, Oliver Selfridge, then a brilliant young disciple of Norbert Wiener, proposed a machine, "Pandemonium," whose name captures his idea of what it might take for intelligent order to emerge.[4] Unfortunately its name also captured what turned out to be the problem with his idea: chaos.

Pandemonium and random networks did not give rise to sufficient order to be useful. But emergence remained a major theme in AI research, although it was increasingly clear that emergent intelligence would come only with more modulated attempts to balance between control and chaos. Some of the best-known early work in AI, such as Newell and Simon's highly controlled and centralized General Problem Solver, led critics to fear that the influence of the discipline would be its pressure toward mechanical models of human psychology.[5] But another thread in AI has developed a way of thinking that Minsky saw reflected in *Tron*. This is an image of a fragmented mind in which intelligence emerges from the interactions of conflicting, competing parts.

Now I take up this thread, first very briefly as it has developed within the technical discipline, and then, more central to my concern, as something that has moved out to influence how people on the periphery of AI think about their minds. I believe that tracing the movement of this idea is important. Jordan is typical of many people I interviewed: the idea of emergence is a key element that breaks down resistance to seeing mind as machine.†

---

* "Emergence" sounds like magic, but nature is rich in examples that serve as metaphors for it. Take the spherical shape of a soap bubble: when you blow the bubble you do nothing, tell it nothing to make the bubble round; its spherical shape emerges from the interaction of its molecules, none of which is individually programmed to be part of a round bubble. Social life too is rich in examples of emergence: conversations produce more than the individual participants could have produced or anticipated.

† This chapter looks at how a few powerful ideas elaborated within the AI world have captured the imagination of people who are not in AI but close enough to it and to computers to be responsive to its influence. I found one such group in Harvard and MIT students in fields other than computer science; another in the community of scientists who meet AI but are not a part of its professional structure; another in a group one might call "Gödel,

The Idea of Emergence

One of the most famous and influential "learning" programs was written by Arthur Samuel in the late 1950s.[6] This program played checkers according to built-in rules. In that sense, it did what it was programmed to do. But it was also programmed to modify its rules based on its "experience." It played many games, against many opponents, and it did get better, finally achieving the status of a "world class" checkers player. But the dramatic moment in this program's life was not the day it beat a champion, but the day it beat its creator. The program became good enough to beat Arthur Samuel at his own game.

Among those struck by the drama of that moment was Norbert Wiener. For the mathematician usually regarded as the founder of cybernetics, the machine triumphing over its creator symbolized a new era. In *God and Golem, Inc.* he suggested that the implications bordered on the theological: "Can God play a significant game with his own creature? Can any creator, even a limited one, play a significant game with his own creature?"[7]

In the checkers program, Samuel took a decisive technical step beyond the Lovelace model of programming. To show how, consider the ways one might determine whether one arrangement of pieces on a checkerboard is more "favorable" than another. One "rule of thumb" is to count pieces. In fact, children often decide whether they are "winning" on this basis alone. Another method would be to look at how many of the enemy pieces are "under attack." A program that acted simply by following either of these two rules would play a very weak game. To make a stronger program you could go in either of two directions. The "Lovelace"

Escher, Bach enthusiasts," people who met AI ideas in that work and felt that something about their way of seeing the world had changed. I also found it useful to follow students through their first programming courses and their first brush with AI. In 1979–80 I looked at three different introductory classes, one at Harvard and two at MIT. I selected twenty students from each university for more intensive study. Most were interviewed several times as their course progressed.

Interviews with "newcomers" proved to be a rich source of materials on the computer as an object that provokes philosophical reflection on how minds might be or not be like machines. This study made my interests known among the local undergraduate community and led to about twenty-five other contacts with Harvard and MIT students.

I met Jean while working on a study that is not discussed in this book, a study of people who meet computers in the world of work. She is here because her conflict focuses a problem: how we are pulled, in spite of ourselves, to blur the line between people and machines.

direction would consist of adding systematic precise rules for measuring "being ahead," rules that would be increasingly subtle and complex. The other way, "heuristic programming," uses a collection of disparate rules of thumb. From this perspective, you take the two "weak" rules (counting pieces and counting threats) together, recognizing that each has a place in the game even though insufficient by itself. Then you might add other rules to make a collection of "agents" within the program, each with a particular point of view, each limited, but valid in its own way.

This was Samuel's strategy. Once he had chosen it, the problem for him, as it would be for the manager of any organization whose individual members are confined to their own specialties, was how to create a structure within which the agents could interact. Samuel's solution was to have them cast weighted votes. What was most innovative about his program was that the program itself modified the weights depending on the track record of the different agents and of the program as a whole. Samuel's program worked on a kind of "society" model. The choice of which move to make was based on a "democratic" process in which a number of agents, each with a partial, limited view of the situation, could vote for or against a particular move, and the majority would win. For this program, "learning" consisted of adjusting the number of votes that could be cast by any particular agent.

In *God and Golem*, Norbert Wiener discussed whether the Samuel program "merely did what Samuel programmed it to do." It did, but in this case the programming had, in a certain sense, instructed it to take off on its own to make its own decisions. Lady Lovelace's dictum begins to have a different feel when obedience means autonomy. For Wiener the working of the Samuel program started to feel like overstepping an ancient taboo: the taboo of speaking of "living beings and machines in the same breath."[8]

The idea of the Samuel-style voting procedures (in more technical language, called "perceptrons") generated excitement as a model for getting machines to make intelligent decisions of all sorts, not just in checkers. But it soon became clear that it was exceptional for a decision procedure to be reducible to a perceptron. Not all learning could be made as simple. What worked for checkers would work for little else.[9]

In the classical perceptron that Samuel used, intelligence emerged by simple addition of "votes." What didn't work out mathematically for a large number of cases was the idea of "simple addition." But what remained a strong metaphor within the AI world was the idea of a society of limited agents whose intelligence is emergent from their interaction, the idea that a computer system as a whole will be significantly, qualitatively different than the sum of its parts. We use this idea when we think about living things and about creation: for example, the DNA that emerged from the inert molecules of the nonliving earth. AI has seized it to think of how intelligence might "grow" in a computer program in a way that might model the way it grows in a child.

"Growing" Intelligence

If we take a simple problem like trying to decide whether there are more black or white marbles on a tabletop, something that very young children can do, it is easy to write a Lovelace-style program that could solve it. Have one part of the program, one subprocedure, count the black marbles, have another subprocedure count the white marbles. Have a third subprocedure compare the numbers and report the color with the greatest number back to the top level of the program.

This Lovelace program does the job. But it presents a problem if you are trying to model how the child does it. In order to decide whether there are more black or more white marbles on the tabletop, the Lovelace system needs to know how to count, how to compare numbers, and, most complicated of all, how to integrate this counting and comparing ability into the solution of its problem. But children can say "which is more" long before they are able to do these things. If you are trying to model a growing mind, it would be more satisfying to imagine how "which is more" could be built up out of the kinds of things that small children can do. In other words, it would be more satisfying to model this piece of intelligence as "emergent."

You can imagine a small child telling the difference between a black marble and a white one, grabbing one of each, and putting them away. In order to tell which is more, all the child needs to do is repeat this action until there are either no marbles left or marbles of only one color. In the latter case, the child can then call out the color of the remaining marbles, and that color will be "more." This description reflects, better than the Lovelace "counting program," the kinds of matching ability young children actually have. Thus, a computer program that follows it will have greater psychological plausibility. Some AI theorists have suggested ways of writing this kind of program. For example, Alan Newell and Herbert Simon, who want to construct theories of human thought in the form of programs, have put forth the idea of a "production system," a style of programming that moves away from Lovelace to get closer in spirit to the child solving the "which is more" problem by grabbing the marbles off the table.

A production system is a little society inhabited by agents each of which can recognize a specific condition and, when it arises, carry out a specific job. A first agent might be able to recognize black and white pairs (its "triggering condition") and put them aside, "grab them off the table." Another agent does nothing unless it sees a tabletop with only white marbles, in which case it says "more white." The third does nothing unless it sees a tabletop with only black marbles, in which case it says "more black." In traditional Lovelace programming, the programmer fixes in advance the order in which instructions will be executed. In a production system, the order in which the agents do their jobs is not determined by the program but by the environment in which the system finds itself.

The Lovelace program had a subprocedure that knew how to count, a relatively advanced ability. None of the three agents here (Newell and Simon call such agents "productions") has anything approaching this degree of smartness. All they can do is follow simple rules about grabbing pairs of marbles or making pronouncements about "more black" or "more white." In the Lovelace program, numerical ability is programmed in. In the production system, it emerges from the interaction of agents who don't have any. In the language of the students I interviewed, intelligence comes from having a number of "dumb agents" that can produce smart behavior when they work together.

Newell and Simon's production system and Samuel's checkers program can both be thought of as societies of agents that are restricted in a particular way. In Samuel's case, agents act only by voting. In the case of the productions, each agent has to wait its turn to act. Marvin Minsky and Seymour Papert have developed a society theory of emergent intelligence in which they lift these restrictions. They see agents with a wide diversity of roles, including the administration and the censoring of other agents.[10]

Papert uses this type of model to explain how children develop conservation of liquids, the knowledge that the quantity of a liquid doesn't change when you pour it from a short, stout glass into a tall, thin one. Young children consistently judge how much water there is by the water level, and so the higher level in the tall glass makes that water seem like "more."

Papert begins by describing three agents, each of which judges quantities in a different simpleminded way. The first judges quantity by height; anything that goes higher is "more." A second agent judges quantity by width, horizontal extent. And a third agent says that quantities are the same if they once were the same. This third agent, which Papert calls a "history" agent, "seems to sound like a conservationist child, but this is an illusion."[11] The history agent knows only how to say that things are the same as they used to be, even things that have in fact changed. When the water is poured from the stout to the thin glass in front of a preconservationist child, "each of the three agents makes its own 'decision' and clamors for it to be adopted." For the preconservationist child, the height agent's voice speaks the loudest, but this changes as the child moves on to the next stage.

Papert believes that the child moves on to the next stage when the height and width agents get into a new relationship: they start to neutralize each other when they give contradictory opinions. This happens because a new agent called a "geometry" agent acts as a referee. When the height and width agents both say either more or less, the geometry agent passes on their common message to the "top level" of the information system that is this child. But if they disagree, the authority of the geometry agent is undermined, in which case the history agent's voice is loudest and the child "has conservation." The geometry agent doesn't know what the programs under it are called or what they do or why. It knows only that before it can make a move it has to hear from them, pass on their message if both are the same, go back to sleep if they are not.

Papert's account makes the appearance of conservation in the child's mind "emergent" from the coming into being of the geometry agent. But this agent was not introduced "in order" to produce conservation. Papert believes that in its most primitive form it was there long before as an agent capable of recognizing disagreement when it saw it. The geometry agent came into being for reasons quite independent of the conservation problem: in Papert's model, conservation is a product, but not the planned product, of materials that happen to be there. This makes it attractive for thinking about building machine intelligence insofar as it suggests you can get intelligence without knowing exactly how to build it.

Some dismiss this as circular. When it requires that something new get done, it posits a new agent to do it. But members of the artificial intelligence culture, and others who have come to accept some of its ground rules, insist that another way of saying circular is to say recursive, self-referential. This computational aesthetic almost always sees self-reference as the solution rather than the problem. For Papert, circularity is a source of power: ". . . like recursive programs . . . the theory derives much of its power from a constructive use of 'circular logic.' "[12]

This kind of theory offers a bridge between the way people think about themselves and a way of thinking about machines. The "emergent-intelligence" idea feels psychologically plausible, and the theory's reliance on self-reference gives it an appealing intellectual tenor. Beyond this, the idea that people as well as programs have many agents within them can be related to our experience of inner conflict—the feeling of being of two, three, many minds.

But there is a certain unreality to this bridge-building between people and programs, since no society model close to the elaborateness of what Papert is talking about can be run on present-day computers which move through a problem one step at a time in strict sequence. They cannot "hear two voices" at once. In order for agents to fight it out in a computational society, a "multiprocessor" machine is needed, a computer that can execute many functions simultaneously. Today, parallel-processing computers with enough capacity are only a dream.[13] Many people speak of the day when there will be "real multiprocessor computers" in a way reminiscent of how others speak of "when the revolution comes" or "after the millennium." People who imagine a multiprocessing computer feel free to develop their own "society theories" and feel freer to describe its mind in terms of how they see their own.

Thinking of Yourself as a Machine

Mark is an MIT junior and a computer-science major. He has always been interested in logic and systems. When asked to think back to his childhood games, he does not talk about playing with other children. He recalls how he "sorted two thousand Lego pieces by color, size, and shape." He liked the feel of sorting the pieces, and he liked making the Legos into complex structures, "things that you would never expect to be able to make from Legos." Although Mark spends most of his time working with computers, he sees himself as a professional in training rather than as a computer hacker. He cares about his schoolwork, gets top grades, and "tries to keep things other than computers in my life." One of these is being "Dungeon Master" for one of MIT's many ongoing games of Dungeons and Dragons. His game has been going for a couple of years, and he is pretty sure it is the best game in the Boston area.

> The people who play my dungeon use it to express their personalities, and also to play out sides of their personalities that they hide in their everyday life. That's one of the things that is so fantastic about the game. But you have to make a great game for that to really happen. You have to hold them in your world, but you have to give them a lot of space to be themselves. It is a very complicated thing, an art.

Mark spends many hours a week preparing for the Sunday-afternoon meeting of his dungeon: "at least five hours of preparation for each hour of play. And sometimes we play for five hours. It's a responsibility. I take it very seriously. It's one of the most creative things I do."

Mark has strong relationships with the members of his dungeon. He is more able to involve himself with them than with people he meets outside of the structure of the game. The dungeon offers him a safe world built on a complex set of rules. Within it he can use his artistry to build social situations much as he built his Lego constructions. Dungeons and Dragons allows Mark to be with people in a way that is as comfortable for him as dealing with things. It is his solution to a familiar dilemma: he needs and yet fears personal intimacy. He has found a way of being a loner without being alone. One might say that for him Dungeons and Dragons becomes a social world structured like a machine.

There is another and more dramatic way in which Mark shows his preference for machinelike systems. He has elaborated a theory of psychology that leads him to see himself and everyone else as a machine. The theory, which he claims to be his own, is made up largely of ideas current at the Artificial Intelligence Laboratory at MIT. We see in Mark how these ideas are appropriated by someone who is not part of the AI world, but who is close enough to be a first link on the chain of these ideas moving out.[14]

Over the past year, he has built up a detailed picture of exactly how the Mark-machine works through a self-consciously introspective method. "Like Freud," he tells me. "I don't follow other people's theories. I just think about myself and make up my own—the way Freud came up with his theories and then looked around him and fit things in." When Freud "looked around" he "fit in" ideas from his scientific culture, from physics and biology. Mark's is a computer culture. He uses computer systems to think about all complex systems, especially to consider the complexity of his own mind.

Mark begins with the idea that the brain is a computer. "This does not mean that the structure of the brain resembles the architecture of any present-day computer system, but the brain can be modeled using components emulated by modern digital parts. At no time does any part of the brain function in a way that cannot be emulated in digital or analog logic." In *Tron*, the programs are complicated, psychological, and "motivated" beings. They do a lot of running around, planning, plotting, and fighting. In Mark's model the computational actors in the brain are simple. Each is a little computer with an even smaller program, and each "knows only one thought." Mark takes the "one thought" limitation seriously. "One processor might retain the visual impression of a computer cabinet. Another might retain the auditory memory of a keyboard being typed at. A third processor might maintain the visual image of a penguin."

In Mark's model, all of the processors have the same status: they are "observers" at a long trough. Everything that appears in the trough can be seen simultaneously by all the observers at every point along it. The trough with its observers is a multiprocessing computer system. Using computer jargon, Mark describes the trough as a "bus," a trunk line that puts actors in contact with each other. Their communication options are very limited. Each looks at the trough and when something appears that relates to what "he" knows, "all he can do is put his knowledge in."

> The trough plus observers make up the central processor of the brain. The consciousness of the brain is only a reflection of what is in the trough at a given time. Consciousness is a passive observer looking at the trough. It does not even see everything in the trough, but only those things which are very strong, either because they were dumped in the trough by more than one observer or they were in the trough for a very long time.

Mark goes on to elaborate this notion of consciousness as a passive observer:

> The processors, the observers, correspond to neurons in the brain. If a researcher on the edge of the brain could sample a number of the neurons and decode what impression was active in the brain at a given time, that researcher could be "seeing" what the brain was thinking. That researcher would be performing the function of the consciousness. Helpless to alter the chain reactions in the brain, this consciousness is rather carried along in the thought process, sensing whatever is the strongest impression at a given time. The consciousness is a helpless observer in the process we call thought. It is a byproduct of the local events between neurons.

Mark does not read philosophy. But his computer model of mind forces him to grapple with some of the oldest philosophical questions: the idea of free will and the question of a "self." Mark's theory has room for neither: the trough and the observers are a deterministic system. What we experience as consciousness is only a "helpless bystander" who gets the strongest signals filtered up to him. "Actions as well as thought," says Mark, "are determined by the cacophony of the processor voices."

There is no free will in Mark's system. The individual's feeling of conscious decision-making is an illusion, or rather an imposture: one of the processors, just as dumb as the others, has arrogated to itself the "seeming" role of consciousness. It has no power of decision, "it could just be a printer, attached to the computer. The strongest messages from the agents would just be printed out." Consciousness is epiphenomenon. Mark says that even if there were agents that could act with "free will," it would still be "them" and not "him" who would have it. In Mark's way of looking at things, there is no "me."

> You think you're making a decision, but are you really? For instance, when you have a creative idea, what happens? All of a sudden, you think of something. Right? Wrong. You didn't think of it. It just filtered through—the consciousness processor just sits there and watches this cacophony of other processors yelling onto the bus and skims off the top what he thinks is the most important thing, one thing at a time. A creative idea just means that one of the processors made a link between two un-associated things because he thought they were related.

In the course of my interview with Mark, creativity, individual responsibility, free will, and emotion were all being dissolved, simply grist for the little processors' mills. I asked Mark if he thought that "mind" is anything more than the feeling of having one. His answer was clear: "You have to stop talking about your mind as though it were thinking. It's not. It is just doing."

Mark takes the idea of agents and runs with it as far as it can take him—to the demolition of the idea of free will, to the demolition of the idea that he has a "responsible" self. And when I ask him about emotions, he says, "OK, let's model it on a piece of paper."*

Even though Mark makes it clear that the world must wait for tomorrow's multiprocessing technology to achieve the working intelligence that he has modeled, he turns his version of the "society theory" into something that uses today's computer parts. His bus and simple processors are doing things that Mark thinks he knows how to make computers do (like recognize an "image of a penguin"). And when something comes up that he doesn't know how to make a computer do, he can postpone the problem by claiming

---

* He makes a sketch that shows emotion corresponding to an overall change in the state of the processor system. He explains that each of the little processors might be able to run in five different states that could correspond to different thresholds for attracting their interest. The "angry" state might desensitize the processors involved in working out logical connections. They would still do their thing, but they do it far less insistently, while other processors, for example those concerned with self-defense, might be sensitized. "Being angry" is not the job of particular agents. It is something that affects the functioning of all of them.

that intelligence will emerge through the interaction of the processors.

Mark finesses problems that would require making his model more complicated or more specific. He talks about intelligence emerging from "two or three or four hundred stupid agents." But considering the highly specific skill that he gives to each of them ("one knows how to recognize a picture of a computer, another knows how to recognize a picture of a computer cabinet"), three or four hundred seem hopelessly few, even to allow the baby to recognize the objects seen from the crib, the playpen, and the high chair. Mark talks about his multiprocessor "model," but what he really has is a multiprocessor metaphor. Despite its generality and vagueness he finds his metaphor powerful. First, he can identify with it directly. He can put himself in the place of the agents. They look, they shout, they struggle, they assert their piece of smartness in the crowd. And it is powerful because Mark's daily experience with computers makes his theory seem real to him. Without the computer Mark's theory would feel to him to be nothing more than "wishy-washy hand-waving," the slur that engineers use to deride the psychological models of the precomputational past. He believes that in his model the problem of intelligence has been reduced to a technical one. Since he sees himself as a technical person, this makes him happy. It gives him a sense of being very powerful indeed. It means the appropriation of psychology by the engineers. What sweet revenge if the "ugly ones" turned out to be the gurus of the mind.

Mark's way of talking is exceptional only because his ideas are elaborated and he has such utter confidence in them. But the idea of thinking of the self as a set of computer programs is widespread among students I interviewed at Harvard and MIT who were familiar with large computer systems. Like Mark, they find that the complexity of these systems offers a way to think about their minds.

Elliot, an MIT biology major, calls his agents the "gallery of stupids" who "input into clusters of special-interest groups inside his brain." And then these special-interest groups fight it out and forward the result of their debates to his conscious self.

> Should I study, should I go to sleep? Most of the time, it comes to a debate. I am aware of the conflict, but the debate gets played

out by the agents. And it continues while I sleep. Sometimes I decide to go to sleep, and I awake with no other thought but to study. The agents have closed their debate. And the signals that are most powerfully coming up to consciousness are the study signals.

Ned, an MIT premedical student, also thinks of his mind as a multiprocessor:

Some of the agents are a little smarter than the others. The way an op-amp is smarter than a transistor, but that still makes them a long way off from having consciousness or free will. Consciousness and free will are illusions created by having many of the smarter processors and many of the dumber processors linked together by billions and billions of neural connections.

Children debating the metaphysical status of computer toys led me to say that computers bring philosophy into everyday life. What made the children's discussions philosophical was not their conclusions, but the structure of their argument, the effort to resolve intellectual tensions. But Elliot and Ned use the computer presence to bypass the mind/body problem: for them the reduction of mind to matter is unproblematic, as is the assertion that free will is an illusion. There is no tension, no need to examine their beliefs. We could say that Elliot and Ned are discussing free will and the mind/body problem, but their way of doing so suggests a qualification: sometimes computers bring philosophy into everyday life only to take it away again.

But if, for them, the mind/body problem does not exist, the reliance of their theories on the idea of multiple agents leaves them with a different problem: does the self exist. Has it been dissolved in the fragmentation of quarreling processors?

Challenging the "I"

A model of mind as multiprocessor leaves you with a "decentralized" self: there is no "me," no "I," no unitary actor. Mark expressed this when he admonished me not to talk about my mind as though "I" was thinking. "All that there is is a lot of processors—

not thinking, but each *doing* its little thing." Elliot put the same thought jokingly: "Nobody is home—just a lot of little bodies."

But theories that deny and "decenter" the "I" challenge most people's day-to-day experience of having one. The assumption that there is an "I" is solidly built into ordinary language, so much so that it is almost impossible to express "anti-ego" theory in language. From the moment that we begin to write or speak, we are trapped in formulations such as "I want," "I do," "I think." Even as we articulate a "decentered" theory there is a pull back away from it, sometimes consciously, sometimes not.

Of course, "mind as multiprocessor" is not the first challenge to the "I" that has encountered the resistance of everyday "common-sense" psychology and everyday speech. The idea of the Freudian unconscious is also incompatible with our belief that we "know what we want." We don't, says Freud. "Our" wishes are hidden from "us" by a complex process of censorship and repression. We are driven by forces quite outside our knowledge or control.

Freud divided the "I," but the theorists who followed him moved toward restoring it. They did so by focusing on the ego turned outward toward reality. They began to see it as capable of integrating the psyche. To them, the ego seemed almost a psychic hero as it battled off id and superego at the same time that it tried to cope with the demands of the everyday. Anna Freud wrote of its powerful artillery, the mechanisms of defense, which helped it in its struggles, and Heinz Hartmann argued that the ego had an aspect that was not tied up in the individual's neurotic conflicts: it had a "conflict-free zone." This "unhampered" aspect of the ego was free to act and choose, independent of constraints. It almost seemed the seat for a reborn notion of the will, the locus of moral responsibility. Intellectual historian Russell Jacoby, writing of psychoanalytic ego psychology's reborn, autonomous "I," described it as the "forgetting of psychoanalysis."[15]

A theory that had called the "self" into question now had a reassuring notion of the ego as a stable "objective" platform from which to view the world. A decentered theory had been recentered. A subversive theory had been normalized. Ego psychology is the version of the unconscious most acceptable to the conscious.

As a theory aspires to move from the world of high science to that of the popular culture, there is a natural pressure to cast it into more acceptable forms. Theories that call the self into question live in a natural state of tension. Although much of their power comes from the fact that they offer concrete images through which to express our sense of being constrained or driven by forces beyond our control, they are also under constant pressure from that other side of our experience—our sense of ourselves as selves. This was true of psychoanalysis. It is true of multiprocessor models of mind.

The Reconstituted Center

Mark begins with the flat assertion that there is no self, no conscious actor. "Consciousness is just a feeling of thinking." But even as he makes his case, the contradictions slip in. He claims that consciousness "just sits there and watches this cacophony of other processors yelling onto the bus and skims off the top what he thinks is the most important thing, one thing at a time." But who is "he"? Could this skimming really be done by a processor that is as "passive as a printer"?

Mark's description of how he developed his theory, his description of his introspective method, illustrates the contradiction in his position.

> My only way to know all this, my only way to tell, is by closing my eyes and trying to figure out what I'm doing at any given time. My theory was not developed as a "neat hack" to explain something, but rather "I thought this was going on" based on the small amount of evidence that filtered through to my consciousness of what's going on in my mind.

Here there is the reappearance of a "subject," something either smart enough to make up the theory itself or able to send ideas that come up "back down the line" for further processing. But according to Mark's theory as he states it rigorously, neither is possible: the consciousness processor is dumb ("just a printer") and, at most, has the power to "send back a bit or two." Mark brings in something like a self despite himself. He would like to accept the pure decentered theory, but this is not easy for anyone. We are pulled back to common-sense ways of thinking that are familiar since childhood and supported by language, ways of thinking that make us feel that there is a self, that the "I" is in control.

Throughout history, philosophers have challenged what seems obvious to common sense. Some have argued that we don't really know that objects exist or that other people have minds, or that there really are relations of cause and effect. The eighteenth-century Scottish philosopher David Hume held to this last view: events might follow one another, but we never have the right to say that one caused the other. While this might be easy enough in the philosophy seminar, in ordinary life we are obliged to act and talk as though we had the right to make such assumptions. And thus we understand Hume's *cri de coeur,* "Skepticism can be thought but not lived."

The decentered theory of mind, whether in psychoanalytic or computational terms, is as hard to live with as Hume's skepticism, and for similar reasons. The cornerstone of ordinary life is that there is an "I" that causes things to happen. A philosopher like Hume takes away the causality. Decentered psychologies take away the "I." Thus one sympathizes when Mark slips and reintroduces the "I." Others who have been caught up in multiprocessor models of mind take more deliberate actions to make them more "livable."

Some "recenter" their multiprocessor models by talking about one of the agents in the society of programs, usually one they call consciousness, as "not quite so dumb as the rest." When this happens, the other agents acquire a new role. Certain kinds of intelligence can still emerge from their interaction, but this intelligence is at the service of the smarter agent.

"I believe that the mind is just a computer," says Susan, "but one of the programs that runs on it gets to see the stuff that filters up from the dumber agents all of the time." This agent might start out "as dumb as all the rest," but, according to Susan, it has certain "pattern-recognition" properties and "it begins to grow in its ability to manipulate data." The dumb agents get to "talk to each other, but the consciousness agent has contact with the whole, and with the outside world, with all of the sensory systems." As a mediator, it develops new abilities. Freud's ego stood between id, superego, and impinging realities. Susan's theory replaces mind with a society of dumb agents, but her "pattern-recognizing" agent is an ego reborn.

According to Andy, one of the things that the "consciousness" agent knows how to do is to "flip off" its connection to the dumb processors. On the computer system he uses, this "interrupt" function is known as Control G. In Andy's model of how his mind works, "Control G-ing" allows whatever bits of information happen to be stored in the consciousness agent to undergo reprocessing, "like putting them in a new stew—they get to mix around, interact more than they usually get to do when they just filter up to consciousness." Compared to the trillions of bits of information in the system at any one time, the bits that are made available for reprocessing are rare. But there are enough of them to allow a sense of free will to emerge. "When the system shuts off you do whatever comes out of the new mix. And it is heavily influenced by messages from your body, whether you are sexually turned on, whether you are tired or feeling exhilarated—it is influenced by all of these chemical things, whereas the dumb processors are usually isolated from all of that." In Andy's picture, the "I" emerges from egoless cognition touched by the sensual and animal.

Some of the students I interviewed think of their minds as computer systems, but they reconstitute an "I" in a more direct way than Andy. It is not just a question of a decentered system being periodically interrupted to allow for a moment of conscious action and free will. They split the system, putting a multiprocessor in charge of all cognitive functions, but reserving the "emotional" things for another power. "I see my mind as two systems that have worked out a process of peaceful or maybe not very peaceful coexistence," says Arlene, a computer-science major who is studying acting in her spare time.

> There is a computational part, that's the part with the agents that somehow through their interaction have real intelligence come through. This part does my reasoning, my logic, my math homework, my ability to learn history. But then I have another system. It is built up from instincts. Evolution. My animal part. It is involved with love, feelings, relating to people. It can't control the computer part. But it lives with it. Sometimes fights with it. And this is the part that gives me the feeling of being me.

Amy is taking her first programming course. Three months into the course, she "discovered it. . . . I realized how good I am at programming" and she became taken with "all the possible analogies between my mind and a computer. I heard about Minsky saying 'the mind is a meat machine,' and I thought that must be right." Now six months into the course, she is modifying her ideas about what kind of machine the mind might be. She thinks that there must be a special agent that intervenes in the messages "that come up from the brain's central processing unit." What makes the agent special is that it has its own sources of information. These sources are not purely rational: "You could think of it as God or you could call it evolution—I think that one of the agents has been influenced by evolution." She says the special agent acts as a "buffer" for final decision-making. The messages from the CPU rest there for a moment.

> In general I see my mind in terms of continual processing by internal programs. But the weight given to the output of these programs can be influenced by emotion. And then when they come up to consciousness, they come up to a level where there is this other kind of agent—the special agent. The one in touch with my history and with evolution.

Theories that challenge the "I" need to be cast in more acceptable forms. We saw how in ego psychology psychoanalysis constructed a version of the unconscious acceptable to the conscious, one that brought psychoanalysis back into line with more traditional and reassuring models of mind. A similar process of normalization is at work in the case of machine models of mind. The students I interviewed used ideas about multiprocessing and emergence to describe how their minds worked. In their hands, the technical ideas that were developed within the artificial intelligence community were cast in nontechnical forms, such as the "agents at the trough." But then, there was a tension because these images of decentered minds do not sit easily with the sense of being a person and acting in the world.

The discrepancy between theory and the experience of the self shows itself in different ways. Mark does not recognize it at all, and it is visible only in the form of inconsistencies in his descriptions of his theory and himself. In the cases of the other students, Susan, Andy, Arlene, and Amy, the strain of fully accepting a computational model of the mind that dissolved the "I" was handled more explicitly. It led them to substantial modifications of the theory. They destroy the purity of the multiprocessing model; they are relying on ad-hoc fixes to soften the theory's fragmentation of self and destruction of the notion of free will.

Frank, a devout Catholic, an MIT junior in computer science who hopes someday to work in artificial intelligence research, does not rely on a "local fix" to make space for other commitments, in his case a commitment to the idea of soul. He thinks that the brain is hardware. He is not put off by Marvin Minsky's description of it as a "meat machine." The brain has some rudimentary capabilities —vision, sensory perception, instinctual reactions—and beyond this there are the familiar computational agents whose interaction could potentially lead to intelligence. But here is the point where Frank parts company with many of his friends. The complexity, the elegance, and the possibilities of the human mind machines are so great that souls come to inhabit them.

> If you go along with a straight computational model, the idea of free will has to get dumped along with the idea that there is a self. That is, to say the least, disturbing to those of us who would like to think that we control our own actions. But wait. We do indeed control our own actions, but only if we consider ourselves to be our souls and not just the collection of neurons that form our individual meat machines. The soul exists. It has free will. It is I.

Frank is skeptical about multiprocessor theories that refer to emergent intelligence as requiring a "critical mass" of agents around. What is needed is not critical mass, but just the right kind of "delicate programming." The combination of perfectly programmed agents is what could make intelligence emerge. There is an analogy with the early bath of organic molecules that gave birth to life. It had to be just the right molecules in the right proportions. The agents of the mind need to be delicately programmed, and this, says Frank, "is the province of the soul." It is the soul that infuses the meat machine with what makes us human. But the soul has only one way of acting, and that is through its interaction with our hardware: "It twiddles a few bits here and there." Frank sees the relationship of soul to brain as not quite a split between spirit and matter. It is more like the hacker to hardware.

> The brain is a computer and the soul sort of programs. I think of it as a combination of doing some rewiring and keying in some bytes, but there's another aspect to that, too. And that is

that the soul, in addition to having the console in front of it, there would also be a direct line through the human form. This part is hard to say. It bothers me. But the soul is not in a simple relationship to the body. It is like a programmer and a computer. There is a harmony. A fit. The soul is sometimes sitting there at the console, at least one part of it is, and part of it is in the machine. It is continuously aware of the state of the machine and can change any part of it at will at any time. So I like to see that as emerging, the soul is not just typing in, it's a spiritual thing which inhabits this computer.

Sometimes when Frank programs he gets the feeling that he is "part of the machine." He knows "it is only like a hallucination," but having had an experience of feeling both programmer and part of the thing being programmed makes it easier for him to imagine this kind of relationship for the soul in the machine. It certainly doesn't seem impossible, not even implausible. When experiences with the computer make him feel he is building something that is also a part of him, he considers them points of contact with the experience of the soul. In this sense, working with computers has become part of his religious practice.

I run into Frank while he is in the middle of an argument with a friend, Mike, who challenges Frank's attempt to reconcile his religious and computational views. If Frank really thinks that souls inhabit only human computers and that this is the natural order of things, isn't artificial intelligence with its project for a non-human mind a doomed project, perhaps even a new kind of blasphemy? Frank's answer surprises Mike and surprises me.

> Souls reside in people because they are special, there hasn't been anything else like them in the world. Nothing else with the computational capacity. But now what I feel is that we might, people might be at the stage where they can replicate their computational capabilities in their own manner. And then, if that happens, it may come to pass, if God allows it to happen, that after we connect together several trillion NAND gates or their equivalents, it may come to pass that some adventurous soul will decide to use that machine as its "receptacle" in this universe.*

---

* NAND gates are one of the elementary "logic components" for building digital circuits. They have a special property: they are universal. In principle, all other logic components can be built out of them.

Until the "soul invasion," the only intelligence we can create will be limited—a good chess program, a slightly better version of ELIZA, programs that operate by stock reasoning, mathematical analysis. But "it's all left-brain stuff—nothing that requires too much of the right brain. What it would not have are those things we cannot quantize. It would not have the ability to feel. It would be unemotional. It would certainly not be self-aware. These uniquely human functions are the province of the soul, and it is the soul that allows us to feel."

Frank has his heroes. Edwin Land, the inventor of instantaneous photography, the creator and until recently chairman of the board of the Polaroid Corporation, is one of them because he was something of a "hacker." In the enthusiasm of his identification with Land, Frank moves Land's alma mater from Harvard to closer to home. "He flunked out of MIT in order to devote himself to the things that MIT stands for. I like that." Marvin Minsky is another hero, and here the relationship is reverential. "The noblest of activities," says Frank, "is to create vessels for the wandering souls, but it can't just be a smart computer with a lot of knowledge stuffed in, a machine with a lot of showy programs and 'bells and whistles.'" The aesthetic has to be right. "You have to want to capture the essence of humanity. What I like about Minsky is that he seems to want to make a computer that a soul would want to live in."

Appropriable Models of Mind

The question of what it takes for people to feel a kinship with computational views of mind is important. When there is this sense of kinship, there is the groundwork for the development of a new psychological culture, a "computational culture" with new metaphors for thinking about the mind as program and information processor. This culture spreads through the diffusion of computational ideas much as the psychoanalytic culture spread through the diffusion of Freudian ideas.

When we interpret our dreams or comment on our friends' slips of the tongue, we are weaving psychoanalysis into the world of the everyday. What kind of processes make theories of mind capable of "moving out" from the scientific and academic environments in which they are born to a larger culture? What makes a science of mind "appropriable"?

Freudian theory suggests the beginnings of an answer, one way to think about its own appeal.

Consider Freud's theory of slips. It is a theory of why people make slips: we try to repress unacceptable wishes, but they break through all the same. By extension, I read it as a theory of why people like to think about slips: they allow us contact with these taboo wishes. And, most central to my concern, I read it as a theory of why people are attracted to Freudian ideas: Freudian interpretations offer us a way to come closer to aspects of ourselves, like sexuality and aggression, which we censor but at the same time want to be in contact with, the uncivilized that makes us human.

Computer models are seductive because they too put us in contact with issues that are both threatening and fascinating. The question here is not which theory, the psychoanalytic or the computational, is true, but rather how these very different ways of thinking about ourselves capture our imagination. Behind the popular acceptance of the Freudian theory was a nervous, often guilty preoccupation with the self as sexual; behind the widespread interest in computational interpretations is an equally nervous preoccupation with the self as a machine. Playing with psychoanalytic and computational theories allows us to play with aspects of our nature that we experience as taboo.

People are afraid to think of themselves as machines, that they are controlled, predictable, determined, just as they are afraid to think of themselves as "driven" by sexual or aggressive impulses. But in the end, even if fearful, people want to explore their sexual and aggressive dimensions; hence, the evocative power and popular appeal of psychoanalytic ideas. Similarly, although fearful, people want to find a way to think about what they experience as the machine aspect of their natures; this is at the heart of the computer's holding power. Thinking about the self as a machine includes the feeling of being "run" from the outside, out of control because in the control of something beyond the self. Exploring the parts of ourselves that we do not feel in control of is a way to begin to own them, a way to feel more whole.

Thus, the "Freudian" explanation for Freud's appeal explains part of the appeal of computational models: each model allows us to think about highly charged materials. Another element that makes many computational models appealing is more dependent on their form than on their content. "Appropriable" theories of mind, ideas that move out into the culture at large, tend to be those in which we can become "actively" involved. They tend to be theories that we can "play with."

In the case of psychoanalysis, what we play with are "Freudian objects" such as dreams, slips, and jokes. We become used to looking for them and manipulating them, both seriously and playfully. And as we do so, psychoanalytic theory, or at least the idea that there is an unconscious, starts to feel "natural." In the case of computational models of mind, there are what I call "carrier objects" that encompass both the physical computer and ideas that grow out of programming.

Recall, for example, what is at work to help people appropriate Donald Norman's computational model of slips and, through it, the idea of mind as computer.[16] According to the model, people, like complex computer programs, become momentarily derailed and make slips. And when people "slip" it doesn't reflect sexual fantasies or forbidden desires. It simply reveals information overload and the mechanisms of computation.

You pour ketchup into your coffee instead of cream. Norman lets you imagine a computer in your place and think of its workings as a process involving numerous subprograms. One program is called up to locate the cream, another to locate the coffee, another to get a fix on the location of the hand, another to get it going in the right direction, and others to check that it is on the right path, to verify that the position of hand, creamer, cup have not changed, and so on. In this buzz of activity it is hardly surprising that one of these programs might go wrong. At a given moment, the program that verifies that the position of X has not changed might "mistakenly" take X to be ketchup instead of cream, because another program on which it depends is still registering ketchup as "the object of greatest salience," a morsel of information left over from a previous phase of the meal during which ketchup was appropriately being poured on a cheeseburger. Once you have identified with the computer you cannot fail to identify with the error, since each of us knows that we make many more when "we" are consciously involved in a scenario as complex as this one. We are able to identify with the programs and so become sympathetic to their confusion.

Norman's slips theory is "appropriable" because its description of how a computer works sounds so much like a confused person that people identify with the computer to the point of believing that it makes slips for the same reason they do. From here it is a small step to feeling that we make slips because we are computers and that we are computers because of the way we make slips.

As a formal, logical argument this is circular. But as a description of how people adopt a point of view, of how they weave it into their intuitions, it is quite straightforward. Norman's theory found its way out of academic journals—a version of it appeared in *Psychology Today* and then in *Reader's Digest*—and was widely read. People easily imagine themselves in the role of the procedures, and acting out these roles feels enough like Norman's theory to give the sense of understanding it. One may forget the details of the theory, but it offers an experience of "playing computer" and of feeling comfortable in the role that has a longer-lasting effect. The experience breaks down resistance to seeing mind as machine.

The computational theory of slips is the kind of theory that passes easily into the general culture. It is able to take a nontechnical form, people can imagine themselves "in the theory," it provides a handle to think about the everyday, and it touches on emotionally charged concerns. Mark's theory of the dumb multiprocessing agents had all of these qualities. Like Norman's, it anthropomorphized machine processes so that it was easy to identify with them, one could put oneself in the place of agents around the trough, it was a way to think about fragmented identity, a problematic aspect of the self. Such experiences are the stuff upon which a computer culture is built.

Mark's computational theory of psychology is personal. He has given little thought to where it stands in relation to other theories. But a growing culture needs something more. It needs to be conscious of itself as a culture, it needs symbols, it needs heroes, it needs antiheroes. Such elements exist in the worlds of computer subcultures. The hackers had LISP as symbol of the true, the beautiful, and the good; IBM's FORTRAN was their symbol of degeneracy. One sure sign of the movement of the computer culture into the larger world is the appearance of a literature that carries these out to a larger public.

Douglas Hofstadter's 1978 *Gödel, Escher, Bach: An Eternal Golden Braid* is an example of that literature. It affirms computation as a culture—along with its symbols, its language, its humor, its ways of breaking down resistance to the idea of mind as machine. Hofstadter begins his book with a declaration of purpose:

> Computers by their very nature are the most inflexible, desireless, rule-following of beasts. Fast though they may be, they are nonetheless the epitome of unconsciousness. How, then, can intelligent behavior be programmed? Isn't this the most blatant of contradictions in terms? One of the major theses of this book is to urge each reader to confront the apparent contradiction head on, to savor it, to turn it over, to take it apart, to wallow in it, so that in the end the reader might emerge with new insights into the seemingly unbreachable gulf between the formal and the informal, the animate and the inanimate, the flexible and the inflexible.[17]

Hofstadter goes about this by providing puzzles, thought experiments, riddles, and dialogues, many of them dedicated to offering a way to address a stumbling block to the idea that the mind is a computer: "If machines are perfect and I am human, how can my mind be a computer?" The answer: the perfect machine is by its nature imperfect.

The mathematician and the logician know this idea in the technical form of Gödel's theorem. After a period in the late nineteenth and early twentieth centuries when a proliferation of increasingly powerful formal methods created hopes of a universal mathematics that could solve all mathematical problems, Kurt Gödel produced a dramatic theorem that scuttled once and for all any hopes that there could be such a thing.[18] In principle, says Gödel, every formal system is limited. Any mathematics that would be sufficiently powerful to seem to promise completeness, universality, would necessarily be incomplete: it would be possible to ask it questions that could not be answered using its methods. This idea that a system is incomplete because it is strong goes against common sense.

Gödel's thoroughly mathematical proof that a formal system (this could be a machine) is vulnerable because strong had been accessible only to a mathematical elite. Hofstadter brings it to a larger circle. His strategies are numerous. Most powerful among them is a technique he borrows from Lewis Carroll: dialogues between characters that Carroll himself used, for example Achilles and the Tortoise, to which Hofstadter adds others as necessary, among these the Crab, a personage who is the subject of an infinitely repeating drawing by Escher.

In my favorite dialogue, Achilles is talking to the Tortoise about whether it is possible to have a perfect phonograph.[19] The answer turns out to be no. And the way of discussing the possibilities for phonograph perfection, like those for mathematical perfection and machine perfection, begins with the idea of self-reference.

A crystal glass can be shattered by a singer who hits exactly the right note. By extension, for any piece of matter, including a phonograph, there is a pitch that will shatter it. If a record whose "song" contains this pitch is played on the phonograph, the machine will "self destruct." Thus any phonograph must be imperfect in one of two ways. It can be imperfect because it is unable to play notes with enough fidelity to reproduce the destructive tone, in which case it does not destroy itself, but is obviously imperfect, imperfect through weakness. Or it can be imperfect through strength, in which case it is able to reproduce notes in full fidelity, and the record with that "certain note" will shatter it to pieces.

The paradox at the heart of Gödel's theorem is this: if the formal system is really powerful there will be a question that can be posed within it which it cannot answer. If the phonograph is really perfect, it will be able to reproduce the sound that would shatter it to pieces. And, indeed, the Tortoise has been driving his friend the Crab to distraction by shattering an increasingly expensive series of phonographs with specially designed records that he calls "Music to Break Phonographs By."

"Music to Break Phonographs By," like the proof of Gödel's theorem, plays on the idea of self-reference.* In the history of mathematics, self-reference has been controversial. Bertrand Russell and Alfred North Whitehead, among many other logicians,

---

* Gödel wanted to prove that arithmetic is "incomplete." The problem is to find a statement about numbers that cannot be proved or disproved. Gödel found one by drawing on the famous paradox of self-reference. If a proposition P says that the proposition P is false, by an argument known since the time of the Greeks such a proposition can be neither true nor false. Assume P is true. P asserts its own falsity. So, if true, it must be false. Assume it is false. It says it is false, so it must be true. Gödel found an arithmetical equivalent of this paradox. He assigned code numbers to propositions in such a way that a certain proposition P says that the proposition whose code number is n cannot be proved. And when we look up the code we find that n is the code number for the proposition P itself. The proposition P thus declares itself to be unprovable. Proving it would be absurd, disproving it equally so.

had placed a ban on it: propositions that referred to themselves (like the statement "This statement is false") were declared meaningless. But Gödel found ways of doing indirectly something akin to what had been outlawed, smuggling enough self-reference back into arithmetic to show that there is at least one proposition in it that cannot be proven true or proven false.

Gödel made a breach in the wall erected by logicians against self-reference, but it remained small because Gödel's propositions seemed esoteric. The computer presence enlarged the breach because, in programming, self-reference is an everyday matter of the greatest practical use, a powerful tool for building complex programs. Within the AI and hacker community, Gödel's theorem became a symbol that "we," the computer culture, had won a battle against "them," the logicians. Gödel's "hack" had broken the system. Hofstadter dramatized the struggle and put his readers in a position to feel participant in the triumph of a new intellectual aesthetic. The mighty had fallen. Russell and Whitehead had been sacrificed on the altar of computational logic.

The growing computer culture draws its strength from awareness of its roots and from aggressive assertion of continuity with the culture into which it is penetrating. By placing self-reference at the center of his intellectual world Hofstadter is able to recruit Bach and Escher into the computer culture. Bach (who used it in his endlessly rising canons) and Escher (who used it in his endlessly rising staircases) are made into cultural heroes just as Russell and Whitehead are made into cultural enemies. After over seven hundred pages of *Gödel, Escher, Bach*, Hofstadter's readers have little sympathy with the traditional logicians, not just because they wanted to ban paradox, but because they belonged to an intellectual culture that saw in paradox problems rather than power. Hofstadter succeeds in getting his readers to sense themselves as part of a new culture, a computer culture, strong enough to shrug off the culture of Russell, Whitehead, and traditional philosophy and logic.

Hofstadter began *Gödel, Escher, Bach* with a declaration of purpose: to bridge the gap between the mental and the mechanical. Through the phonograph story—if you are sufficiently strong you are by definition vulnerable and incomplete—and his many other examples of what he calls "strange loops," Hofstadter gives people a language for talking about the questions that come up when we consider whether we are machines. "If we are machines, are we perfect?" asks Frank, the student who put the soul into the machine. No, he comes back saying, "if we are the most powerful kind of machines, the kind that God would create," we are limited, vulnerable, weak. "You see, Professor Turkle, what Achilles and the Tortoise and the Crab are saying is that if we are machines, we are human."

CHAPTER 9

The Human Spirit in a Computer Culture

Ours has been called a culture of narcissism.[1] The label is apt but can be misleading. It reads colloquially as selfishness and self-absorption. But these images do not capture the anxiety behind our search for mirrors. We are insecure in our understanding of ourselves, and this insecurity breeds a new preoccupation with the question of who we are. We search for ways to see ourselves. The computer is a new mirror, the first psychological machine. Beyond its nature as an analytical engine lies its second nature as an evocative object.

I have described groups of people chosen for the intensity of their involvement with computers, where the computer's second nature—as reflective medium and as philosophical provocateur—is writ plain. Some of them were involved with the computer professionally, but many were not. They came to the computer on their own, or perhaps it is better to say that the computer came to them. For what is new in the 1980s is that intense involvement with computers, largely confined to computer subcultures when I began my study in 1976, has become a popular phenomenon. Today, when computer companies project their sales of personal computers, they think in tens of millions. This means that for middle-class Americans, and soon for their counterparts in much of the world, if you don't have a computer at home you have a friend or colleague or neighbor who does. We are living in a culture that invites us all to interact with computers in ways that permit us to become intimate with their second nature. And as this happens, the relationships between people and machines that we have seen in the computer subcultures become harbingers of new tensions and the search for new resolutions that will mark our culture as a whole in the almost immediate future.

For example, the computer offers hackers something for which many of us are hungry. Hysteria, its roots in sexual repression, was the neurosis of Freud's time. Today we suffer not less but differently. Terrified of being alone, yet afraid of intimacy, we experience widespread feelings of emptiness, of disconnection, of the unreality of self. And here the computer, a companion without emotional demands, offers a compromise. You can be a loner, but never alone. You can interact, but need never feel vulnerable to another person.

The hackers illustrate another facet of our emerging relationships with machines. Their response to the computer is artistic, even romantic. They want their programs to be beautiful and elegant expressions of their uniqueness and genius. They recognize one another not because they belong to the same "profession," but because they share an urgency to create in their medium. They relate to one another not just as technical experts, but as creative artists. The Romantics wanted to escape rationalist egoism by becoming one with nature. The hackers find soul in the machine—they lose themselves in the idea of mind building mind and in the sense of merging their minds with a universal system. When nineteenth-century Romantics looked for an alternative to the mechanism and competition of society, they looked to a perfect society of two, "perfect friendship," or "perfect love." This desire for fusion has its echo today, although in a new and troubling form. Instead of a quest for an idealized person, now there is the computer as a second self.

The images of the computer offering a new expressive medium and of the computer offering a "schizoid compromise" between loneliness and fear of intimacy are emblematic of the encounter between the machine and our emotional lives. Along with this encounter comes another: between computers and our philosophical lives, in particular our thinking about human nature. Because they stand on the line between mind and not-mind, between life and not-life, computers excite reflection about the nature of mind and the nature of life. They provoke us to think about who we are.

They challenge our ideas about what it is to be human, to think and feel. They present us with more than a challenge. They present us with an affront, because they hold up a new mirror in which mind is reflected as machine.

The effect is subversive.[2] It calls into question our ways of thinking about ourselves: most dramatically, if mind is machine, who is the actor? Where is responsibility, spirit, soul? There is a new disorder. *Newsweek* magazine runs a cover story on the mind and begins it with an old joke, one that expresses a long-standing and reassuring dualism:

> "What's the matter?"
> "Never mind."
> "What is mind?"
> "No matter."[3]

By the end of the article that describes advances in brain chemistry and in artificial intelligence, *Newsweek* reports that the age of such reassurances is over: its reporters have researched the territory and find that neuroscience and silicon chips are on their way to providing technical solutions to the mystery of mind. We are chemistry and program. *Newsweek*'s tone is matter-of-fact, but for the people I have studied things are not that simple. Even those who accept the idea that as humans they are computers find ways to think of themselves as something more as well.

When Copernicus ousted earth and its travelers from their illusion of a central place in the universe, his assertion went beyond physics: it called into question our privileged relationship to God. It was as if the status of humankind had been reduced—from the center of creation to an inhabitant of a speck of dust in the vastness of space. It was unthinkable, and yet, with time, the unthinkable becomes taken for granted. This is not just because people get used to the new idea, or get tired of fighting against it. Something else happens as well. What happens is that ways are found to reassert a centered view of the human within the new context.

One such way has been described by the scientist and philosopher Michael Polanyi. Since Copernicus writers have exhorted us to abandon "sentimental egoism and see ourselves objectively in the true perspective of time and space," but Polanyi is skeptical.

"No one—scientists included—looks at the universe this way whatever lip service is given to objectivity. Nor should this surprise us. For, as human beings, we must inevitably see the universe from a center lying within ourselves . . ."[4] For Polanyi, this center is the human mind. We recenter ourselves as thinkers, at the intellectual if not the physical center of the universe.

This pattern of challenge and reassertion has been repeated time and time again. A first reaction to the Darwinian idea that humans are descended from animals was moral repulsion. Again, we were taken from a privileged position and turned into something that, this time, seemed not so much insignificant as ignoble. But here too, after the shock comes a fresh reassertion of the uniqueness of humanity: we may be animals, kin to the others, but we are the crown of the evolutionary process.

The computational model of mind is yet another blow to our sense of centrality. Copernicus and Darwin took away our special role as the centerpiece of creation, but we could still think of ourselves as the center of ourselves. Now the computer culture, like the psychoanalytic culture before it, threatens the very idea of "self." Freud's notion of the unconscious challenges thinking about personal responsibility and life decisions. Psychoanalysis asks us to confront the fact that our choices—even and especially our most consequential choices about love and work, career and spouse—are repetitions of a primitive scenario, are determined by our earliest experiences. But the Freudian unconscious has a certain abstract quality. It allows people to slide easily between "I am my unconscious" and the more acceptable "I am influenced by my unconscious."

The theorists who followed Freud reasserted an active autonomous ego, making it easier for psychoanalysis to enter the general culture as a triumph of reason over the uncivilized within each of us. The computer's threat to the "I" is in many ways similar, but far more relentless. The computer takes up where psychoanalysis left off. It takes the idea of a decentered self and makes it more concrete by modeling mind as a multiprocessing machine. Where the Freudian vision seemed speculative to some, literary to others, the computational model arrives with the authoritative voice of science behind it—and with the prospect that someday there will be a thinking machine whose existence will taunt us to say how we are other than it.

In response, a quest has already begun for ways to hold on to an understanding of human mind as other than machine.

Joseph Weizenbaum's controversial book *Computer Power and Human Reason* argued that the computer—linear, logical, and rule-governed—encourages this kind of thinking in us and magnifies the place of instrumental reason in our culture.[5] Weizenbaum fears that the psychological theories that might be derived from artificial intelligence would lead to a flattened, mechanical view of human nature.

Weizenbaum's response is to value as most human what is most different from the computer. As emblematic of the human essence, he chooses what the computer cannot do, the things "we know but cannot tell": the glance that a mother and a father wordlessly share as they stand over the bed of their sleeping child.

Weizenbaum is critical of some aspects of the culture of artificial intelligence. But his idea that what is essentially human is the uncodable is shared by many who are far more sympathetic to AI theories of mind. It is also expressed by many people without theoretical interests who when they meet the psychological machine define the human in opposition to it.

Psychoanalysis has taught us that resistance to a theory is part of its cultural impact. Resistance to the idea of the unconscious and the irrational leads to an alternative view of people as essentially logical beings. Resistance to a computational model of people as programmed information systems leads to a view that what is essential in the human is what is ineffable, uncapturable by language or formalism. It is as if we need to strike a balance. When we use information-processing models to explain larger and larger slices of our behavior, we seem impelled to isolate as our "core" something we can think of as beyond information. We met this idea in Weizenbaum's assertion that the human is the uncodable, and in a more elaborated form in John Searle's argument that no matter how perfect, a computer simulation of thought is not thought, because the computer will simply be following rules that "it" does not understand.[6]

When people give allegiance to Searle's argument, when they say that he has done "something important" by "taking on" artificial intelligence, they are doing more than assenting to his specific arguments. They are using Searle to help themselves reassert a set of deeply felt commitments: a commitment to a "centered" self, to the "real" as distinct from any simulation, to the human as unique.

Arguments about human uniqueness based on what computers can't do leave us vulnerable to technical progress and what clever engineers might come up with. Searle separates the issues. No matter what a computer can do, human thought is something else. For Searle, thought is the product of our specific biology, the product of a human brain.

When Searle talks about biology he means neurons and the chemistry of the synapse. Most people have a more personal view of what it means to be "biological." What makes us biological is our life cycle: we are born, we are nurtured by parents, we grow, we develop sexually, we become parents in our turn, we die. This cycle is what gives meaning to our lives. It brings us the knowledge that comes from understanding loss—from knowing that those we love will die and so will we. A being that is not born of a mother, that does not feel the vulnerability of childhood, a being that does not know sexuality or anticipate death, this being is alien. We may be machines, but it is our mortality that impels us to search for transcendence—in religion, history, art, the relationships in which we hope to live on.

There is something familiar in all of these reassertions of an "essentially human." The response is romantic. It is provoked by the new technology, the ultimate embodiment of universal logic, just as the nineteenth-century Romantic movement was provoked by the triumph of science and the rule of reason. As a self-conscious response to Enlightenment rationalism, what Romanticism longed for was clear: feelings, the "law of the heart."[7]

So, too, in the presence of the computer, people's thoughts turn to their feelings. As the children tell it, we are distinguished from the machines by love and affection, by spiritual urges and sensual ones, by the excitement that attaches to heroism, and by the warmth and familiarity of domesticity. The twelve-year-old programmer David summed up these sentiments: "When there are computers who are just as smart as people, the computers will do a lot of the jobs, but there will still be things for the people to do. They will run the restaurants, taste the food, and they will be the ones who will love each other, have families and love each other. I guess they'll still be the ones who go to church." Adults who work closely with computers often end up with similar images. In the style of David, some find it sufficient to say that machines are reason and people are sensuality and emotion. But most find it necessary to take greater account of human reason and to seek more nuanced formulations. Then the dichotomy that David used to separate computers and people becomes a way to separate the elements of what is human. One student speaks of his "technology self" and his "feelings self," another of her "machine part" and her "animal part."

In Greek times, the experience of the divided human was captured in Plato's image of a driver of two horses, white and black, reason and passion. The ride was uneven. With and without the computer, people have found ways to describe this uneven ride. They use different languages: there are reason and passion, logic and emotion, ego and id. The computer makes a new contribution. Along with a new urgency, it provides a new discourse for describing the divided self. On one side is placed what is simulable; on the other, that which cannot be simulated. People who say they are perfectly comfortable with the idea of mind as machine assent to the idea that simulated thinking is thinking, but often cannot bring themselves to propose further that simulated feeling is feeling.

The new romantic reaction is not made by people who reject the computer in the way that the nineteenth-century Romantics rejected science. The reassertions of feeling and of the "ineffable" that I speak of here come from people who have and accept the technology, not by those who are fleeing from it.

In this it is different from the romanticism of the 1960s, when people set themselves in opposition to technology and rationalism. Sixties values—simplicity, self-expression, and the authenticity of pure emotion—were asserted in a global protest against cold science. Mysticism and Eastern religion were arms against instrumental reason. The computer presence gives new legitimacy to a set of values that many people did not find comfortable as long as they were associated with the East and opposed to science and reason.

Cultures are fluid, conflictual, and contradictory. The computer gives support to those who see human psychology in mechanistic terms, and also, in a paradox that is increasingly important for our culture, it is a point of reference for those who place greatest value not on rationality but on affect. We cede to the computer the power of reason, but at the same time, in defense, our sense of identity becomes increasingly focused on the soul and the spirit in the human machine.

Before the computer, the animals, mortal though not sentient, seemed our nearest neighbors in the known universe. Computers, with their interactivity, their psychology, with whatever fragments of intelligence they have, now bid for this place. We met children who seemed ready to give it to them. These children defined themselves not with respect to their differences from animals, but by how they differ from computers. Where we once were rational animals, now we are feeling computers, emotional machines. But we have no way to really put these terms together. The hard-to-live-with, self-contradictory notion of the emotional machine captures the fact that what we live now is a new and deeply felt tension.

As they grow up, will children of the computer culture follow Searle back around his circle, reasserting the primacy of biology? Will they remain where we saw them, split between a mechanical vision of intelligence and a mystical vision of pure emotion? More probably, the challenge of the computer will inspire them to invent new hybrid self-images, built up out of the materials of animal, mind, and machine.

One thing is certain: the riddle of mind, long a topic for philosophers, has taken on new urgency. Under pressure from the computer, the question of mind in relation to machine is becoming a central cultural preoccupation. It is becoming for us what sex was to the Victorians—threat and obsession, taboo and fascination.

On Method:
A Sociology of Sciences of Mind

The style of inquiry of this work is ethnographic. Like the anthropologist who lives in an isolated village in a far-off place to get to know its inhabitants, their ways of seeing and doing things, their myths and rituals, their economy and artifacts, I lived within worlds new to me, tried to understand what they are about, and tried to write about my understandings so that the worlds I studied could come alive for others.

This kind of enterprise stands in an ambiguous relationship to science and art. The research is systematic: one informant's account of how something is done is checked and rechecked against the accounts of others; careful note is taken of what people do so that this can be compared with what they say they do. But at the same time, the very process of research is interpretive. In writing about ethnography, Clifford Geertz has stressed this fundamental fact: ". . . what we call our data are really our own constructions of other people's constructions of what they and their compatriots are up to. . . . Right down at the factual base, the hard rock, insofar as there is any, of the whole enterprise, we are already explicating; and worse, explicating explications. Winks upon winks upon winks."[1]

I began this work shortly after joining the faculty of the Massachusetts Institute of Technology. I came to the job with training and experience as both a sociologist and a clinical psychologist. I considered myself a member of the "culture" of humanists; I had never touched a computer. Thus, this book is a product of something that anthropologists call *dépaysement*, which refers to the dislocation and change of perspective that makes being a stranger in a foreign place both difficult and exciting.

Soon after I arrived at MIT, an incident occurred which captures my shock of recognition that I was in a different world. In the morning I had worked with a patient in psychotherapy who, for many months, had been using the image of "being a machine" to express his feelings of depersonalization, emptiness, and despair. That evening I went to a party for new MIT faculty. I met a young woman, a computer-science major and one of my students, who was listening to a heated conversation about whether machines could ever think. She was growing impatient: "I don't see what the problem is—I'm a machine and I think." She believed herself to be a "collection of programs," which operated independently and produced "her" through their interaction. My patient of the morning was unhappy, unable to form close relationships. In his culture, describing oneself as a machine was an expression of pain. The cheerful young woman at the party was from a different culture. She differed from the young man (and from me) in the meaning she ascribed to the language of machines: for my patient it was charged with negative associations; for her it was an unproblematic "fact of science." She differed from me in another way as well: where I would have used a language drawn from psychoanalytic thought to talk about my problems and my decision-making, she used metaphors drawn from programming, cybernetics, and information processing.

Social scientists use many different terms to describe the ideas and assumptions people use to organize their experience of the world and of themselves: *Zeitgeist,* world view, frame, world-taken-for-granted. Such phrases are the standard language of the sociology of knowledge. In one of its major traditions, inspired in large measure by European phenomenology, reality is not "out there" to be perceived. Rather, it is "socially constructed"—built by individuals in cultures.[2] I came to MIT and to my conversation with this young woman with an interest in this process of construction of meanings and with a special interest in ideas that provide ways of thinking about the self—particularly in how "sciences of mind" influence the general culture.

When I met the young woman at the party in 1977 I was finishing a book that dealt with a sociology of a particular "science of mind," psychoanalysis. *Psychoanalytic Politics* is a study of how France, a country traditionally resistant to psychoanalytic ideas, had been swept by an "infatuation with Freud" in the late 1960s.[3] The movement began in the hothouse climate of the Parisian intelligentsia, and this was where I first studied it. But the story went far beyond intellectuals and their fickle taste. There was a fit between a psychoanalytic way of thinking and a social demand. Psychoanalytic language spread into the rhetoric of political parties, into training programs for schoolteachers, into advice-to-the-lovelorn columns. I became fascinated with how people were picking up and trying on this new language for thinking about the self. I had gone to France to study the psychoanalytic community and how it had "rein vented" Freud for the French taste, but I was there at a time when it was possible to watch a psychoanalytic community become a "psychoanalytic culture."

My experiences at MIT impressed me with the fact that something analogous to the development of a psychoanalytic culture was going on in the worlds around computation. At MIT I heard computational metaphors used to think about politics, education, social process, and, most central to the analogy with psychoanalysis, about the self. MIT is, of course, a special kind of environment—a setting deeply immersed in the scientific state of the art. What I was hearing there could only be a first step in the cultural assimilation of a new way of thinking. But it soon became clear that computational ideas, like psychoanalytic ideas, had the power to move beyond specialized settings. Early in my study the point was made dramatically by the public reaction to Douglas Hofstadter's *Gödel, Escher, Bach*. Hofstadter took a computational idea, the idea of recursion, and used it as a way to think about mind, music, literature, biology, epistemology—even as a way to think about God. The idea of recursion which had lived an isolated life in the worlds of scientists and mathematicians entered the wider culture. It had a public resonance. Early in my study I interviewed many readers of *Gödel, Escher, Bach* for whom it was an introduction to computational ideas. *Gödel, Escher, Bach* has a special place in the evolution of my work because reactions to the book were among my first evidence that people who are not particularly involved with computers are drawn to using computational ideas for thinking about themselves.

In my work in France on psychoanalytic culture, my concerns had turned to the question of how to do an ethnographic study of a culture of self-reflection, an ethnography of a science of mind. The essential question in such work is how ideas developed in the world of "high science" are "appropriated" by the culture at large. In the case of psychoanalysis, how do Freudian ideas "move out" to touch the lives of people who have never visited a psychoanalyst, people who are not even particularly interested in psychoanalysis as a theory? In the study of the nascent computer culture, the essential question was the same: how were computational ideas moving out into everyday life?

Investigating this kind of question—for psychoanalytic ideas as for computational ones—calls for a genre of field research with some special qualities.

First and foremost, the research requires particularly close attention to the experience of individuals. Psychoanalytic ideas enter into people's sense of moral responsibility, their sense of the meaning and consequence of their actions. Similarly, in the case of computation, the idea of "mind as program" enters into people's sense of who is the actor when they act. Both sciences provide models of mind which have something to say about the degree to which we are determined by outside forces.[4] They both influence how people think about their frustrations and disappointments, their relationships with their families and with their work. Thus, my style of interviewing had to borrow from the clinical interview because understanding the roles of psychoanalysis and of computation in a person's life demands a detailed and empathic understanding of that person. Only this kind of close understanding makes it possible to appreciate how particular ideas about the self fit into individual lives, serving particular social and psychological needs. In every case, these needs influence how ideas are picked up and how they are reshaped.

This kind of study of the role of ideas is not a survey of *opinion* on psychoanalysis or computation. I am interested in thoughts and feelings that are often not articulated as stable opinions or preferences. Indeed, they are often not articulated at all, but manifest themselves in the expression of ideas through action. My desire to understand ideas that are reflexive—those which the individual uses to think and work through his or her own situation—also influenced my choice of a clinical interviewing style.

And yet, my focus is not individual psychology. From hundreds of cases, patterns emerge which support generalizations about the cultural implications of the presence of psychoanalytic and computational ideas in everyday life. In the case study of psychoanalysis in France in the late 1960s and early 1970s, it was apparent that psychoanalytic ideas took on great urgency as a way of thinking through a new relationship between the personal and the political. Similar themes emerged in the study of computation: in thinking about politics and education, people use metaphors borrowed from their experiences with computers. But these political themes were not the most widespread or salient. In the case of computation in the late 1970s and early 1980s in America, I found the emphasis more solidly rooted in the personal—the personal development of a metaphysics, of a sense of personal mastery, and the development of a personal language for thinking about identity.

Ideas about mind, like ideas about anything else, are not transported directly from the professionals who develop them to the waiting individual. These ideas are mediated by family, friends, business acquaintances, and most significantly, by the social groups to which an individual belongs. In the terms of this study, ideas about mind are mediated by culture, in a more technical sense, by participation in subcultures. Thus, in my study of both psychoanalysis and computation, I pay special attention to the rule of subcultures. In the case of psychoanalysis, I was interested in how ideas were taken up by the worlds of medicine, political activism, and the university. These subcultures appropriated psychoanalytic ideas selectively and reinterpreted them in the process of presenting them to their members. In the case of computation, I also looked at different subcultures—at personal computer owners, at hackers, and at the world of artificial intelligence—and found similar processes at work. The meanings of computation for the individual are shaped by the group which emphasizes and mythologizes certain modes of relating to the computer (for example, the hacker and the idea of "winning," the hobbyist and the idea of "transparency").

Thus, understanding the relationship between people and psychoanalytic or computational ideas requires understanding the subcultures of which they are participants. But my reporting of what I found in the investigation of these subcultures has a particular focus: what ethnographers traditionally refer to as "cosmology," the knowledge and belief systems that contribute to the coherency of the group.

For example, in my chapter on hackers, I refer to this community's social setting, its rites of initiation, its economic niche, but my primary concern is with how its relationship with an artifact provides a metaphor for what is important in life as this is expressed in the group's mythology and dominant ideas about human relationships. The same priorities hold in my treatment of other computer subcultures. For example, what interests me in the artificial intelligence community is not its history and social organization as a profession, but how the idea of program and of "mind building mind" influences what a group of people come to see as most important about the human.

The parallels in the study of psychoanalytic and computational culture are numerous, but in the case of computation there is also something new, something that provided a handle for pursuing my questions in a new way. The social study of computation is the study of a nascent culture that has an object as a central actor. The computer culture is carried not only by ideas, not only by the writings of its theorists, not only by articles in magazines or programs on television, but by a machine that people bring into their homes, give to their children, use to play games, to write letters, and to help them in the management of time and money.

This means that in this book, the focus is on people's relationships with an object and on how these relationships themselves become building blocks of culture.

Of course, among technologies, the computer is not alone in its ability to evoke strong feelings, carry personal meanings, and create a rich, expressive environment for the individual. People develop intense and complex relationships with cars, motorbikes, pinball machines, stereos, and ham radios. And subcultures have formed around all these technologies. If computers are an exception to the general rule that there is a subjective side to people's relationships with technology, it is insofar as they raise this commonly known phenomenon to a higher power, and give it new form as well as new degree.

In this book we have seen the computer serve as a Rorschach, a projective screen for other concerns. Other technologies—knives, for example —can also serve as this kind of screen: do we associate knives with butter or with blood? But we can come close to having people agree that before it is a part of eating or killing, a knife is a physical object with a sharp edge. By contrast, we have seen that the elusiveness of computational process and of simple descriptions of the computer's essential nature undermines any such consensus and makes the computer an exemplary "constructed object"—a cultural object which different people and groups of people can apprehend with very different descriptions and invest with very different attributes. Ideas about computers become easily charged with personal and cultural meanings.

The influence of the computer as a cultural object is not confined to adults. The machine has become commonplace in the lives of children. Understanding its influence required a study of children as they grow up with it. This study became an increasingly important part of my work as two things became clear. First, that the computer provides a new window onto developmental processes. For example, the child's passage from what I call a "metaphysical" to a "mastery" stage is made transparent through the child's relationship with the computer when interest shifts sharply from philosophizing to "winning." The relationship with the computer reveals more than developmental sequence: it is also a projective screen for different personality styles. Second, the computer, because of its interactivity, its "animation" (the fact that it speaks, plays, wins, "knows" things), and the possibilities it offers for working with issues of control and mastery, actually *enters into* both cognitive and emotional development. It offers a medium for growth and, in certain cases, a place for "getting stuck."

I began my work with children through participant observation, watching them and playing with them. Their conversations gave clues about what they thought and felt. Pursuit of what they thought led me to supplement participant observation with a Piagetian-like method of investigation—for example, the question of the computer's status as a living or not-living thing.* Pursuit of what they felt led me to use a more clinical style of interviewing and psychological tests such as the Rorschach, the TAT, and tests to measure locus of control.

---

* See "Children's Psychological Discourse: Methods and Data Summary" for further discussion of this work.

My discoveries about the individuality of computer relationships as a function of personality and cognitive style, and as a function of distinct moments in the life cycle, exclude simplistic notions about a "modal response" to the computer. My efforts at synthesis are at a different level. I do not attempt to characterize an "average" relationship between people and computers. I identify the significant dimensions along which people differ, and I present cases that mark off these dimensions.

I interviewed more than two hundred children and more than two hundred adults. I interviewed broadly, attempting to meet with people who had a variety of reasons for using the computer, a range in their degree of computer use, and a range in the social context of that use. Some of the people I met saw the computer as a tool and used it only "instrumentally." Things went no further. But for many more, things did go further. In one way or another, and to varying degrees, a relationship with the computer entered into their way of thinking about themselves and other people. My book is about them. My effort is to provide evidence for the "subjective" impact of the computer and to provide concepts to organize thinking about it.

In the study of the very young children and computer toys and games, I report work done with a sample of children from ages 4 to 14 who were chosen at random from school, day-care centers, and informal play groups. The rest of the people I describe in this book have made computers a larger part of their lives than many others in our society. But they are selected less for the intensity of their involvement than because they indicate the range of relationships that people forge with computers. I consider one of my most important contributions to be my conceptualization of frameworks for thinking about this range of relationships.

One framework is my identification of metaphysics, mastery, and identity as three modes of relating to computation. These modes are not exclusive—people can relate to the machine in all three ways. But for many people, one or another of them becomes predominant, a selective effect that is a function of age and personality, and of the social world in which they meet the computer. In this book I chose to sharpen the reader's appreciation of these three modes by presenting them first as dominant themes in the chronology of individual development, and then as dominant themes in the construction of different computer cultures— metaphysics in the world of artificial intelligence, mastery for the hacker, identity for the home computer owner.

Metaphysics, mastery, and identity provide a classification system. Within each of them, there are profound individual differences. For example, the fourth graders Jeff and Kevin were both dealing with mastery when they programmed, although they did so in very different ways; the same was true for the eighth-graders Deborah and Bruce, where issues of identity were most salient. I state the dimensions that distinguish people's ways of handling metaphysics, mastery, and identity in terms of polar oppositions, in which the poles represent "pure types" and the range of responses in between form a continuum. I discuss hard versus soft mastery and risk versus reassurance in programming, transparency versus complexity as a way of experiencing the computer, and I present case material that defines the poles.

When Max Weber first used the notion of ideal types, he associated it with the construction of pure cases to illustrate a conceptual category. In this sense, ideal types are fictions. In this book I have isolated real cases that serve much the same function. The examples I chose describe the poles that define the dimensions for thinking about people whose responses are less "pure."

My conceptual distinctions have several practical functions. They have diagnostic utility. The idea of "Computer as Rorschach" is more than a metaphor. An individual's way of relating to a flexible programming environment is a window onto personality and cognitive style. Deborah's "30-degree world," Bruce's out-of-control spirals, Jeff's "master plan," Kevin's negotiations, Henry's identification with the life of the machine —all these responses enrich our understanding of these children. My distinctions also have pedagogical utility: teaching people about computers should not and need not be the imposition of a standard curriculum; introductory experiences with computers can be tailored to the individual's preferred style of interaction. Finally, my most recent investigations suggest that the conceptual distinctions I have isolated have a use in therapeutic practice. Therapists working with children have always used such materials as toys, clay, and paint to elicit emotional response and to give children a medium for working through their concerns. The computer provides a new and evocative medium; the range of responses to them provides rich material whose meaning can become grist for the therapeutic mill, to be analyzed and worked through in the relationship between therapist and patient.

As I have worked on this book I have often been asked, "Are computers good or bad?" The question was usually asked in regard to children, but as home computers moved aggressively into the marketplace, I was increasingly asked to answer this question in regard to adults. The question deserves some comment. No one asks whether relationships with people are good or bad in general. Rather, we seek out the information to build our own model of a particular relationship. Only then do we make judgments about the possible effects of the relationship. We have long experience with this kind of model building of relationships between people, but we are only beginning to think in this more textured way about our relationships with technology.

Computers are not good or bad; they are powerful. It is a commonplace to say that they are powerful in their instrumental use. The modes of relating to computers and the oppositions I use to organize the material in this book are a contribution to understanding the computer's subjective power in a more nuanced way. If the reader is surprised by the intensity or the range of responses I report, this is only to the good if it leads to a critical reexamination of what each of us takes for granted about "The Computer" and to an attitude of healthy skepticism toward any who propose simple scenarios about the "impact of the computer on society."

Children's Psychological Discourse: Methods and Data Summary

The Question of "Really Alive"

Like all the research reported in this book, my research with children was ethnographic. The observation of styles of programming, of emotional response to the animate qualities of computer toys, the weaving of computer experiences into the development of identity—all these phenomena are accessible through interviews and observation in natural settings. So is the existence of a pervasive anthropomorphism in children's dealings with computers. Children often talk about computers as if they were people. They attribute a psychology to them. And so they treat computers as though the machines were, in a certain sense, alive. I met this phenomenon in my ethnographic investigations, but took a more structured approach to determine its extent and its evolution with children's age and computer experience. Here I report on my investigation and discuss its relationship to other research.

I come to the study of the child's attribution of lifelike qualities to the computer with a very different set of interests from those which underlie a long tradition of research on child animism. This tradition has been dominated by controversy around the question "Do children *really* think inanimate objects are alive?" Jean Piaget is widely associated with the position that they do.[1] He has been supported in this by numerous studies of which the most widely cited is Monique Laurendau and Adrien Pinard's *Causal Thinking in the Child.*[2] Other investigators have argued against Piaget. I. Huang and H. W. Lee find that only a small proportion of the children they studied regarded inanimate objects as living, and even when they did so, they very often denied them lifelike traits, such as the capacity to will or to feel pain.[3] Virginia Holland and Nicholas

Rohrman believe that "animistic thinking is not a genuine phenomenon but linguistic confusion . . ." and note that a child who attributes "alive" to a cloud may not believe that the cloud eats or breathes or dies. They also note that children who respond positively when asked whether certain objects are alive never list them when asked to "name some living things."[4] Thus, from their perspective, children do not consider inanimate objects such as clouds to be alive in the full sense in which a plant or an animal is alive, and conclude that child animism reflects confusion about the use of the word "alive" rather than beliefs about what is alive and what is not.

My own observations agree with those of the many investigators who stress the complexity and ambiguity of animistic judgments. Where my approach differs is that I am not concerned with a yes/no answer to the question "Do children really believe that this or that object is alive?" From my perspective, focused on the computer as an element of culture, the discussion evoked by the issue of aliveness is interesting in itself.

When I describe how Anne says that computers are "sort of alive," I am reporting a response that would not count as "animistic" on many contemporary researchers' criteria. For example, Anne does not think that computers eat or sleep or breathe. But from my perspective, what is important here is that Anne's "sort of alive" response leads her into a particular kind of discussion of the computer. Specifically, the computer is "alive enough" to lead her to discuss its psychology. That this discussion takes place is interesting for two reasons. First, the discourse surrounding an object contributes to building the culture of which it is a part. Second, Anne is becoming more comfortable thinking in psychological terms. I am interested in how the computer is entering her development as a psychological thinker and theory builder.

My observations of Anne were part of an ethnographic study of children in a computer-rich school environment. My effort there was to try to understand her as a unique individual and member of the school culture, to understand how her anthropomorphization of the machine fit in with her personal traits as shown by psychological tests and clinical interviews. But as I met more and more children who, like Anne, psychologized and anthropomorphized computers, two questions arose: How widespread is the tendency to use a psychological discourse in the anthropomorphization of computational objects? And how does it relate to children's age and sophistication about computational objects? To begin to answer these questions, I embarked on a more structured investigation of 88 children aged from 4 through 14, focused on the question of the "aliveness" of computational objects.[5]

Evocative Situations

I constructed a set of situations designed to get children talking about their notions of life. I asked the children to draw pictures of "alive" and "not alive" things, and used these drawings as a basis for conversation. I presented the children with a set of cards with pictures of objects (the sun, an alarm clock, a cloud, a dog, an automobile, an airplane, Superman, a Muppet, an insect, a tree, a snake, a bicycle, a telephone, a television set, a typewriter) and asked them to sort these into piles of "alive" and "not alive" things. The children were asked to explain their choices, so that the "sorting game" also became a precipitant of conversation. A third kind of situation was giving children an opportunity to play with a variety of objects—some of them objects met in the sorting game, some of them familiar toys such as dolls and trucks, and some of them computer toys.[6] I observed the children's spontaneous play and interaction with all these objects and raised the question of their "aliveness." I also observed how children introduced the computer toys to their friends, and how the toys entered group play and group discussion.

Some of the children in my sample had been working with computers in school. I used the same method with them except that here I used the computer itself as well as computer toys as a precipitant of conversation. In my sample of children, 63 were "newcomers" to computational objects of any kind (I began this research in 1978, just as the new toys were first appearing on the market, and so it was not difficult to find children who were meeting the toys for the first time with me), and 25 were "experienced," having a computer toy at home or having worked for a term with a computer at school.

The Two Sides of Animism

The study of child animism has two aspects: the study of children's judgments about the "aliveness" of objects and the study of how the attribution of aliveness (or properties of life) to inanimate objects enters into children's thinking.

The Judgment: Alive or Not Alive

Piaget presents his study of children's judgments on what is alive in terms of a stage theory.

> During the first stage everything is regarded as living which has activity or a function or a use of any sort. During the second stage, life is defined by movement, all movement being regarded as in a certain degree spon-

taneous. During the third stage, the child distinguishes spontaneous movement from movement imposed by an outside agent and life is defined by the former. Finally, in the fourth stage, life is restricted either to animals or to animals and plants.[7]

I have noted that some investigators reject the very idea of child animism, claiming, in essence, that when it appears, it is not something the child believes, but simply a mistake, much as a bird is in error when it flees from a scarecrow. The scarecrow is not seen as a living thing distinct from the farmer; it is simply confused with him. But even researchers (including Laurendau and Pinard) who support Piaget in his thesis of child animism raise an objection: animism may exist, but children's criteria for aliveness are not nearly as systematic as Piaget indicates in his stage theory.

In my own investigation, I found many children who justified their judgments about the aliveness of traditional objects by reference to motion. But like other researchers, I also found children at all ages who used other criteria. So did Piaget. I noted in Chapter 1 that when Piaget reports the presence of criteria other than motion for deciding about life, he sets them aside as "adventitious" and holds on to his stage theory based on motion. To appreciate why, we must understand that for Piaget the stages expressed something more than a way to organize empirical results.

Piaget's assertion that motion is the basis for judgment is at least in part a theoretical interpretation in which motion is assigned a privileged status among all the criteria children use. As I read him his principal reason for according motion this status is not the frequency with which children use it as the basis for judgment (although undoubtedly he sees its frequency as an important confirmation of conclusions reached for deeper reasons). Motion has a privileged role because Piaget sees the refinement of theories of motion as a growing point in the child's world view just as it was of scientific history—and for Piaget the convergence of "ontology" and "phylogeny" in intellectual development has always been an important theme. Since adventitious criteria do not fit into a larger picture, Piaget notes their existence but denies them theoretical importance.[8] My thinking follows Piaget in the sense that one of the reasons I believe psychological criteria are important as the child thinks about the computer is that with the computer presence, these criteria seem to enter into a larger enterprise of theory building, this time not about physics but about psychology.

In analyzing my results, I divide the reasons children give for their judgments about the "aliveness" of objects into seven categories: movement (from point A to point B), other action ("The kettle is alive; it boils"), realism ("Superman is not alive; he is not real"), moral ("Spiders are not alive; you can step on them"), biological ("It's alive; it grows"), psychological ("Alarm clocks are alive; they remember"), and a category of "other responses" which included the mention of origins other than biological ones (such as "Computers aren't alive; they're programmed").

For traditional (noncomputational) objects, I found movement to be the most frequently cited criterion for deciding an object's "aliveness": 53 out of 88 children used it. Only 13 of the 88 children used movement as a criterion for the aliveness of computational objects. Thus, I found Piaget's motion criterion quite useful in dramatizing a sharp difference between the way children discuss the aliveness of traditional and computational objects. However, I found more satisfying a slightly different cut at the data in which I put movement together with other physical action ("The kettle boils" and "The top spins") and contrast all of these with psychological criteria, criteria having to do with intention, will, emotion, and intellect. My major finding here is that physical criteria dominate the discussion of the aliveness of traditional (noncomputational) objects until they give way to standard biological criteria (breathing, growing, metabolism), while *psychological criteria dominate the discussion about computational objects for young children and persist even after the child consistently uses biological language to talk about the aliveness of traditional objects.* Taking my sample of 88 children, ages 4 through 14, as a whole, 68 percent use physical criteria and 11 percent psychological criteria for discussing the aliveness of traditional objects. For computational objects, the relationships are reversed: 17 percent use physical criteria and 67 percent use psychological criteria.[9]

An important aspect of children's response to traditional and computational objects emerges when we look at the evolution of "aliveness" criteria with age. This aspect can be seen even from a very simple analysis. I recalculated the percentages noted above for two groups of children: those aged 8 or under and those over 8. In deciding the question of aliveness, both groups used physical criteria more frequently for traditional objects and psychological criteria more frequently for computational objects. But while the percentages of children who used physical criteria for traditional objects *declined* from 85 percent for those 8 or under to 30 percent for those over 8 (a shift that represents children's increasing use of standard biological criteria for discussing aliveness), the percentage using psychological criteria in discussing the aliveness of computational objects *increased* from 62 percent for children 8 or under to 78 percent for children over 8.[10]

How does attributing life to inanimate objects enter into children's thinking?

If we are to believe Piaget, the world of the child has always been populated with inanimate objects that have a kind of "psychology"—that is to say, intentionality. The child says, "The ball rolls to get here" or "The sun rises to keep us warm"—with the understanding that these objects *want* to take these actions. Given this, does what I found about the child's view of the computer point to anything new? Is the computer-related "psychologizing" different from what has been reported before? It is. It is different from "traditional animism" in at least three ways.

First, there is a different relationship between the attribution of a psychology to the inanimate object and the question of that object's aliveness. In the typical pattern for traditional objects, a child may explain the movement of a ball by saying what it wants to do, but when asked, "Is the ball alive?" answers in physical terms—for example: "It's alive because it rolls." Even though children attribute psychological qualities to traditional objects, they do not usually cite these qualities as reason for believing that these objects are alive. This is not the case for the computer. Here, psychological characteristics or their lack are explicitly given as justifications for saying that the machine is alive or not alive.

Second, there is a difference of developmental course. My study, like Piaget's, and like most follow-up studies of Piaget's work, focuses on subjects in the age range 4 through 11 or 12.[11] During this period, the animism discussed by Piaget is on the decline as the child moves toward "causal" reasoning. But as noted above, during this same period the psychological discourse I observed in discussions of the question of the computer's aliveness actually becomes more prominent. And in Chapter 1 I noted that it also becomes more sophisticated. So, for example, a twelve-year-old might discuss why the computer is not alive in terms of its lack of intentionality, desire, feelings, or ability to *really* understand.

Third, there is a difference in the way these two patterns relate to a child's theory building. Piaget, I think correctly, related the evolution of the child's concept of life to the child's growing sophistication and grasp of physical concepts. For example, as the child attains a clearer understanding of the origins of movement, a distinction between autonomous and imposed movement can be made, and with it a corresponding refinement in the concept of life. There is room for questions about the distribution of cause and effect in this development, but it is clear that the refinement is taking place in the physical rather than the psychological domain.

A child might say that a river is alive long after relegating rolling stones to the category of the nonliving because it requires considerable physical knowledge to understand what makes the river flow. Puzzling about the flowing river and how its movement is like or unlike that of the stones could feed into the development of the child's understanding of how gravity works. But thinking about the river's intentionality is not likely to feed into the development of more sophisticated ideas about psychology. By contrast, thinking about the "minds" of computers can raise increasingly refined questions about psychological matters. Can one cheat without knowing one is cheating? Could feelings be programmed? Are feelings and thinking different—and if so, how? Do you really know something if you are "programmed" to think it? What, after all, could it mean for a person to be programmed?

Other Windows onto the Development of the Psychological

As my study of children progressed, two issues that I had not anticipated in planning my research became increasingly salient: the child's perception of whether or not computers "cheat" and the question of how computers differ from people. Both were suggested by spontaneous discussions among children during my early field observations. And both provided windows onto the child's "construction of the psychological."

Twenty-five children (age range 4 through 11) of the 88 in the aliveness study spontaneously raised the question of whether or not computers cheat. (The most usual precipitant of such discussion was a session with Merlin, the tic-tac-toe–playing computer which frustrates many children by beating them so steadily.) My major finding here is that as children grow older they move from physical to behavioral and finally to psychological rationales for their opinions on whether the computer cheats. Sixty-seven percent of the children from ages 4 to 6 gave a physical reason for why the computer did or did not cheat ("Merlin can't cheat; it doesn't have hands"; "Merlin can cheat because he has tiny, tiny little eyes"). At ages 7–8, physical criteria were used by only 33 percent of the children (at this stage largely to *deny* the possibility of the computer's cheating for lack of having the required "body parts" such as hands or eyes), but behavioral criteria were used by 50 percent of them (largely to affirm the computer's cheating: "Merlin cheats—he goes twice. He has his own special way of cheating" or "Merlin cheats by pressing down real quick"—with no mention of Merlin's body parts). In a third stage, 80 percent of the children 9 years old and above gave a psychological reason for their decision about cheating.[12]

Another window onto the development of children's psychological reasoning is provided through an analysis of the reasons children give for how the computer differs from people. Thirty-two children (age range 5 through 14) of the 88 in the aliveness study spontaneously offered an opinion on what made computers different from people. Of these 32 children, 20 percent of those 8 years old or younger thought that "feelings" marked the difference between computers and people. Most children at this age said that the difference between computers and people is physical—as in "Computers are made of wire; people are made of bones and blood"—or due to different origins—as in "Computers are made in factories; people are made by God." But 88 percent of the children over 8 said that the difference between computers and people is that people have "feelings," most often expressed as a variant of "Computers are smart, but they don't have feelings" or "Computers are good at games and puzzles and math, but they could never have emotions."[13] In Chapter 1 I comment on this data as relevant to children's growing ability to make psychological distinctions, in this case a distinction about cognition and affect.

The Problem of Novelty

I did my study of computer toys and personal computers in the first five years after the introduction of these technologies into the lives of children. Moreover, these technologies were new not only to the children but to the culture around them. As the presence of the computer in all of its forms becomes more familiar, so might conventional answers to many questions about it. Our culture will develop ways of thinking about the computer that, in a sense, require no thought. As these reach the ears and minds of children, they may change the child's discourse about these objects.

To me, one of the most interesting aspects of what I found is that faced with a computer and the question of its life, children struggle to find a handle on the question: they give the impression of thinking hard. When computers become more common, children may simply resort to answers such as "It's not alive; it's just a machine"—a response which usually comes out like a long-established truth, something picked up "ready-made" rather than thought through.

Critics of Piaget have used the idea of novelty to call his idea of animism into question, claiming for example, that "animistic thinking is not a genuine phenomenon but linguistic confusion elicited by novel objects and unfamiliar events."[14] The idea of novelty also suggests a limitation on my findings. I may have tracked the first reaction to a marginal object at a point when reactions are most clear.

It is, however, important to note that the psychological discourse I observed does not depend on unfamiliarity as such.

My sample of 88 children in the aliveness research included children of different degrees of familiarity with computational objects. I divided my sample into two groups: 63 "newcomers" who had no previous contact with computers or computer toys and 25 "experienced" children who either had computer toys at home or had had contact with computers for at least a term at school. The degree of experience with computational objects had no significant impact on the use of psychological criteria to discuss the aliveness of traditional objects (they were used by 11 percent of the "newcomers" and 12 percent of the "experienced" group). But the degree of experience with computational objects did have an impact on the use of psychological criteria in discussing the aliveness of computers and computer toys. The use of psychological criteria for discussing the aliveness of computational objects increased from 57 percent for the newcomers to 92 percent for the experienced children. And in Chapter 1 I note that the psychological discourse increased not only in its frequency but in its level of sophistication.

But there is a difference between individual familiarity—which allows for and even encourages the elaboration of ideas—and cultural familiarity, which provides ready-made answers. To see the effects of the latter we shall have to wait—perhaps not very long, given the speed of development of the computer culture. My conjecture is that even though in a computer-rich world children might no longer find evocative the direct question "Is the computer alive?" and might give it a conventional answer ("No, it's just a machine"), in subtler ways they will continue to be touched by the psychological issues that the computer raises, just as is the case for adults today.

Source Notes

Introduction: The Evocative Object

1. Roger Shattuck, *The Forbidden Experiment* (New York: Farrar, Straus, and Giroux, 1980).
2. See, for example, Lewis Mumford, *Technics and Civilization* (New York: Harcourt, Brace and World, 1934), particularly the classic discussion of time in "The Monastery and the Clock," pp. 12–18.
3. My discussion of personalized computer worlds builds on the notion of "microworlds" for learning developed by Seymour Papert in *Mindstorms: Children, Computers, and Powerful Ideas* (New York: Basic Books, 1980).
4. The classic discussion of how children develop the concept of life is found in Jean Piaget, *The Child's Conception of the World*, trans. by Joan and Andrew Tomlinson (Totowa, N.J.: Littlefield, Adams, 1975), especially "The Concept of Life," pp. 194–206.
5. For a discussion of psychoanalytic "stage theory" recast in a social as well as a psychological perspective, see Erik Erikson, *Childhood and Society* (New York: Norton, 1963), and "Identity and the Life Cycle," *Psychological Issues* 1 (1959). Erikson refers to the school age as dominated by "industry."
6. Erikson's writing on adolescence has become the classic presentation of the concept of "identity." See *Childhood and Society* and "Identity and the Life Cycle."
7. See, for example, Max Weber, "The Social Psychology of World Religions," in H. H. Gerth and C. W. Mills, eds., *From Max Weber: Essays in Sociology* (New York: Oxford University Press, 1946), p. 24.
8. An example of the "determinist" view is expressed by anthropologist Leslie White: "Social systems are functions of technologies and philosophies express technological forces and reflect social systems. The technological factor is therefore the determinant for the cultural system as a whole." See Leslie White, *The Science of Culture* (New York: Farrar, Straus, and Giroux, 1949), p. 336. An example of the nondeterminist view is expressed by historian Lynn White: "As our understanding of history increases, it becomes clear

that a new device merely opens a door, it does not command one to enter."
See Lynn White, *Medieval Technology and Social Change* (New York: Oxford
University Press, 1966), p. 28.

Not all positions are as polarized. Although sociologist Daniel Bell gives a
privileged status to technology as a motor of change, he describes a complex
relationship between technical and social factors. See Daniel Bell, *The Coming
of Post-Industrial Society* (New York: Basic Books, 1973). But in the popular
culture and in the popular literature on technology and its effects, the "pure"
technology-driven position is rampant. See, for example, Marshall McLuhan,
Understanding Media (New York: New American Library, 1973), John Nais-
bitt, *Megatrends* (New York: Warner Books, 1982), and Alvin Toffler, *Future
Shock* (New York: Random House, 1970).

The question of technological determinism, characterized as a debate over
"engines of change," is discussed in Langdon Winner, *Autonomous Technology*
(Cambridge, Mass.: MIT Press, 1977), pp. 44–106. Marshall Sahlins makes a
distinction related to the debate on technological determinism when he contrasts materialist/rationalist explanations and explanations that look to the
centrality of symbols. See Marshall Sahlins, *Culture and Practical Reason* (Chicago: University of Chicago Press, 1976).

9. My analysis of the computer as an "object-to-think-with" grew out of my
appreciation of the way several other authors discussed the relation between
artifacts and thought. In particular, I was influenced by Claude Lévi-Strauss'
discussion of *bricolage* in *The Savage Mind* (Chicago: University of Chicago
Press, 1968), Mary Douglas' discussion of objects in *Purity and Danger* (London: Routledge and Kegan Paul, 1966), and Seymour Papert's description of
a relationship to gears as crucial to his development as a mathematician. See
Seymour Papert, "The Gears of My Childhood," in *Mindstorms*. Sharon Traw-
eek's recent work on the culture of high-energy physicists in the United States
and Japan includes a fascinating discussion of the relationship of physicists
to their tools; see *Uptime, Downtime, Spacetime, and Power: An Ethnography of the
Particle Physics Community in Japan and the United States,* unpublished Ph.D.
dissertation, University of California at Santa Cruz,1982.

10. For a discussion of the role of psychological theories as they enter into every-
day life and become materials for the construction of personal biography, see
Peter L. Berger and Thomas Luckmann, *The Social Construction of Reality: A
Treatise in the Sociology of Knowledge* (New York: Doubleday, 1967), Peter L.
Berger, "Towards a Sociological Understanding of Psychoanalysis," *Social
Research* 32 (Spring 1965), pp. 26–41, Peter L. Berger, *Invitation to Sociology:
A Humanistic Perspective* (New York: Anchor, 1963). See also Jerome Bruner,
"Freud and the Image of Man," in Jerome Bruner, *On Knowing: Essays For the
Left Hand* (Cambridge, Mass.: Belknap, 1962). For one of the first essays
sensitive to the computer as metaphor, see Ulrich Neisser, "Computers as
Tools and as Metaphors," in Charles Dechert, ed., *The Social Impact of Cyber-
netics* (Notre Dame, Indiana: The University of Notre Dame Press, 1966). For
a more extended discussion of my use of the term "psychoanalytic culture"
see Sherry Turkle, *Psychoanalytic Politics: Freud's French Revolution* (New York:
Basic Books, 1978).

11. My analysis of the computer as an evocative object because of its "betwixt and between" nature owes much to Victor Turner's work on liminal objects; see especially *The Ritual Process: Structure and Antistructure* (Chicago: Aldine, 1966) and Mary Douglas' observations about marginality in *Purity and Danger.*

Chapter 1: Child Philosophers

1. These studies are reported in Jean Piaget, *The Child's Conception of the World,* trans. by Joan and Andrew Tomlinson (Totowa, N.J.: Littlefield, Adams, 1960). See especially Chapters 5, 6, and 7: "Consciousness Attributed to Things," "The Concept of Life," and "The Origins of Child Animism, Moral Necessity and Physical Determinism," pp. 169–252. I refer to these studies as background throughout this chapter and I shall not repeat the formal citation.

2. Piaget states that the relationship of affect to intelligence is "only functional" where "affectivity would play the role of an energy source on which the functioning but not the structures [cognitive] would depend. It would be like gasoline, which activates the motor of an automobile but does not modify its structure." Jean Piaget, *Intelligence and Affectivity: Their Relationship During Child Development,* trans. and ed. by T. A. Brown and C. E. Kaegi (Palo Alto, Calif.: Annual Reviews, 1981), p. 5. I too see emotional issues as fuel, serving to direct the attention of the child, but I believe that they do more as well, entering into the development of thought.

   Psychologist Martin L. Hoffmann supports Piaget's position on the role of affect when it comes to "cognition in the physical domain," but argues that cognition in the social domain seems to present a different case "in which affect appears to be not only the driving force, but also a source of crucial information." See Martin L. Hoffmann, "Perspectives on the Difference Between Understanding People and Understanding Things: The Role of Affect," in John H. Flavell and Lee Ross, eds., *Social Cognitive Development: Frontiers and Possible Futures* (Cambridge, England: Cambridge University Press, 1981). In this chapter I extend Hoffmann's point to cognition in the domain of computer–human interaction, a kind of interaction which (in terms of the issues it raises for the child) stands precisely and evocatively between the physical and the social.

3. On this point, see the provocative paper by Marvin Minsky, "Jokes and the Cognitive Unconscious," MIT AI Memo No. 603 (November 1980).

4. See Joseph Weizenbaum, *Computer Power and Human Reason: From Judgment to Calculation* (San Francisco: W. H. Freeman, 1979), especially pp. 1–16 and 188–91, for Weizenbaum's description of initial reactions to the ELIZA program.

5. Piaget looks to children's perception of logical contradictions in their models to drive forward theory construction. For example, a seven-year-old child might explain that clouds are not alive "because they are pushed by the wind," but on a different occasion she might say that "the wind is made by clouds pushing the air." The contradiction could lurk for a long time without

coming to her awareness. When it does, she will try to do something. In this case, the inconsistency may push her toward doubts about her version of the "motion" theory that she used to accord life to the clouds. My emphasis on the role of the affective offers a way to understand how a child's attention can become riveted on points of tension in his or her theories: children's emotionally charged fascination with marginal objects draws their attention to the lines between conceptual categories.

6. In his work, Piaget talks of "stages." Of course, no one is graduated into the next stage at a predetermined moment. The "stage" language that I use here and elsewhere in this book must be read as heuristic, as approximations to a more complex reality.

7. In reviewing children's thoughts about animate and inanimate objects, Rochel Gelman and Elizabeth Spelke characterize animate objects as "entities that know, perceive, emote, learn, and think," and state: "In these respects, inanimate objects have no counterpart. A machine may undergo complex transformations of states that are internal and unseen. But it lacks the capacity for mental transformations and processes." And then they note: "Here, as elsewhere in the text, the reader will surely ponder the status of a computer. For purposes of exposition, we disregard or set aside modern man-made machines that mimic in one way or more ways the characteristics of man." Their intuition is right: the marginal computer does upset the child's constructed boundaries between thing and person. See Rochel Gelman and Elizabeth Spelke, "The Development of Thoughts About Animate and Inanimate Objects: Implications for Research on Social Cognition," in Flavell and Ross, eds., *Social Cognitive Development*.

8. In the pilot tests and early phases of this study I was assisted by Jaffray Cuyler, Sani Kirmani, and Artemis Papert, whose patience, rapport with children, and creative suggestions added immeasurably to the work. I also owe a debt to Pearl Levy for her careful observations of children's discourse during their introduction to programming computers.

9. There are several kinds of criticism of Piaget's discussion of childhood animism. Some claim that there isn't any such thing. For example, Virginia Holland and Nicholas Rohrman argue that that animistic thinking is not a genuine phenomenon but a linguistic confusion elicited by novel objects and unfamiliar words; see "Distribution of the Feature [+ Animate] in the Lexicon of the Child," *Journal of Psycholinguistic Research* 8 (July 1979), pp. 367–78. Other critics grant the fact of childhood animism but question its extent or Piaget's interpretation of criteria used by children. For example, S. Honkavaara reports that children from five to eight are more likely to attribute life to things they like; see "The Dynamic-Affective Phase in the Development of Concepts," *Journal of Psychology* 45 (1958), pp. 11–25. Others, for example N. W. Sheehan, et al., argue that animism can be found at all ages; see "The Nature of the Life Concept Across the Life Span," *International Journal of Aging and Human Development* 12, 1 (1980–81), pp. 1–13. And many have criticized Piaget's acceptance of verbal answers as reflecting children's real reasons for their beliefs and actions. My argument here is focused on the nature of the discourse that children use to discuss the question of life. It is

not necessary to settle all questions about Piaget's methods and interpretation to document that children's discourse about life is different for computational and traditional objects. For more on this point see my note "Children's Psychological Discourse: Methods and Data Summary."

10. Rochel Gelman and Elizabeth Spelke stress the relationship between understanding and the nature of the object that is being understood: "Children's understanding of a given domain depends not only on the logical structure of the tasks used to assess competence and the level of development of some general set of cognitive structures. Their competence depends as well on the nature of the objects about which they must reason." Thus, it is to be expected that a "psychological object" would push forward "psychological reasoning." See Gelman and Spelke, "The Development of Thoughts About Animate and Inanimate Objects: Implications for Research on Social Cognition."

11. Readers who are familiar with the role that Piaget and others attribute to childhood animism in the development of causal thinking must be careful of a possible confusion. When children are asked to explain physical phenomena such as a stone falling, their answers sometimes imply they think that the stone has a "will," such as "It wants to be on the ground," or as if they think it has a moral sense of duty, such as "It has to be on the ground," or in other ways behaves for reasons applicable only to people or animals. Giving physical objects psychological attributes in this way is different from the use of psychological discourse I have been describing. First, the children who attribute "will" to a stone do not usually reply positively to a question such as "Is it alive?" And if asked to explain their answer they will not refer to ways in which the stone's psychology is like or unlike human psychology. An animistic explanation of physical events is not the same as using psychological criteria to discuss whether an object is alive. Second, and perhaps most important, the animistic physics uses psychological concepts in a very simple form. Contrast the complexity of "the stone wants to be on the ground" with "the computer is sort of alive because it is smart, but it can't feel." And the animistic explanation of physical events is on its way out just at a time when the psychological discourse about computational objects is becoming increasingly nuanced. By age ten or eleven few children still use the animistic explanations in any systematic way. But this is the time children reach a high level of sophistication in their handling of psychological ideas to make distinctions between computers and people. For discussion on this point see "Children's Psychological Discourse: Methods and Data Summary."

12. Among the children I spoke with, most at stage one thought the computer didn't cheat for lack of a body part. Stage two children, unconcerned about machines' anatomical "parts," were divided on whether the machines cheated. Then, during the "psychological" stage three, they move back to the idea that the machine does not cheat. This is a common progression in the development of other kinds of reasoning: more sophisticated children use more sophisticated theories to get "wrong" answers more of the time. For example, when children distinguished between endogenous and exogenous motion, they began to classify clouds as alive because they could not identify the "outside push" that activates the clouds. Progressions in theory do not

always correspond to progressions in the percentage of "right answers." For details of the responses on cheating see "Children's Psychological Discourse: Methods and Data Summary."

13. See, for example, John Searle, "Minds, Brains, and Programs," *The Behavioral and Brain Sciences,* 3 (1980), pp. 417–24, Daniel C. Dennett, *Brainstorms: Philosophical Essays on Mind in Psychology* (Montgomery, Vt.: Bradford, 1981), and Joseph Weizenbaum, *Computer Power and Human Reason.*

14. I do not deal here with children's new mythic heroes, many of which are hybrids between people and machines. One of the most striking of these is a character called Goldorak, introduced in a comic strip in Japan in 1975 and in France in 1978. The robot Goldorak is an extension of a man, Actarus, a scientist from a now-destroyed planet. Two things make this hero particularly interesting. First, his deepest commitment is to the defense of the pastoral— the defense of the land and of the simple, good life. Typically, Actarus' friends reward him with a plant or a flower after an intergalactic battle as Goldorak. The pastoral theme is resonant with my finding of a "romantic reaction" in children's responses to computer technology. Second, the body parts of the man/robot Goldorak are given names which borrow both from human anatomy and from machine images: retrolaser, clavicogyre, carneful-gur, fulgurpoing.

15. For a discussion of how children build up categories by defining "neighbors" which share salient features, see Susan Carey, "The Child's Concept of Animal," unpublished manuscript (1977). See also Gelman and Spelke, "The Development of Thoughts About Animate and Inanimate Objects," and Hoffmann, "Perspectives on the Difference Between Understanding Persons and Understanding Things."

16. T. S. Eliot, "The Metaphysical Poets," in *Selected Essays 1917–1932* (New York: Harcourt, Brace and Co., 1932), pp. 241–50.

Chapter 2: Video Games and Computer Holding Power

1. Woody Allen, "The Kugelmass Episode," *The New Yorker,* May 2, 1977.

2. *Principles of Compiler Design,* by computer scientists Alfred V. Aho and Jeffrey Ullman (Reading, Mass.: Addison Wesley, 1977), has the following illustration on its cover: a knight (named Syntax Directed Translation) on a steed (named Data Flow Analysis) fights a dragon (named Complexity of Compiler Design). The knight's weapon is a lance called LALR Parser Generator. I show this cover illustration to my students majoring in computer science. Their comment: "Oh, sure, a lot of compiler people are into D and D."

3. Psychologist Mihaly Csikszentmihalyi studied people's inner states while pursuing activities that appear to contain rewards in themselves—chess, rock climbing, dance, sports, surgery. He discovered that central to all of them is an experience which he calls "flow." Its most marked characteristic is the "merging of action and awareness." Csikszentmihalyi's analysis of flow experiences closely parallels many issues I found at the heart of the "holding power" of both video games and computer programming. See Mihaly Csiks-

zentmihalyi, *Beyond Boredom and Anxiety* (San Francisco: Josey Bass, 1975). For a cognitive perspective on the psychology of game use, see also Thomas W. Malone, "What Makes Things Fun to Learn? A Study of Intrinsically Motivating Computer Games," Xerox Palo Alto Research Center, Cognitive and Instructional Sciences Series (August 1980).

Chapter 3: Child Programmers

1. Marshall McLuhan, *Understanding Media* (New York: New American Library, 1973).
2. Leo Marx's *The Machine in the Garden* (New York: Oxford University Press, 1964) portrays the literary associations of children and the pastoral within the American context.
3. Jean-Jacques Rousseau, *Essay on the Origin of Writing*, trans. by John Moran (New York: Frederick Ungar, 1966).
4. There is a growing literature on children learning to program. See Seymour Papert, Daniel Watt, Andrea diSessa, and Sylvia Weir, "Final Report of the Brookline Logo Project," MIT AI Memo No. 545 (September 1979); Daniel Watt, "A Comparison of the Problem Solving Styles of Two Students Learning Logo, A Computer Language for Children," *Proceedings of the National Educational Computing Conference* (1979); R. D. Pea and D. M. Kurland, "On the Cognitive and Educational Benefits of Teaching Children Programming: A Critical Look," in *New Ideas in Psychology*, Vol. 1 (Elmsford, N.Y: Pergammon, 1983); and Joan Hawkins, "Learning Logo Together: The Social Context," Center for Children and Technology, Bank Street College of Education, Technical Report No. 13 (1983).
5. Logo was primarily developed by a research group led by Seymour Papert at MIT. Essential to its philosophy was the assumption that children would have access to personal computers that could support a powerful programming language. The group made a language that needed such machines at a time when small, powerful, and inexpensive machines did not yet exist. Another effort with a similar philosophy—design a powerful language and assume that the hardware will be there to support it when the time comes—was pursued by Alan Kay and his research group at the Xerox Palo Alto Research Laboratories. Although it was never commercially distributed, their language, Smalltalk, was used in experiments teaching children to program. See Alan Kay and Adele Goldberg, "Personal Dynamic Media," *Computer* 10 (March 1972).
6. Seymour Papert, *Mindstorms: Children, Computers, and Powerful Ideas* (New York: Basic Books, 1980).
7. The classification "hard" and "soft" is related to several other distinctions. Herman Witkin introduced an influential dichotomy by defining two basic cognitive styles: field independent and field dependent. The former implies firmer barriers between self and nonself and a greater tendency to rely on internal referents. Another related dichotomy is J. B. Rotter's concept of locus of control. Individuals have internal locus of control when they tend to

believe that they make events happen; they have external locus of control when they tend to see events as "happening to them." Internal locus of control is conceptually closer to hard than to soft. It is also empirically closer. Locus of control tests were administered to the children at Austen and the hards showed an internal and the softs an external locus. See Herman Witkin, *Cognitive Styles in Personal and Cultural Adaptation* (Worcester, Mass.: Clark University Press, 1978); J. B. Rotter, *Social Learning and Clinical Psychology* (New York: Prentice-Hall, 1954); and J. B. Rotter, "Generalized Expectancies for Internal versus External Control of Reinforcement," *Psychological Monographs* 80 (1966). Other dichotomies that suggest themselves for further correlative study include convergent/divergent, verbal/spatial, and "left brain"/ "right brain."

The concept of hard and soft had its roots in Papert, Watt, diSessa, and Weir, "Final Report of the Brookline Logo Project." The authors make a distinction between the cognitive styles of planners and tinkerers. In my work, hard and soft refers also to a quality of interaction with the computer and a quality of identification with computational objects.

8. Claude Lévi-Strauss, *The Savage Mind* (Chicago: University of Chicago Press, 1968).
9. David Shapiro, *Neurotic Styles* (New York: Basic Books, 1965), p. 28.
10. *Ibid.*, p. 114.
11. See D. W. Winnicott, *Playing and Reality* (New York: Basic Books, 1971).
12. See Evelyn Fox Keller, "Gender and Science," *Psychoanalysis and Contemporary Thought* 1 (1978), pp. 409–33. My studies of women were deeply influenced by the work of Nancy Chodorow; see *The Reproduction of Mothering: Psychoanalysis and the Sociology of Gender* (Berkeley: University of California Press, 1978) and Carol Gilligan; see *In a Different Voice: Psychological Theory and Women's Development* (Cambridge, Mass.: Harvard University Press, 1982).
13. Keller, "Gender and Science."
14. *Ibid.*, p. 427. In a classic work in the sociology science, Ian Mitroff studied the relationship of Apollo moon scientists to their work. He notes the "intense masculinity" and "aggressiveness" of these scientists: "It is an aggressiveness that not only deeply infuses their relationships with one another, but, as we have seen, their abstract concept of science. . . . They were free and quick in displaying aggressive or harsh emotions; they were far less free, however, in displaying more affective or soft emotions. In this sense they do avoid complex human emotion. They displayed only one half of the sphere of human emotionality and that hemisphere with such an intensity that it tended to obliterate the other." See Ian Mitroff, *The Subjective Side of Science* (New York and Amsterdam: Elsevier Scientific Publishing, 1974), pp. 144–145.
15. Keller, "Women, Science, and Popular Mythology," unpublished manuscript. See also Evelyn Keller, *A Feeling for the Organism: The Life and Work of Barbara McClintock* (San Francisco: W. H. Freeman, 1983).
16. Keller, "Women, Science, and Popular Mythology."
17. Winnicott, *Playing and Reality*, p. 2.
18. *Ibid.*, p. 5.
19. Mitroff's study of the Apollo moon scientists showed that although the sci-

entists were "masculine" in their aggressivity and judged affective and inter-
personal dimensions as irrelevant to their concept of the "Ideal Scientist,"
they also "insisted that it was not an either/or between analysis and speculation, rationality and intuition, and so on." *The Subjective Side of Science*, p. 143.
Mitroff takes up this theme in "Passionate Scientists," *Society* (September–
October 1976), pp. 51–57.

20. Philip J. Davis and Reuben Hersch write about a session with an interactive
computer graphics system that is reminiscent of Ronnie's experience of mathematics as felt intuition. The authors describe the difficulties of imagining a
"hypercube," an object that exists in four-dimensional space. A movie that
shows the hypercube in motion leaves them disappointed; manipulating the
cube in an interactive computer environment has an altogether different
effect: "I tried turning the hypercube around, moving it away, bringing it up
close, turning it around the other way. Suddenly I could feel it! The hypercube had leaped into palpable reality, as I learned how to manipulate it,
feeling in my fingertips the power to change what I saw and change it back
again. The active control at the computer console created a union of kines-
thetics and visual thinking which brought the hypercube up to the level of
intuitive understanding." See Philip J. Davis and Reuben Hersch, *The Mathematical Experience* (Boston: Houghton Mifflin, 1981), p. 404.

21. Alan Wheelis makes the following observation about the changes in psychiatric symptoms: "Many elements of motivation which were commonly repressed in the nineteenth century are now rarely repressed. The evidence
concerning aggression is equivocal, but there is no doubt about the liberation
of sexuality. The diminished incidence of hysteria is in line with these observations, and is similarly a matter of fact. Hysteria depends upon repression,
and is becoming rare; character disorders reflect warped ego-functioning,
and are becoming common. As clear-cut symptom neuroses disappear, vague
conditions of aimlessness and futility become prevalent." See Alan Wheelis,
The Quest for Identity (New York: Norton, 1958), p. 128. On the relationship
between culture and symptom, see also Ilza Veith, *Hysteria: The History of a
Disease* (Chicago: University of Chicago Press, 1965), and Christopher Lasch,
The Culture of Narcissism (New York: Norton, 1979), which takes the shift in
styles of suffering as a central premise. On schizoid process, there is of course
a large psychiatric and psychoanalytic literature. For an introduction to some
major positions, see Herbert A. Rosenfield, *Psychotic States* (New York: International Universities Press, 1965); Melanie Klein, *Contributions to Psychoanalysis* (New York: McGraw-Hill, 1964); Otto Kernberg, *Borderline Conditions and
Pathological Narcissism* (New York: Jason Aronson, 1975).

Chapter 4: Adolescence and Identity

1. In discussing children at play Erik Erikson says: "It is true that the content of
individual play often proves to be the infantile way of thinking over difficult
experiences and of *restoring a sense of mastery*, comparable to the way in which
we repeat, in ruminations and in endless talk, in daydreams and in dreams

during sleep, experiences that have been too much for us." See Erik Erikson, "Identity and the Life Cycle," *Psychological Issues* 1 (1959), p. 85.

2. *Ibid.*, especially pp. 101–64. For a discussion of adolescents somewhat older than those in this chapter, one where the focus is on using politics (rather than computation) to think through questions about the self, see Kenneth Keniston, *The Young Radicals: Notes on Committed Youth* (New York: Harcourt, Brace and World, 1960). See also Kenneth Keniston, *The Uncommitted: Alienated Youth in American Society* (New York: Delta, 1967), especially for the discussion of what Keniston calls "the technological ego."

In this chapter I discuss people's use of theories to help them think through their experience under the rubric of identity. John Flavell has used the term "metacognition" to refer to the ideas people have about their own thinking, the knowledge they have of how they know. See John H. Flavell, "Metacognition and Cognitive Monitoring: A New Era of Psychological Inquiry," *American Psychologist* 34 (1979), pp. 906–11. The Piagetan school relates the ability to think about one's thinking to the emergence of the formal stage. See, for example, Barbel Inhelder and Jean Piaget, *The Growth of Logical Thinking from Childhood to Adolescence* (New York: Basic Books, 1958).

3. For a description of Turtle Geometry see Seymour Papert, *Mindstorms: Children, Computers, and Powerful Ideas* (New York: Basic Books, 1980), and Harold Abelson and Andrea diSessa, *Turtle Geometry: Computation as a Medium for Exploring Mathematics* (Cambridge, Mass.: MIT Press, 1982).

4. On ego psychology and the American neo-Freudians, see Chapter 8, note 15.

5. John Seeley Brown and Richard R. Burton write about debugging strategies in learning as "paving the way for students to see their own faulty behavior not as a sign of their stupidity, but as a source of data from which they can understand their own errors." Brown and Burton also speculate on possible deeper psychological implications of debugging metaphors. See John Seeley Brown and Richard R. Burton, "Diagnostic Models for Procedural Bugs in Basic Mathematical Skills," *Cognitive Science* 2 (1978), pp. 155–92.

Chapter 5: Personal Computers with Personal Meanings

1. The early hobbyist movement is best seen as a technical subculture. The literature on the sociology of subcultures offers an approach to its study and is also useful for comparative purposes. On subcultures see Howard Becker, *The Outsiders: Studies in the Sociology of Deviance* (Glencoe: Free Press, 1963), and David Arnold, ed., *The Sociology of Subcultures* (Berkeley: Glendessary Press, 1970). Paul Willis, *Profane Culture* (Berkeley: University of California Press, 1981), and Hunter Thompson, *Hell's Angels* (New York: Ballantine Books, 1967), deal with subcultures around a technological object, the motorbike. On machines as cultural objects, see also Robert Pirsig, *Zen and the Art of Motorcycle Maintenance* (New York: William Morrow, 1975); Tracy Kidder, *The Soul of a New Machine* (Boston: Little, Brown, 1982); and Frederick P. Brooks, Jr., *The Mythical Man-Month: Essays on Software Engineering* (Reading, Mass.: Addison-Wesley, 1979).

The concept of computing worlds as cultural worlds is taken up in Rob Kling and Elihu Gerson, "Patterns of Segmentation and Communication in the Computer World," *Symbolic Interaction* 1 (1978), pp. 24–43; Rob Kling and Walt Scacchi, "Computing as Social Action: The Social Dynamics of Computing in Complex Organizations," *Advances in Computers*, Vol. 19 (New York: Academic Press, 1980), pp. 150–327; Lee S. Sproull, Sara Kiesler, and David Zubrow, "Encountering an Alien Culture," unpublished manuscript (August 1983); Shoshanna Zuboff, "New Worlds of Computer Mediated Work," *Harvard Business Review* 60 (1982), pp. 142–52; Sherry Turkle, "Computer as Rorschach," *Society* 17 (1980), pp. 15–24; and Sherry Turkle, "The Subjective Computer: A Study in the Psychology of Personal Computation," *Social Studies of Science* 12 (1982) pp. 173–205. Some of the material on first-generation users that appears in this chapter was presented at the 1980 meetings of the International Federation of Information Processors; see Sherry Turkle, "Personal Computers and Personal Meanings," in S. H. Lavington, ed., *Information Processing 80* (New York and Amsterdam: North Holland, 1980).

2. See Karl Marx, "Machinery and Modern Industry," in Robert C. Tucker, ed., *The Marx-Engels Reader* (New York: Norton, 1978), pp. 291ff.

3. This chapter touches on the question of computers and alienation through the experience of programmers. On this subject, see Philip Kraft, *Programmers and Managers: The Routinization of Computer Programming in the United States* (Berlin, Heidelberg, and New York: Springer-Verlag, 1977). But the issue of computers and alienation goes beyond changes in the work life of programmers. See, for example, Thomas B. Sheridan, "Computer Control and Human Alienation," *Technology Review* 83,1 (October 1980), pp. 60–67; David Noble, "Social Choice in Machine Design: The Case of Automatically Controlled Machine Tools, and a Challenge for Labor," *Politics and Society* 8 (1978), pp. 313–47; Harley Shaiken, *Work Crisis: Automation and Work in the Computer Age* (New York: Holt, Rinehart, and Winston, forthcoming); and David Noble, *Forces of Production* (New York: Knopf, forthcoming).

4. The political charge on the early personal computer movement was only one aspect of its cultural life. Its strongest roots as an organized movement were in the California Bay Area. There it grew up with role-playing fantasy games, with holistic health, and with humanistic psychology. Many of these themes emerged in the discourse of early personal computer utopians, in the early literature of the hobbyist movement, and in the proceedings of the first generation of personal computer "Faires," sponsored by the organizers of the San Francisco Homebrew Computer Club.

5. The distinction between risk and reassurance brings us into a discussion of the psychology of programming for adults. On this subject see Gerald M. Weinberg, *The Psychology of Computer Programming* (New York: Von Nostrand Reinhold, 1971). For more recent work, see Beau Shiel, "The Psychological Study of Programming," *ACM Computing Surveys* 13,1 (1981), pp. 101–41, and Richard E. Mayer, "The Psychology of How Novices Learn Computer Programming, *ACM Computing Surveys* 13,1 (1981), pp. 121–41. Mayer's study is part of a growing literature on novice programming. See also E.

Solloway, "Cognition and Programming: Why Your Students Write Those Crazy Programs," *Proceedings of the National Education Conference* (1981); E. Soloway, K. Ehrlich, J. Bonar and J. Greenspan, "What Do Novices Know About Programming," in B. Schneiderman and A. Badre, eds., *Directions in Human–Computer Interactions,* (Hillsdale, N.J.: Ablex, 1982); and Sproull, et al., "Confronting an Alien Culture."

6. For a quantitative study of the factors that lead this next generation to buy a home computer, see Everett M. Rogers, Hugh M. Daley, and Thomas D. Wu, "The Diffusion of Home Computers: An Exploratory Study," Institute for Communication Research, Stanford University (October 1982).

Chapter 6: Hackers

1. In this chapter I owe a great debt to my student Justin Marble, who did a series of interviews with student hackers. This chapter situates the hacker within the MIT engineering culture. Other social and psychological studies of this surrounding culture provide useful background. See, for example, Benson Snyder, *The Hidden Curriculum* (Cambridge, Mass.: MIT Press, 1971) and Kenneth Keniston, "The Unpracticed Heart: Youth and High Technology," invited address to the American Psychiatric Association, Toronto, Ontario, May 19, 1982. Keniston divides MIT engineering students into two categories: "the craftsman engineer" and "the passionate engineer." The hackers I describe here belong to his second category, characterized by Keniston as the engineer who "becomes" his project.

2. Robert Pirsig, *Zen and the Art of Motorcycle Maintenance* (New York: Bantam, 1975). Robert Florman, *The Existential Pleasures of Engineering* (New York: St. Martin's Press, 1976).

3. Tracy Kidder, *The Soul of a New Machine* (Boston: Little, Brown, 1981), p. 291.

4. Joseph Weizenbaum, *Computer Power and Human Reason: From Judgment to Calculation* (San Francisco: W. H. Freeman, 1976), p. 116.

5. "The Hacker Papers," *Psychology Today*, August 1980, pp. 62–69.

6. Tom Wolfe, *The Right Stuff* (New York: Bantam, 1980).

7. Cited in Don B. Parker, *Fighting Computer Crime* (New York: Charles Scribner's Sons, 1983), p. 146. Parker's book contains a section on system hackers. It is important to note that the hackers I describe in this chapter have committed no crimes. This does not mean, however, that understanding their relationship to the machine "as puzzle" does not illuminate the motives of those who do.

8. Bruno Bettelheim, *The Empty Fortress: Infantile Autism and the Birth of the Self* (New York: The Free Press, 1967), p. 234. For a classic discussion of the machine and psychotic process, see Victor Tausk, "The Influencing Machine," in Robert Fliess, ed., *The Psychoanalytic Reader* (New York: International Universities Press, 1973), pp. 31–64.

9. Bettelheim, *The Empty Fortress*, p. 234.

10. *Ibid.*, p. 238.

Chapter 7: The New Philosophers of Artificial Intelligence

1. Hubert Dreyfus, "Alchemy and Artificial Intelligence," The Rand Corporation (December 1965).
2. Arthur Samuel, "Some Studies in Machine Learning Using the Game of Checkers," *IBM Journal of Research and Development* 3 (July 1959), pp. 210–99.
3. The predictions that Herbert Simon made in his 1957 talk were published in Alan Newell and Herbert Simon, "Heuristic Problem Solving: The Next Advance in Operations Research," *Operations Research* 6 (January–February 1958). For an impassioned and critical look at these AI predictions, see Hubert Dreyfus, *What Computers Can't Do: The Limits of Artificial Intelligence*, 2nd ed. (New York: Harper and Row, 1979), pp. 81ff. and Chapter 4.

   For a general discussion of many of the AI theories dealt with in this chapter, see Margaret Boden, *Artificial Intelligence and Natural Man* (New York: Basic Books, 1977), and Pamela McCorduck, *Machines Who Think* (San Francisco: W. H. Freeman, 1979). A more technical but highly readable survey of the field is Patrick Winston, *Artificial Intelligence* (Reading, Mass.: Addison-Wesley, 1977). A collection of early classic papers in artificial intelligence appears in Edward Feigenbaum and Julian Feldman, eds., *Computers and Thought* (New York: McGraw Hill, 1963). See also Alan Ross Anderson, ed., *Minds and Machines* (Englewood Cliffs, N.J.: Prentice-Hall, 1964), and John Haugeland, ed., *Mind Design* (Cambridge, Mass.: MIT Press, 1981). The philosophical and metaphysical issues involved in artificial intelligence work are also raised in Douglas R. Hofstadter's *Gödel, Escher, Bach: An Eternal Golden Braid* (New York: Basic Books, 1978); Douglas R. Hofstadter and Daniel C. Dennett, *The Mind's I: Fantasies and Reflections on Self and Soul* (New York: Basic Books, 1981); Daniel C. Dennett, *Brainstorms: Philosophical Essays on Mind and Psychology* (Montgomery, Vt.: Bradford, 1981). See also Martin Ringle, ed., *Philosophical Perspectives on Artificial Intelligence* (Atlantic Highlands, N.J.: Humanities Press, 1979), and Aaron Sloman, *The Computer Revolution in Philosophy* (Brighton, England: Harvester, 1979).

   This chapter presents artificial intelligence as an emergent science. Other literature on the emergence of new disciplines is relevant to understanding its ideological tone and emphasis on strong personalities. See Warren Hagstrom, *The Scientific Community* (New York: Basic Books, 1965); Nicholas Mullins, "The Development of a Scientific Specialty: The Phage Group and the Origins of Molecular Biology," *Minerva* 10 (1972), pp. 451–65; J. Ben David and R. Collins, "Social Factors in the Origins of a New Science: The Case of Psychology," *American Sociological Review* 31 (1966), pp. 451–65; David Edge and Michael Mulkay, *Astronomy Transformed* (New York: John Wiley. 1976); and G. Lemaine, R. MacLeon, M. Mulkay, and P. Weingart, eds., *Perspectives on the Emergence of Scientific Disciplines* (Chicago: Mouton, 1976).
4. In *Machines Who Think*, McCorduck's account of what she calls "L'Affaire Dreyfus" is partisan, but has the great merit of conveying through interviews the complicated motivations of the adversaries.

5. Early discussions of chess are found in Claude Shannon, "Programming a Digital Computer for Playing Chess," *Philosophy Magazine* 41 (March 1950), pp. 356–65, and Alan Turing in B. B. Boden, ed., *Faster Than Thought* (London: Pitman, 1953), pp. 288–95. Of leading AI theorists, Newell and Simon have taken chess most seriously as a test bed for the development of ideas. An early important paper is Alan Newell, J. C. Shaw, and Herbert Simon, "Chess Playing Programs and the Problem of Complexity," *The IBM Journal of Research and Development* (October 1958), pp. 320–35. See also Alan Newell and Herbert Simon, *Human Problem Solving* (Englewood Cliffs, N.J.: Prentice-Hall, 1973). Not all AI theorists have seen game playing as a rich area for research. Although Richard Greenblatt wrote MacHack at MIT, he did so as a "hacker." Games have been notably absent from the official research agenda of the MIT AI lab.

6. A technical overview of most topics in artificial intelligence can be found in Avron Barr, Edward A. Feigenbaum, and Paul R. Cohen, *The Handbook of Artificial Intelligence*, 3 vols. (Los Altos, Calif.: William Kaufmann, 1981). On expert systems, see also Frederick Hayes-Roth, Donald A. Warterman and Douglas B. Lenat, eds., *Building Expert Systems* (Reading, Mass.: Addison-Wesley, 1983).

7. AI is a complex field, with many different schools of thought. Whether expertise can be achieved before common sense is a subject of debate.

8. The influence is most substantial in the field that has come to be known as cognitive science. For an extensive survey of the use of computational paradigms see Marc De Mey, *The Cognitive Paradigm* (Dordrecht: D. Reidel, 1982). Also see Boden, *Artificial Intelligence and Natural Man*. For a more popular treatment of contemporary cognitive science, see Morton Hunt, *The Universe Within* (New York: Simon and Schuster, 1982). George A. Miller has written a personal account of the birth of the new discipline of cognitive science in which he singles out "The Second Symposium on Information Theory," a conference held at MIT in September 1956, as a turning point. There were papers by Claude Shannon, Alan Newell and Herbert Simon, and Noam Chomsky. "What is important to me," says Miller, "is that I went away from the Symposium with a strong conviction, more intuitive than rational, that human experimental psychology, theoretical linguistics, and the computer simulation of cognitive processes were all pieces from a larger whole, and that the future would see a progressive elaboration and coordination of their shared concerns." See George A. Miller, "A Very Personal History," MIT Center for Cognitive Science Occasional Papers, No. 1 (September 1979). See also the "Historical Addendum" to Newell and Simon, *Human Problem Solving*.

An example of an idea that has recently moved out from AI to cognitive psychology is the notion of "Scripts." See Roger Schank and Robert Abelson, *Scripts, Plans, Goals and Understanding* (Hillsdale, N.J.: Lawrence Erlbaum, 1977); Robert Abelson, "Psychological Status of the Script Concept," *American Psychologist*, July 1981, pp. 715–29; and G. Bower, J. Black, and T. Turner, "Scripts in Text Comprehension and Memory," *Cognitive Psychology* 11 (1979), pp. 177–220.

Ideas from AI have also been taken up by researchers working in personality theory and social psychology. See Michael Apter, *The Computer Simulation of Behavior* (New York: Harper and Row, 1970); J. S. Carrol and J. W. Payne, eds., *Cognition and Social Behavior* (Hillsdale, N.J.: Erlbaum, 1976); John Loehlin, *Computer Models of Personality* (New York: Random House, 1968); and Kenneth Colby, "Simulation of Belief Systems," in Roger Schank and Kenneth Colby, eds., *Computer Models of Thought and Language* (San Francisco: W. H. Freeman, 1973).

9. See Newell and Simon, *Human Problem Solving*, and Herbert Simon, *Models of Thought* (New Haven and London: Yale University Press, 1979).

10. Some of the best-known medical programs for medical diagnosis are MYCIN, for meningitis and blood infections; ABEL, for acid-base electrolyte disorders; and CADUCEUS, for internal medicine. For a discussion of medical systems in the context of other expert systems, see Barr, Feigenbaum, and Cohen, *The Handbook of Artificial Intelligence*, Vol. 3.

11. Donald Norman, "Post-Freudian Slips," *Psychology Today*, April 1980, pp. 44–50, "Slips of the Mind and an Outline of a Theory of Action," Center for Human Information Processing, University of California, San Diego, November 1979, and "Categorization of Action Slips," *Psychological Review* 88 (January 1981).

12. The dictionary analogy is my example, constructed to convey Norman's way of using computation to think about mind.

13. See Sigmund Freud, "The Psychopathology of Everyday Life," *The Standard Edition of the Complete Psychological Works of Sigmund Freud*, trans. and ed. by James Strachey (London: The Hogarth Press, 1960), vol. VI.

14. Marvin Minsky, "Jokes and the Cognitive Unconscious," MIT AI Memo No. 603 (November 1980).

15. Cited in Jeremy Bernstein, *Science Observed* (New York: Basic Books, 1982), pp. 96–97.

16. Of course, the "invaded" fight back. See, for example, Jerry A. Fodor, *Representations: Philosophical Essays on the Foundation of Cognitive Science* (Cambridge, Mass.: MIT Press, 1981), particularly in Chapter 8, "Tom Swift and His Procedural Grandmother." Zenon W. Pylyshyn has often played the role of mediator of the debate between AI and those it is attempting to colonize. See, for example, his "Computation and Cognition: Issues in the Foundation of Cognitive Science," *The Behavioral and Brain Sciences* 3 (1980), pp. 111–32.

17. Danny Hillis is a graduate student at MIT working on a machine called "the Connection Machine," which will contain a very large number (on the order of a million) of separate processors working in parallel. As an undergraduate at MIT, Hillis built the Tinkertoy computer I refer to in the next chapter, made contributions to Logo, and to computer graphics. See W. Daniel Hillis, "Active Touch Sensing," MIT AI Memo No. 629 (April 1981), and "The Connection Machine," MIT AI Memo No. 646 (September 1981).

18. Gerald Sussman is best known for his program HACKER, capable of debugging simple programs, and for his work on new programming languages of which the latest is a dialect of LISP called SCHEME. See Gerald Jay Sussman, *A Computer Model of Skill Acquisition* (New York: American Elsevier, 1975),

and Gerald Jay Sussman and Harold Abelson, *Structure and Interpretation of Computer Programs* (Cambridge, Mass.: MIT, forthcoming). Sussman's hobbies illustrate one aspect of the AI culture: he loves playing with mechanisms and can outdo most professional watch repairmen. Characteristically, he is devoting his 1983–84 sabbatical year to learning a new field, galactic physics.

19. This lecture was delivered in January 1981 as part of MIT's Independent Activities Program.

20. Roger Schank is best known for developing the idea of "Scripts" as a principle both for AI programming and for understanding human intelligence. See note 8 above.

21. Cited in Bernstein, *Science Observed*, pp. 110–11.

22. Gary Drescher has made contributions to programming, notably in the implementation and extension of Logo, and to AI theory in proposing a computational version of Piaget's theory of infant development, which he calls "Genetic AI."

23. Edward Fredkin is a leading figure in another branch of "computational imperialism," this one not directed at the human sciences, but at physics.

24. Cited in McCorduck, *Machines Who Think*, p. 346.

25. *Ibid.*, pp. 352–53.

26. Hubert Dreyfus, *What Computers Can't Do: The Limits of Artificial Intelligence*, 2nd. ed. (New York: Harper and Row, 1979).

27. John Searle, "Minds, Brains, and Programs," *The Behavioral and Brain Sciences* 3 (1980), pp. 417–24. For other philosophical discussion relevant to this problem, see Dennett, *Brainstorms*, the essays collected in Dennett and Hofstadter, *The Mind's I;* Hilary Putnam, *Mind, Language, and Reality: Philosophical Papers*, Vol. 2 (Cambridge, Eng.: Cambridge University Press, 1975); Fodor, *Representations;* and Richard Rorty, "Mind as Ineffable," in Richard Q. Elvee, *Mind in Nature* (San Francisco: Harper and Row, 1982).

28. Alan Turing, "Computing Machines and Intelligence," reprinted in Feigenbaum and Feldman, eds., *Computers and Thought*.

29. John Searle, "The Myth of the Computer," *The New York Review of Books*, April 29, 1982, p. 5.

30. *Ibid.*

31. *Ibid.*

32. *Ibid.*

Chapter 8: Thinking of Yourself as a Machine

1. Edgar Allan Poe went to see an "automatic" chess player and wrote about the experience. Poe's "proof" that the machine was a fake is a fascinating commentary on the image of the machine at that time. For Poe, the chess machine was proved to be a not-machine because it sometimes lost a game. "The Automaton does not invariably win the game," Poe explains. "Were the machine a pure machine, this would not be the case—it would always win." "Maelzel's Chess Player," in *The Complete Tales and Poems of Edgar Allan Poe* (New York: The Modern Library, 1938), p. 433.

2. The AI message is carried directly by such works written for the general public as Douglas R. Hofstadter's *Gödel, Escher, Bach: An Eternal Golden Braid* (New York: Basic Books, 1978); Douglas R. Hofstadter and Daniel C. Dennett, *The Mind's I: Fantasies and Reflections on Self and Soul* (New York: Basic Books, 1981); Pamela McCorduck, *Machines Who Think* (San Francisco: W. H. Freeman, 1979); by profiles of AI figures such as Jeremy Bernstein on Marvin Minsky in *Science Observed* (New York: Basic Books, 1982) and Philip J. Hilts on Stanford AI scientist John McCarthy in *Scientific Temperaments: Three Lives in Contemporary Science* (New York: Simon and Schuster, 1982); and by the numerous articles on artificial intelligence which appear in popular magazines such as *Omni, Psychology Today, Time,* and *Newsweek.* Recently, an important channel for the dissemination of AI ideas has been Hofstadter's regular column in *Scientific American.* An early and extremely thoughtful essay on the public reception of AI ideas is Paul Armer, "Attitudes Towards Intelligent Machines," in Edward A. Feigenbaum and Julian Feldman, eds., *Computers and Thought* (New York: McGraw-Hill, 1963).

3. In response to a Lovelacian description of the functioning of a computer by Arthur Samuel, Marvin Minsky said: "His argument, based on the fact that reliable computers only do what they are instructed to do, has a basic flaw; it does not follow that the programmer therefore has full knowledge of (and therefore responsibility and credit for) what will ensue. For certainly the programmer may set up an evolutionary system whose limitations are for him unclear and possibly incomprehensible." See Marvin Minsky, "Steps Toward Artificial Intelligence," in Feigenbaum and Feldman, eds., *Computers and Thought,* p. 447.

4. Oliver G. Selfridge, "Pandemonium, A Paradigm for Learning," in D. V. Blake and A. M. Uttley, eds., *Proceedings of the Symposium on Mechanization of Thought Processes,* 2 vols. (London: H. M. Stationery Office, 1959).

5. The GPS model is discussed in Alan Newell and Herbert Simon, *Human Problem Solving* (Englewood Cliffs, N.J.: Prentice-Hall, 1973). For a critical voice about its implications, see Joseph Weizenbaum, *Computer Power and Human Reason: From Judgment to Calculation* (San Francisco: W. H. Freeman, 1976).

6. Arthur Samuel, "Some Studies in Machine Learning Using the Game of Checkers," *IBM Journal of Research and Development* 3 (July 1959), pp. 210–29.

7. Norbert Wiener, *God and Golem, Inc.* (Cambridge, Mass.: MIT Press, 1964), p. 17. Wiener's other work on the moral and social consequences of computation is *The Human Use of Human Beings: Cybernetics and Society* (Boston: Houghton Mifflin, 1950).

8. Wiener, *God and Golem, Inc.,* p. 5.

9. Marvin Minsky and Seymour Papert, *Perceptrons* (Cambridge, Mass.: MIT Press, 1969).

10. Marvin Minsky and Seymour Papert, "The Society of Mind," unpublished manuscript (1977). See also Marvin Minsky, "Plain Talk about Neuro-Developmental Epistemology," MIT AI Memo No. 430 (June 1977), and "K-Lines: A Theory of Memory," MIT AI Memo No. 516 (June 1979).

11. Seymour Papert, *Mindstorms: Children, Computers, and Powerful Ideas* (New York: Basic Books, 1980), p. 167.
12. *Ibid.*, p. 169.
13. A key goal in the Japanese plan to make a fifth-generation "supercomputer" is achieving an unprecedented degree of multiprocessing.
14. Marvin Minsky has commented on this process of ideas moving out and generated his own list of computational ideas that have "moved out" into psychology:

"New concepts grow from older ones so stealthily that one wonders if any are ever really new. I believe, however, that the concepts of computer science are so novel as to change qualitatively the prospect of understanding how minds work. In the past our reservoir of ways to describe complex processes was too feeble, I think, to deal with human mental processes and their development. (It remains to be seen, of course, whether we now have enough such ideas.) Let me cite, only by name, a few new concepts, familiar to AI programmers and cognitive psychologists, which have no substantial technical counterparts in traditional psychology or philosophy:

symbol table	subroutine	calling sequence
dispatch table	breakpoint	time-sharing
memory protect	trace	functional argument
property list	data type	format matching
hash coding	microprogram	pushdown stack
interpreter	production	garbage collector
list structure	syntax-directed	priority interrupt
content address	paging	indirect address
call-by-name	exec program	pure procedure

"There are actually several hundred such terms, each standing for some clear and well-developed conceptual model, in contrast to the handful of quasi-mechanical concepts from mechanics, hydraulics, and Newtonian dynamics at the root of earlier thinking about thinking. Concepts like these are surely important in the functioning of nervous systems, but we should note that very little is actually yet understood about how brains work. In fact, there is no established (or even generally believed) theory of how information is stored in and retrieved from human memory."

See Marvin Minsky, "Computer Science and the Representation of Knowledge," in Michael L. Dertouzos and Joel Moses, eds., *The Computer Age: A Twenty-Year View* (Cambridge, Mass.: MIT Press, 1979), p. 393.
15. On ego psychology, see Anna Freud, *The Ego and the Mechanisms of Defense* (New York: International Universities Press, 1946); Heinz Hartmann, *Ego Psychology and the Problem of Adaptation* (New York: International Universities Press, 1958), and "Comments on the Psychoanalytic Theory of the Ego," in Ruth Eissler, et. al., eds., *The Psychoanalytic Study of the Child*, Vol. 5 (New York: International Universities Press, 1950).

The American Neo-Freudians (Erich Fromm, Karen Horney, Clara Thompson, Harry Stack Sullivan) shifted the emphasis of dynamic psychology from the unconscious to the conscious, from id to ego, and most generally from depth psychology to cultural psychology; in doing so they gave psycho-analysis a more optimistic tone. In a sense, they did their job too well, and the next generation of American theoreticians usually referred to as the "post-Freudians" (Abraham Maslow, Gordon Allport, Carl Rogers) were not responding to Freud but contented themselves with revising his revisionists. On this point, see Russell Jacoby, *Social Amnesia: A Critique of Contemporary Psychology from Adler to Laing* (Boston: Beacon Press, 1975). Jacoby's book deals with the "forgetting of psychoanalysis" and the emergence of a primar-ily American "conformist psychology."

There were, of course, theorists who viewed these developments with alarm, fearing the dilution of Freud's revolutionary message. Among the most active critics of ego psychology was France's Jacques Lacan. See, for example, his *Ecrits: A Selection*, trans. by Alan Sheridan (New York: Norton, 1977). For a discussion of the process of "normalization" in psychoanalysis and of the French attempt to "return" to an early and, to their way of think-ing, more "subversive" Freud, see Sherry Turkle, *Psychoanalytic Politics: Freud's French Revolution* (New York: Basic Books, 1978).

16. Donald Norman, "Post-Freudian Slips," *Psychology Today*, April 1980, pp. 44–50, "Slips of the Mind and an Outline of a Theory of Action," Center for Human Information Processing, University of California, San Diego, Novem-ber 1979, and "Categorization of Action Slips," *Psychological Review* 88 (Jan-uary 1981).
17. Hofstadter, *Gödel, Escher, Bach*, p. 26.
18. Kurt Gödel, *On Formally Undecidable Propositions* (New York: Basic Books, 1962). This is a translation of Gödel's 1931 paper.
19. Hofstadter, *Gödel, Escher, Bach*, pp. 75–81.

Chapter 9: The Human Spirit in a Computer Culture

1. See Christopher Lasch, *The Culture of Narcissism* (New York: Norton, 1979).
2. The classic statement of the passage to a radically new way of seeing is Thomas Kuhn's *The Structure of Scientific Revolutions*, 2nd ed. (Chicago: Uni-versity of Chicago Press, 1970). Herbert Simon has eloquently stated that he believes that the subversive dimensions of the computational revolution add up to a change of the kind that Kuhn is talking about: "Perhaps the greatest significance of the computer lies in its impact on Man's view of himself. No longer accepting the geocentric view of the universe, he now begins to learn that mind, too, is a phenomenon of nature, explainable in terms of simple mechanisms. Thus the computer aids him to obey, for the first time, the ancient injunction, 'Know thyself.'" See Herbert Simon, "What Computers Mean for Man and Society," *Science* 195 (March 18, 1977), pp. 1186–91. See also Bruce Mazlish, "The Fourth Discontinuity," in Zenon W. Pylyshyn, ed., *Perspectives on the Computer Revolution* (Englewood Cliffs, N.J.: Prentice-Hall, 1970), pp. 195–207.
3. *Newsweek*, February 7, 1983.
4. Michael Polanyi, *Personal Knowledge* (Chicago: University of Chicago Press, 1969), p. 3.

5. Joseph Weizenbaum, *Computer Power and Human Reason: From Judgment to Calculation* (San Francisco: W. H. Freeman, 1976).
6. John Searle, "Minds, Brains, and Programs," *The Behavioral and Brain Sciences* 3 (1980), pp. 417–24.
7. On the Romantic reaction to science see Walter Jackson Bate, *From Classic to Romantic: Premises of Taste in Eighteenth Century England* (New York: Harper and Row, 1961); M. H. Abrams, *The Mirror and the Lamp* (New York: Oxford University Press, 1977); and Alfred North Whitehead, *Science and the Modern World* (New York: Macmillan, 1953).

On Method: A Sociology of Sciences of Mind

1. Clifford Geertz, "Thick Description: Toward an Interpretive Theory of Culture," in *The Interpretation of Cultures* (New York: Basic Books, 1973), p. 9.
2. See, for example, Peter L. Berger and Thomas Luckmann, *The Social Construction of Reality: A Treatise on the Sociology of Knowledge* (New York: Doubleday, 1966).
3. Sherry Turkle, *Psychoanalytic Politics: Freud's French Revolution* (New York: Basic Books, 1978).
4. Both psychoanalysis and computation challenge commonsense understandings of action and responsibility because they get people thinking about the idea of a "decentered" self—a self that is not a unitary, responsible agent. In this sense, the cultural appropriation of psychoanalysis and computation provides case studies not only in the sociology of sciences of mind, but also in the sociology of subversive sciences which undermine commonsense ways of thinking about the self. See Turkle, *Psychoanalytic Politics*.

Children's Psychological Discourse: Methods and Data Summary

1. Jean Piaget, *The Child's Conception of the World* (Totowa, N.J.: Littlefield, Adams, 1975).
2. Among the early confirmations of Piaget are those of R. W. Russell, "Studies in Animism: II. An Investigation of the Concepts Allied to Animism," *Journal of Genetic Psychology* 55 (1940), pp. 389–400; R. W. Russell and W. Dennis, "Studies in Animism," *Journal of Genetic Psychology* 57 (1940), pp. 57–63; W. Dennis, "Piaget's Questions Applied to a Child of Known Environment," *Journal of Genetic Psychology* 60 (1942), pp. 307–20. Monique Laurendau and Adrien Pinard's *Casual Thinking in the Child* (New York: International Universities Press, 1962) sets the confirmation of Piaget's position on animism in the context of a comprehensive reconsideration of Piaget's work on pre-causal thinking.
3. I. Huang and H. W. Lee, "Experimental Analysis of Child Animism," *Journal of Genetic Psychology* 66 (1945), pp. 69–74.

4. See Virginia Holland and Nicholas Rohrman, "Distribution of the Feature [+ Animate] in the Lexicon of the Child," *Journal of Psycholinguistic Research,* 8 (1979), pp. 367–78.

5. These children were drawn from several kinds of settings: day-care centers, informal play groups, and schools. Most of the elementary-school children in the sample were drawn from urban public schools. The sample is of a racially and ethnically mixed middle-class population. It should be noted, however, that the "sophistication" of these urban children may make them something of a special population.

6. I used four computers toys in this study: Merlin, Simon, Speak and Spell, and Big Trak.

7. Jean Piaget, *The Child's Conception of the World,* pp. 194–95.

8. There is, of course, another criticism of Piaget which follows from the fact that from reading his account of his investigation, one gets no idea how often these "adventitious" criteria appeared.

9. I am reporting percentages of children who give at least one argument based on physical activity or psychology. Some children used both physical and psychological criteria, and they are counted twice. Some children used neither of these criteria, and these children are not counted at all. Thus the percentages, here and elsewhere in this note when I report·on children's criteria for judgment, do not necessarily add up to 100 percent. All percent ages are rounded off to the nearest whole number.

10. The percentages of children using psychological criteria for traditional objects and physical criteria for computational objects is small for all ages and does not change as dramatically. For traditional objects, psychological criteria were used by 15 percent of the younger group and by 4 percent of the older group, reflecting children's increasing reliance on biological criteria for justifying the judgment of "aliveness." For computational objects, physical criteria were used by 16 percent of the younger group and 19 percent of the older group. There was a tendency for older children who did discuss computational aliveness in terms of physical criteria to also mention the origins of computers as a way to classify them as "not alive" (for example, "The computer isn't alive because it is made in a factory").

11. My study included two children over 12.

12. Children of 9 and above use a psychological reason to deny the possibility that a computer could cheat, most often through the assertion that cheating required *knowing* one was cheating or that cheating required a moral sense which computers lacked.

13. Of course, some of these children gave other answers as well, referring to biology; to the fact that computers are not self-aware, conscious; or to the fact that computers are "programmed" but people are not—a distinction between having "psychology from the inside" and "psychology from the outside" analogous to the Piagetian division between endogenous and exogenous motion.

14. Holland and Rohrman, "Distribution of the Feature [+ Animate] in the Lexicon of the Child," p. 367.

INDEX